Access™ 2007 FOR DUMMIES®

by Laurie Ulrich Fuller,
Ken Cook & John Kaufeld

Wiley Publishing, Inc.

Access™ 2007 For Dummies®

Published by
Wiley Publishing, Inc.
111 River Street
Hoboken, NJ 07030-5774
www.wiley.com

Copyright © 2007 by Wiley Publishing, Inc., Indianapolis, Indiana

Published by Wiley Publishing, Inc., Indianapolis, Indiana

Published simultaneously in Canada

For general information on our other products and services, please contact our Customer Care Department within the U.S. at 800-762-2974, outside the U.S. at 317-572-3993, or fax 317-572-4002.

For technical support, please visit www.wiley.com/techsupport.

Wiley also publishes its books in a variety of electronic formats. Some content that appears in print may not be available in electronic books.

Library of Congress Control Number: 2006934825

ISBN-13: 978-0-470-04612-8
ISBN-10: 0-470-04612-0

Manufactured in the United States of America

10 9 8 7 6 5 4 3

1B/QV/RS/QW/IN

WILEY

About the Authors

Laurie Ulrich Fuller has been writing about and teaching people to use Microsoft Office since the 1980's. Her teaching career goes back to the time before Microsoft Windows – which means she also remembers the first time she taught people to use a Windows-based application, and a student picked up the mouse and aimed it at the computer screen as though using a TV remote. Nobody laughed (except Laurie, after class), because everyone was new to the mouse back then. As new as the mouse was, so was the idea of keeping a database on a computer that could fit on your desk — and Laurie's been there through every new version of Access — as Office has evolved to meet the needs of users from all walks of life — from individuals to huge corporations, from growing business to non-profit organizations.

Since those early days of Office and Windows, Laurie has personally trained more than 10,000 people to make better, more creative use of their computers, has written and co-written more than 25 nationally-published books on computers and software — including several titles on Microsoft Office. In the last few years, she's also created two video training courses — one on Word 2003, and the other on the entire Office 2003 suite. She runs her own company, Limehat & Company, offering training, educational materials, and web development services. She invites you to contact her at laurie@ limehat.com, and to visit her personal website, www.planetlaurie.com, for more information.

Laurie would also like you to know that despite being able to remember the world before Windows, she does not remember a time before cars, television, or fire.

Ken Cook has built and managed a successful computer consulting business since 1990 serving clients in New Jersey, New York, Pennsylvania, and California. He began as a trainer - training numerous users (too many to count!) on a variety of software packages — specializing in Microsoft Office. Currently, he "dabbles in training" but his main focus is creating expert Microsoft Office solutions and Microsoft Access database solutions for Fortune 500 and small business clients.

He can be contacted through his Web site www.kcookpcbiz.com or email: ken@kcookpcbiz.com.

Publisher's Acknowledgments

We're proud of this book; please send us your comments through our online registration form located at www.dummies.com/register/.

Some of the people who helped bring this book to market include the following:

Acquisitions, Editorial, and Media Development

Project Editor: Pat O'Brien
  (Previous Edition: Susan Pink)

Acquisitions Editor: Steve Hayes

Copy Editor: Andy Hollandbeck

Technical Editor: Michael Alexander

Editorial Manager: Kevin Kirschner

Media Development Specialists: Angela Denny, Kate Jenkins, Steven Kudirka, Kit Malone, Travis Silvers

Media Development Coordinator: Laura Atkinson

Media Project Supervisor: Laura Moss

Media Development Manager: Laura VanWinkle

Media Development Associate Producer: Richard Graves

Editorial Assistant: Amanda Foxworth

Sr. Editorial Assistant: Cherie Case

Cartoons: Rich Tennant (www.the5thwave.com)

Composition Services

Project Coordinator: Erin Smith

Layout and Graphics: Jonelle Burns, Carl Byers, Lavonne Cook, Denny Hager, Joyce Haughey, Barbara Moore, Barry Offringa, Alicia South, Julie Trippetti, Erin Zeltner

Proofreaders: Johnna VanHoose Dinse, John Greenough, Christy Pingleton

Indexer: Techbooks

Publishing and Editorial for Technology Dummies

  Richard Swadley, Vice President and Executive Group Publisher

  Andy Cummings, Vice President and Publisher

  Mary Bednarek, Executive Acquisitions Director

  Mary C. Corder, Editorial Director

Publishing for Consumer Dummies

  Diane Graves Steele, Vice President and Publisher

  Joyce Pepple, Acquisitions Director

Composition Services

  Gerry Fahey, Vice President of Production Services

  Debbie Stailey, Director of Composition Services

Contents at a Glance

Table of Contents

Introduction

· ·

You've picked up this book and are hoping it will teach you to use Microsoft Access. Of course, as the authors, we believe that it was some sort of divine intervention that led you to our pages, and we're quite certain that this is The Book For You. We could be wrong, but that happens so infrequently that we're hardly considering it. No, the reason you picked up this book is that you want to learn Access, and this is the best place to do that. Really. No kidding.

Of course, being a normal human being, you probably have work to do, and whether we're right about this being The Book For You or not, you need Access. You need it to organize your data. You need it to store and allow you to use all the information that's currently spilling out of notebooks, file drawers, your pockets, your glove compartment, everywhere. You need it so you can print out snappy looking reports that make you look like the genius you are. You need it so you can create cool forms that will help your staff enter all the data you've got stacked on their desks — and in a way that lets you know that the data was entered properly, so it's accurate and useful. You need Access so you can find little bits of data out of the huge pool of information you need to store. You just need it.

About This Book

Because with all the power that Access has (and that it therefore gives *you*), there comes a small price: complexity. Access isn't one of those applications you can just sit down and use, "right out of the box". It's not scarily difficult or anything, but there's a lot going on and you need some guidance, some help, some direction, to really use it and make it sing and dance. And that's where this book, a "reference for the rest of us" comes in.

So you've picked up this book. Hang on to it. Clutch it to your chest and run gleefully from the store (stop and pay for it first, please). And then start reading — whether you begin with Chapter 1 or whether you dive in and start with a particular feature or area of interest that's been giving you fits on your own. Just read, and then go put Access through its paces.

Conventions Used in This Book

As you work with Access, you're going to need to tell it to do things. You'll also find that at times, Access has questions for you, usually in response to your asking it to do something. This book will show you how to talk to Access, and how Access will talk to you. To show the difference between the two sides of that conversation, we format the commands as follows:

This is something you type into the computer.

```
This is how the computer responds to your command.
```

Because Access *is* a Windows program, you don't just type, type, type — you also mouse around quite a bit. Here are the mouse movements necessary to make Access (and any other Windows program) work:

- ✔ **Click:** Position the tip of the mouse pointer (the end of the arrow) on the menu item, button, check box, or whatever else you happen to be aiming at, and then quickly press and release the left mouse button.

- ✔ **Double-click:** Position the mouse pointer as though you're going to click, but fool it at the last minute by clicking twice in rapid succession.

- ✔ **Click and drag (highlight):** Put the tip of the mouse pointer at the place you want to start highlighting and then press and hold the left mouse button. While holding down the mouse button, drag the pointer across whatever you want to highlight. When you reach the end of what you're highlighting, release the mouse button.

- ✔ **Right-click:** Right-clicking works just like clicking, except that you're exercising the right instead of the left mouse button.

What You Don't Have to Read

Now that we've told you that you should read the book, we're telling you don't have to read *all* of it. Confused? Don't be. This section of the introduction exists to put your mind at ease, so you won't worry that you have to digest every syllable of this book in order to make sense of Access. And more than just being a required section of the introduction, this is true. You don't have to read the whole book.

You should read the chapters that pertain to things you don't know, but you can skip the stuff you do know or that you're fairly sure you don't need to know. If the situation changes and you eventually *do* need to know something, you can go back and read that part later.

If you only use Access at work, and you're using an Access database that some geek in your IT department created, chances are you can't tinker with it. Therefore, if you only need to know about using an existing Access database, you can skip the chapters on designing databases.

On the other hand, it might be nice to know what's happening "behind the scenes", but you don't have to read those chapters if you don't want to.

Foolish Assumptions

You need to know only a few things about your computer and Windows to get the most out of *Access 2007 For Dummies*. In the following pages, we presume that you:

  ✔ Know the basics of Windows — how to open programs, save your files, create folders, find your files once you've saved them, print, and do basic stuff like that.
  ✔ Want to build your own databases.
  ✔ Want to work with databases that other people have created.
  ✔ Want to use and create queries, reports, and an occasional form.
  ✔ Have either Windows XP with Service Pack 2 or Windows Vista.

    If your computer uses Windows 98 or 2000, you can't run Office 2007.

You don't have to know (or even care) about table design, field types, relational databases, or any of that other database stuff to make Access work for you. Everything you need to know is right here, just waiting for you to read it. Of course, you may *want* to know what's going on under the hood (so to speak). You'll find that information within this book's pages.

How This Book Is Organized

Here's a breakdown of the parts in this book. Each part covers a general aspect of Access. The part's individual chapters dig into the details.

Part 1: Basic Training

In this first part of the book, you'll find out what Access is, what it isn't, how it works, and how you open it up and start using it. You'll find out how to navigate and tame the Access workspace, and for people who've used previous versions of Access, you'll find out about all the new doo-dads that are part of Access 2007.

Part I also takes you through the process of planning your database — deciding what to store, how to structure your database, and how to use some of Access 2007's very helpful tools for starting a database with templates — cookie cutters, if you will — for a variety of common database designs. Be prepared to pick up some helpful jargon, as you learn a bit about a few specialized terms that you really need to know.

Part II: Getting It All on the Table

Part II takes you a bit deeper, starting out with a chapter on setting up more than one table to store related data — and moving on with chapters on setting up relationships between those tables, customizing the way data is stored in your tables, and ways to control how data is entered into the tables in your database.

Part III: Data Mania and Management

You'll find out all about forms, the customized interfaces you create to make it easier to enter, edit, and look at your database. You'll also discover cool ways to share your Access data with other programs and how to bring content from Word documents and Excel worksheets into Access to save time, reduce the margin for data entry errors, and build consistency within all the work you do in Microsoft Office. You'll also find out about using Access tables on the web, and how to publish your database to the internet. Look out world!

Part IV: Ask Your Data, and Ye Shall Receive Answers

In Part IV, you'll discover how to ask questions like "How many customers do we have in Peoria?" and "How long has that guy in Accounting worked here?" Of course, you already know how to form sentences that go up at the end (so people know you're asking a question), but when you ask a question in Access, the pitch of your voice rarely makes any difference. You'll need, therefore, to know how to sort, filter, and query your data to get at the information you're storing in your Access database.

Part V: Plain and Fancy Reports

Reports are compilations of data from one or more tables in your database. That statement might sound a bit scary, because "compilations" has four syllables and you might not be sure what a table is yet. Have no fear, however, because Access provides some cool automatic tools that let you pick and choose what you want in your report, and then it goes and makes the report *for you.* How neat is that?

Automatic reports weren't good enough for you, eh? If your jobs relies upon reports not only being informative but also attractive and attention-grabbing, Part V will be like opening a birthday present. Well, not really, but you'll find out about charts, printing labels, and putting page numbers on your reports.

Part VI: More Power to You

Part VI gives more power in the form of the Access Analyzer, a tool that tunes up your database for better performance. It also gives you more power by showing you how to create a user interface that controls what people see, which tables they can edit, and how they work with your database overall.

Part VII: The Part of Tens

The format of these chapters is designed to give you a lot of information in a simple, digestible fashion so you can absorb it without realizing you're actually learning something. Sneaky, huh?

Appendix: Getting Help

This isn't really a whole part, but it's darn useful. Remember how your mom told you the only foolish question is the one you don't ask? In this appendix, you'll find out about the online and built-in help that Access offers.

Icons Used in This Book

When something in this book is particularly valuable, we go out of our way to make sure that it stands out. We use these cool icons to mark text that (for one reason or another) *really* needs your attention. Here's a quick preview of the ones waiting for you in this book and what they mean:

Tips are incredibly helpful words of wisdom that promise to save you time, energy, and the embarrassment of being caught swearing out loud, while you're alone. Whenever you see a tip, take a second to check it out.

Some things are too important to forget, so the Remember icon points them out. These items are critical steps in a process — points that you don't want to miss.

Sometimes we give in to the techno-geek lurking inside of us and slip some technical babble into the book. The Technical Stuff icon protects you from obscure details by making them easy to avoid. On the other hand, you may find them interesting.

The Warning icon says it all: *Skipping this information may be hazardous to your data's health.* Pay attention to these icons and follow their instructions to keep your databases happy and intact.

Where to Go from Here

Now nothing's left to hold you back from the delights and amazing wonders of Access. Hold on tight to this copy of *Access 2007 For Dummies* and leap into Access.

- ✔ If you're brand new to the program and don't know which way to turn, start with the general overview in Chapter 1.
- ✔ If you're about to design a database, I we salute you — and recommend flipping through Chapter 4 for some helpful design and development tips.
- ✔ Looking for something specific? Try the Table of Contents or the Index.

Now, go. Have fun. And look both ways before crossing the street.

Part I
Basic Training

The 5th Wave   By Rich Tennant

"Once I told Mona that Access was an 'argument' based program, she seemed to warm up to it."

In this part . . .

Don't worry, even though this part of the book is called "Access Basic Training", nobody's going to shout at you, demand you call them "Sir!", or make you do pushups. I promise. Instead, you'll find out what Access is, what it does, and how to get started using it.

The three chapters in this part of the book introduce you to the Access 2007 workspace, and show you how to start building your first database. You'll also find out about some essential terms and concepts that will help you make better use of the rest of the book and any other print, online, or even in-person discussions of databases. This will help you talk about your database needs at work, with clients, or if you're trying to bore people to death at a party.

Ready? Then let's get started!

Chapter 1

Getting to Know Access 2007

In This Chapter

▶ Deciding when to use Access

▶ Unlocking the basics of working with Access

▶ Figuring out how to get started

*A*ccess 2007, the most recent version of Microsoft Office's database application, is a very robust and powerful program. You probably already know that, and perhaps that power, or your perceptions of all that Access can do, is what made you reach for this book. Good decision!

For all of Access's power, it's important to note that Access is also very — pardon the expression — *accessible*. It's pretty easy to use at the edges, where a new user will be; you don't have to venture all the way in to its core to get quite a lot out of the software. In fact, with just the basic functionality that you'll discover in this book, you'll be able to put Access through many of its most important paces, yet you'll be working with wizards and other on-screen tools that keep you at a comfortable arm's distance from the software's inner workings, the things that programmers and serious developers play with.

You don't need to use every feature and tool and push the edges of the Access envelope. In fact, you can use very little of everything Access has to offer and still have quite a significant solution to your needs for storing and accessing data — all because Access can really "do it all" — enabling you to set up a database quickly, build records into that database, and then use that data in several useful ways. Later on, who knows? You may become an Access guru.

In this chapter, you'll discover what Access does best (and when you might want to use another tool instead), you'll see how it does what it does, and hopefully you'll begin to understand and absorb some basic terminology. Now, don't panic — nobody's expecting you to memorize any vocabulary or anything scary like that. The goal here (and in the next two chapters) with regard to terms is to introduce you to some basic words and concepts that will help you make better use of Access in general and in the subsequent chapters in this book, too.

What Is Access Good For, Anyway?

What *is* Access good for? That's a good question. Well, the list of what you can do with it is a lot longer than the list of what you *can't* do with it — of course, only if you leave things like "paint your car" and "do the dishes" off the "can't do" list. When it comes to data organization, storage, and retrieval, Access is at the head of the class.

Building big databases

What do I mean by *big database?* I mean any database with a lot of records. And by *a lot,* I mean hundreds. And certainly if you have thousands of records, you need a tool like Access to manage them. Although you can use Microsoft Excel to store lists of records, you are limited as to how many you can store (the number of rows in a single worksheet) and you can't set up anything beyond a simple list that can be sorted and filtered. So anything with a lot of records is best done in Access.

Some reasons why Access handles big databases well:

- ✔ Typically, a big database has big data entry needs to go along with it. Access offers forms, or more accurately, the ability for you to create a quick form through which someone can enter all those records. This can make data entry easier and faster and can reduce the margin for error significantly. Check out Chapter 5 for more information on building forms.

- ✔ When you have lots and lots of records, the margin for error within them — duplicate records, records with misspellings, records with missing information — is great. So you need an application like Access to ferret out those errors and fix them. See Chapter 9 to see how Access lets you find and replace errors and search for duplicate entries.

- ✔ Big databases mean big needs for accurate, insightful reporting. Access has powerful reporting tools that allow you to create printed and on-screen reports that include as few or as many pieces of your data as you need, and to include data from more than one table in the report. You can tailor your reports to your audience, from what's shown on the reports pages to the colors and fonts used.

- ✔ Big databases are hard to wade through when you want to find something. Access provides several tools for sorting, searching, and creating your own specialized tools (known as *queries*) for finding the elusive single record or group of records you need.

✔ Access saves time by giving you great tools for importing data from other sources, such as Excel worksheets (if you started in Excel and have maxed out its usefulness as a data storage device) and Word tables. This saves you from re-entering all your data and allows you to keep multiple data sources consistent.

Creating databases with multiple tables

Whether your database holds 100 records or 1,000 records (or more), if you need to keep separate tables and relate them for maximum use of the information, you need a *relational* database — and that's Access. How do you know whether your data needs to be in separate tables? Think about your data — is it very compartmentalized? Does it go off on tangents? Consider the following example and apply the concepts to your data and see if you need multiple tables for your database.

The Big Customer database

A large contracting business has a database of customers — past, present, and potential clients — and wants to keep track of a lot of information on them. For the current and past clients, the bigwigs want to store information about the work that was done, what materials were used — paint colors, tile designs, carpet styles, preferred fixtures, and so on. For potential customers, they want to keep track of when and how they've contacted them with mailings, phone calls, and visits from sales reps. Imagine keeping all of that in a single table — with everything from the customer's name to what wallpaper was used in the bedroom.

For a complex database like this one, you'd need multiple tables, as follows:

✔ One table would house the customer contact information — names, addresses, phone numbers, fax numbers, and e-mail addresses. A field one might also include would be customer number, which makes each record unique, and in that number, one or more of the characters could be used to differentiate between different customer types — past, current, or potential.

✔ A second table would contain the customer number again (as a way to link or connect the two tables) and also the customer's status information — what work was done (kitchen, bathroom, painting, restoration, any number of established classifications) and what was charged for the work.

✔ A third table, again containing the customer number, would include the customer's preferences for paint manufacturers and colors, wallpaper, tile, countertops, fixtures, carpet, and so on. Because you don't have to fill in every field in a record, if no carpeting was done for a particular customer, for example, that field can be left blank.

With these three tables in place, any type of customer (past, current, or potential) can be entered into the database, and only the table or tables that apply to that customer need be populated with data. When a potential customer becomes a current one, relevant data can be entered into the appropriate table(s). If a potential customer never buys, he or she can be deleted when a prescribed length of time has elapsed, or perhaps a fourth table, with archived customer records, can be set up. The options are limited only by your needs and intended use of the data.

Failure to plan? Plan to fail

If you think carefully about your database and how you use your data and what you need to know about your customers, products, or whatever you're storing information about, you can plan

✔ How many tables you'll need

✔ Which data will go into which table

✔ How you'll use the tables together to get the reports you need

Feel free to sketch your planned database on paper, drawing a kind of flow chart with boxes for each table and lists of fields that you'll have in each one. Draw arrows to show how they might be related — sort of like drawing a simple family tree — and you're well on your way to a well-planned, useful database.

Here's a handy procedure to follow if you're new to the process of planning a database:

1. **On paper or in a word processing document, whichever is more comfortable, type the following:**

   • A tentative name for your database

   • A list of the pieces of information you get from that database on a daily or regular basis

2. **Now, based on that information, create a new list of the actual details you could store:**

   List every piece of information you can possibly think of about the customers, products, ideas, cases, books, works of art, students — whatever your database pertains to. Don't be afraid to go overboard — you can always skip some of the items in the list if they don't end up being things you really need to know or can possibly find out about each item in your database.

3. **Take the list of fields — that's what all those pieces of information are — and start breaking them up into logical groups.**

How? Think about the fields and how they work together:

- If the database keeps track of a library of books, for example, perhaps the title, publication date, publisher, and ISBN (International Standard Book Number, which is unique for each book), price, and page count can be stored in one group, and author information, reviews, and lists of other titles by the same author or books on the same topic can be stored in another group. These groups become individual tables, creating your relational database of books.

- Figure out what's unique about each record. As stated in the previous point, you need a field that's unique for each record, and while Access can create this for you if no unique data exists for each record in your database, it's often best if you actually have or create one yourself. Customer numbers, student numbers, book ISBNs, catalog numbers, serial numbers — anything that won't be the same for any two records will do.

With a big list of fields and some tentative groupings of those fields at the ready, and with an idea of which field is unique for each record, you can begin figuring out how to *use* the data.

4. **Make a list of ways you might use the data:**

    - Reports you'd like to create, including a list of which fields should be included for each report.

    - Other ways you can use the data — labels for mailings, product labels, catalogue data, price lists, contact lists, and so on.

5. **List all the places your data currently resides — on slips of paper in your pocket, on cards in a box, in another program (such as Excel), or maybe through a company that sells data for marketing purposes.**

With this planning done, you're ready to start building your database. The particulars of that process come later in this chapter and in subsequent chapters, so don't jump in yet. Do pat yourself on the back, though, because if you read this procedure and applied even some of it to your potential database, you're way ahead of the game, and I feel very positive about your ability to make good use of all that Access has to offer.

Databases with user forms

When planning your database, consider how the data will be entered:

- If you'll be doing the data entry, perhaps you're comfortable working in a spreadsheet-like environment, known in Access as *Table view*, where the table is a big grid, and you fill it in row by row (each row is a record).

    Figure 1-1 shows a table in progress in Table view. You decide — is it easy to use, or can you picture yourself forgetting to move down a row and entering the wrong stuff in the wrong columns as you enter each record?

✔ You may want to use a *form* (shown in Figure 1-2), a specialized interface for data entry and editing and for viewing your database one record at a time, if

- Someone else will be handling data entry
- Typing row after row of data into a big grid seems mind-numbing.

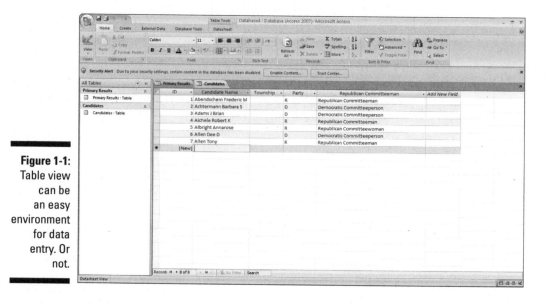

Figure 1-1: Table view can be an easy environment for data entry. Or not.

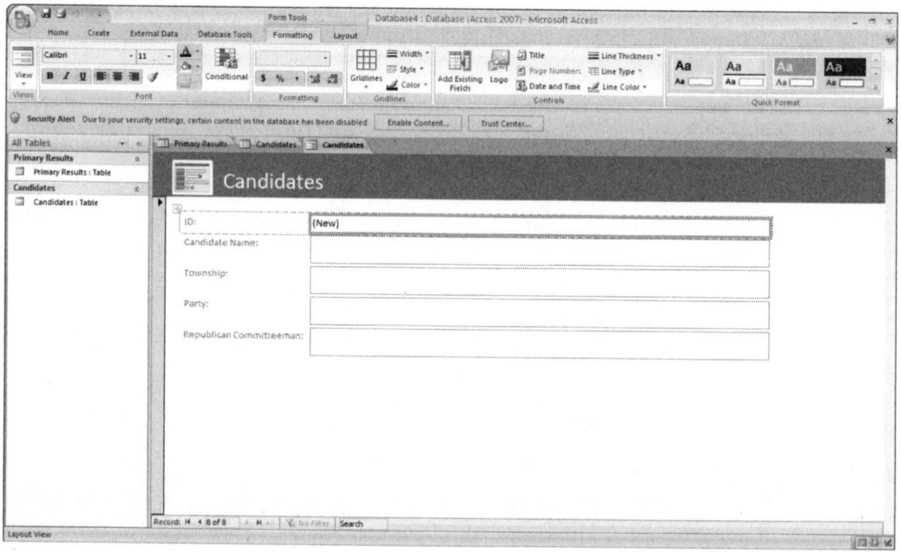

Figure 1-2: A form for entering new records or reviewing existing ones can be a great tool.

You can find out all about forms in Chapter 5, and if your database is large enough to require help doing the data entry, or if it will continue to grow over time and an on-going data entry process is likely, Access is the tool for you. The fact that it offers simple forms of data entry and editing is reason enough.

Databases requiring special reporting

Yet another reason to use Access is its ability to create customized reports quickly and easily. Some database programs, especially those designed for single-table *flat file* databases, have some canned reports built in, and that's all you can do — just select a report from the list and run the same report every other user of that software runs.

If you're an Excel user, your reporting capabilities are far from easy or simple, and they're not designed for use with large databases — they're meant for spreadsheets and small, flat-file lists. Further, you have to dig much deeper into Excel's tools to get at these reports. Because Access is a database application, reporting is a major feature.

An example? In Excel, to get a report that groups your data by one or more of the fields in your list, you have to sort the database first, using the field/s to sort the data, and then you can create what's known as a subtotal report. To create it, you use a dialog box that asks you about calculations you want to perform, where to place the results, and whether you're sorting and subtotaling on more than one field. The resulting report is not designed for printing, and you have to tinker with your spreadsheet pagination (through a specialized view of the spreadsheet) in order to control how the report prints out.

In Access? Just fire up the Report Wizard, and you can sort your data, choose how to group it, decide which pieces of data to include in the report, and pick a visual layout and color scheme — all in one simple, stream-lined process. Without your doing anything, the report is ready for printing. Access is built for reporting, because it's a database application — and reports are one of the most, if not *the* most important way you'll use and share your data.

Because reports are such an important part of Access, you can create them quickly and easily, but you can also customize them to create powerful documentation of your most important data:

- Build a quick, simple report that just spits out whatever's in your table in a tidy, easy-to-read format. See Figure 1-3 for a sample.

- Create a customized report that you design step-by-step with the Report Wizard. See Figure 1-4.

- You can really roll up your sleeves and design a new report or play with an existing one, adding all sorts of bells and whistles. Figure 1-5 shows this happening in Design view.

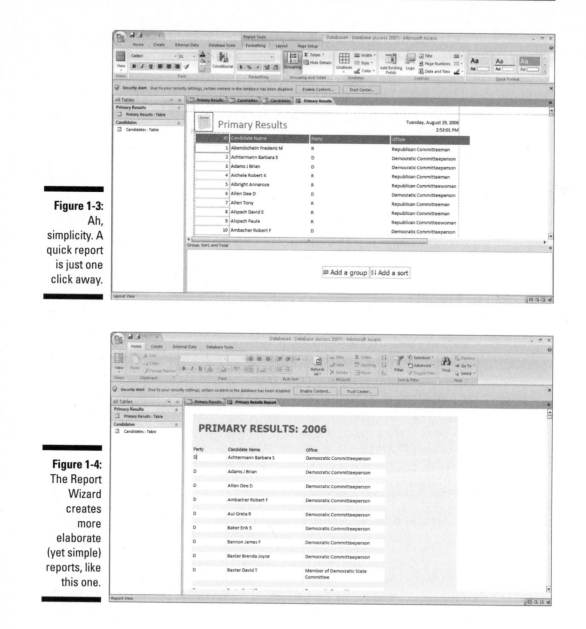

Figure 1-3:
Ah,
simplicity. A
quick report
is just one
click away.

Figure 1-4:
The Report
Wizard
creates
more
elaborate
(yet simple)
reports, like
this one.

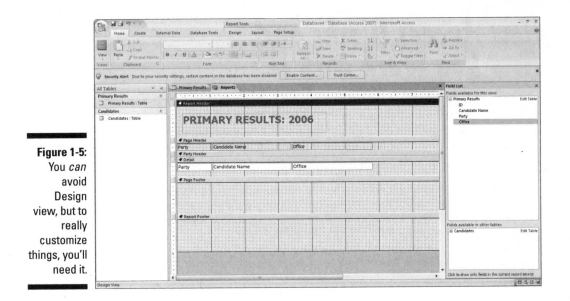

Figure 1-5:
You *can*
avoid
Design
view, but to
really
customize
things, you'll
need it.

So, you can create any kind of custom report in Access, using any or all of your database tables and any of the fields from those tables, and you can group fields and place them in any order you want:

- ✔ With the Report Wizard, you can choose from several preset layouts for your report, and it can all be customized row by row, column by column.

- ✔ Quick Format buttons apply preset designs to existing reports.

- ✔ If you want to place your personal stamp on every aspect of your report, you can use Design view to

  - Add titles, instructional or descriptive text boxes, and graphics.

  - Set up customized headers and footers to include any information you want to appear on all the report's pages.

If all this sounds exciting, or at least interesting, then you're really on the right track with Access. The need to create custom reports is a major reason to use Access, and you can find out about all these reporting options in Chapters 14 through 17. That's right: four whole chapters on reporting — it *must* be a big feature in Access!

How Access Works and How You Work with It

When you look at all the applications in Microsoft Office — Word, Excel, PowerPoint, Outlook, and of course, Access — you'll see some features that are consistent throughout the suite. There are big differences, too, and that's where books like these come in handy, helping you deal with what's different or not terribly obvious to a new user.

Access has several features in common with the rest of the applications in the Microsoft Office suite. You'll find the same buttons on several of the tabs, and the Quick Access toolbar, demonstrated in Chapter 2, appears in all the applications, as do the items on the menu.

If you already know how to open, save, and print in, say, Word, you're probably ready to do the same things in Access without any difficulty.

To make sure you're totally Access-ready, here are the basic procedures to make sure that you have a solid foundation on which to build.

Opening Access

Access opens in any one of several ways. So, like a restaurant with a very comprehensive menu, some people will love all the choices, and others will say, "I can't decide! There are just too many things to choose from!" Of course, the multiple ways to open Access aren't designed to suit any diner's palate, but to accommodate all the different situations Access users find themselves in.

Now, you'll run into situations in which one of the ways is the glaringly best choice — hands down, that one will be the way to go. But what if you've never heard of it? You'll be trying to find my phone number (I'm unlisted — ha!) so you can give me a piece of your mind. So to acquaint you with *all* your choices, so you'll be ready for any situation, here are all the ways that you can open Access:

✔ Click the Start menu button (in the lower-left corner of the screen) and choose All Programs⇨Microsoft Office⇨Microsoft Office Access 2007.

  Figure 1-6 shows my Start menu. I have a lot of programs, many of which you may not have; don't worry about that — just focus on the Microsoft Office submenu and make your choice from that.

✔ If you've recently used Access, it's listed on the left side of the Start menu (see Figure 1-7). Just choose Start⇨Microsoft Office Access 2007, and Access opens.

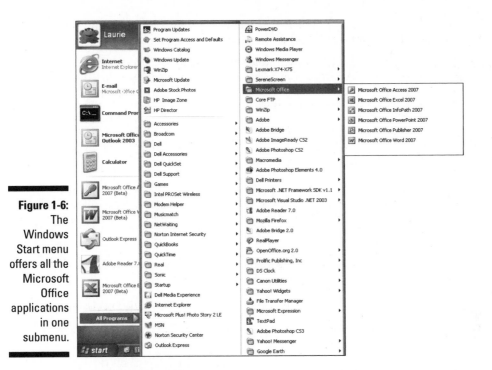

Figure 1-6:
The
Windows
Start menu
offers all the
Microsoft
Office
applications
in one
submenu.

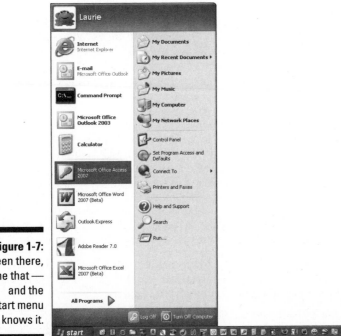

Figure 1-7:
Been there,
done that —
and the
Start menu
knows it.

✔ Double-click any existing Access database file on your Desktop or in a folder (as shown in Figure 1-8). Access opens automatically.

Access 2007 will open the database files you created with previous versions of Access, and should support whatever features are employed within the database. All your tables should open properly, and reports, forms, and queries should all work fine, too.

✔ If some helpful person has added Access to the Quick Launch toolbar (on the Windows Taskbar), you can click the Access 2007 icon (it looks like a pink key) and there you go. Access opens for you right then and there.

Does having an Access icon on the Taskbar sound extremely convenient? It is! To add the icon, follow these steps:

1. **Choose Start⇨Microsoft Office.**

2. **Hold down the Ctrl key and click and drag the Access menu command down to the Quick Launch bar.**

   A black I-beam will appear where you point with your mouse on the bar, indicating where the new icon will go.

3. **Release the mouse button and then the Ctrl key**

   You've got yourself single-click access to, well, *Access.*

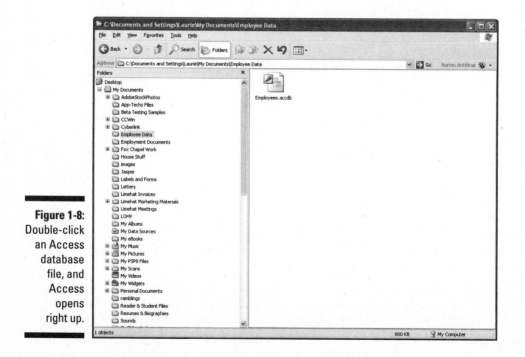

Figure 1-8: Double-click an Access database file, and Access opens right up.

Selecting a starting point

So Access is open, and assuming you opened it from the Start menu or from
the Quick Launch bar, you're staring at the Access interface, which includes
some features whose purposes may elude you or that you may not know how
to use. Hey — don't worry — that's why you're reading this book!

You can find out more about all the tabs and buttons, panels and menus, and
all that fun stuff in Chapter 2 — for now, just look at the ways Access lets you
get started with your database, be it an existing one that needs work or a new
one you have all planned out and ready to go.

Opening an existing database

Well, this is the easy one. If a database already exists, you can open it by
selecting it from the Open Recent Database list on the far right side of the
Access window (see Figure 1-9). Just click once on the database in the list
and it opens, listing its current tables, queries, reports, and forms on the far
left side of the window.

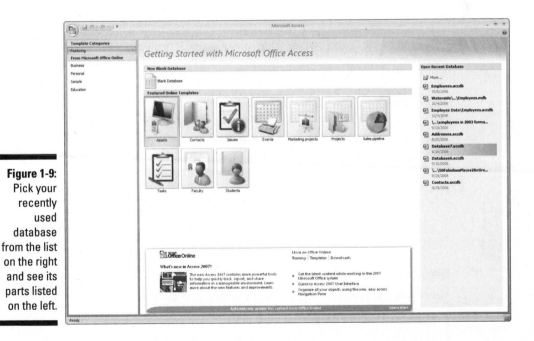

Figure 1-9:
Pick your
recently
used
database
from the list
on the right
and see its
parts listed
on the left.

When the database is open, you can open its various parts just by double-
clicking them in that left-most panel, and whatever you open appears in the
main, central part of the window. Figure 1-10 shows a table, ready for editing.

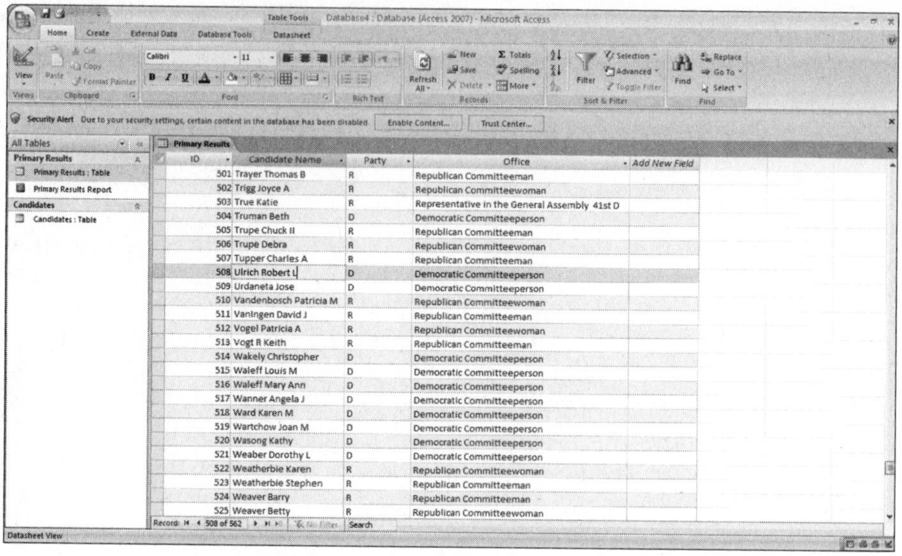

Figure 1-10:
An existing
table, ready
for records.

After you open a table, you can begin entering or editing records — and you can read more about how that's done in Chapter 6, where the different ways to edit your data and tweak your tables' setups are demonstrated. If you want to tinker with any existing queries, these, too, open just by clicking them in the list on the left side of the workspace. For more information on queries, check out Chapters 11 and 12. You can do simple sorting and look for particular records with the skills you'll discover in Chapter 9.

Starting a new database from scratch

So you don't have a database to open, eh? Well, don't let that stop you. To start a new one, all you have to do is open Access using any of the techniques listed earlier in this chapter — except the one that starts Access by opening an existing database file.

A database file holds *all* your database components. Everything associated with the data is part of the database, including

- ✔ All the tables that house your data
- ✔ Queries that help you search and use the data
- ✔ Reports that show what your data is and what it means
- ✔ Forms that allow people to view, enter, and edit data

After Access is open, you can click the Blank Database button (shown in Figure 1-11) to get started. Clicking that button opens a panel on the far right, which allows you to name your database and select a home for it. For the specific steps in this process, read on:

1. **With Access open and the "Getting Started with Microsoft Access" screen displayed, click the Blank Database button under the heading New Blank Database.**

   A panel appears on the right side of the Access window asking for a name for your new database (see Figure 1-11).

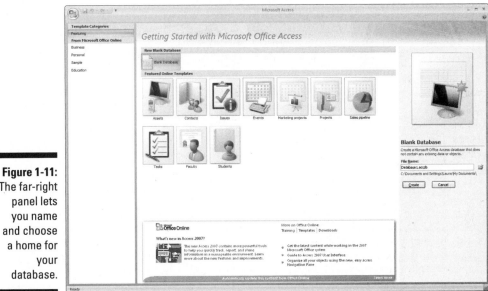

Figure 1-11:
The far-right panel lets you name and choose a home for your database.

2. **Replace the default** `DatabaseX.accdb` **with whatever name you want to use.**

   The X in the preceding filename represents a number — Access assigns a consecutive number to the default names, based on any previously created databases.

   If this is your absolute first one in a fresh installation of Access, the filename offered in this panel will be `Database1.accdb`. Note that the "accdb" extension appears automatically — you don't need to type that yourself.

3. **As needed, choose a new location for the database file by following these steps:**

   a. *Click the little file folder (with an arrow on it) found to the right of the File Name box.*

   This opens the File New Database dialog box, shown in Figure 1-12, which you can use to navigate to the drive/folder where your database should live.

   b. *Use the Save In drop list or the panel on the left side of the dialog box to choose a folder for your database. Once you're looking at a list of* folders, click once to select the one in which you want to store your database.

c. As needed, click the New Folder button (a folder with an asterisk on it) and name your new folder — click OK to return to the File New Database dialog box.

d. Click OK — the name you gave the file in Step 2 is applied, and the file is saved to the location you chose.

4. Click the Create button.

A blank table opens with the first cell in the grid (the first field in the first record) selected.

At this point, you can begin entering records into your first table or begin naming your fields and setting them up. The field names go in the topmost row (the "ID" field is already created), and "Add New Field" is atop the column with the active cell. If you choose to save your table now (right-click the Table1 tab and choose Save), you can name your table something more useful than "Table1."

Starting with a template

Access provides templates, or database cookie-cutters, for your new database needs. You'll find a list of template categories on the left side of the Access window when you first open the application. As shown in Figure 1-13, you can choose a template category on the left (which changes the displayed icons in the center of the workspace), or pick a particular template from the icons representing the templates available at Microsoft Office Online. Everything from Assets and Inventory to Marketing to Accounting and Finance is represented, so chances are, you'll find just what you need.

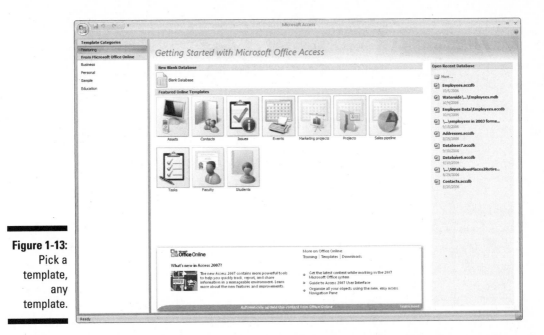

Figure 1-13:
Pick a
template,
any
template.

What about those big icons in the middle of the Access window? As shown in Figure 1-15, there's also a big Microsoft Office Online tab in the middle of the window, with three icons: Customer Service Database, Marketing Projects Database, and Gradebook Database. Covering everyone from someone in sales to a school teacher, these templates are also accompanied by a link to more online templates (see "More on Microsoft Office Online" and the three links beneath it, also shown in Figure 1-14).

When you click a template category in the left-hand list "From Microsoft Office Online," the center area in the workspace changes. It shows the name of the category you clicked and a series of template icons for that category. For example, if you click Business, you see the icons shown in Figure 1-15, where you can pick from different business databases — Assets, Contacts, Events, Issues, and so on.

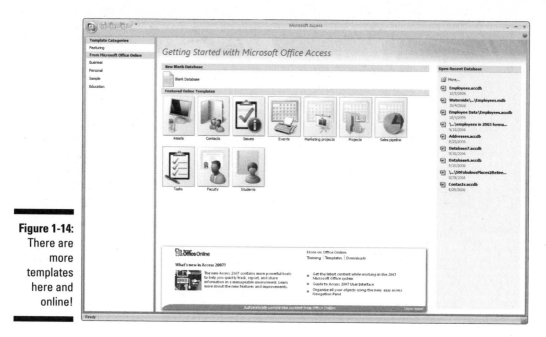

Figure 1-14:
There are
more
templates
here and
online!

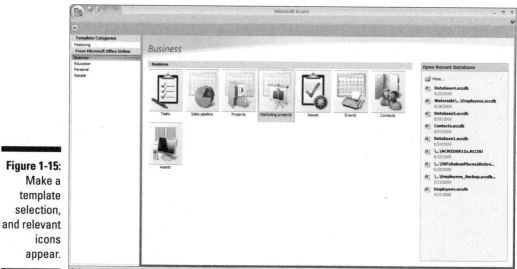

Figure 1-15:
Make a
template
selection,
and relevant
icons
appear.

If you click an icon (such as Marketing Projects), the right-hand panel discussed earlier (when we started with a new, blank database) activates, and you can now give your new database a name and click the Download button to download it from the Web (see Figure 1-16).

After the template is downloaded (or if it was a template that was available within your installed copy of Access and no download was needed), you can start building data into it. What's different than the previous procedure that uses this right-side panel to build a database from scratch (naming it, choosing a place to store it) is that instead of having a blank "Table1" and nothing else, the template gives you pre-made tables, reports, queries, and forms (in various combinations and numbers, based on the template you chose) and they're all set up — all *you* have to do is start entering records. Figure 1-17 shows the populated list of database components — a table and three reports — that comes with the Contacts database template.

Just like the table you built from scratch, the template-based tables need to be populated with data. You can change field names (see Chapter 5 for directions) and add and remove fields, too. After you tweak them to be appropriate for *your* database, you can begin entering records, one field at a time.

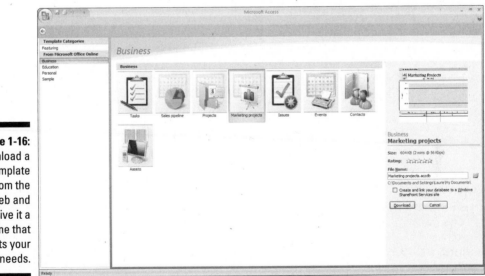

Figure 1-16: Download a template from the Web and give it a name that suits your needs.

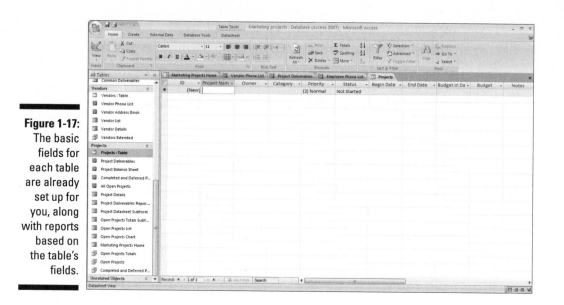

Now what?

So you've got a new database started. What do you do now? You leaf on over to Chapter 2, where you can find out more about all the tools that Access offers — tools that are on-screen almost all the time and those that are specific to the way you chose to dig in and start that database.

In Chapter 3, you actually begin building a database, setting up tables and the fields that give them structure. And you'll figure out which tables you need to set up, putting that great plan that this chapter helped you build to work!

Chapter 2

Finding Your Way Around Access

*I*f you ever used Access 2003 or any of its predecessors, or if you've used any of the Microsoft Office suite before the 2007 edition, you're probably surprised by the new 2007 interface. I say you're probably surprised because in at least the last two or three versions of Office, Microsoft hasn't introduced any major changes to the look and feel of the software. In fact, many people felt that there was no big change between any of the versions of Office since Office 97, and a lot of people chose to stick with whatever version they were using when new versions came out. You may, for example, be upgrading to Office 2007 after having used Office 2000 for several years, never having seen the need to move to Office XP or 2003.

Whatever version of Office (and therefore Access) you've been using, the new Office 2007 interface is strikingly different:

✔ Menus have given way to tabs and buttons in what's known as the *Ribbon*.

✔ Toolbars are no longer made up of distinct, 3-D buttons. Instead, there are buttons and graphic examples of formatting, pictures of what the buttons create, and drop-down lists.

Figure 2-1 shows the Access 2007 interface for a new, blank database with an as-yet-unpopulated table on its own tab. In this image, the Datasheet tab is active, but you can see the Home, Create, External Data, and Database Tools tabs to the left of the active tab.

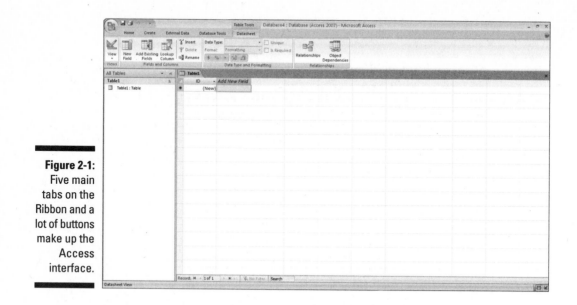

Figure 2-1:
Five main
tabs on the
Ribbon and a
lot of buttons
make up the
Access
interface.

You also get new features on the sides of the workspace, which change
depending on what you're doing or which button you've clicked:

- If you're starting a new database, options for doing so appear in the
  center panel and on the right side of the workspace.

- If you're working with an existing database, its parts are listed in a panel
  on the left side of the workspace.

- Panels also open up along the bottom of the workspace when specific
  activities are taking place.

I won't go into every possible combination of on-screen features in this
chapter — you get to know a lot of them in the subsequent chapters.
For now, I'll show you the basic workspace in three states:

- When Access first opens up

- When a new database is being built, either from scratch or when you've
  started with one of Access's database templates

- When you're working on an existing database

As you read through the following sections, you can refer solely to the accom-
panying figures or, if you want, try to work along with the procedures — you'll
find doing what you see described here boosts your confidence when you're
using Access later, on your own.

The Getting Started Window

So you're ready to dive in. Good for you! It's easy to start Access. You can start the application in multiple ways, accommodating nearly any situation you're in. Whether you're starting Access to view and edit an existing Access database (which gives you what you see in Figure 2-2) or are about to create your own (which opens the application and displays the Getting Started window, shown in Figure 2-3), you can get to the tools you need quickly and easily. Figure 2-2 shows an existing database open to one of its tables, its other components listed on the left side of the workspace.

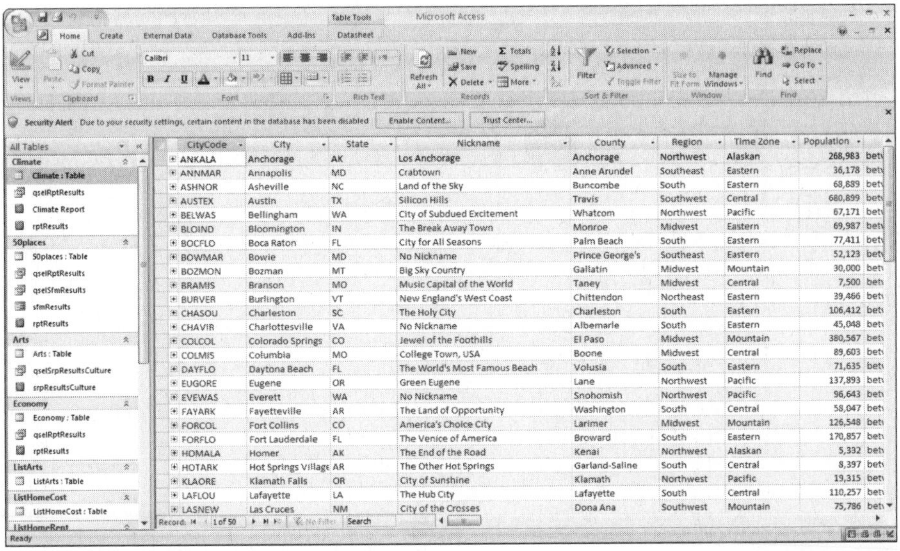

Figure 2-2: Open Access *and* your existing database in one fell swoop.

When you first open the application, as you also discover in Chapter 1, you're presented with a workspace that offers three basic ways to make that swan dive into the pool that is Access. You can pick which part of the existing database you want to work with, you can start a new, blank database from scratch, or you can start out with one of the Access templates.

Figure 2-3 shows the Getting Started window with the Blank Database icon highlighted. Beneath that button are the Featured Online Templates icons, for using various preset databases as your jumping-off point.

If you opened Access by using the Start menu or a Desktop/Taskbar icon and *now* you want to open an existing database, note the list of files on the right side of the window — in the Open Recent Database panel. Click any one of the files and the database opens, displaying its parts on the panel on the left side of the workspace. If you don't see the file you want there, you can click Open from the Quick Access toolbar — click the big Office logo button in the upper-left corner of the workspace, as shown in Figure 2-4. The figure also shows the resulting Open dialog box.

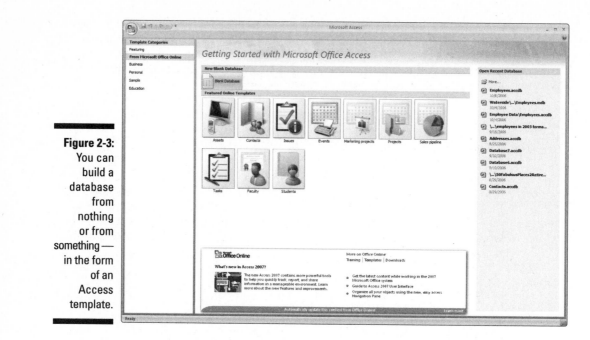

Figure 2-3:
You can
build a
database
from
nothing
or from
something —
in the form
of an
Access
template.

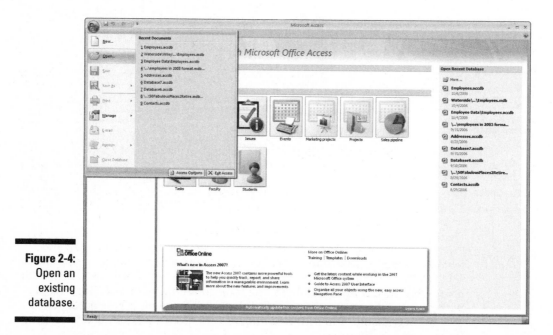

Figure 2-4:
Open an
existing
database.

So that's it, really — any way you want to get started is represented in the appropriately named Getting Started window. After you get working, however, it's time to use the on-screen tools that don't appear until you open a database. Read on for a whirlwind tour of the Access workspace, including views and explanations of all the major bells, whistles, and buttons.

Working with Access's On-screen Tools

When you open a database — be it an existing one or one you're just starting from a blank database or a template — the workspace changes, offering the Ribbon and its five tabs, shown in Figure 2-5. These tabs are not to be confused with the database components tabs, which appear in the center of the workspace for whichever tables, reports, queries, or forms you have chosen to open from the list on the left.

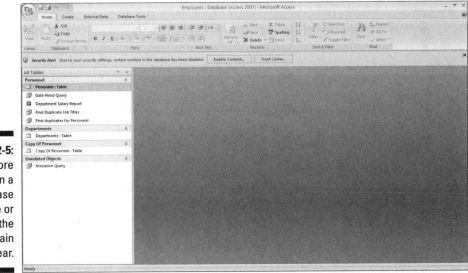

Figure 2-5:
Even before you open a database table or report, the five main tabs appear.

When the Ribbon tabs first appear, many of their buttons are dimmed — because they don't become available until you're doing something that warrants their use. For example, if you haven't opened any tables, forms, reports, or queries in your open database, the tools for editing or formatting your database will appear on the tabs, but they'll be dimmed, which indicates that they're unavailable. Tools for creating new components are available on the Create tab, but anything that works with existing data will be dimmed.

After you open a table, report, query, or form, the tools become available, as shown in Figure 2-6.

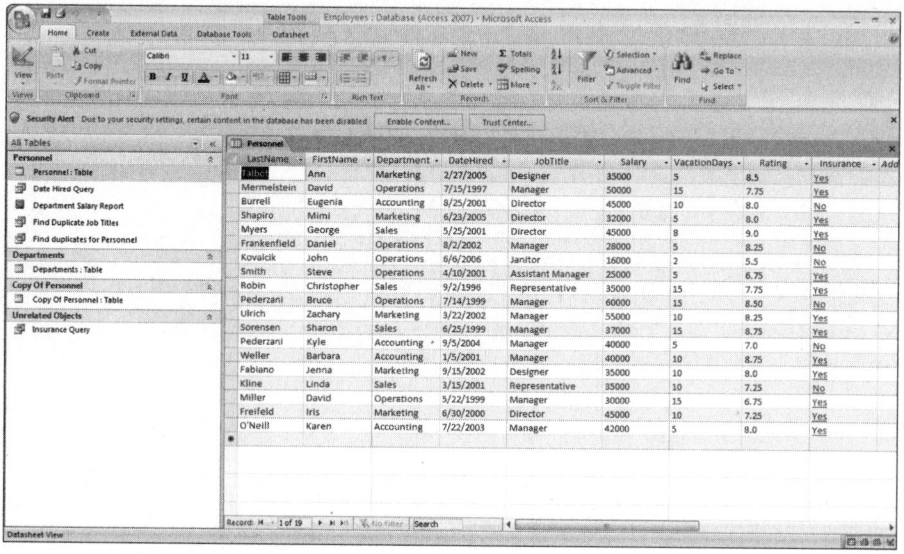

Figure 2-6: The buttons relevant to what's open and active in your database are available when you need them.

When anything other than a table is open in the workspace, you have only four tabs — the Datasheet tab disappears when a report, form, or query is open.

Clicking tabs

To move from one tab on the Ribbon to another, simply click the tab's name. It's easy to see which tab is currently open — as shown in Figure 2-7, the tab is bright, and you can see all of its buttons. When you mouse over a tab (in the Figure 2-7, the Create tab is active, but the mouse is pointing to the Home tab in anticipation of clicking it) a glow forms around and inside the tab. That glow appears on the Home tab which indicates that the mouse is pointing to it.

When you have a table open, the Datasheet tab is displayed, and it has a tab above it entitled Table Tools. The Table Tools tab doesn't do anything other than offer further identification of the content and purpose of the Datasheet tab, and nothing happens when you click it.

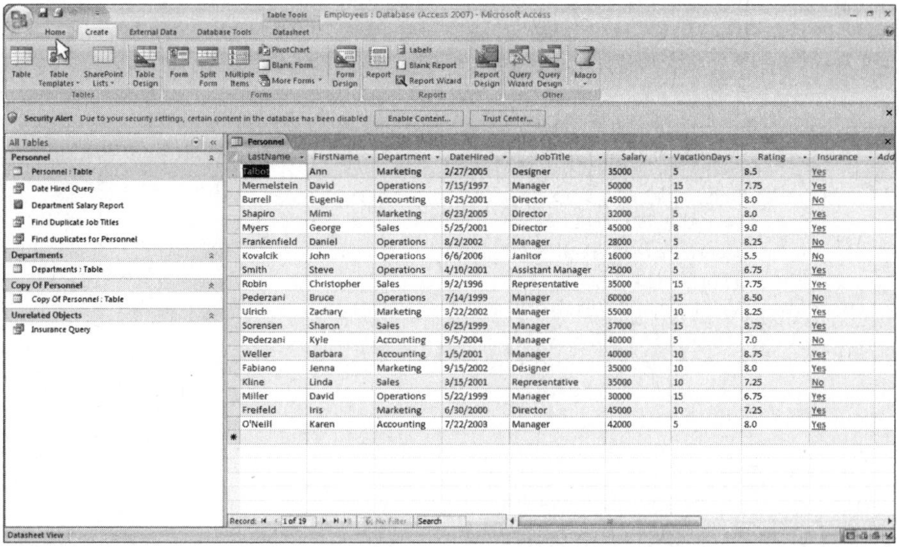

Figure 2-7:
You can easily tell the active tab from the inactive ones. The tab about to become active is obvious, too.

Using buttons

Access buttons come in two varieties:

✓ **Buttons that do something when they're clicked,** either opening a dialog box or wizard or performing some change or task in your open table, report, query, or form

✓ **Buttons that represent lists or menus of choices.** This latter variety comes in two flavors of its own:

  • Drop-down list buttons are accompanied by a small, down-pointing triangle, appearing to the button's right. When you click the triangle, a list of options appears, as shown in Figure 2-8.

  • Some buttons have a down-pointing triangle at the bottom of the button (as shown in Figure 2-9). Click anywhere on the button (not necessarily on the triangle), and a menu appears.

The Quick Access menu and toolbar

If you've used previous versions of Office, you may notice that there's no File menu in Access 2007. This menu contained key actions and features. The File menu was where you went to *print, save, open,* and *close* files. You'd miss these actions if there were no Office 2007 equivalent.

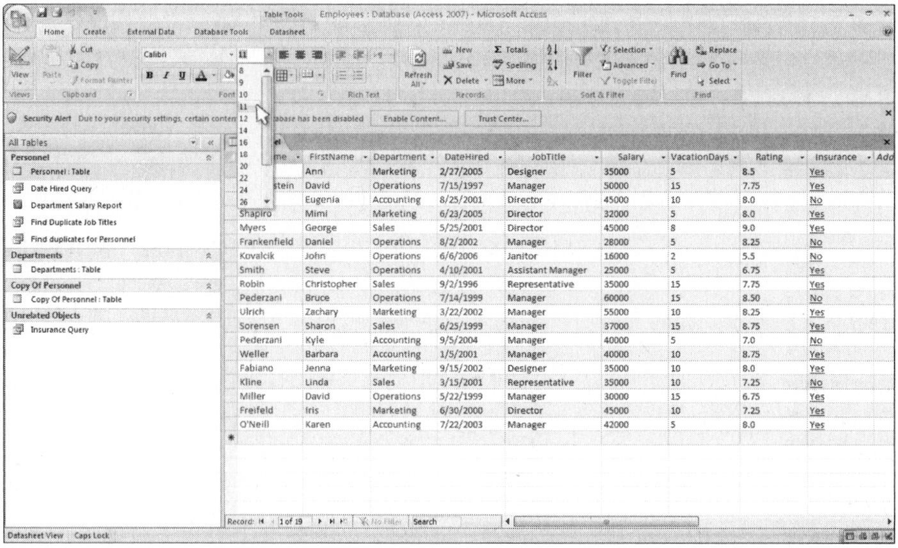

Figure 2-8:
Click the triangle to the right of the button and make a choice.

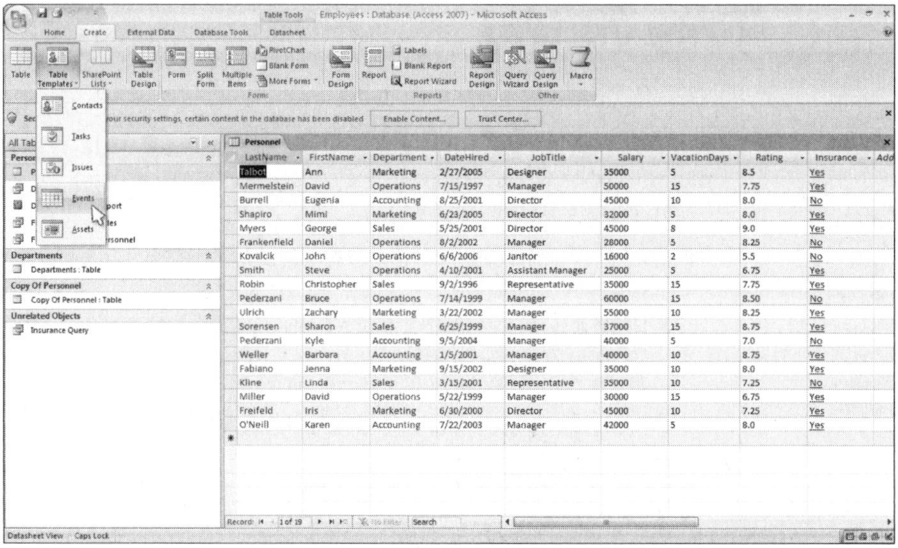

Figure 2-9: Menu buttons display a — surprise! — menu when clicked.

Panic not, dear Office user. Replacing the File menu, and incorporating some of the Edit menu's commands, is the Quick Access menu and toolbar. Note the big button with the Office logo on it in the upper-left corner of the Access (and other Office applications') workspace. Next to it are three buttons and a drop-down list arrow. Clicking the big button spawns a menu (see Figure 2-10), and the buttons next to that big button perform common tasks, such as saving, printing, and "undoing" (found previously in the Edit menu).

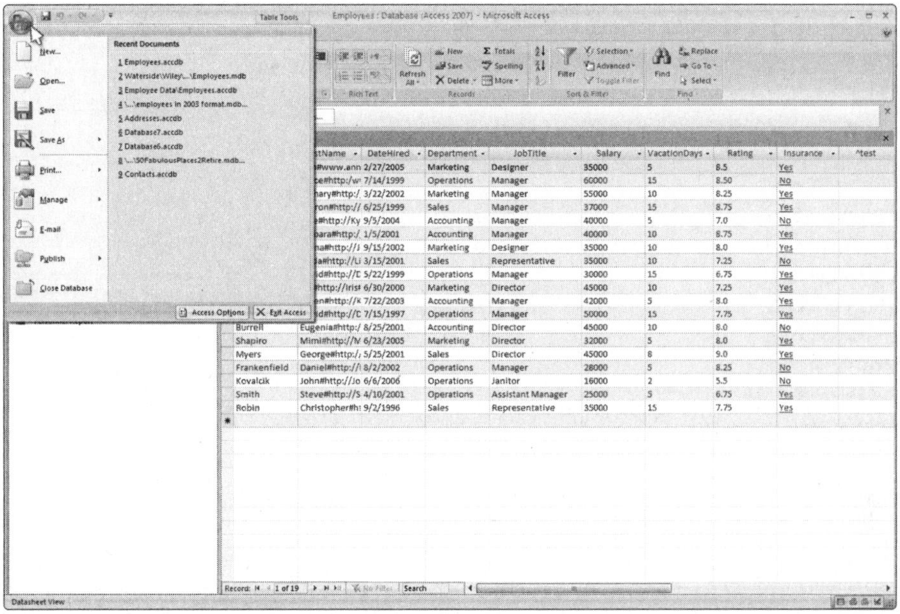

Figure 2-10: Craving the File menu's tools? Look no further than the Quick Access button and toolbar.

What's that triangle at the end of the Quick Access toolbar? It offers a pop-up menu with two choices: Customize Quick Access Toolbar and Place Quick Access Toolbar Below the Ribbon. You can get the same pop-up by right-clicking any tab or button on the Ribbon. These commands are demonstrated in the next major section of this chapter.

Accessing panes, panels, and context-sensitive tools

Depending on what's going on within the workspace — that is, what you've just done in terms of editing your table, report, query, or form, or which button you've clicked on one of the Ribbon tabs — Access offers relevant on-screen tools and panels. As an example of this context-sensitivity, if you open a table and click the Report button on the Create tab (see the Reports section of the Create tab), not only does a report appear, but you also get a Group, Sort, and Total panel across the bottom of the workspace, as shown in Figure 2-11.

To find out more about reporting, including the ability to group, sort, and total your data, see Chapters 14 through 17.

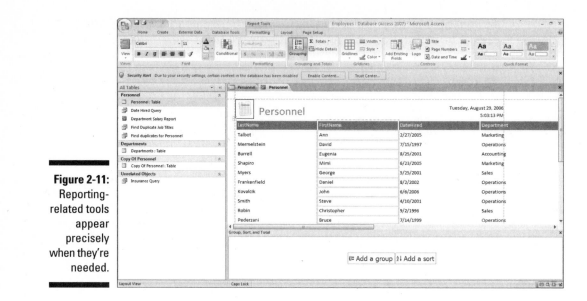

Figure 2-11:
Reporting-related tools appear precisely when they're needed.

The five main tabs (four tabs, if you don't have a table open) are joined by additional tabs, depending on what you're up to:

✔ If you create a report, Formatting and Layout tabs appear under a Report Tools heading following the Database Tools tab.

✔ If you create a form (by clicking the Form button on the Create tab), you get a Formatting and Layout tabs, under a Form Tools heading (as shown in Figure 2-12)

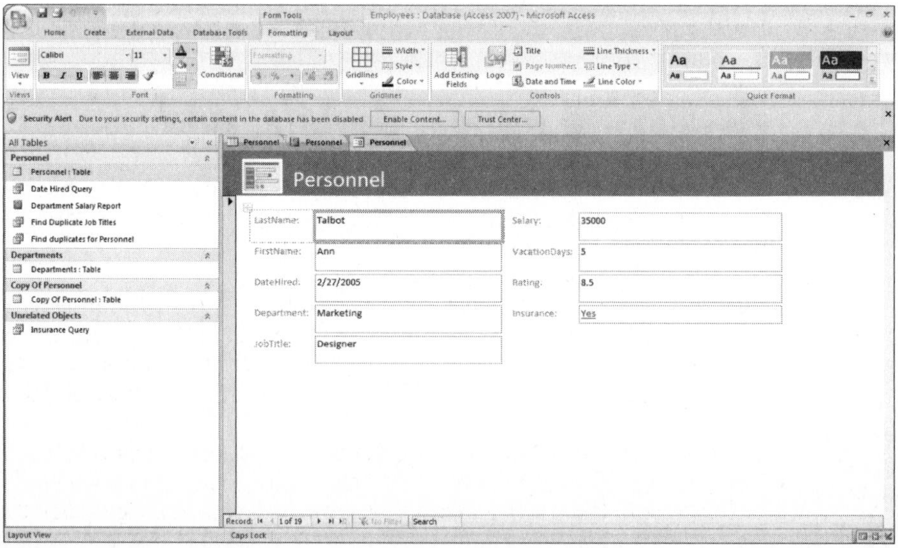

Figure 2-12:
Access is aware of your actions and supplies the right tools for the job at hand.

As you work with Access, you'll get a feel for what's going to appear when you do certain things. Things appear and disappear as you work because Access offers you just what you need for the task you're performing or feature you're using.

Customizing the Access Workspace

Any good application provides some capability for the user to customize the workspace — from adding and rearranging buttons on the toolbar to dragging toolbars and panes around to optimize the layout.

Access is certainly a good software application so it does allow you to customize the workspace. You can move the Quick Access toolbar, you can add buttons from the main tabs to the Quick Access toolbar, you can resize the Ribbon, you can tweak the status bar, and you can decide how or if your ScreenTips are displayed as you mouse over tools.

There's no need to do any customization, really — the default settings for toolbar locations, button combinations, and on-screen help are designed with the average or most common user in mind, and they're pretty good. On the other hand, you may just want to tweak things to feel at home. Think of the times you've fluffed the pillows on the couch before lying down — they may not have needed it, but you want to make your mark on your environment, right? Right.

Repositioning the Quick Access toolbar

For the position of the Quick Access toolbar, you have two choices:

- **Above the Ribbon, which is the default location**
- **Below the Ribbon**

To move the Quick Access toolbar, simply right-click it and choose Place Quick Access Toolbar Below the Ribbon. Figure 2-13 shows the pop-up menu with this command available.

When you place the Quick Access toolbar below the Ribbon, you'll notice that the same command (viewed by right-clicking the toolbar in its new location) is now Place Quick Access Toolbar Above the Ribbon. So it toggles like that, switching from Above to Below, depending on its current location.

You don't have to right-click specifically the Quick Access toolbar in order to reposition it. The aforementioned command (Place Quick Access Toolbar . . .) is available in the pop-up menu that appears when you right-click the tabs, too.

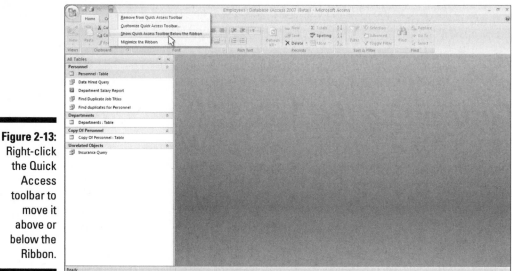

Figure 2-13:
Right-click
the Quick
Access
toolbar to
move it
above or
below the
Ribbon.

Adding buttons from the tabs to the Quick Access toolbar

Speaking of the Quick Access toolbar and all the ways you can access commands for customizing it, try this to add commands:

1. **With any database open (so that the Ribbon tabs are displayed), right-click any of the buttons on any of the tabs.**

   You can also right-click the Quick Access toolbar or any Ribbon tab.

2. **Choose Customize Quick Access Toolbar.**

   The Access Options dialog box opens (shown in Figure 2-14), with its Customization options displayed.

3. **Click the Choose Commands From drop-down list and choose a command category.**

   File is chosen by default, and the main Ribbon tabs as well as some of the context-sensitive tabs (for reports and forms) are listed.

4. **From any (or each) category, choose the commands you want to see at all times in the Quick Access toolbar by clicking them one at a time and then clicking the Add>> button.**

   As you click the Add>> button, the command you chose is added to the list on the right.

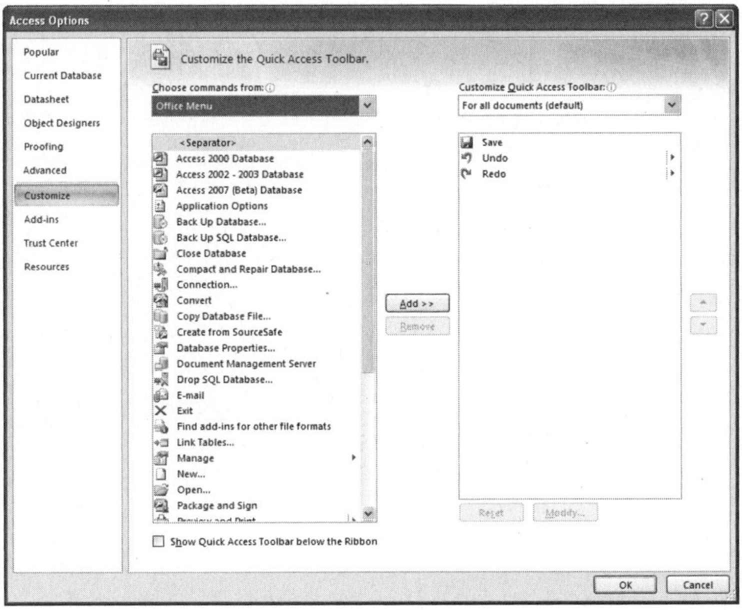

Figure 2-14:
Pick a
command
category
and a com-
mand to add
to the Quick
Access
toolbar.

5. Continue selecting categories and commands on the left and using the Add button to add them to the list on the right.

Not all of the commands will be usable at all the times that the Quick Access Toolbar is displayed. For example, if you choose to place a button from the Create tab on the Quick Access toolbar, the button won't be available until and unless a table, query, report, or form is open.

6. When you've added all the commands you want to add, click OK to add them and close the dialog box.

When you click OK, the changes to the Quick Access toolbar are applied. The toolbar's space on the top of the workspace grows to accommodate all the new buttons (Exit, Open, and Print Preview in this case), as shown in Figure 2-15.

If you want to quickly add a specific button to the Quick Access toolbar, and you're looking right at the button you want to add, just right-click the button and choose Add to the Quick Access Toolbar. The button you right-clicked instantly appears on the toolbar *and* remains in the tab where it was living when you right-clicked it.

Why would you use the Access Options dialog box? Because it gives you the ability to select buttons from all the tabs in one place — no need to go hunting on the tabs for the buttons you want to add. But when there's just one you want and you can see it at the time, the right-click method can't be beat.

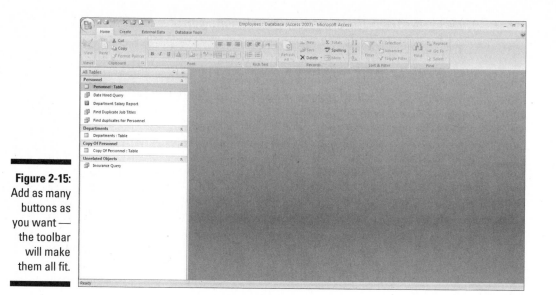

Figure 2-15:
Add as many
buttons as
you want —
the toolbar
will make
them all fit.

Removing buttons from the Quick Access toolbar

Want to remove a command from the Quick Access toolbar? It's easy:

1. **Point to the unwanted button on the Quick Access toolbar and right-click.**

2. **Choose Remove from Quick Access Toolbar from the pop-up menu (see Figure 2-16).**

   Voilà! It's gone.

Because the button remains on the tab where it originally lived, it's not lost — it's just not taking up space at the top of the Access workspace.

Be careful not to remove the default buttons — Save, Print, and Undo. Why? Because they're used so often it's silly to remove them from such a great location. If you do remove them, you'll have to use the Quick Access menu button and select them from that menu. That's two steps (opening the menu and making a selection) instead of one, and who wants to increase steps by 100%? Not me!

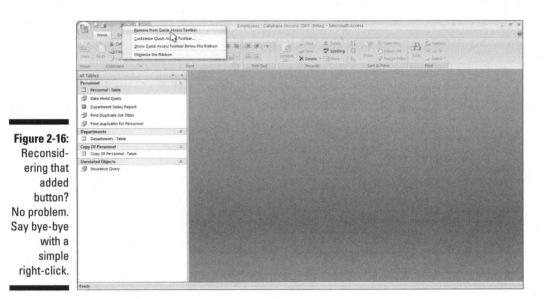

Figure 2-16:
Reconsid-
ering that
added
button?
No problem.
Say bye-bye
with a
simple
right-click.

Minimizing the Ribbon

Need more elbow room? If you need to spread out and want more workspace, you can make the Ribbon smaller, reducing it to just a strip of the tab titles (whichever tabs are in place at the time you choose to minimize the Ribbon). Once it is minimized, you can bring it back quickly and easily.

To minimize the Ribbon, follow these steps:

1. **Right-click anywhere on the Ribbon.**

   A pop-up menu appears. Note that you can click on a button, a Ribbon tab, along a section name (such as "Reports" on the Create tab, or "Font" on the Home tab) and the appropriate pop-up menu will appear.

2. **Choose Minimize the Ribbon.**

   The Ribbon is reduced to a long bar with just the tab titles on it, as shown in Figure 2-17.

3. **To bring the Ribbon back to its full glory, right-click the reduced Ribbon bar, and choose Minimize the Ribbon.**

   Note that the command is now checked (as also shown in Figure 2-17), indicating that the Ribbon is currently minimized. Performing this step — reselecting the command — toggles this setting off, and the Ribbon returns to full size.

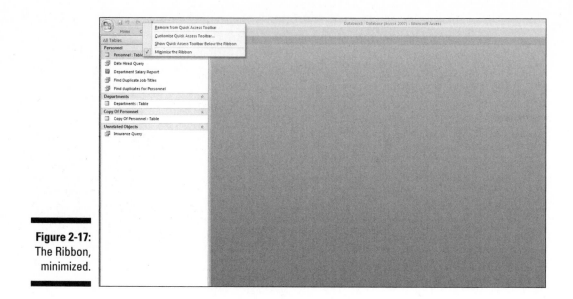

Figure 2-17:
The Ribbon,
minimized.

Working with ScreenTips

ScreenTips are the little names and brief descriptions of onscreen tools that appear when you mouse over buttons, commands, menus, and many of the other pieces of the Access workspace.

Not all onscreen features have ScreenTips, but for anything you can click and make something happen — a dialog box opens, Access performs some task for you, something is created — these things typically have associated ScreenTips that you can choose to view or not view, and if you choose to view them, you can choose to see very brief or more elaborate tips.

To tinker with Access' ScreenTips settings, follow these steps:

1. **Click the Quick Access menu button.**

   The Quick Access Menu opens.

2. **Click the Access Options button at the bottom of the menu, as shown in Figure 2-18.**

3. **From the list on the left side of the Access Options dialog box, select Popular.**

   The dialog box options change to show options related to ScreenTips, file formats and folders, and how your name and initials are stored.

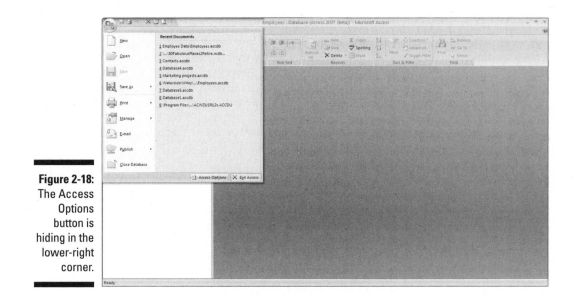

Figure 2-18:
The Access
Options
button is
hiding in the
lower-right
corner.

4. **In the first section of the dialog box, click the ScreenTip Scheme drop-down list, as shown in Figure 2-19.**

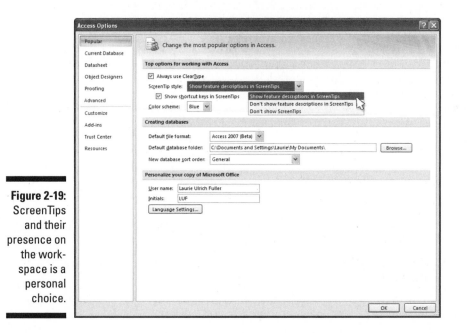

Figure 2-19:
ScreenTips
and their
presence on
the work-
space is a
personal
choice.

5. Choose from the following options:

- *Show Feature Descriptions in ScreenTips:* This option displays ScreenTips with extra information, as shown in Figure 2-20. Here you see that in addition to the name of the button, a brief description of how it works or its effect is displayed for your benefit. It even points to more assistance and information — in this case, the ScreenTip
references the use of the F1 key to open Access's Help files.

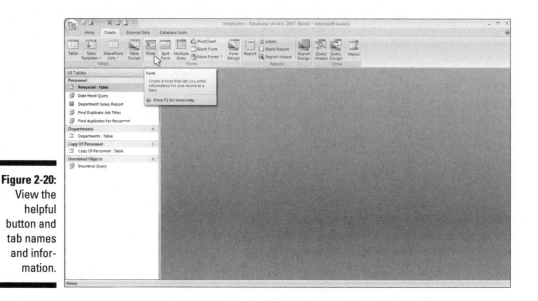

Figure 2-20:
View the helpful button and tab names and information.

- *Don't Show Feature Descriptions in ScreenTips:* If you want just the facts, ma'am, this is for you. ScreenTips will show just get the button name and no further explanation.

- *Don't Show ScreenTips:* Want to go it alone? Turn off ScreenTips.

6. Click OK to close the Access Options dialog box.

You can choose whether or not to include keyboard shortcuts in ScreenTips. This is on by default, and it's pretty useful — that is unless you plan to tape the Cheat Sheet from the front of this book to your shirt so it's always there to remind you of the various keyboard shortcuts Access has to offer. If that idea isn't appealing (or practical!), leave this option on.

Correcting your screen resolution for maximum visibility

If you find that the workspace tools in Access are too small to read, or if they're so big that you often have to scroll from side to side or up and down in tables just to see a handful of records or more than a few fields at a time, it's a good time to think about adjusting your Windows display settings.

To change your screen resolution, get back to your Windows Desktop (click the Show Desktop button on the Quick Launch toolbar or minimize all your open windows) and then follow these steps:

1. **Right-click an empty spot on the Desktop.**

   Don't click on or right next to any icons, or the resulting pop-up menu will relate to the icon, not to the Desktop.

2. **Choose Properties.**

   The Display Properties dialog box opens.

3. **Click the Settings tab.**

   The dialog box changes to show your screen resolution and your display color settings, as shown in Figure 2-21.

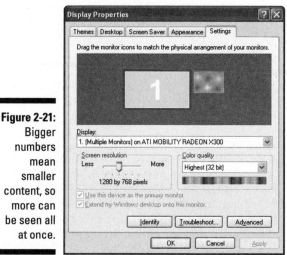

Figure 2-21:
Bigger numbers mean smaller content, so more can be seen all at once.

4. **Drag the Screen Resolution slider to the right to shrink the content of your window (so you can see more stuff at once) or to the left to make your on-screen items bigger.**

   Windows offers only the settings that work for the monitor you're using.

5. **Click Apply to see the new resolution.**

   The screen will go black for a second, and the new resolution is applied.

6. **In the resulting dialog box, click Yes to keep the new setting or No to go back to the previous setting.**

   If you don't like the setting, clicking No keeps the Properties dialog box open, and you can re-drag the Screen Resolution slider and repeat Steps 5 and 6 until you find a resolution you like.

Be sure Access is open while you're doing this so you can immediately hop back to Access and see the impact of your resolution change on the application workspace — bigger or smaller text, buttons, tabs, and so on.

The change to the Windows display setting will affect all your applications, the Windows Desktop, taskbar, and all operating system dialog boxes and menus. What makes Access more comfortable to look at may create problems elsewhere, so be prepared to adjust your resolution again to meet your visual needs in other applications.

Mousing Around

Access, like all Windows applications, is meant to be used with the mouse. The mouse is assumed to be your main way of communicating with the software — clicking Ribbon tabs, buttons, and drop-down lists, and making choices in dialog boxes to use things like the Report Wizard and the Access Options dialog box discussed in the previous sections of this chapter.

You can left-click to make standard choices from on-screen tools and right-click to access pop-up menus, also known as context-sensitive menus. They're considered *context-sensitive* because the menu choices vary depending on what was right-clicked. If you right-click a Ribbon tab or button, you get choices for customizing toolbars and buttons. If you right-click a database component tab (say the table tab while that table is open), you get choices related to the table.

Not a big fan of the mouse? Check out the Cheat Sheet in the front of this book. It's full of powerful keyboard shortcuts.

Navigating Access with the Alt Key

If you like to use the keyboard as much as possible when you're working with software, Access makes it somewhat easy to do that. I say *somewhat* because you need to use a special key in order to make the rest of the keyboard work as a commander.

When you want to switch tabs and issue commands with the keyboard (rather than with the mouse), press the Alt key. As shown in Figure 2-22, pressing Alt causes numbers and letters to appear in small squares on the Quick Access toolbar and the Ribbon's tabs. When the numbers and letters are visible, you can press one of those characters on your keyboard to issue a command (such as pressing 1 to Save) or to switch to a tab (such as pressing C to get to the Create tab).

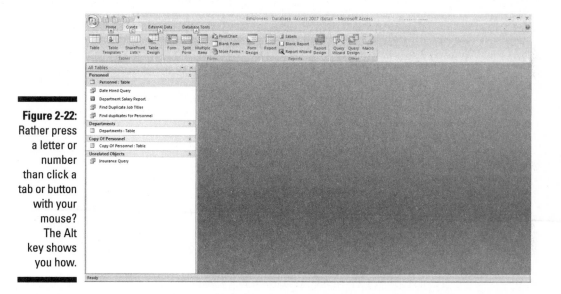

Figure 2-22:
Rather press a letter or number than click a tab or button with your mouse? The Alt key shows you how.

After you're on a tab, the individual buttons on that tab have their own keyboard shortcuts displayed. Instead of single numbers or letters, however, now you're looking at pressing key combinations, such as W+1 (displayed as W1 on-screen) to activate the Report Wizard. Figure 2-23 shows the keyboard shortcuts for the Create tab.

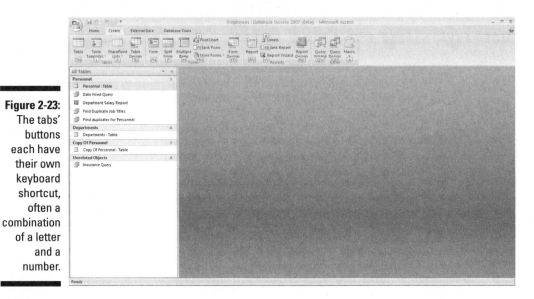

Figure 2-23:
The tabs'
buttons
each have
their own
keyboard
shortcut,
often a
combination
of a letter
and a
number.

The goal is not to try to press the two keys (such as W1 for the Report Wizard or L1 to display table templates) at the exact same time. Instead, press the first one listed, and with that key still pressed, tap the second key. Voilà!

Chapter 3

Database Basics

In This Chapter

▶ Getting to know some basic terms and concepts

▶ Outstanding in your field(s)

▶ Flat file? Relational? You decide.

▶ Getting a table started

*T*his may be the single most important chapter in this book. After you've read about why Access is the right tool for you (in Chapter 1) and how to get around in the Access interface (Chapter 2), it's time to really nail down how Access works and how to start building your database.

Database Lingo

Now, if the section heading ("Database Lingo") is making you panic that I want you to memorize a bunch of database jargon, don't worry. Just relax. Breathe normally. The next section, and many throughout this chapter, simply uses some terms you need to know so you can figure out what Access is referring to in various dialog boxes and on the tabs (the tabs you use to get at the commands in the Access workspace) . Knowing these terms will, therefore, help you get around and get things done in Access.

Unfortunately, you simply must know technical terms — there's no two ways about it. I'm talking about only a handful of words, though, some of which you probably already know and maybe even use in reference to information in general — words like *record* and *database*. See? Nothing high-tech, just some basic words and concepts you really need to absorb so you can move on and use Access effectively.

The terms in this section appear in size order, starting with the smallest piece of a database — the data — and advancing to the largest — the entire database itself. I've done it this way so you get the big picture, a little bit at a time, and see that the big picture is made up of smaller items. Seeing how they all fit together (and what to call each piece) is what this chapter's all about.

Data, no matter how you pronounce it

Data is the stuff that Access stores. Information you may store in your head one way will be stored in a different way in a database program like Access. For example, you may think of someone's name as *John Smith,* or you may only ever think of the guy as *John* — either because you don't know his last name or because you never use his last name. A database, however, stores his name as either *John Smith,* in a *field* called Name, or as two pieces — Last Name (Smith) and First Name (John). The latter approach is best because it gives you more freedom to use the data in more ways. You can sort the data by Last Name, for example, which is hard to do if you've just stored the entire name as one chunk.

Get the idea? As I say in Chapter 1, where you plan out your database, it's a good idea to break the data down as much as possible. No matter how you pronounce it — "day-tah" or "dat-tuh" — it's your information, and you want to be able to get at it in the simplest, most logical way possible. As you read on in this chapter, and when you review Chapters 1 and 2, you'll see that Access gives you all the tools you need to do just that — it's just a matter of using them!

Fields of dreams (or data)

Because people don't want their data to wander around homeless, the technical wizards created *fields* — places for your data to live. Each field holds one kind of data. For example, to track information about a baseball card collection, your fields might include Manufacturer, Player Name, Position, Year, Team, and Average (or ERA, for pitchers). If you have a name and address database, it might consist of Last Name, First Name, Middle Initial, Address1, Address2, City, State, Zip, Phone, Cell, and Email. When you think about it, it's pretty logical. What are all the things you can know about a baseball player? A client? A product? These *things* become *fields*.

As with the term *data,* other database programs, such as FoxPro and FileMaker, all agree on what a field is. However, larger database packages, such as Oracle and Microsoft SQL Server, use the term *column* instead of *field.* And to make things more exciting, Microsoft Excel stores your fields (when you use Excel to store a list) in columns. The tabular structure of a database table is what leads Oracle and SQL to refer to columns rather than fields, but for heaven's sake — couldn't they have stuck to a term we all know?

Records

Having fields is a good start, but if you stop there, how do you know which last name works with which first name? Something needs to keep those unruly fields in order — something like a *record*. All the fields for one baseball card — or one client or one product — are all collectively known as a *record*. If you have two baseball cards in your collection, you have two records in your database, one for each card. Fifty clients? Fifty records.

For a little more about records, check out the following:

- ✔ FoxPro and FileMaker concur on the term *record*. Oracle and Microsoft SQL Server use the term *row* instead. Again, this comes from the tabular (table-like) structure of the tables in which their records . . . er, rows . . . are stored.

- ✔ Each record in a *table* contains the same fields but (usually) has different data in those fields. And not every record has to have data in every field. If someone doesn't have a cell phone, you can't very well have any data in the Cell field for that person, right?

- ✔ A single record contains all the information you need about a single item (accounting entry, recipe, or whatever) in your table. That's all there is to it.

Tables

A *table* is a collection of records that describe similar data. The key phrase to remember in that last sentence is *similar data*. All the records in a single table contain fields of similar data. The information about that baseball card collection may fit into a single table. So would the client or product data. However, a single table would *not* handle both baseball cards *and* clients because they're unrelated databases. You wouldn't put the records for your car's repairs in the folder where you keep your Christmas cookie recipes, right?

Why? Because if anyone else needed to know when you last had the tires rotated, they aren't going to know to look in the same place one finds the best recipe for Ginger Snaps. *You* might remember that they're stored in the same place, but it's just too confusing for anyone else. And too limiting. Access lets you write reports and queries based on your data, and if the data in your database isn't all related, it'll be chaos trying to write a report or generate a query that pulls data from that database. You could end up with a recipe that calls for motor oil or a maintenance schedule that tells you to preheat the car to 350 degrees. Such a report might be amusing, but it's hardly useful.

The database

An Access *database*, or *database file* (the terms are interchangeable), is a collection of everything relating to a particular set of information. The database contains all the tables, queries, reports, and forms that Access helps you create to manage and work with your stuff. Instead of storing all those items *individually* on the disk drive, where they can become lost, misplaced, or accidentally erased, they're grouped into a single collective file.

Here's an important point: All those parts — the tables, the reports, queries, and forms — all cumulatively make a database. And that's before you even enter any records into the tables. The database, therefore, is more than the data; it's the tools that store, manipulate, and allow you to look at the data, too.

Field Types and Uses

A field, you remember, is where your data lives. Each field holds one piece of data, such as Last Name or Batting Average.

Because there are so many different kinds of information in the world, Access offers a variety of field types for storing it. In fact, Access puts ten field types at your disposal:

- ✔ Text
- ✔ Memo
- ✔ Number
- ✔ Date/Time
- ✔ Currency
- ✔ AutoNumber
- ✔ Yes/No
- ✔ OLE Object
- ✔ Hyperlink
- ✔ Attachment

Don't worry about figuring out what each one is or does based on its name — I go over each one shortly. As you can see, though, the list covers just about any type of data you can imagine. And remember, each one can be customized extensively, resulting in fields that meet your needs exactly. If you absolutely cannot wait to find out about modifying all the specs for your fields, check out Chapter 4.

Below is a breakdown of the ten field types and how they're used. You'll also find out a little bit about how you can tweak them to meet your specific needs:

- ✔ **Text:** Stores up to 255 characters of text — letters, numbers, punctuation, and any combination thereof.

  Numbers in a text field aren't numbers; they're just a bunch of digits hanging out together in a field. Be careful of this fact when you design the tables in your database.

  Text fields have one setting you need to know about: size. When you create a text field, Access wants to know how many characters the field holds. That's the field *size.* If you create a field called First Name and make its size 6, *Joseph* fits into the field, but not *Jennifer.* This restriction can be a problem. A good general rule is to make the field a little larger than you think you need. It's easy to make the field even larger if you need to, but it's potentially dangerous to make it smaller. Surgery on fields is covered in Chapter 4.

- ✔ **Memo:** Holds up to 64,000 characters of information — that's almost 18 pages of text. This is a *really big* text field. It's great for general notes, detailed descriptions, and anything else that requires a lot of space.

- ✔ **Number:** Holds real, for-sure numbers. You can add, subtract, and calculate your way to fame and fortune with number fields. But if you're working with dollars and cents (or pounds and pence), use a currency field instead.

- ✔ **Date/Time:** Stores time, date, or a combination of the two, depending on which format you use. Use a date/time field to track the whens of life. Pretty versatile, eh?

- ✔ **Currency:** Tracks money, prices, invoice amounts, and so on. In an Access database, the bucks stop here. For that matter, so do the lira, marks, and yen. If you're in the mood for some *other* kind of number, check out the number field.

- ✔ **AutoNumber:** It does just what it says: It fills itself with an automatically generated number every time you make a new record, and each number is unique. As you find out later, it's important that each table in your database have a unique field in each record, and AutoNumber can create a field just for that purpose. You can use it when you add a customer to your table — Access generates the customer number automatically!

- ✔ **Yes/No:** Holds Yes/No, True/False, and On/Off, depending on the format you choose. When you need a simple yes or no, this is the field to use.

- ✔ **OLE object:** OLE Stands for Object Linking and Embedding — a powerful, geeky technology that's pronounced "o-lay." An OLE object can be just about anything — from a Word document, an Excel spreadsheet, and a Windows bitmap (a picture) to a MIDI song. If you embed an OLE object in your table, your database automatically "knows" how to use the object.

✔ **Hyperlink:** Thanks to this field type, Access understands and stores the special link language that makes the Internet such a powerful place. If you use Access on your company's network or use the Internet extensively, this field type is for you. You'll find out more about hyperlinks and other neat ways Access and the Internet play well together in Chapter 8.

To help you start thinking about your database and your data and to begin imagining the fields you could use for some common types of data, I present, in Table 3-1, a breakdown of field types and ways you might use them.

Table 3-1	Common Fields for Everyday Tables		
Name	**Type**	**Size**	**Contents**
Title	Text	4	Mr., Ms., Mrs., Mme., Sir
First Name	Text	15	Person's first name
Middle Initial	Text	4	Person's middle initial; allows for two initials and punctuation
Last Name	Text	20	Person's last name
Suffix	Text	10	Jr., Sr., II, Ph.D., and so on
Job	Text	25	Job title or position
Company	Text	25	Company name
Address 1, Address 2	Text	30	Include two fields for the address because some corporate locations are pretty complicated these days
City	Text	20	City name
State, Province	Text	4	State or province; apply the name appropriately for the data you're storing
Zip Code, Postal Code	Text	10	Zip or postal code; note that it's stored as text characters, not as a number
Country single country	Text	15	Not needed if you work within a
Office Phone	Text	12	Voice telephone number; increase the size to 17 for an extension

Name	*Type*	*Size*	*Contents*
Fax Number	Text	12	Fax number
Home Phone	Text	12	Home telephone number
Cellular Phone	Text	12	Cell phone or car phone
E-mail Address	Text	30	Internet e-mail address
Web Site	Hyperlink		Web page address; Access automatically sets the field size
Telex	Text	12	Standard Telex number; increase the size to 22 to include answerback service
SSN	Text	11	U.S. Social Security number, including dashes
Comments	Memo		A freeform space for notes; Access automatically chooses a field size

Fun with field names

Of all the Windows database programs out there, I think Access has the simplest field-naming rules. Just remember these guidelines to make your field names perfect every time:

✔ **It's a good idea to start with a letter or a number.** While Access won't stop you from using certain characters at the beginning of or within your field name, it's not a good idea. First, it can make things confusing for other people who might use your database, and symbols are hard to read if the type is very small. They also have limited logical use in terms of identifying the content of the field — what would "^Address" tell you that "Address" wouldn't? Of course, after the first character you might find logical uses for symbols such as plus signs and underscores. You can include spaces in field

names, too. Oh — and which symbols are no-nos? See Table 3-2.

✔ **Make the field name short and easy to understand.** You have up to 64 characters for a field name, but don't even think about using all that space. However, don't get stingy and create names like N1 or AZ773 unless they mean something particular to your company or organization.

✔ **Use letters, numbers, and an occasional space in your field names.** Although Access lets you include all kinds of crazy punctuation marks in field names, don't do it. Keep it simple so that the solution you develop with Access doesn't turn into a problem on its own.

All these field types listed as samples in Table 3-1 are really *text* fields, even the ones for phone numbers. This is because Access sees their content as text rather than a number. Of course, some of the field types (listed in the Type column) are not Text fields — you also see a Memo field and a Hyperlink field. These, too, are considered text, but these alternate types of text fields give you options for the specific kind of text that will be stored in such fields. If all this text versus numbers stuff is confusing you, remember that computers think there's a difference between a *number* (that you'd use in a calculation) and a string of digits, such as the digits that make up a phone number. When it comes to different kinds of text fields, it's a matter of how much text will be stored in the field, and if it needs any special formatting in order to work properly in the database.

Table 3-2	Prohibited symbols
Symbol	*Name*
/	Forward slash
*	Asterisk
;	Semicolon
:	Colon
!	Exclamation point
#	Pound sign
&	Ampersand
?	Question mark
-	Dash
"	Double quotes
'	Single quote
$	Dollar sign
%	Percent

Choosing between Flat and Relational Databases

Unlike ice cream, databases come in just two flavors: flat file and relational. Also unlike ice cream, it's not really a matter of preference as to which one you choose. Some databases require a relational approach, and others would be overwhelmed by it. Read on to figure out how to tell the difference.

Isolationist tables

In a *flat* system (also known as *flat file*), all the data is lumped into a single table. A phone directory is a good example of a flat file database: Names, addresses, and phone numbers (the data) are crammed into a single place (the database). Some duplication occurs — if one person has three phone lines at home, his or her name and address are listed three times in the directory — but that's not a big problem. Overall, the database works just fine.

Tables that mix and mingle

The *relational* system (or *relational database*) uses as little storage space as possible by cutting down on the duplicated (also known as *redundant*) data in the database. To accomplish this, a relational database splits your data into several tables, with each table holding some portion of the total data.

Borrowing the preceding phone book example, one table in a relational database can contain the customer name and address information, while another can hold the phone numbers. Thanks to this approach, the mythical person with three phone lines has only one entry in the "customer" table (after all, it's still just one customer) but has three distinct entries in the "phone number" table (one for each phone line).

The key to relational databases

The *key field* (or *linking field*) is the key to this advanced technology. All related tables in a relational database system contain this special field. The key field's data identifies matching records from different tables.

The key field works just like the claim stub you receive when you drop off your dry cleaning. To pick up your dry cleaning when it's finished, you present the claim check, complete with its little claim number. That number identifies (or *links*) you and your cleaning so that the clerk can find it.

Likewise, in the phone book example, each customer can have a unique customer ID. The "phone number" table stores the customer ID with each phone number. To find out who owns a phone number, you look up the customer ID in the "customer name" table. Granted, it takes more steps to find someone's phone number than it does in the plain flat file system, but the relational system saves storage space (no more duplicate names) and reduces the chance of errors at the same time.

If this process seems complicated, don't feel bad. Relational databases *are* complicated! But that's mostly behind the scenes, where Access is doing the stuff it does when you make a selection in a tab or ask it to run a Wizard for you. A good deal of the complexity is invisible to you; all you see is the power it gives you. When you're ready to find out more about all that behind-the-scenes stuff, check out Chapter 4.

But do your tables need to relate?

Now you at least have an idea of the difference between flat file and relational databases. But do you care? Yes, you do. Each approach has its unique pluses and minuses for your database:

- **Flat file systems are easy to build and maintain.** A Microsoft Excel spreadsheet is a good example of a flat file database. A list of records is stored, one record per row, and you have as many records as can fit on the worksheet. Simple, easy, and in many cases the way to go if your database is simple and easy, too.

- **Relational systems shine in big business applications such as invoicing, accounting, or inventory.** They're also a big help if you have a small business — your customer data, for example, could require several tables to store customer names and addresses, purchase history, and credit information. Storing everything you need to store about customers could be too big a job for a single, flat file database.

I don't recommend that you set off to build a relational database system all by yourself after reading just some or all of this book. It's a big job, and you'll likely just end up discouraged if you dive in too quickly. If you're sure that you need one, enlist some help in the form of a friend or colleague who's had some experience building databases. He or she can walk you through it the first time, and then, with this book (and Access help files) at your side, you can try it on your own later.

Although Access is a relational database program, it does flat file systems quite nicely because even though it lets you set up several tables and set up relationships between them, it's also quite happy to set up a single flat file table. Whether you choose flat file or relational for your database project, Access is the right program.

Building a Database

So you've read a few chapters here at the beginning of the book, and maybe you've leafed ahead where I've referred to other chapters, and now you feel ready. You want to dive in and start building a database. Keeping in mind my previous advice to take it slowly, you can take a whack at it here.

In the following procedure, you set up a new database and then use the Table Wizard to build the first table in the database. Ready? Here we go . . .

1. **If Access is not already running, take a moment to start it.**

   I show you how to do this in Chapter 2.

   In the Access workspace, the words *New Blank Database* appear across the central section of the window, with a Blank Database button beneath it.

2. **Click Blank Database.**

   A Blank Database panel appears on the right, as shown in Figure 3-1.

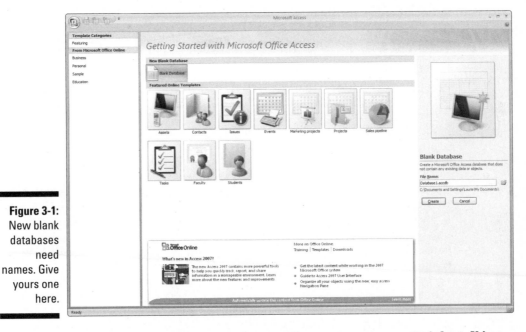

Figure 3-1:
New blank databases need names. Give yours one here.

3. **Type a name to replace the generic** `DatabaseX.accdb` **(where X is the number assigned chronologically to the database).**

   You don't need to type the file extension (`.accdb`), and if you accidentally delete it while changing the file name, don't worry — Access will add that to the file name you type.

   Just beneath the File Name text box is the contents of the currently-selected folder into which your database will be saved when you click Create.

4. **If you don't like the folder that Access picked out for you, click the little folder icon and choose where to store the new database.**

   As shown in Figure 3-2, when you click that little folder icon, the File New Database dialog box opens. From here, you can navigate to anywhere on your local system or on a network to which you're connected and select the drive and folder on which to store your new database. When you've finished selecting a spot for your new database, click OK to return to the workspace.

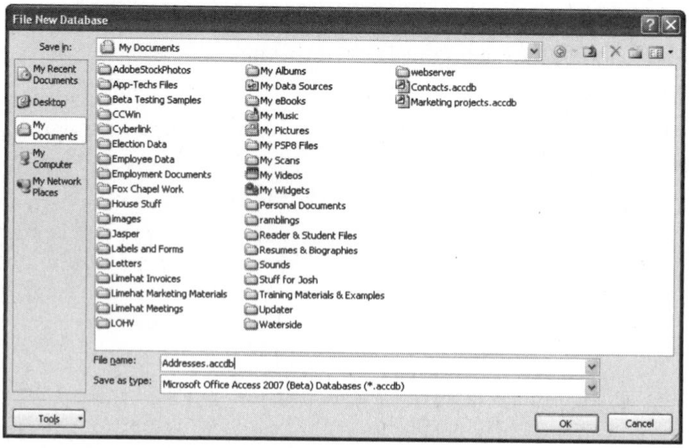

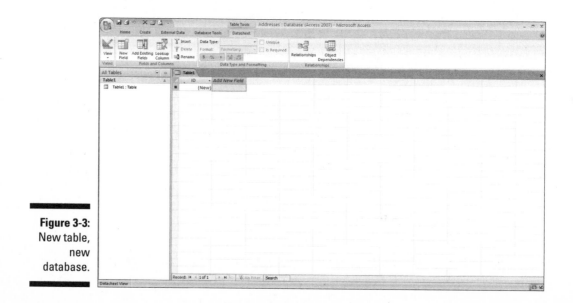

Figure 3-2:
Select a
home for
your new
database.

5. **Click the Create button.**

A blank table, called Table1, appears in the central section of the workspace, and on the left, a panel lists the parts of your database (there's just one part so far). Figure 3-3 shows your new table and the left-hand panel.

Figure 3-3:
New table,
new
database.

When you click Create, if a dialog box pops up and asks whether you want to replace an existing file, Access is saying that a database with the name you entered is already on the disk.

- If this is news to you, click No and then come up with a different name for your new database.

- If you *intended* to replace that old database with a new one, click Yes and proceed.

6. **Begin naming your fields in the table by double-clicking the Add New Field box at the top of the second column in the table and then typing a field name.**

What's that ID field in the first column? It's there by default and will contain a unique number for each record you create (when you start entering records, later). This provides the unique field that each table requires, especially if you're going to relate your tables. You can change its name by double-clicking the name "ID" and changing it to, for example, Customer Number.

Later on, after you've set up your tables and established relationships between them, you can reassign what's known as the *primary key* (another name for a unique field in a table), and at that point, the ID field can go bye-bye.

7. **Press Enter to save the new field name and create the next new field.**

As soon as you press Enter, a new field appears, with a blank at the top, awaiting a name.

Repeat these Step 6 and Step 7 until you have all the fields you think you'll need in this table. You can always rename them later (by double-clicking the current names), so don't worry about perfection at this point. Just start setting up fields so you can start entering data. Figure 3-4 shows a new field name in place.

8. **To save your new table and the entire database, press Ctrl+S or click the Save button on the Quick Access toolbar.**

It's a good idea to save each time you've done something important, like building a table, updating some fields, adding records, and so on — essentially after anything you'd hate to have to do over again.

Rarely is "Table1" a really useful name for a table. Before or after saving your database, renaming a table is easy. Just follow these steps:

1. **Right-click the Table tab.**

2. **Choose Save from the pop-up menu.**

3. **Type a name for the table in the resulting Save As dialog box.**

4. **Click OK to keep the name.**

5. **Resave your database to include this change.**

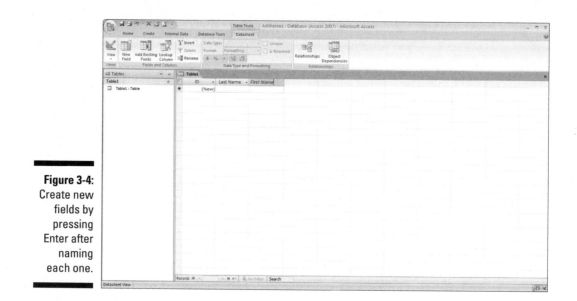

Figure 3-4:
Create new
fields by
pressing
Enter after
naming
each one.

Adding and Removing Tables

Nobody's expecting perfection at this stage of the game. Certainly not in your first foray into database creation, and not even on your second or third attempt. Even seasoned experts forget things now and then, realizing after they've built a table that they didn't need it, or after they've started setting up reports and queries that they've forgotten a table that they needed. It can happen to anyone.

What to do? Use Access's simple interface to add the tables you want and delete the tables you don't.

One more, please

If, after you start building your database, you decide that your database warrants more than one table — in other words, if you realize you need a relational database — you need to add another table. If you already knew that your database was going to need multiple tables, after building the first one the only thing to do is build the rest, one by one.

To add new tables to an existing database, repeat the following steps for each new table:

1. **Click the Create tab.**

   The Create tab's buttons appear, as shown in Figure 3-5.

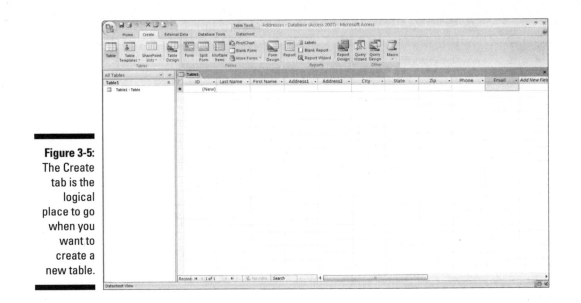

Figure 3-5:
The Create
tab is the
logical
place to go
when you
want to
create a
new table.

2. Click the Table button on the Ribbon.

A new table, blank and awaiting the name for the first field, appears, as shown in Figure 3-6.

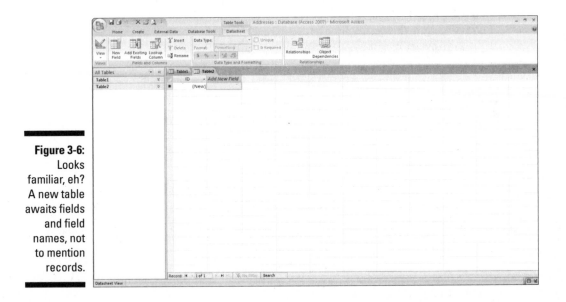

Figure 3-6:
Looks
familiar, eh?
A new table
awaits fields
and field
names, not
to mention
records.

3. **Build and name the fields for this new table as shown in the previous procedure.**

   Save your database periodically as you work.

4. **Continue adding tables, using Steps 1 through 3, for as many tables as you need in the database.**

   You don't have to do this perfectly from the start — you can always go back to rename fields and add or remove tables (more on how to do that in a second). The goal here is to just *do it* — just get started and get the database going, so you can see what you have and start working with it.

Oops, 1 didn't mean to do that

So you have a table you didn't want. Maybe you realize after building Table C that you really only need Tables A and B — or that Table D, which you've also created, really makes Table C unnecessary. Whatever the reason, tables, even ones with records in them, are easy to get rid of.

Let me state that again: Tables are easy to get rid of. Perhaps too easy. Before you delete a table, check and recheck your database to make sure you aren't deleting information that you need to keep. When a table is deleted, all connections to it — relationships, references in queries and reports — are deleted, too. A prompt appears when you choose to delete a table, reminding you of this.

1. **With your database open, look at the panel on the left side of the workspace.**

   You should see a list of your tables in that panel, each one represented by a long, horizontal button, as shown in Figure 3-7.

2. **Click the pair of down-pointing arrows at the right end of the button for the table you want to get rid of.**

   The table name is repeated on a bar that appears beneath the original button.

3. **Right-click the table name on that new bar and choose Delete from the pop-up menu, as shown in Figure 3-8.**

4. **Click Yes in response to the resulting prompt if, in fact, you do want to delete the table.**

   All gone!

Figure 3-7:
Each table
has its own
button,
emblazoned
with the
name you
gave the
table.

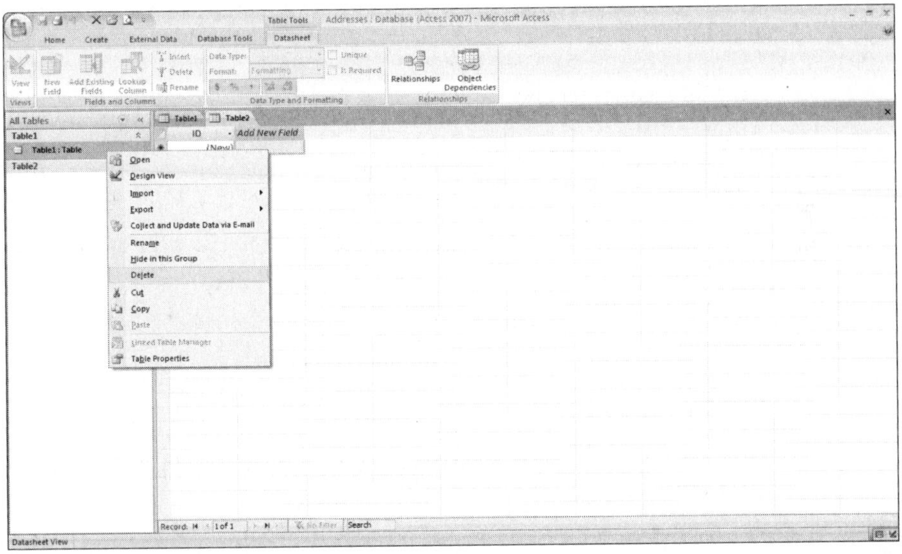

Figure 3-8:
Choose
Delete to
get rid of the
unwanted
table.

Now, you probably think it's time to start entering records, but no, I don't advise that. Before you start populating your tables with data, it's a better idea to set up your table relationships, establish the key fields that will connect your relational tables, and define the specs for each of your fields — taking advantage of those field options I've mentioned earlier in this chapter.

Even if your database will be a flat file database, you need to iron out the settings for your fields before you start entering data — establishing the rules for entering names, numbers, dates, and so forth — so that what you enter is graciously accepted by the fields you've set up.

Chapter 4 helps you prepare your database for its relational duties. In Chapter 5 and Chapter 6, you'll discover the process of customizing your fields to suit your needs. After that's done, you can enter your data and begin taking advantage of Access's forms, queries, and reports — all the stuff covered in the *rest* of the book!

Part II
Getting It All on the Table

The 5th Wave   By Rich Tennant

"Your database is beyond repair, but before I tell you our backup recommendation, let me ask you a question. How many index cards do you think will fit on the walls of your computer room?"

In this part . . .

So by now you've started your database, or at least you've read about how that's done, and you're ready to start thinking about setting up your tables and filling them with data. Or maybe you just kept turning pages in Part I and you ended up here. Hey — you might as well keep reading, right?

If you decide to keep turning pages (and reading, hopefully), this part of the book will show you how the tables that make up a database are built, how they work together, and how you can customize them to become perfect homes for your very important data.

From Chapter 4's explanation of how tables relate to Chapters 5 and 6 that show you what's going on and how to control what's happening behind the scenes with your tables and their data, Part II will help you start building your database, one table at a time.

Chapter 4

Keys, Relationships, and Indexes

*L*ife in today's world is all about doing things faster and more efficiently to increase productivity. Isn't that what your life is about? Oh, you have a life outside the office, too? Maybe you have a relationship? This chapter is about making your databases faster and about building good relationships (the database kind, not the human kind!).

As with any good relationship, the end result is often harmony and happiness. Making your Access tables work well together will make things so much easier in so many ways as you move on to build your queries, forms, and reports. The good news is that building relationships in Access takes a lot less time than building human relationships.

How can you make Access work faster and more efficiently? With key fields and indexes, that's how! Each table should have that one special field assigned as a *primary key*. A primary key prevents duplicate records from being entered into a table — hence, more efficient data entry. (I love the word *hence!*) To retrieve your data faster, you need to create the proper balance of indexes for each table. Not enough indexes, and querying 100,000 records will take forever; too many, and the same could be true. So, assigning indexes to the correct fields is an art form. You find out all about the art of indexes in this chapter.

The Primary Key to Success

A table's primary key is a special field in your table. You use this field to uniquely identify each record in the table.

Usually, the primary key is a single field. In *very* special circumstances, *two or more* fields can share the job. The technical term for this type of key is a *multifield key.*

The lowdown on primary keys

Before we discuss how to create a primary key, you'll need to know some rules and guidelines for their use. This section contains the when, where, and why of the primary key.

Uses

Almost every table you create should have a primary key. Here's why:

> ✔ **A primary key organizes your data by *uniquely* identifying each record.**
>
> That's one reason why a primary key makes your database work a little faster. For an explanation of indexes and their creation, see the section "Indexing for Faster Queries," later in this chapter,
>
> For example, in a Customer table, the Customer Number would be the primary key. If your Customer table contains a dozen Jane Smiths, you need a way to tell them apart. The customer number *uniquely* identifies each Jane Smith — and every other customer, too.
>
> ✔ **Tables by default are sorted by primary key.**
>
> This helps Access find a particular record much faster.
>
> ✔ **Your database could freak out if you don't have a primary key.**
>
> Without a primary key, finding the requested records can be difficult for Access. For example, if you have a customers table and you are querying on customer John Smith that lives in New York City, it's possible you'll have two or more John Smiths in New York City. How does Access know which one you want? A unique primary key for each customer will solve that problem for Access by uniquely identifying each John Smith.

Rules

Before you create a primary key, you need to know a few guidelines.

Location

Access doesn't care where the primary key field appears in the table design. The key can be the first field, the last field, or buried in the middle.

Always make the primary key field the first field in your table. It makes relationship building easier (as you'll see later in this chapter).

The key to table happiness

What makes a good key field? How do you find the right one? Good questions! In fact, they're the two most important questions to ask about a primary key.

Primary key values must be unique for each record. Leaving a primary key field blank is not an option. So start by looking at some sample data that will go into your table. Is there something like a phone number, customer number, or Social Security number that will be unique for each record? If so, you've just found your primary key field. If not, then an AutoNumber field is the way to go. When you designate a field data type as AutoNumber, Access sequentially numbers each record entered into the table. Isn't our good pal Access a peach?

AutoNumber fields always create a unique identifier for each record. When you delete a record with an AutoNumber field, Access even keeps track of those numbers and will not use them again. Access, you are quite a pal indeed!

Defaults

Access tries to save you time and trouble with its default primary key actions:

> ✔ **Access really, really *wants* you to have a primary key in your table.**
>
> • If you create a new table in table design mode without a primary key, Access adds a primary key field when you save the table design.
>
>   Access gives this automatic primary key field a wildly creative name — ID — with an AutoNumber data type.
>
> • If the first field you add in a table is an AutoNumber type, Access automatically makes that AutoNumber field the primary key.
>
> ✔ **Access automatically indexes the primary key field.**

Restrictions

You can't create primary keys willy-nilly. Access imposes these limits:

> ✔ **A table can have only one primary key.**
>
> ✔ **You can't use the memo, OLE object, or hyperlink field types for a primary key.**
>
>   Avoid using the *yes/no* field type in a primary key. You can have only two records in such a table: *Yes* and *No*.
>
> ✔ **All primary key indexes must have a name (just like all fields have a name).**
>
>   Access automatically names all primary key indexes *Primary Key*.

Creating a primary key

To create a primary key, follow these steps:

1. **Open the table in design view.**

   If you just said to yourself "how do I do that?" then it might not be time to create a primary key. Chapter 3 shows you the table basics you'll need before you can create a primary key.

2. **Click the field name for the primary key.**

   Don't know which field to select for your primary key? See the sidebar, "The key to table happiness."

   The preceding section, "Rules," relates the guidelines for selecting a primary key.

3. **On the Ribbon, click the giant button with the key on it (shown in Figure 4-1).**

   A key symbol appears on the button next to the field name you selected.

The primary key is set!

Click here to set the primary key field.

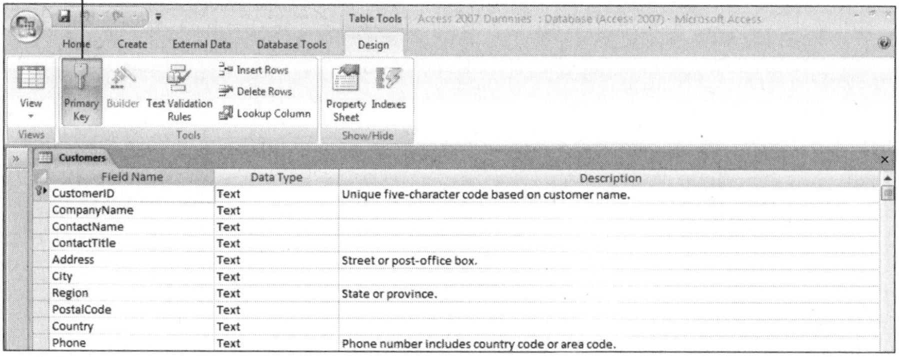

Figure 4-1:
The
completed
primary key.

Field Name	Data Type	Description
CustomerID	Text	Unique five-character code based on customer name.
CompanyName	Text	
ContactName	Text	
ContactTitle	Text	
Address	Text	Street or post-office box.
City	Text	
Region	Text	State or province.
PostalCode	Text	
Country	Text	
Phone	Text	Phone number includes country code or area code.

Making Tables Get Along

Relational databases split data among two or more tables. Access uses a linking field, called a *foreign key,* to tie related tables together. For example, one table may contain customer names and addresses while another table tracks the customer order history. The order information is tied to the customer information with a linking field, which (in this example) is probably a customer number.

Why is this important? Suppose you needed to print an invoice for customer Anita Cash's latest order. By placing the customer number in the orders table and relating the orders table to the customers table via the customer number, you can pull Anita Cash's name and address information for the invoice without placing that information in the order table.

Rules of relationships

Keep this in mind when relating tables:

✔ Tables you want to relate must have at least one field in common. While the field name need not be identical, its data type must be the same in each table. For example, you can't relate a text field to a number field.

Keep the names consistent between your tables. If you don't, that ball of confusion will roll your way at some point down the road.

✔ Usually, the linking field is one table's primary key but rarely the primary key in the other table.

The Customer table, for example, is probably arranged by customer number, while the order data is likely organized by order number.

✔ After the two tables have been created and share a common field, you're not done. You still have to build that relationship.

You find out how to build a relationship in the later section, "Building Table Relationships."

Relationship types

There is more than one type of table relationship in Access. When you relate two tables, you can choose one of three possible relationship types.

Unless you want to be an Access expert, you only need to understand the one-to-many table relationship. It's the most common.

One-to-many

One-to-many relationships connect one record in the first table to *many* records in the second table. This is the default and by far the most common relationship type.

One customer may make many purchases at the store, so one customer record is linked to many sales records in the Transaction table.

One-to-one

One-to-one relationships link one record in the first table to *exactly* one record in the second table.

One-to-one relationships aren't common. Tables that have a one-to-one relationship can be combined into one table, which usually happens.

Many-to-many

Many-to-many relationships link *many* records in one table to *many* records in another table.

Here's a common example of a many-to-many relationship:

- ✔ A customer order database contains separate tables for

  - Customers

  - Individual products

- ✔ Every individual product needs to be available to every customer.

  In other words, *many* customers need to be able to order *many* of the same products. The database needs to satisfy *both* of these inquiries:

  - Every customer who ordered the same product.

  - Every product that one customer ordered.

In Access 2007, there are two ways to link *many* customers to *many* of the same products: *multivalue fields* and *junction tables*.

Multivalue fields

Access 2007 allows the creation of many-to-many relationships between two tables via *multivalue* fields.

Multivalue fields are a new capability in Access 2007. In previous versions of Access, many-to-many relationships between two tables were bad — so bad that Access didn't allow them. Older versions of Access required a third table called a junction table to accomplish a many-to-many relationship.

A multivalue field can store many similar data items. Adding a multivalue field ends the need for creating multiple records to record multiple products ordered on one customer order. For example, you can add a multivalue field called ProductID to the Order Detail table. All products ordered can be stored in one field, so only one record per order is required.

Multivalue fields are not all peaches and cream. Use a junction table if you need to query or sort the data stored in the multivalue field.

Junction tables

A *junction table* is a special table that keeps track of related records in two other tables:

- The junction table has a *one-to-many* relationship with both tables.
- The result works like a direct *many-to-many* relationship between both tables.

For example, a junction table called Orders can connect the customers to the order details for a particular order. The junction table has a one-to-many relationship with *both* the Customer and Order Details tables.

Building Table Relationships

If you can drag and drop, you can build a table relationship.

Keep these three limitations in mind:

- **You can relate only tables that are in the same database.**
- **You can relate queries to tables, but that's unusual.**
- **You need to specifically tell Access how your tables are related.**

When you're ready to play the matchmaker between your amorous tables, here's how to do it.

The Relationships window

To build a table relationship, first open the Relationships window. Follow these steps:

1. **Click the Database Tools Ribbon tab.**

   The Show/Hide tool group appears on the Ribbon (see Figure 4-2).

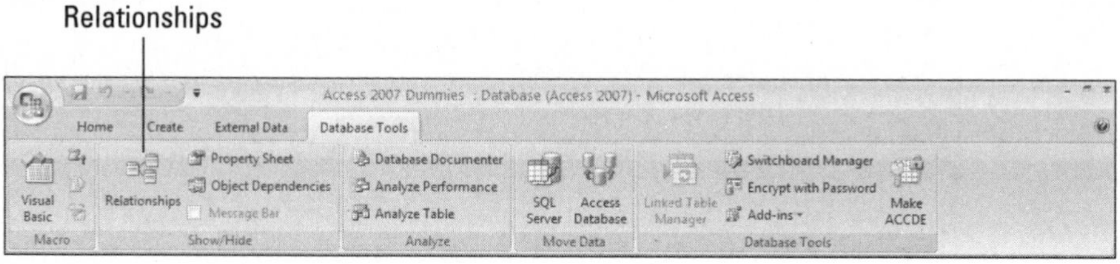

Figure 4-2:
The
Advanced
Tools
Ribbon tab
and the
Analyze tool
group.

Relationships

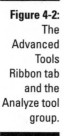

2. In the Show/Hide tool group, click the Relationships tool.

The Relationships window appears.

If some tables are already listed in the window, someone (or some wizard) has already defined relationships for this database. If you're not sure how they got there and if more than one person is working on your database, stop and consult all database developers before changing the relationships. What might work for you could be disastrous for your colleagues.

When the Relationships window is open, you can select and relate tables.

Table relationships

For each pair of tables you relate, you must select the tables then join their common fields. The following sections show you how.

Selecting tables

To select tables to relate open the Relationships window (find out how in the preceding section) and follow these steps:

1. Choose Show Table from the Relationships Ribbon group.

The Show Table dialog box appears, listing the tables in the current database file.

2. For each pair of tables you want in the relationship, follow these steps:

a. Click the table.

b. Click Add.

In the big Relationships workspace, a little window lists the fields in that table. As you add tables to the layout, a separate window appears for each table. You can see these windows on either side of the Show Table dialog box in Figure 4-3.

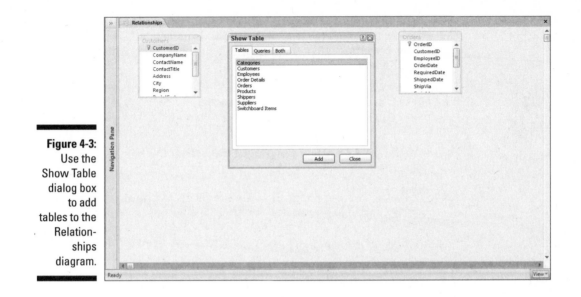

Figure 4-3:
Use the
Show Table
dialog box
to add
tables to the
Relation-
ships
diagram.

Repeat Step 2 for each pair of tables you want to relate. If one of the tables in the pair is already present due to an existing relationship it has with another table, you do not need to add it again.

3. After you finish adding tables, click the Close button.

When you have all the tables present, you're ready for these tables to get to know each other. The following sections show how to relate the tables.

Managing relationships

This section contains all the information you'll need to create, edit, and delete your table relationships..

Creating relationships

After you select the tables (as shown in the preceding instructions), follow these steps to create a relationship between two tables:

1. Decide which two tables you want to relate.

Since the one-to-many relationship is the most common, these instructions pertain to it. The two tables in a one-to-many relationship are designated as

- *Parent:* In the parent table, the related field will be the primary key. Each record in the parent table will be uniquely identified by this related field.

• *Child:* In the child table, the related field contains the same information as the field in the parent table. Typically it shares the same name with the field in the parent table as well although this is not a requirement.

To make relating tables easier, put related fields near the beginning of the field list. In Access, you must see the related fields on the screen before you can make a relationship. If the related fields are not at the beginning of the field list, you have to do a lot of scrolling to find them.

2. **Follow these steps to select the parent field from the list:**

   a. *Put the mouse pointer on the field you want to relate in the parent table.*

   Usually, the field you want to relate in the parent table is the primary key.

   b. *Hold down the left mouse button.*

3. **While holding down the mouse button, follow these steps to join the parent field to the child field:**

   a. *Drag the mouse from the parent field to the child table.*

   A plus sign appears at the base of the mouse pointer.

   b. *Point to the related field in the child table.*

   c. *Release the mouse button.*

   The Edit Relationships dialog box appears, detailing the soon-to-be relationship, as shown in Figure 4-4.

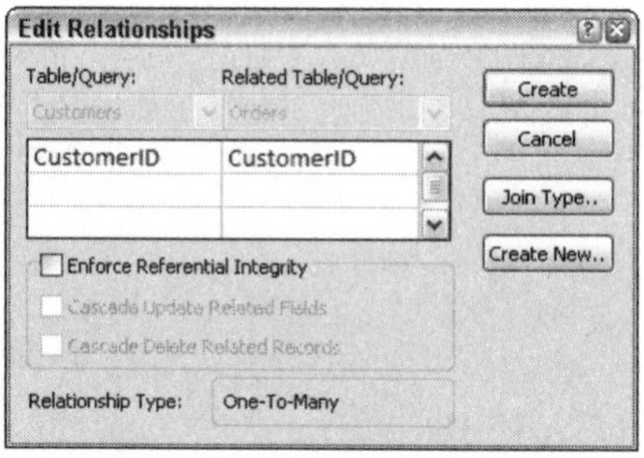

Figure 4-4:
The Edit Relationships dialog box details how Access connects two tables.

Be very careful before releasing the mouse button. Put the tip of the mouse pointer *directly* on the child field before you let go.

• If you drag between the two fields correctly, the Edit Relationships dialog displays the parent and child fields side by side, as shown in Figure 4-4.

- If you miss, cancel the Edit Relationships dialog box and try Step 3 again.

4. **In Edit Relationships dialog box, select the Enforce Referential Integrity option.**

5. **Double-check that your field names are the correct ones and then click Create.**

Access illustrates the new relationship in the Relationships window:

- A line between the related fields shows you that the tables are related.

- If you checked the Enforce Referential Integrity option in the preceding step, Access places a 1 next to the parent in the relationship and an infinity symbol next to the child, as shown in the full set of relationships in Figure 4-5.

To relate another pair of selected tables, repeat the preceding Steps 1-5.

Access also provides tools for modifying and removing relationships. The following section shows how to use them.

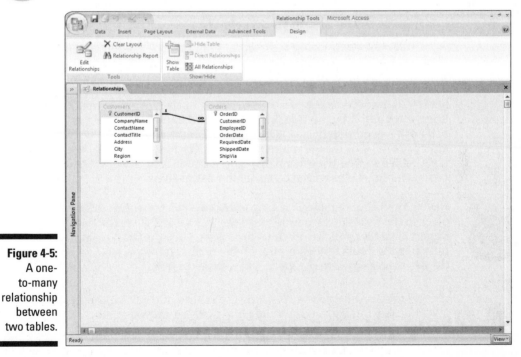

Figure 4-5:
A one-to-many relationship between two tables.

Children's Protective Services

Enforce Referential Integrity sounds harsh, doesn't it? It simply means that Access makes sure that a record is present in the parent table before you can add one to its child table. (Shouldn't every child have a parent watching?)

For example, with Referential Integrity enforced, Access won't let you enter an order in the orders table for a customer that is not present in the Customers table.

Modifying relationships

After you relate tables, you can see, organize, and remove the relationships.

If you create a relationship you don't want, open the Relationships window and follow these steps to delete the relationship:

1. **Click the relationship line connecting the two tables.**

   If you were successful, the line will thicken. That means the line is selected.

2. **Tap the Delete key on your keyboard.**

   Voilà! The relationship is gone.

If you are relating many tables together, the Relationships window may look a little messy because relationship lines will cross each other. This makes it difficult to determine which tables are related to each other. To rectify this situation, click and drag the title bar of a table window to another part of the screen. It's good practice — although not always possible — to show parents either *above* or to the *left* of their children. Try to arrange the parent and child tables so that the lines between the parent and child tables do not cross over lines illustrating other table relationships.

Having trouble understanding your relationships? Are you scrolling all over the place in the Relationships window to see everything? If so, the Relationship Report is just for you. To preview this report, click the Relationship Report button in the Tools Ribbon group. All the related tables in your database will display in an easy-to-read report. Okay, *easier* to read!

Indexing for Faster Queries

You may find yourself sitting for a minute or two waiting for a query or report to run. I've sat longer than that for some reports during the development stage. So what can be done to speed up your queries? Add *indexes* to your tables, that's what.

An Access table index works just like the index in a book. It helps Access find a record in a table just as a book index helps you find a topic in a book.

Indexes dramatically speed up queries and sorts. When you sort or query a table on an indexed field, the index has already done most of the work.

The benefit of an index depends on the number of records in the table:

- ✔ If you have 100 customers, an index won't improve performance much.
- ✔ If you have tens of thousands of customers, an index will make a significant performance improvement.

Create your own index

Here's the skinny on indexes:

- ✔ Each field in a table can be indexed if it isn't one of these field types: *hyperlink, memo,* and *OLE object.*
- ✔ Like the primary key, an index may have a unique name that's different from the field name.
- ✔ You don't have to name your index; Access does that for you.
- ✔ Indexes either *allow* or *prevent* duplicate entries in your table.

How an index works

An index is essentially a copy of the table that's already *sorted* on the indexed field.

When a table is indexed properly, queries run faster because the indexes help Access locate the data faster.

Here's an example. Suppose you needed to produce a list of all your Pennsylvania customers, and you often query your customer table by state:

- ✔ If you index the State field in your Customers table, all of the Pennsylvania customers will be in one place. When Access reaches the Pennsylvania customers, it can stop there and return them to you in your query.
- ✔ Without the index, Access must scan every record in the table to return the desired results.

Here are some guidelines on deciding which fields to index:

✔ Start by querying the table whose query performance you'd like to improve. Make note of the time it took to run the query.

✔ Next, index each field that you know you'll query frequently. For example, in a contacts table, you might query by contact ID, contact last name, and contact state.

✔ Finally, query the newly indexed table. If the query time improves, your indexes are correct. If your query time worsens, try removing an index one at a time starting with the field you think you will query the least from the group of indexed fields. Rerun your query and note performance.

✔ When you've optimized performance, your indexing is complete.

The sidebar "To duplicate or not to duplicate" shows which index type to apply.

✔ To list the table's indexes, follow these steps:

1. **Open the table in design view.**

2. **Click the Indexes button in the Show/Hide Ribbon group (see Figure 4-6).**

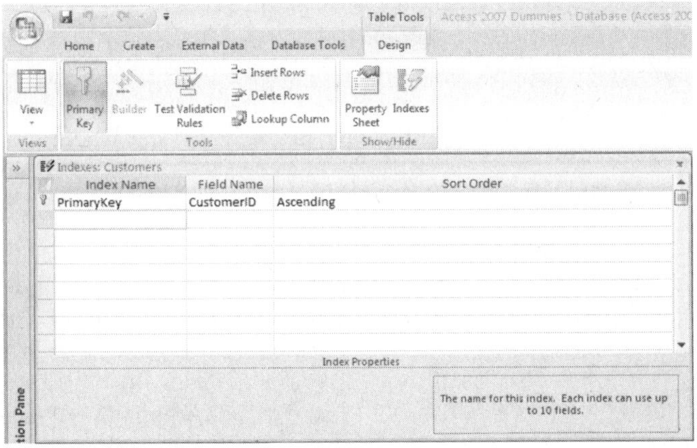

Figure 4-6:
The Indexes window with the Indexes button above it on the Ribbon.

Building too many indexes in a table slows down some tasks. Adding records to a table with several indexes takes a little longer than adding records to an un-indexed table. Access spends extra time updating all those indexes behind the scenes. The trick is to get the right number of indexes assigned to the right fields. Sometimes it comes down to trial and error to optimize query performance via indexes.

To duplicate or not to duplicate

When you create an index, you have two options for handling duplicate values:

✔ If records can have the same value in this field, click *Yes (Duplicates OK)*.

Yes (Duplicates OK) is the most common choice.

✔ If every record needs a unique value in this field (such as customer numbers in your Customer table), click *Yes (No Duplicates)*.

The No Duplicates setting tells Access to make sure that no two records have the same value in the indexed field.

Access automatically indexes primary key fields as No Duplicates when you designate the primary key.

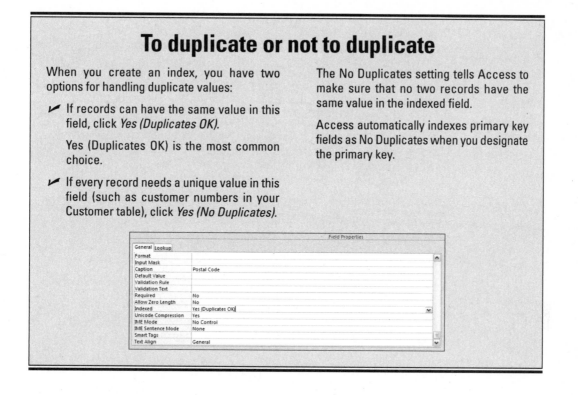

Adding and removing indexes

After you decide on the correct fields to index (as outlined previously in this section), creating an index is a snap.

In the following instructions, Step 4 can *delete* an existing field index. You delete a field index if it is hindering data input more than it is enhancing query performance.

To add or remove field indexes, open the table in design view and follow these steps:

1. **Click the name of the field you want to index.**

   The blinking cursor lands in the field name.

2. **In the General tab of the Field Properties section, click the Indexed box.**

Now the cursor moves into the Indexed box, and a down arrow appears on the right end of the box.

If the Indexed display has no entry, this field type doesn't work with indexes. You can't index *hyperlink, memo,* or *OLE object* fields.

3. Click the down arrow at the end of the Indexed box.

A list of index options appears:

- *Yes (Duplicates OK)*
- *Yes (No Duplicates)*
- *No*

The previous sidebar "To duplicate or not to duplicate" shows how to decide on the correct index setting.

4. Select the index type you want from the list.

To remove an existing index from the selected field, click No.

5. To make the change permanent, click the Save button on the Quick Access toolbar.

If your table contains thousands of records, Access may take a few moments to create the index.

Chapter 5

Remodeling Your Data

*F*rom remembering to change your car's oil every 3,000 miles to cleaning out your rain gutters or mowing the lawn, everything in your surroundings needs a little maintenance now and then. Most of that maintenance involves tidying up, getting rid of old or unwanted things, or making improvements. Sometimes *all* of these things are part of the maintenance process.

Well, it's no different for your database — an Access database needs a tune-up now and then, just to keep things running right. This can be as simple as checking for blank fields where you need to plug in missing data, as common as purging old or inaccurate records, or a matter of changing the names of tables and fields so that your database makes more sense to those who use it.

Unlike getting your car serviced or cleaning out your gutters, however, maintaining your database isn't expensive or difficult. Of course, *not* keeping your database in good working order *can* get expensive — in terms of your time, of the potential impact of inaccurate records on your business, of wasting time and paper printing reports that include obsolete data, and of confusing those who use your database by having incorrect or vague field and table names.

Don't worry, though — for all those doomsday potentialities, the solution is as simple as a few clicks, a couple double-clicks, and a little bit of typing — and it's free!

Opening a Table for Editing

Of course, before you can edit a table you have to open it. And that requires opening the database of which the table is a part. This is a very simple process, assuming you know where your database is stored and which database (if you have more than one) contains the table you need to maintain.

When you open Access 2007, as I discuss in Chapters 1 and 2, the workspace contains several features for getting started — templates you can call upon to help you build a new database, a list of recently opened databases, and one-click access to the Access main menu, which contains commands such as Save, Print, and Open. All of these options are visible in Figure 5-1.

Of course, to open a database (and then the table or tables within it) you probably need that Open command I just mentioned. But you have other choices, which you'll use depending on the situation.

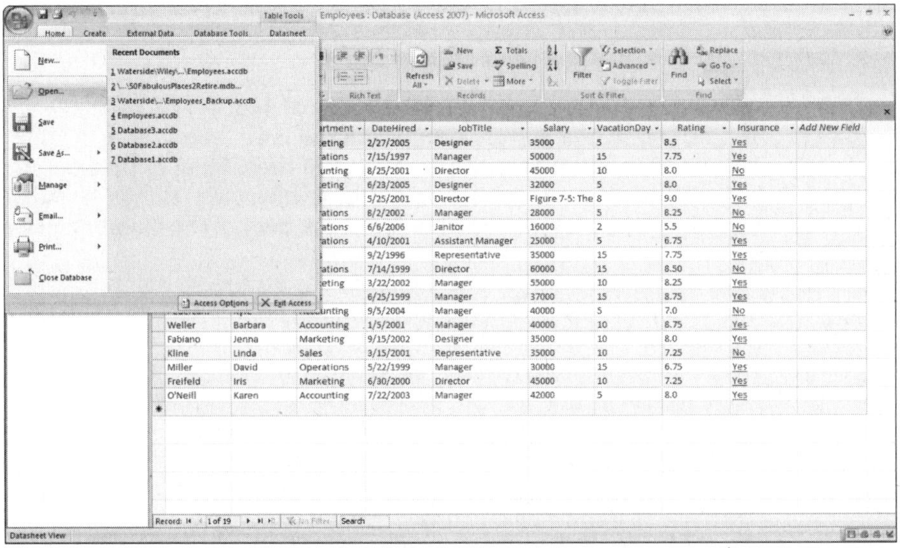

Figure 5-1:
The Access workspace makes opening a database easy.

To expand on those options, check out the following list — you can open a database in any of the following ways:

✔ **If you've recently used the database,** choose your database from the list entitled Recent Documents, opened by choosing Open from the Office button menu.

To open a database from the list, just point to it and click once — the items in the list work like links (your mouse pointer will turn into a pointing hand).

✔ **If you don't remember where your database is stored,** click the Windows Start button and choose Search. A Windows Search window opens (see Figure 5-2), through which you can search for files based on their name, date last modified, size, file type . . . just about any attribute that you *do* know. Assuming your database appears in the Search Results, just double-click it (and note where it's stored so you don't have to go searching again).

✔ **If you remember where your database is stored, but it isn't in the Open Recent Database list,** use the following procedure to use the Open dialog box to navigate to and open your database:

   1. *Click the main button on the Quick Access toolbar and choose Open from the list of commands.*

   The Open dialog box pops onto the screen, as shown in Figure 5-3.

   By default, the Open dialog box goes to the My Documents folder, which may contain your database.

   2. *If the database isn't in the My Documents folder, use the buttons on the left side to check your Desktop, local hard drive, or network drives.*

   3. *When you find the database, open it by double-clicking its name.*

   The database file opens immediately, as shown in Figure 5-4.

   An introductory screen of some kind (known as a *switchboard*) may appear instead of the tabbed dialog box. Access is telling you that your database either contains some custom programming or was created by the Database Wizard. You probably have some special forms that help you interact with the information in your database. If you want to find out how to create your own switchboard, check out Chapter 21.

   4. *Below the All Tables button on the left side of the workspace, look for the table you want to open.*

   Each table has its own button.

   5. *Double-click the table you want to edit.*

   The table opens in Table view, and you can begin your maintenance of the data. You can add or remove fields or change the names of your fields — topics I discuss later on in this information-packed chapter.

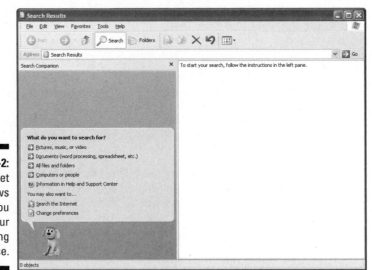

Figure 5-2:
Let
Windows
help you
find your
missing
database.

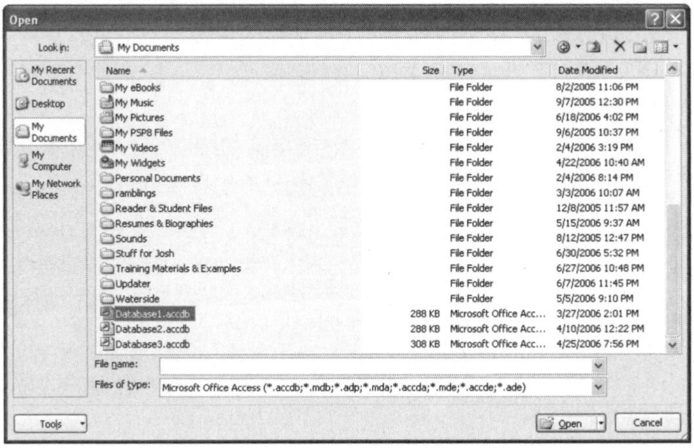

Figure 5-3:
Use the
Open dialog
box to open
your
database.

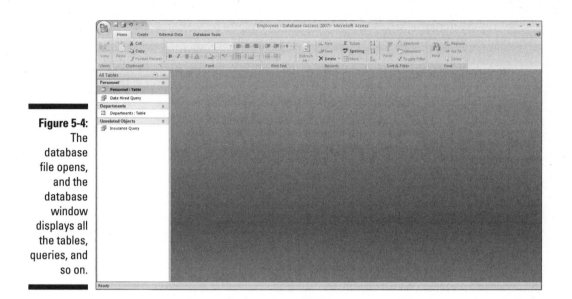

Figure 5-4:
The
database
file opens,
and the
database
window
displays all
the tables,
queries, and
so on.

Inserting Records and Fields

Ever gone on vacation and forgotten your toothpaste? Sure, you can probably just pick up a tube at a drug store in the place you're visiting, but it's still a pain. The same "Darn!" feeling overcomes you when you realize you've left something out of your database suitcase, too (although you might use a different four-letter word, but this is a family publication).

Luckily, like making a quick trip to the drug store for that forgotten toothpaste, adding a forgotten record or field to your table is easy — so easy that you may find that "Darn!" (or any other word expressing regret) is no longer your reaction to discovering a missing field. Instead, you'll calmly launch into the following steps — one set for inserting a missing record and one set for inserting a missing field.

Adding a record

To add a record, follow these steps:

1. **In the Table view of the table that's missing a record, click inside the empty cell at the bottom of the table — below the last displayed record in the table.**

   Your cursor blinks in the first field in that record as shown in Figure 5-5.

2. Type your information for the first field.

If the first field is an AutoNumber type, press Tab and begin typing in the second field. As soon as you start typing, the AutoNumber field generates a new number and displays it in the field.

Don't panic if the AutoNumber field seems to skip a number when it creates an entry for your new record. When an AutoNumber field skips a number, it means that you probably entered (or at least started to enter) a record and then deleted it.

Figure 5-5:
A new record sits ready for its data.

LastName	FirstName	Department	DateHired	JobTitle	Salary	VacationDay	Rating	Insurance	Add New Field
Talbot	Ann	Marketing	2/27/2005	Designer	35000	5	8.5	Yes	
Mermelstein	David	Operations	7/15/1997	Manager	50000	15	7.75	Yes	
Burrell	Eugenia	Accounting	8/25/2001	Director	45000	10	8.0	No	
Shapiro	Mimi	Marketing	6/23/2005	Designer	32000	5	8.0	Yes	
Myers	George	Sales	5/25/2001	Director	45000	8	9.0	Yes	
Frankenfield	Daniel	Operations	8/2/2002	Manager	28000	5	8.25	No	
Kovalcik	John	Operations	6/6/2006	Janitor	16000	2	5.5	No	
Smith	Steve	Operations	4/10/2001	Assistant Manager	25000	5	6.75	Yes	
Robin	Christopher	Sales	9/2/1996	Representative	35000	15	7.75	Yes	
Pederzani	Bruce	Operations	7/14/1999	Director	60000	15	8.50	No	
Ulrich	Zachary	Marketing	3/22/2002	Manager	55000	10	8.25	Yes	
Sorensen	Sharon	Sales	6/25/1999	Manager	37000	15	8.75	Yes	
Pederzani	Kyle	Accounting	9/5/2004	Manager	40000	5	7.0	No	
Weller	Barbara	Accounting	1/5/2001	Manager	40000	10	8.75	Yes	
Fabiano	Jenna	Marketing	9/15/2002	Designer	35000	10	8.0	Yes	
Kline	Linda	Sales	3/15/2001	Representative	35000	10	7.25	No	
Miller	David	Operations	5/22/1999	Manager	30000	15	6.75	Yes	
Freifeld	Iris	Marketing	6/30/2000	Director	45000	10	7.25	Yes	
O'Neill	Karen	Accounting	7/22/2003	Manager	42000	5	8.0	Yes	

3. Press Tab to move through the fields and enter all the data for this new record.

4. When you finish entering data into the last field for the new record, you're finished!

Because Access automatically saves the new record while you're typing it, you have nothing more to do. Pretty neat, eh?

If you want to add another record, press Tab and type away.

If you change your mind and want to kill the new addition, you have a couple of options:

✔ Press Ctrl+Z and then click Yes when Access asks about deleting the record.

✔ Right-click the cell to the far left of the record (the empty cell to the left of the first field). From the resulting pop-up menu, choose Delete Record. Click Yes when asked whether you're sure about the deletion.

Inserting a field

With the field-challenged table open, follow these steps to add the field you're missing:

1. **In Table view, find and click the field heading aptly called *Add New Field* (see Figure 5-6).**

   The entire column beneath the heading is highlighted.

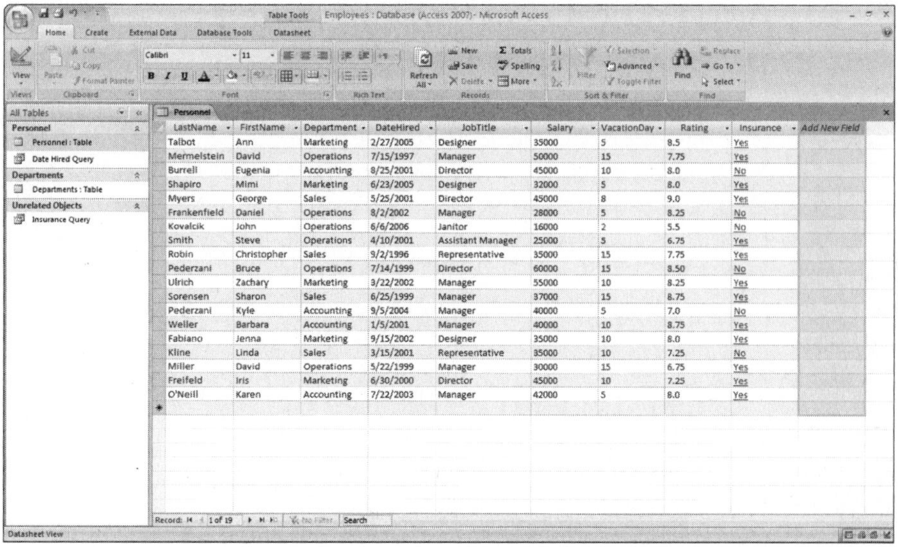

Figure 5-6:
Right there in the table is a new field, awaiting creation.

2. **Double-click the instructional Add New Field heading.**

   The heading disappears, and your cursor blinks in the heading cell.

3. **Type the name of your new field and press Enter.**

   Your new field is created.

4. **To rearrange your fields so that the new field is where you want it among the existing fields, click once on the field name and then click again.**

   Your mouse pointer turns into a white, left-pointing arrow.

5. **Drag to the left or right depending on where you want to drop your new field.**

   A thick vertical line follows you indicating where the field will appear as soon as you release the mouse (see Figure 5-7).

6. **When you're happy with the intended location of the field, release the mouse.**

Your field is relocated.

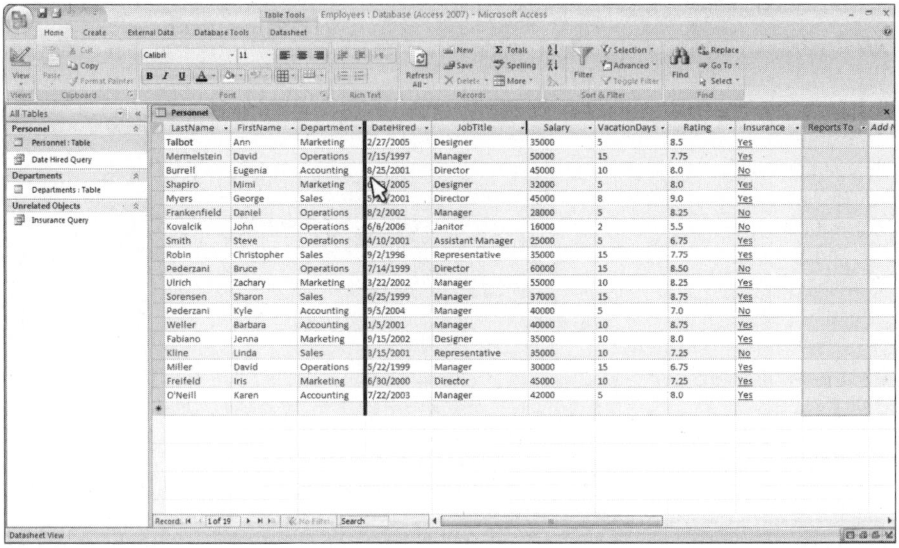

Figure 5-7:
Drag and drop your field to reposition it amongst the other fields in the table.

By default, all fields created in Table view are Text fields. If this isn't the type of field you need, you can change the Data Type (as well as other settings) for the new field:

1. **With the field selected, click the Datasheet tab.**

2. **In the Data Type and Formatting section of the tab, click the Data Type drop-down arrow.**

3. **Choose a format from the resulting list (as shown in Figure 5-8).**

You can also tinker with settings that go with the Data Type you choose — for example, if you choose a number format, you can choose how many decimal places will display or apply a Currency format by using the buttons below the Data Type drop-down list.

Deleting a field

Getting rid of a field is no big deal — in fact, it might be too easy, although Access does give you a little nudge (in the form of a dialog box) to make sure you're positive you want to get rid of the field in question.

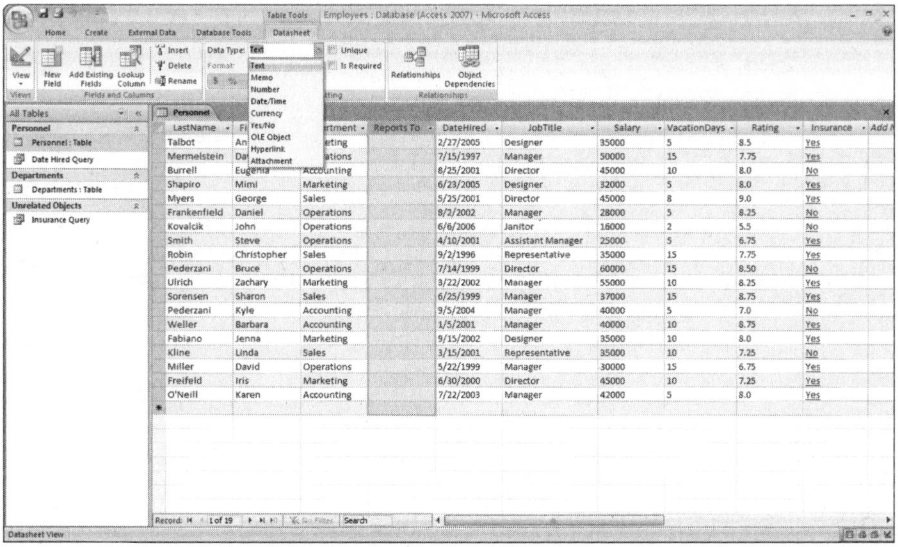

Figure 5-8:
Need a type
of field other
than the
default Text
data type?
The
Datasheet
tab gives
you options.

To get rid of an existing field that you no longer need, follow these steps:

1. **Right-click the heading for that field column.**

2. **From the resulting pop-up menu, shown in Figure 5-9, choose Delete Column.**

3. **When prompted, click Yes to confirm your desire to complete the delete.**

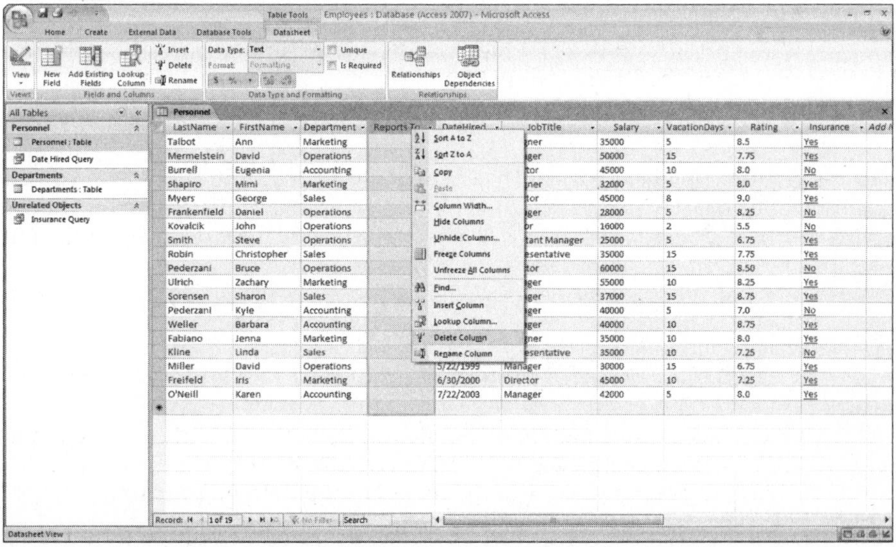

Figure 5-9:
Fields go
bye-bye
with ease.

Modifying Field Content

Although your stuff is safely tucked away inside a table, you can reach in and make changes easily. In fact, editing your data is so easy that I'm not sure whether this is a good feature or a bad one.

Whenever you're browsing through a table, please be careful! Access doesn't warn you before saving changes to a record — even if the changes are accidental. (If I were one of those preachy authors, I'd probably make a big, guilt-laden point about how this "feature" of Access makes regular backups all the more important, but that's not my style.)

To change something inside a record, follow these steps:

1. **Scroll through the table until you find the record that needs some adjusting.**

2. **Click the field that you want to change.**

   The blinking toothpick cursor pops into the field.

   If your mouse has a wheel button, use the wheel to quickly spin through the table. For such a small innovation, that wheel is a big time-saver!

3. **Change the field.**

   - *Replace the entire field:* Press F2 to highlight the data and then type the new information. The new entry replaces the old one.

   - *Repair a portion of the data in a field:* Click the field and then use the right- and left-arrow keys to position the toothpick cursor exactly where you want to make the change.

     Press Backspace to remove characters to the left of the cursor; press Delete to remove characters to the right. Insert new characters by typing.

   If you're in a time/date field and want to insert the current date, press Ctrl+; (semicolon). To insert the current time, press Ctrl+Shift+; (semicolon).

   If you change your mind and want to restore the original data, press Esc or Ctrl+Z to cancel your edits.

4. **When you're finished with the record, press Enter to save your changes.**

   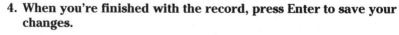

   Don't press Enter until you're positive about the changes you typed. After you save them, the old data is gone — you can't go back.

Name Calling

You've built your table, and maybe you've done a stellar job from the get-go — you didn't forget any fields, you put the fields in the right order, and you set up the fields to house the right kind of data. Pat yourself on the back!

Of course, nothing in life is that simple, is it? It's not uncommon to realize, after building your table (and patting yourself on the back for having done such a great job) that you need to make a few changes. You may need to change the table's name or you might need to change one or more of the field names in the table. Or both! If this happens, it doesn't mean you messed up or anything, it just means you're a human being who, with even the most scrupulous planning and preparation, can make a mistake or change your mind. Luckily, Access makes it easy to make either kind of change.

Renaming fields

Oh, no! Now that you think about it, you really shouldn't have abbreviated that field name. The "Dept" field might be confused with the "Depth" field in the table that lists product specifications. So now you want to change "Dept" to "Department" so there's no chance of confusion if someone other than you (or you, before your coffee) works with the database. This sort of field-naming dilemma is common when you're setting up a table for the first time, and can even crop up later on, when working with a table that has been around and in use for a while. The need to edit field names can arise for any reason, at any time, and it's never too early or to late to edit them.

So, for whatever reason, you need to edit a field name. What to do?

 Access makes it incredibly easy to rename a field — and to keep it simple, we'll do it in Table view. The simplicity doesn't end with how the actual renaming takes place, either — as soon as you rename a field, Access automatically updates

✔ All connections from that field to other tables (if you've already set up your table relationships, as discussed in Chapter 4)

✔ All queries, reports, and other goodies that already use the field

What could be easier than that?

Table view

So when you're ready, follow these steps:

1. **Double-click the field name, as shown in Figure 5-10.**

   The current name is highlighted and moves to the left side of the cell.

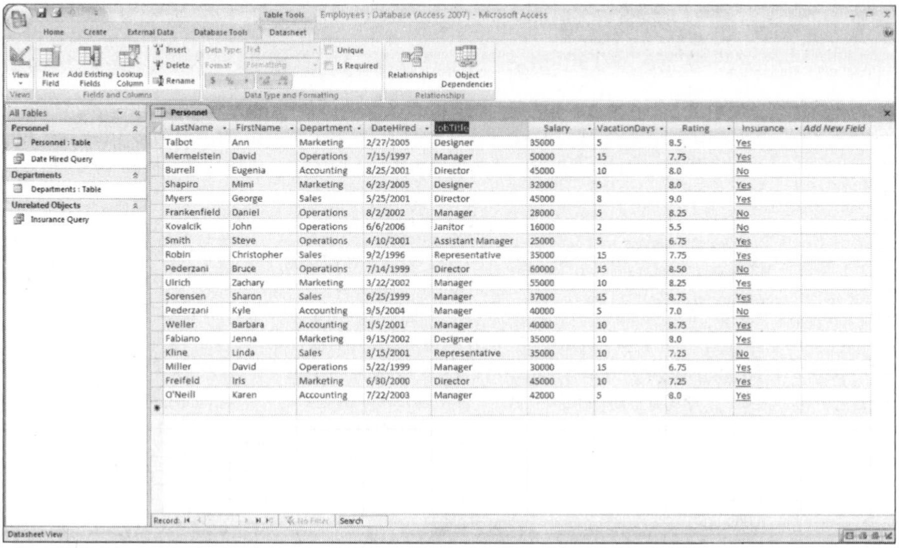

Figure 5-10:
A selected
field name is
ripe for
editing.

2. **Edit the name as needed:**

   • *To replace the current name entirely,* type the new name while the current name is still highlighted.

     While the field name is highlighted, the very next thing you type will replace the current name — so only if you need to replace the entire name should you begin typing at that point.

   • *To edit the name (leaving some of the current name in place),* click inside the existing, selected name and then insert or remove characters as needed.

3. **When you like the name you see, click in any cell in the table.**

   The new name appears at the top of the column, and you're ready to do whatever you need:

   • Enter new records.

   • Edit another field.

   • Save the table and close it (if you've finished working).

Datasheet tab

To rename a field in the Datasheet tab in Table view, follow these steps:

1. **Click the field name that you want to edit.**

   You can also click in any cell in that column — just give Access some way of knowing which field you want to rename.

2. **Click the Datasheet tab.**

3. **In the Fields and Columns section, click Rename, as shown in Figure 5-11.**

   The current field name is highlighted and will be replaced by the next thing you type.

4. **Type the replacement.**

5. **Press Enter or click in any other cell in the view.**

   This tells Access to accept your change.

Renaming a table

Renaming an entire table is not as common as needing to rename a field, but it can happen. Maybe you misspelled the name. Maybe the name you gave it is too long, too short, or is misleading to people who need to guess which table to open when they're looking for something in particular.

To edit the name of a table, follow these steps:

1. **Open the database that contains the table you want to rename.**

   With that database listed on the left side of your Access workspace, be sure all of its tables are listed, too.

Don't open the table itself. It can't be open during the renaming process.

2. Right-click the table name.

3. Choose Rename from the pop-up menu, as shown in Figure 5-12.

The name is highlighted.

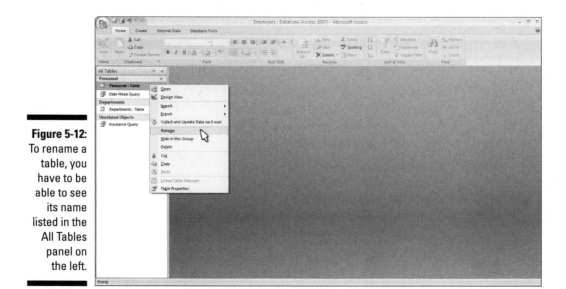

Figure 5-12:
To rename a table, you have to be able to see its name listed in the All Tables panel on the left.

4. Change the table name.

You can either

- Type the new name.

- Modify the current name (use your arrow keys to move within the name and your Backspace and/or Delete keys to edit).

After you've renamed your table, all the items that link to or use it within your database will be updated to use the same table with the new name. You don't need to re-create any of your queries, reports, forms, or relationships.

Turn Uh Oh! into Yi Hah!

I have only three suggestions for picking up the pieces from a bad edit. Unfortunately, none is a super-cool elixir that magically restores your lost data. I wish I had better news to close the chapter, but I'm fresh out of headlines:

✔ **You can recover from one add or edit with the Undo command.** Unfortunately, you cannot Undo the deletion of a record. Access will warn you, though, if you attempt to delete one or more records, and you can choose not to proceed if you're not absolutely sure.

✔ **Double-check any change you make before saving it.** If the change is important, triple-check it. When you're sure that it's right, press Enter and commit the change to the table. If you're not sure about the data, don't save the changes. Instead, get your questions answered first and then feel free to edit the record.

✔ **Keep a good backup so that you can quickly recover missing data and get on with your work.** Good backups have no substitute. If you make good backups, the chance of losing data is greatly reduced, your boss promotes you, your significant other unswervingly devotes his or her life to you, and you may even win the lottery.

Chapter 6

What's Happening Under the Table?

*I*f you have a sound table structure but poor data collection, your database won't report anything of interest to its intended audience. You know the old saying "garbage in, garbage out"? This chapter helps you limit the garbage that is put into your tables with four tools Access puts at your disposal. Access doesn't call them tools however; instead, it calls them *properties*.

You don't want the task of going back and cleaning up your data after it has all been typed. Better to type it correctly the first time. This chapter shows you how to use formatting, input masks, required fields, and validation to keep your data nice and tidy.

Access Table Settings

This chapter shows how to use these four properties to help keep incorrect data out of your database:

- ✔ **Formatting:** Control how your data appears without changing the way it is stored.

- ✔ **Input mask:** Force data entry to follow the correct structure, such as typing phone numbers in the (###) ###-#### format.

- ✔ **Required:** Force the entry of data in the field before the record can be saved.

✔ **Validation:** Require that data be typed in a field following a specific set of rules, such as a number between 0 and 100.

All four properties are in the same place: the Table Design window's General tab. Use the following steps to access and modify the four properties:

1. **Open the database file and then click the table you want to adjust.**

2. **Right-click the table and choose Design View (see Figure 6-1).**

   The table flips into Design view, showing its fields and field properties.

   If the table you want is already on the screen in Datasheet view, just click the Views tool from the Home tab of the Ribbon. This toggles between Design and Datasheet views.

3. **Repeat these steps for each field whose properties you want to alter:**

   a. *Click the name of the field.*

      The General tab in the Field Properties section (the bottom half of the window) displays the details of the current field, as shown in Figure 6-2. You're ready to do your thing!

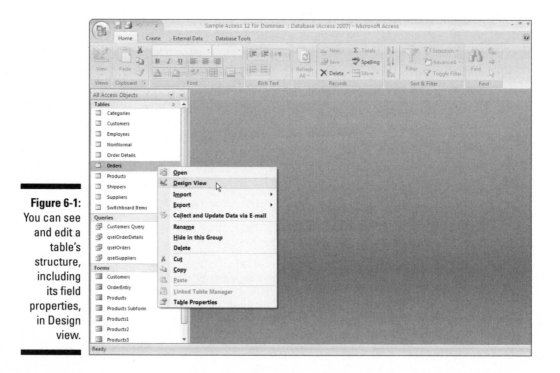

Figure 6-1:
You can see and edit a table's structure, including its field properties, in Design view.

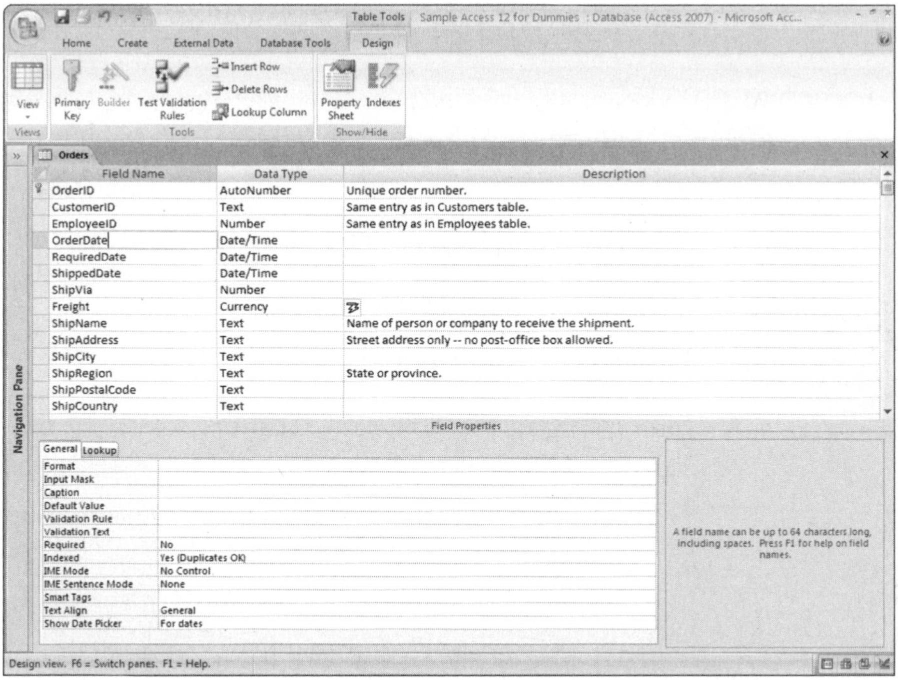

Figure 6-2:
Working on
the order
date field.

b. *In the Field Properties section, click in the Format, Input Mask, Validation Rule, or Required boxes and type your changes.*

In the remainder of this chapter, I delve into these properties in more detail so you'll understand what they do and how to modify them to suit your needs.

Validation Text has a box, too. It goes with the Validation Rule box (kind of like coffee and cream). The "Making your data toe the line with validation" section, later in this chapter, explains how these two properties work together to prevent the entry of unwanted data.

4. **When you've made all necessary property changes, click the Save button on the Quick Access toolbar to keep your changes.**

To *reject* your changes, close the table (click the x in its upper-right corner) and click No in the resulting dialog box.

Using formats, masks, required fields, and validations involves many more details, but use the preceding steps to get started. These steps are the same no matter which property you apply.

The following sections tackle each property individually.

Field Data Formats

Formatting helps you see data in a recognizable, clear arrangement. Formats only change the way you *see* your data on the screen, not how your data is *stored* in the table.

Some field data types require different formatting codes than others. For example, text formatting uses different codes than numeric formatting. The following sections cover formats for the most common field data types.

If your format command doesn't work the first time, follow these steps to troubleshoot it:

1. **Double-check the field type.**

2. **Review the format commands and make any necessary changes.**

   For example, if you see percent signs and your intention was dollar signs, just flip the format from Percent to Currency by using the Format Property drop-down list.

Text and memo fields

Text and memo fields can be formatted in four ways that affect *capitalization, spacing,* and *punctuation.*

Access does not have predesigned formats for text and memo fields, but you can make your own. Just string together some special characters to construct a formatting string that Access can use to display the text in a standardized way.

Table 6-1 lists the special characters that you can use to build your text and memo formats.

Table 6-1	Text and Memo Field Formatting Codes
Character	*Display Option*
>	Show whole field as uppercase (capital letters).
<	Show whole field as lowercase.
@	Show a space in this position if there isn't a data character.
&	Display a character if there is one; otherwise, don't do anything.

Apply formatting, minimize data entry errors

Although formatting won't stop inaccurate data entry, it can make data entry errors more recognizable. Here's how formatting can cut down on errors:

✔ **Make errors more visible.**

For example, suppose you need to type the number *one million* into a numeric field. Without formatting, you see this: 1000000. (Uh, how many zeros are in that?) With standard formatting, you see this: 1,000,000.

✔ **Cut down on typing during data entry.**

For example, phone numbers are often seen as (111) 222-3333. With text formatting applied to a phone number field, simply type **1112223333**. Access displays the phone number with the parentheses and the dash. Can you say "fewer keystrokes"?

Here's what you need to know about the formatting codes in Table 6-1.

Capitalization

By default, Access displays text fields with the actual capitalization of the stored data. However, Access can automatically display a field in all *uppercase* (capital) or *lowercase* letters, regardless of how the data is stored.

Masks using the greater-than and less-than symbols for capitalization require you to enter the symbol only once to affect the capitalization of the whole field.

Uppercase

The *greater-than* symbol (>) makes all the text in that field appear in uppercase (capital) letters, regardless of how the text was typed. To use this option, type a single greater-than symbol in the Format text box.

This is great for U.S. state abbreviations that normally are seen as uppercase.

Lowercase

The *less-than* symbol (<) makes all the text in that field appear in lowercase, regardless of how the text was typed. To use this option, type a single less-than symbol in the Format text box.

Spacing and punctuation

Access allows you to format the spacing and punctuation of typed text. Through formatting, you can add extra spaces or special characters like dashes.

When using the @ or & character in a format, always include one @ or & to represent *each typed character* in the field.

Show filler spaces

The *at sign* (@) forces Access to display either a character or a space in the field. If the typed field data is shorter than the formatting code, Access adds extra spaces to fill the format.

For example, if a field uses @@@@@@ as its format, but the field's data is only three characters long (such as *Tim* or *now*), Access displays three spaces and *then* the data. If the field data is four characters long, the format pads the beginning of the entry with two spaces.

Don't show filler spaces

The *ampersand* (&) means "display a character if there's one to display; otherwise don't do anything."

This is the default format.

You can use this to create special formats. For example, a Social Security number can use this format: &&&- &&- &&&&

If someone types **123456789** in that field, Access applies the format and displays 123-45-6789, adding the dashes in the middle of the numbers by itself.

Formatting changes only the appearance of data, not the data itself. Therefore, if you intend to export the data to another program, such as Excel, the formatting won't necessarily come with it. So, if you type **pa** in a State field and apply the > formatting code to that field, the data will appear as PA in Access but will export to Excel as pa.

Make Access see red so you don't

Here's a great tip for highlighting missing text data in a record: When typing data, sometimes you need to skip a text field because you don't have that particular information at hand. Wouldn't it be great if Access automatically marked the field as blank as a reminder for you to fill in the info later?

Access can create such a custom text format. For example, the following character string displays the word *Unknown* in red if the field doesn't contain a value. Type the following command in the field's Format text box exactly like this (there

are no spaces between the characters in the string) and punctuation:

    @;"Unknown"[Red]

It's easy to customize the above formatting example to suit your needs:

✔ **Text:** Between the quotes, substitute any display text you want instead of Unknown.

✔ **Color:** Between the square brackets, substitute any display color you want instead of Red.

Number and currency fields

Microsoft makes it easy for you to apply numeric formats to your numeric fields. They built the seven most common formats into a pull-down menu right in the Format text box.

To set a number or currency field format, follow these steps:

1. **With your table in Design view, click the Format text box for the field you'd like to format.**

2. **Click the down arrow that appears at the right side of the box and select a format for your field.**

   Figure 6-3 shows the drop-down menu, which is divided in half:

   • The left side shows each format's given name.

   • The right side shows a sample of how each format looks.

Numeric formats change only the appearance of the number, not the number as it is stored. So, if you choose Standard to format a field that contains the number 1.235678, you see 1.24 on the screen. However, Access stores 1.235678 in the field. Any calculations done with the numbers in that field will use the actual typed number, not the formatted number seen on screen.

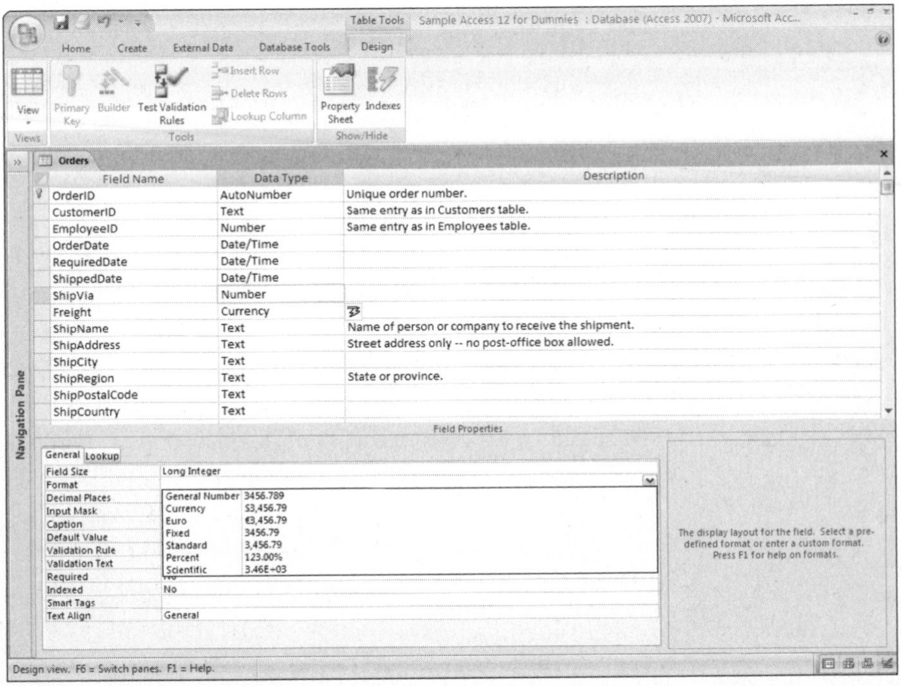

Figure 6-3:
The number format list.

The following sections describe Access's built-in numeric formats.

General Number

The General Number format is the Access default. It merely displays whatever you put in the field without making any editorial adjustments to it.

Currency formats

The currency formats make a standard number field look like a currency field.

Some numeric fields store decimal characters, and others do not — it all depends on the field size you select. So, decimal formatting is irrelevant if you select a field size like long integer that does not store decimal places. Chapter 3 covers number fields and field sizes in more detail.

These two formats show the data with two decimal places (the "cents" part of a dollar amount), substituting zeros if decimals aren't already present:

 ✔ **Currency:** Show the local currency sign and punctuation (based on the Regional Settings in the Windows Control Panel).

 The Currency formats do not automatically perform an exchange rate conversion for the selected currency. They merely display the selected currency symbol in front of the value typed in the field.

 ✔ **Euro:** Use the Euro symbol (ε) regardless of the Regional Settings.

Scientific, Percent, and Decimal formats

The remaining built-in formats are used for a variety of purposes, from displaying a large number in scientific notation to showing decimals as percents:

 ✔ **Fixed:** Shows the decimal value without a comma as a thousands separator.

 ✔ **Standard:** Shows the decimal value with a thousands separator.

 For either Fixed or Standard format, you can adjust the number of decimal places that appear:

  • By default, Fixed and Standard round the display to two decimal places.

  • To specify a different number of decimal places, type a number between 0 and 15 in the Decimal Places setting right below the Format setting.

 ✔ **Percent:** This format turns a simple decimal like .97 into the much prettier 97%.

Type the data as a decimal (for example, type **.97** for 97 percent). Otherwise Access displays some awesomely *wrong* percentages!

If your percentages are displayed only as 0.00% or 1.00%, the sidebar "What happened to my percentages" has a solution.

✔ **Scientific:** Displays numbers in *scientific notation* (the first *significant digits* plus the number of places where the digits belong on the left or right side of the decimal point)

Scientific notation is mostly for very *big* numbers (like the distance light travels in a year) and very *small* numbers (like the distance light travels in a trillionth of a second) that are hard to measure precisely or read at a glance.

Date/time fields

Microsoft provides you with a pull-down menu full of ready-to-use date and time formats. Here's how to apply a date/time format to a field:

1. **With your table in Design view, click the Format text box for the field you'd like to format.**

2. **Click the down arrow that appears on the text box's right side.**

   The menu shown in Figure 6-4 pops down to serve you.

3. **Select the format you want to use.**

What happened to my percentages

When you create a field with the Number data type, Access assigns the Long Integer field size by default. Because by definition integers are whole numbers, Access rounds any decimal number entered in such a field. So, if you enter **0.25** in a field with the Percent format, and Access displays your entry as 0.00%, your entry:

✔ Automatically rounds to the nearest whole number (in my example case, 0)

✔ Always displays zeros in the decimal places

The solution? Change the Field Size setting (right above Format) from Long Integer to Single. This setting tells Access to remember the decimal part of the number.

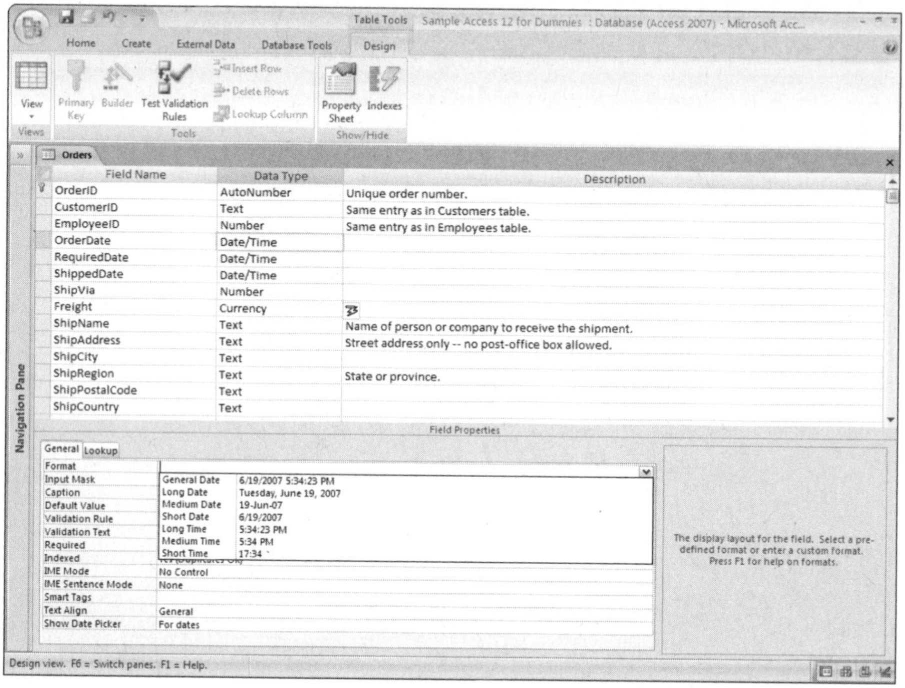

Figure 6-4:
The ever-popular date format list.

Keep these tips in mind when you apply a date/time format:

- ✔ When you use one of the longer formats, such as General Date or Long Date, make sure that the datasheet column is wide enough to display all the information. Otherwise, you'll see a wacky date that makes no sense.

- ✔ If more than one person uses the database, choose a format that provides *more* information, not *less* information.

My clients often ask me to provide a date in the m/d/yy format with a two-digit year (such as 1/1/07 instead of 1/1/2007). To display a date with a two-digit year, type the following in the format box: **m/d/yy**.

Yes/No fields

You can say only so much about a field with three options. Oddly, yes/no fields are set to the Yes/No formatting by default.

If you want the ability to type Yes/No, True/False, or On/Off in the field, make sure that Display Control in the Lookup tab (next to the General tab) is set to Text Box. Otherwise, you will have check boxes in your field since Check Box is the default display for a Yes/No field.

Allowable Yes/No field entries

Here's what you can type in a Yes/No field (see Figure 6-5):

✔ Yes and No (this is the default)

✔ On and Off

✔ True and False

Yes and No is the default, but you can change how a Yes/No field formats its content. Here's how:

1. **With your table in Design view, click the Format text box for the field you'd like to format.**

2. **Click the down arrow that appears on the text box's right side.**

   The menu of three Yes/No formats pops down for your inspection.

3. **Select the format you want to use.**

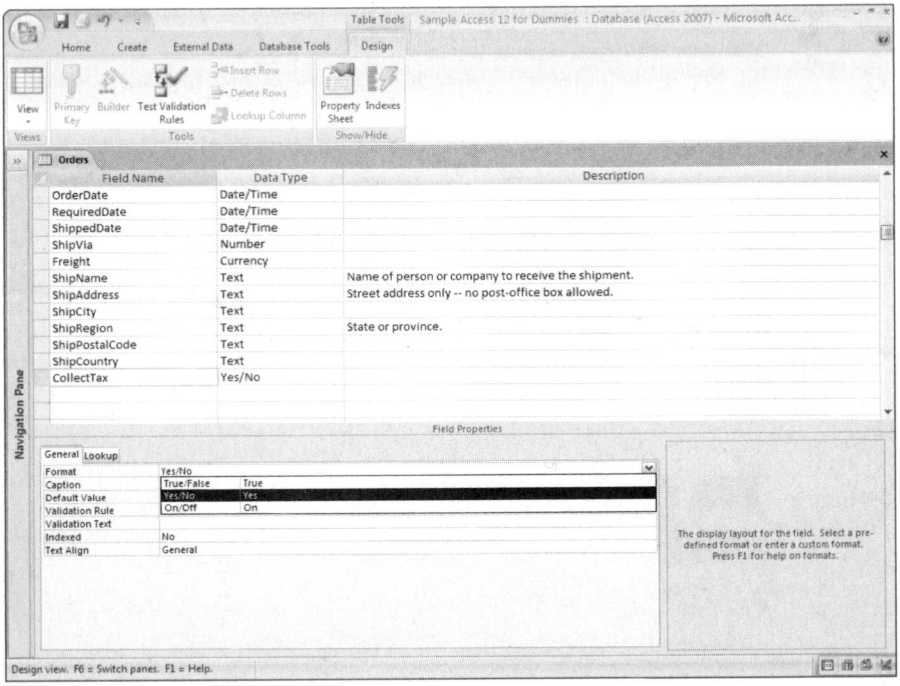

Figure 6-5:
Not much to
talk about
with Yes/No
formatting.

Create your own Yes/No format

To display your *own* choices instead of a boring *Yes* and *No,* type a customized entry in the Format box. A good example format looks something like this:

```
"REORDER"[Red]; "In stock"[Green]
```

The No and Yes parts of the format are separated by a semicolon (;)

- ✔ The part on the left appears if the field is equal to No.
- ✔ The part on the right appears if the field is equal to Yes.

With the preceding example, type **Yes** in the field and the text *In stock* appears in green. Type **No** in the field and *REORDER* screams a warning in bright red.

A custom Yes/No format simply changes the way the typed data appears. A Yes/No field will still only accept the entries as outlined in the previous section "Allowable Yes/No field entries" regardless of what custom format is applied to it.

You can type any words between the quotes and any Access-allowed color names between the square brackets. Who knew that formatting could be so much fun!

Gaining Control of Data Entry

The remaining sections in this chapter explore Access field properties that allow you to control what data is entered in a field. The more you control the data that goes into your tables, the less you'll need clean it up after it has been entered.

You really need to put a mask on those fields

The *input mask* actually prevents users from typing data that does not fit the mask.

An input mask is a series of characters that tells Access what data to expect in a particular field. If you want a field to contain all numbers and no letters, an input mask can do the job. It can also do the reverse (all letters and no numbers) and almost any combination in between.

Formatting (shown previously in this chapter) can make some data entry errors *visible,* but formatting doesn't *block* errors. Input masks, on the other hand, keep that bad data out.

Input masks are stored in the Input Mask property box of the field's General tab. (The beginning of this chapter shows steps to access the General tab.)

Add these masks to fields that contain dates, times, phone numbers, Social Security numbers, and zip codes, among other things. You'll be so glad you did. If you don't, expect to see plenty of phone numbers like 111-123 and zip codes like 0854.

Input masks work best with *short, consistent* data. Numbers and number-and-letter combinations that follow a consistent pattern are excellent candidates. Phone numbers, dates, and zip codes are common examples of data that follow a consistent pattern.

You create an input mask in one of two ways:

- ✔ **Ask the Input Mask Wizard for help.**

    The Input Mask Wizard can't possibly contain every mask for every situation. It only knows about text and date fields, and offers just a few options.

    Always start with the wizard. If it doesn't have your solution, then you need to manually build the mask.

- ✔ **Type the mask manually.**

    Create the mask manually if your data follows a consistent pattern (such as a six-digit part number) yet is not a choice offered by the Input Mask Wizard.

Using the Input Mask Wizard

The Input Mask Wizard gladly helps if you're making a mask for text fields (like *phone numbers, Social Security numbers* and *United States zip codes),* or simple *date and time fields.*

If your data doesn't fit one of the masks that the wizard provides yet follows a consistent pattern, the next section shows how to create a mask manually.

To ask for the wizard's help, follow these steps:

1. **With the database file open, right-click the table you want to work with and choose Design View.**

    The table flips into Design view.

2. Click the name of the field you want to apply an input mask to.

You can use the wizard only with text and date/time fields.

The General tab in the Field Properties section (the bottom half of the window) displays the details of the current field.

3. Click the Input Mask box.

The cursor monotonously blinks away in the Input Mask box. To the right of the box, a small button with three dots appears. That's the Builder button, which comes into play in the next step.

4. Click the Builder button.

The wizard appears, offering a choice of input masks, as shown in Figure 6-6.

Input Mask Wizard

Which input mask matches how you want data to look?

To see how a selected mask works, use the Try It box.

To change the Input Mask list, click the Edit List button.

Input Mask:	Data Look:
Long Time	1:12:00 PM
Short Date	9/27/1969
Short Time	13:12
Medium Time	01:12 PM
Medium Date	27-Sep-69

Try It:

Edit List   Cancel   < Back   Next >   Finish

5. Scroll through the list of input masks to find what you want.

6. Click the input mask you want.

To play with the mask a bit and see how it works, click the Try It area at the bottom of the dialog box and then type a sample entry.

7. Click Finish to close the wizard and use the mask with your field.

If you click Next instead of Finish, the Wizard gives you more options, but we recommend avoiding them. The sidebar "The rest of the Input Mask Wizard" has the details.

The chosen mask appears in the Input Mask area in the table design screen, as shown in Figure 6-7.

The rest of the Input Mask Wizard

This sidebar shows my recommendations for the last two steps of the Input Mask Wizard. If you click Next instead of Finish at the end of my steps, the Input Mask Wizard continues asking you about changing some obscure settings that are best left at the defaults:

✔ **The placeholder character for the input mask.**

The placeholder character in the mask represents the actual typed character by the user. The default is a dash. You can change from the default to a # or %.

✔ **Storing the data with the symbols included within the input mask.**

For example, a Social Security number could be stored with or without the dashes.

The default is No (for *don't store the symbols*). I recommend you keep it that way. The mask takes care of the data display. Why store extra characters in your database?

Figure 6-7:
The Input
Mask
Wizard
completes
its master-
piece.

Field Name	Data Type	Description
OrderID	AutoNumber	Unique order number.
CustomerID	Text	Same entry as in Customers table.
EmployeeID	Number	Same entry as in Employees table.
OrderDate	Date/Time	
RequiredDate	Date/Time	
ShippedDate	Date/Time	
ShipVia	Number	
Freight	Currency	
ShipName	Text	Name of person or company to receive the shipment.
ShipAddress	Text	Street address only -- no post-office box allowed.
ShipCity	Text	
ShipRegion	Text	State or province.
ShipPostalCode	Text	
ShipCountry	Text	

Field Properties

General | Lookup

Format	
Input Mask	99/99/0000;0;
Caption	
Default Value	
Validation Rule	
Validation Text	
Required	No
Indexed	Yes (Duplicates OK)
IME Mode	No Control
IME Sentence Mode	None
Smart Tags	
Text Align	General
Show Date Picker	For dates

A pattern for all data to be entered in this field

Design view. F6 = Switch panes. F1 = Help.

Making a mask by hand

It's not uncommon to need a mask that the Input Mask Wizard doesn't provide. If your fingers can string together a seemingly nonsensical string of characters on the keyboard, then you can make your own input masks. The trick is making sense out of all the nonsensical characters.

Table 6-2 shows the codes that you can use in an input mask and an explanation of what characters they represent:

✔ **Required Code:** User must type that type of character (whether they actually want to or not).

✔ **Optional Code:** User can type or not type the kind of character mentioned in the first column.

Table 6-2	Codes for Input Masks	
Kind of Characters	*Required Code*	*Optional Code*
Digits (0 to 9) only	0 (zero)	9
Digits and + and -	(not available)	# (U.S. pound sign)
Letters (A to Z) only	L	? (question mark)
Letters or digits only	A	a (must be lowercase)
Any character or space	& (ampersand)	C
Any character typed into the mask fills it from right to left	!	None
Any literal character	\ (* displays as just *)	None
All characters typed into the mask are forced to lower case	<	None
All characters typed into the mask are forced to upper case	>	None

You must use the input mask codes to design an input mask.

Designing an input mask

Before you can create a mask, you must determine what mask codes you'll need to build the mask. Here's how:

1. **On a piece of paper, write several examples of the data that the mask should let into the table.**

   If the information you're storing has subtle variations (such as part numbers that end in either a letter/number or letter/letter combination), include examples of the various possibilities so that your input mask accepts them all. You can't build a mask if you don't know your data.

2. **Write a simple description of the data, including which elements are required and which are optional.**

   For example, if your sample is a part number that looks like 728816ABC7, write *six numbers, three letters, one number; all parts are required.*

   Remember to allow for the variations, if you have any. The difference between *one number* and *one letter or number* can be crucial.

   If you need to include a special character in your mask, like a dash or parentheses or a combination of static characters, use this list for guidance:

   - **Dash, slash, or parenthesis characters:** Put a backslash (\) in front of it, like \ – for a dash.

   - **Multiple characters:** Put quotation marks around them.

     For example, an area code may be separated from the rest of the number by *both* a parenthesis and a space, like this: (567) 555-2345

     The corresponding mask has quotes around the parenthesis and the space, like this: !\(999"-) "000\-0000

   The phone number mask also begins with an exclamation point. The exclamation point forces the typed data to fill the mask from right to left versus the default left to right. What's the big deal about that? Some phone numbers don't require an area code, while others do. Suppose you had to type a seven-digit phone number. If not for the right-to-left entry, you'd have to move the cursor past the area code (###) placeholder part of the mask to get to the beginning of the seven digit part.

   If your field includes letters and you want them to be stored as all upper-case, add a greater-than symbol (>) to the beginning of your mask To store the letters as all lowercase, use a less-than symbol (<) instead.

3. **Write the mask codes that represent the elements you've written in Step 2.**

   In Step 2, if you wrote "six numbers, three letters, one number; all parts are required," then you'd need the mask codes `000000LLL0`. Refer to Table 6-2.

Putting on your input mask

Now that you have your mask written on paper, it's time to enter it in Access. Here's how:

1. **With the database file open, right-click the table you want to work with and choose Design View.**

   The table flips into Design view.

2. **Click the name of the field you want to adjust.**

3. **Click the Input Mask box.**

   The cursor blinks in the Input Mask box.

4. **Carefully type your finished mask into the Input Mask area of the Field Properties (as shown in Figure 6-8).**

   If you don't know what to type here, see the preceding section.

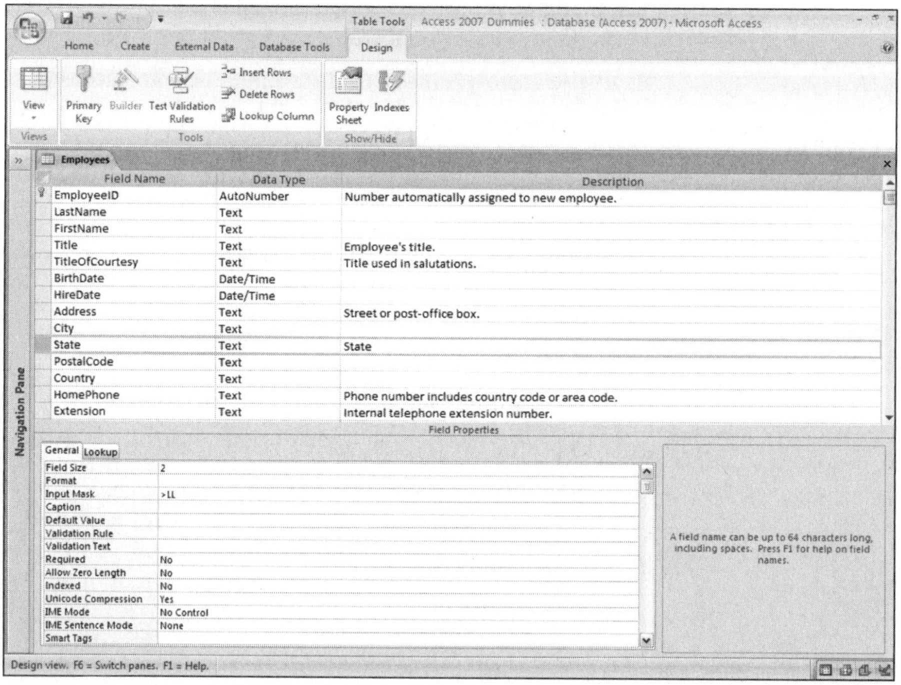

Figure 6-8: Putting a capitalization mask on the State field.

5. **At the end of the mask, add ; ; _ (two semicolons and an underscore character).**

These three characters tell Access to display an underscore where you want each character to appear. The placeholder is not required, but it does make the mask easier to understand for the data entry person.

6. **Click the View button on the Ribbon and place the cursor in the masked field to check out your new mask.**

When prompted to Save, click Yes so you don't lose your work.

When you've entered the mask and have saved the table, try these tests:

a. *Type something unacceptable into the masked field.*

The input mask should prevent you from typing an incorrect value (see Figure 6-9).

b. *Try an acceptable entry.*

The mask should accept your entry.

c. *Try all the variations you identified in the mask planning process.*

All should be accepted by the mask. If they are not, switch back to Design view and tweak your mask until all possible variations of your entry are acceptable to the mask.

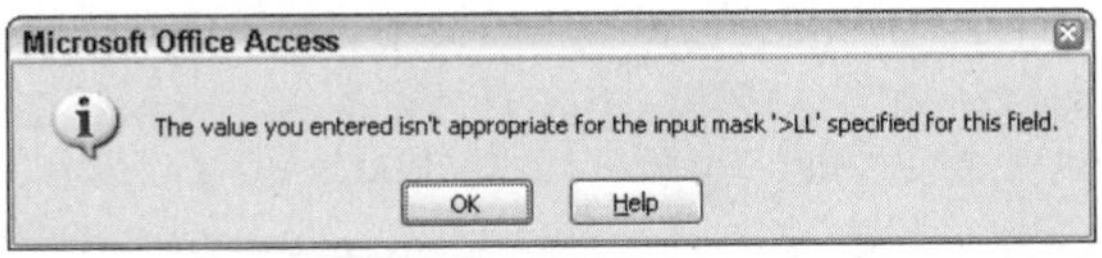

Figure 6-9:
I have
violated the
input mask.

> **Microsoft Office Access**
>
> (i) The value you entered isn't appropriate for the input mask '>LL' specified for this field.
>
> [OK]   [Help]

If you're adding a mask to an existing table with data, Access doesn't report to you on existing records that fail the mask; it gives that data a free pass to exist as typed. To enforce the mask on existing records, repeat these steps for each record:

1. **Click the field in the record.**

2. **Edit the data.**

You can delete the last character and then retype it.

When you move the cursor out of the field, you'll see the warning if the data doesn't comply with the mask.

To require or not to require

There are many occasions when you won't want a record typed until all the facts are in. For example, you certainly wouldn't want an order typed without an order date, customer, and product information. The *Required* property prevents records that are missing essential data from being saved to a table.

The Required property has two settings:

- ✔ **Yes:** The user cannot leave the record without putting something in the field.
- ✔ **No:** Anything goes. (This is the default.)

To require data entry in a field, follow these simple steps:

1. **While in table Design view, click the field in which you want to require data entry.**

2. **Click in the Required box on the General tab in the Field Properties section.**

   An arrow appears at the end of the box. By default, the box reads No.

3. **Click the arrow and select Yes from the list, as shown in Figure 6-10.**

   Watch out, the field is now required!

4. **Switch to Datasheet view and test your work.**

   Type a new record, omitting data entry in the required field. You should see a message box admonishing you for forgetting the required data.

Don't get overzealous with the Required property and set it to Yes for nonessential fields. For example, a contact without a fax number and job title is usually better than no contact at all.

Making your data toe the line with validation

With a *validation,* Access tests the incoming data to make sure that it's what you want in the table. If the data isn't right, the validation displays an error message (you get to choose what it says) and makes you try the entry again.

Figure 6-10:
The
Required
property is
set to Yes.

Like the other options in this chapter, validations are stored in the General tab of the Field Properties area. Two options relate to validations:

✔ **Validation Rule:** The rule is the validation itself.

✔ **Validation Text:** The text is the error message you want Access to display when some data that violates the validation rule is typed.

Validations work best with number, currency, and date fields. Creating a validation for a text field is possible, but the validations usually get very complicated very fast.

Tables 6-3 and 6-4 contain some ready-to-use validations that cover the most common needs. These are ready to type in the General tab of the Field Properties area.

Table 6-3	Common Number Field Validations
Validation Rule	*What It Means*
`> 0`	Must be greater than zero
`<> 0`	Cannot be zero
`> 0 AND < 100`	Must be between 0 and 100 (non-inclusive)
`>= 0 AND <= 100`	Must be between 0 and 100 (inclusive)
`<= 0 OR >= 100`	Must be less than 0 or greater than 100 (inclusive)

Table 6-4	Common Date Field Validations
Validation Rule	*What It Means*
`>= Date ()`	Must be today's date or later
`>= Date () OR Is Null`	Must be today's date, later, or blank
`< Date ()`	Must be earlier than today's date
`>= #1/1/2000# AND <= Date ()`	Must be between January 1, 2000 and today (inclusive)

Here's how to enter a validation rule:

1. **With the database file open, right-click the table you want to work with and choose Design View.**

   The table flips into Design view.

2. **Click the name of the field you want to adjust.**

3. **Click the Validation Rule box.**

   The cursor blinks in the Validation Rule box.

4. **Type the validation rule that matches your data.**

   For example, if you want to allow only numbers between 0 and 1,000 into the field, type **>0 AND <1000**.

5. **Click in the Validation Text field.**

   The cursor blinks in the Validation Text box.

6. **Type the message you'd like the user to see if he breaks the validation rule.**

   For my example in Step 4, you might type **Please enter a number greater than 0 and less than 1,000.**

When you apply a validation rule to a field, watch out for these gotchas:

✔ When using AND, both sides of the validation rule must be true before the rule is met.

✔ With OR, only one side of the rule needs to be true for the entire rule to be true.

✔ Be careful when combining >= and <=. Accidentally coming up with one that can't be true (such as <= 0 AND >= 100) is too easy!

Part III
Data Mania and Management

The 5th Wave   By Rich Tennant

I told Russell he should data model before we go any further.

Miss Claudia Schiffer, please.

In this part . . .

1 admit it. The word "mania" was added just to make this section sound more exciting. How thrilling would it be if it were simply entitled "Data Management"? I'm yawning just thinking about it. Of course, if you really want to understand how to use and control your Access database, you'll read this section of the book – regardless of the perceived potential for inducing sleep.

Actually, in this Part, you'll find out about some really neat features – like Forms, which can be used for building, editing, and viewing your database, ways to import and export data (making building a table-ful of records go *much* faster), how to edit your database automatically, ferreting out duplicate records, misspellings, and other data atrocities, and you'll also — drum roll, please — learn about how your Access data can find a home on the web.

What can be more exciting than that? Well, lots of things could be, but how likely is it that you'll win the lottery, anyway?

Chapter 7

Creating Data Forms

· ·

· ·

Access forms are similar to paper forms in that they are used in part to collect data. Access forms go beyond paper forms by having a direct connection to the database tables that store the collected information. In the "old days," after you completed a paper form, some poor soul had to manually organize and file each form in a file cabinet or tabulate results by hand. With the advent of electronic databases like Access, data is typed into an electronic form and simultaneously placed in the file cabinet (the table) connected to that form.

Like reports and queries, forms are named and stored in the database file. Forms are full-fledged Access objects so you can have your way with them (and nobody gets hurt!).

This chapter shows what forms can do for you, shows you how to make forms, and provides tips for customizing forms so that they're exactly what you need.

Generating Forms

Depending on your needs, you can create forms in three ways:

✔ The AutoForm tools make attractive forms with a click of the mouse.

✔ The Form Wizard asks some questions and then produces an attractive form based on your answers.

Why use forms?

Access forms have all kinds of advantages over old-fashioned paper forms — and they'll spoil you if you're used to wandering through your data in Datasheet view (where the data appears in a spreadsheet format).

Here are the most important reasons for using Access forms to manage your data:

✔ **Say goodbye to Datasheet view:** Maintaining your data in Datasheet view isn't much fun. The constant scrolling back and forth and up and down can make you dizzy. With a form, you focus on one record at a time with all the data laid out on a single screen. Maintaining your data becomes a snap, and your datasheet-induced headaches disappear.

✔ **Modify at will:** When your needs change, update the form in Design view. When you need to collect a new piece of data, just add a field to the appropriate table and to the form associated with that table.

✔ **See your data any way you want:** Access lets you take one set of data and maintain it with as many different forms as you want. Create a special form for the data-entry department, another for your manager, and a third for yourself. Each form can display just the fields that those people need to see. Well-designed forms give the right information to the right people without revealing unnecessary data.

✔ **View the entries in a table or as the results of a query:** Forms pull information from tables or queries with equal ease.

✔ **Combine data from multiple tables:** One form can display data from several related tables. Forms automatically use the relationships built into your database. So you can, for example, see a list of customers and their corresponding orders all on one form.

The Form Wizard and AutoForm tools are a time saving gift from your friends at Microsoft. Use them to create your forms. They happily do the hard stuff so that all you have to do is provide the finishing touches. Some people (especially computer geeks) think wizards are for sissies and that *real men* (and women) build everything from scratch. Well, I don't. If I am given a gift, I accept it with a thank you and a smile. *Thanks, Microsoft!*

Use these criteria to determine which form building tool to use:

✔ Use AutoForm if:

- You want all fields in the selected table or query on the report,
- You don't want control over the type of style that is applied to the form.

✔ Use the Form Wizard (covered later in this chapter) if:

- You want to select specific fields for your form.

- You want to select fields from more than one table or query.

- You want choose from a list of styles for your report.

Keeping it simple: AutoForm

I have good and bad news about the AutoForm tools:

✔ **Good news:** They're fast, and don't ask any questions or talk back!

✔ **Bad news:** They're extremely inflexible little fellas.

You want a larger font and a different background color? Keep it to yourself. AutoForm tools decide what font, colors, and layout you get.

After you create a form with an AutoForm tool, you can *modify* the form. In this chapter, "Rearranging the Parts" gives you the straight scoop.

Meet the AutoForms

There are three kinds of AutoForms:

✔ **A Simple Form** displays one record at a time. If the data source you select for the form has a related child table, the Simple Form tool shows that data as well.

Suppose you have an Orders table and an Order Details table related by an OrderID field (see Chapter 4 for an explanation of table relationships). If you select the Orders table before you click the Simple Form tool, you get a form that also displays customer and order data.

✔ **Split Forms** display all records as a datasheet on the top half of the form and the currently selected record from the top half in an easy-to-read format on the bottom half.

Use a Split Form if you want to browse and edit multiple records in a user-friendly fashion. The split screen format lets you easily browse records in the datasheet portion (top half) of the form and see and edit each record's detail in the currently selected record portion (bottom half) of the form.

✔ **Multiple Items** shows all records from the data source in a beautiful datasheet-like format.

Create a Multiple Items form if you'd like to see all records at a glance. This usually works best with tables that contain a small number of fields since each field translates into a column on your screen.

To use AutoForms, open your database and follow these steps:

1. **From the Navigation Pane, select the table or query that contains the data your new form should display.**

2. **Click the Create tab on the Ribbon.**

   Several tool groups appear on the Ribbon, including the Forms group. (See Figure 7-1.)

Figure 7-1: The Create tab of the Ribbon holds the Forms tools.

3. **Click the AutoForm tool of your choice from the Forms tools.**

   The sidebar "Meet the AutoForms" shows the best AutoForm tool for your data.

   A beautiful form appears before your eyes! (And in Figure 7-2!)

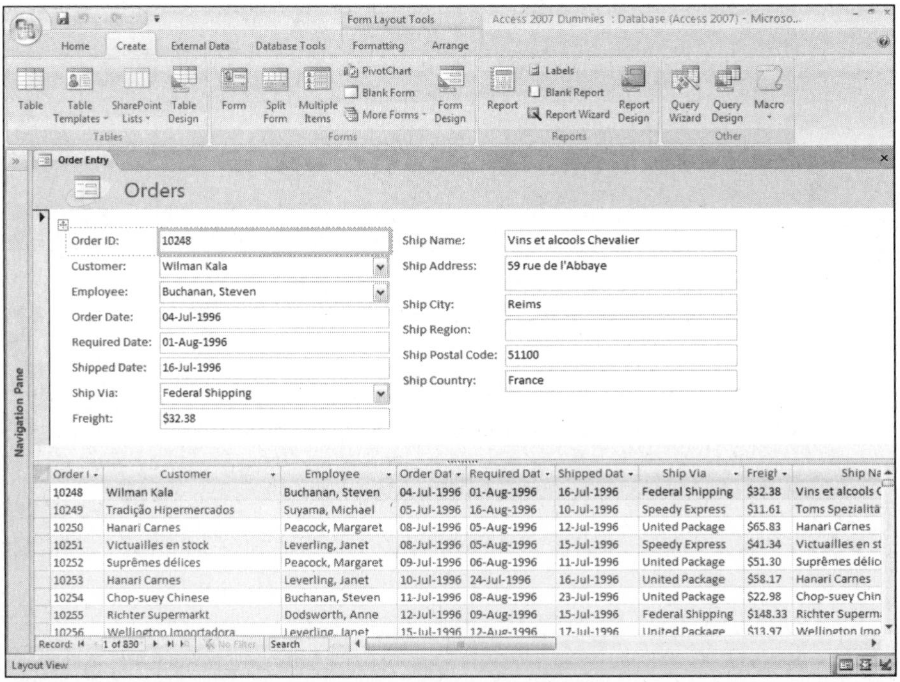

Figure 7-2: Form based on the Orders table using the Split Form tool.

4. **To finish your form, follow these steps:**

   a. *Click the Save button on the Quick Access toolbar.*

   The Save As dialog box appears.

   b. *Type a name for the form in the dialog box, and click OK.*

   Your form name appears on the Navigation Pane.

Granting most wishes: Form Wizard

When you want to control field selection and the style of form design, use the Form Wizard.

As with all Access wizards, the Form Wizard steps you through the creation process. To use the Form Wizard, follow these steps:

1. **Open your database file.**

2. **Click the Create tab on the Ribbon.**

   Several tool groups appear on the Ribbon, including the Forms group.

3. **Click the More Forms button and select Form Wizard from the resulting drop-down list, as shown in Figure 7-3.**

   The Form Wizard springs into action.

4. **In the Tables/Queries box, select the source of the form's fields:**

   a. *Click the down arrow to list the database's tables and queries.*

   b. *Select the table or query that contains the fields you want to view with this form.*

   The Form Wizard lists the available fields.

   Feel free to select fields from different tables, provided the tables are related properly. The Wizard will not let you select fields from unrelated tables.

5. **Select the fields you want.**

   • To select *individual* fields, double-click each field you want in the Available Fields list. (see Figure 7-4).

   • If you want to add *all* the fields from your table or query to your form, click the >> button in the middle of the screen.

   Feel free to select fields from different tables, provided the tables are related properly. The Wizard will not let you select fields from unrelated tables.

To remove a field that you accidentally chose, double-click its name in the Selected Fields list. The field jumps back to the Available Fields side of the dialog box.

Form Wizard

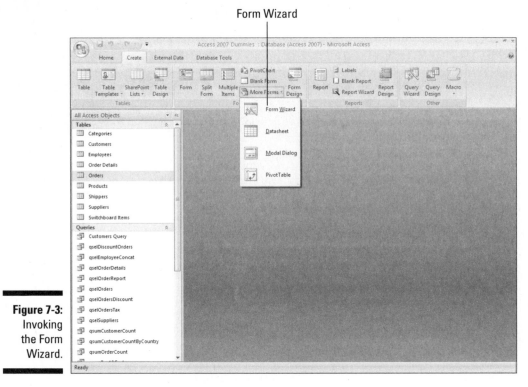

Figure 7-3:
Invoking the Form Wizard.

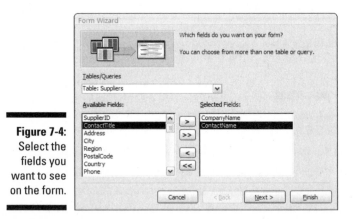

Figure 7-4:
Select the fields you want to see on the form.

Giving forms the right look

Depending on the data you select for your form (for example, whether you use more than one table), you have different options for displaying your data:

- **Columnar:** A classic, one-record-per-page form.

  Most data entry forms are Columnar.

- **Tabular:** A multiple-records-per-page form.

  This layout is best for tables with few fields, like the form based on the Shippers table (shown on the left side). For tables with a larger number of fields, be prepared to scroll back and forth if you select Tabular.

- **Datasheet:** A spreadsheet-like grid.

  Essentially, this is an Access datasheet view embedded in a form. It's appropriate when an Excel-style presentation suits your needs.

- **Justified:** The data is laid out across the whole form over multiple rows (as shown on the right side).

  This layout may be especially useful when you have memo fields.

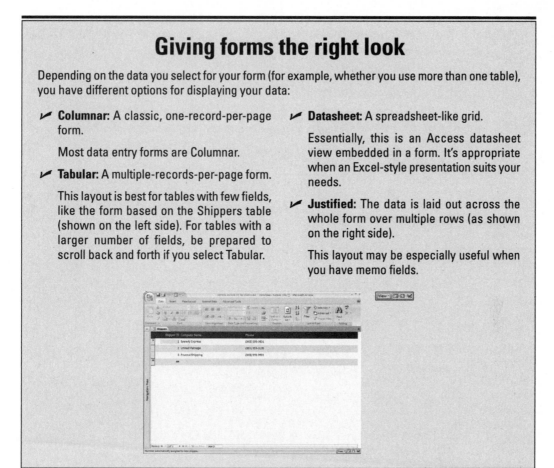

6. **After you've selected all the fields you want to include on your form, click Next.**

   If you selected fields from more than one table, the Form Wizard takes a moment to ask how you want to organize the data in your form. If you choose to organize your data by the parent table (Chapter 4 shows how), you'll be asked to show the child table data as either

   - *Subform:* Shows all data from both tables on one form.

   - *Linked form:* Creates a button that, when clicked, will take you to a new form that displays the child table data.

7. **When the wizard asks about the form layout, choose one of the following layouts and then click Next:**

   - *Columnar:* Records are shown one at a time.

- *Tabular:* Multiple records are shown at one time with an attractive style applied to the form.

- *Datasheet:* Multiple records are shown at one time in a rather unattractive spreadsheet-like way.

Don't know which layout is best? Check out the "Giving Forms the Right Look" sidebar.

8. **Choose a form style (as shown in Figure 7-5) and then click Next.**

   Forms with fancy styles (such as Theme 1 Rich) usually take longer to load. If speed is your thing, choose a simple style such as None.

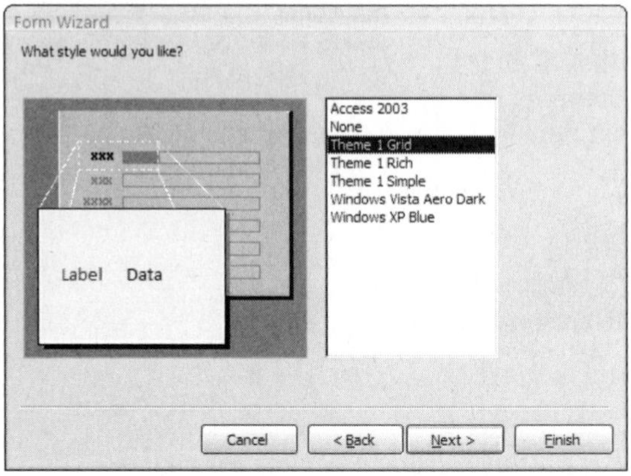

Figure 7-5:
Select a design style for your form.

9. **Enter a descriptive title in the What Title Do You Want for Your Form? box at the top of the Form Wizard screen.**

   There are good reasons to give your form a descriptive title instead of the default name (which is the data source):

   - Tables and forms that share the same name are confusing.

   - The name you type is used to save your form. Letters and numbers are allowed in form names.

10. **Click Finish.**

    Your new form appears on the screen, as shown in Figure 7-6.

    The Form Wizard automatically saves the form as part of the creation process. You don't need to manually save and name it.

The rest of this chapter shows how to customize forms you've created with the Form Wizard.

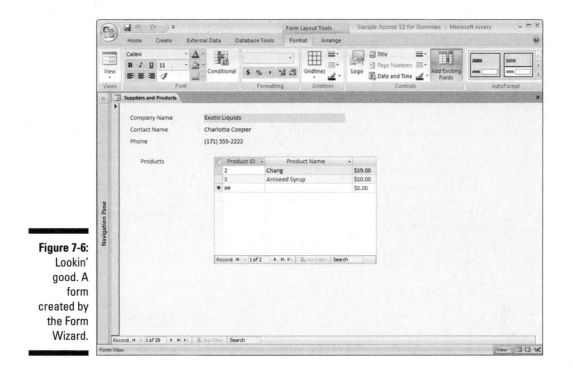

Figure 7-6:
Lookin'
good. A
form
created by
the Form
Wizard.

Customizing Form Parts

The Access 2007 AutoForm tools and Form Wizard do a great job building forms. In fact, for the typical user they do just about everything. However, they don't always do it all. So you may need to do some form tweaking.

If you know some form design basics you can clean up most of the ills left behind by the AutoForm tools and Form Wizard.

The rest of this chapter shows how to move and size controls, edit control labels, and format *controls* on your forms. (A *control* is any design element, (such as a line, label, or data entry box on a form.)

Taking the Layout view

You can make form design changes in either Design or Layout view.

The sidebar "A form with a view" explains these views.

A form with a view

Access forms are a bit schizophrenic. They can be displayed in several ways, called *views*. Each view serves a purpose in using or maintaining the form.

Use the view buttons on the right side of the Status Bar to switch between these views. (This figure shows the form view tools on the status bar.)

Here are the most common views:

- **Design:** Sound familiar? Every Access object has Design view.

  In this view you can modify the layout and appearance of the objects (called *controls*) on the form.

- **Layout:** Use this view to see data on the form and edit its layout and appearance simultaneously. Now if that isn't fun, I don't know what is!

  This view is very helpful for stuff like sizing controls properly and choosing fonts.

- **Form:** Yes, a form has a Form view. Bizarre but true.

  This view displays the data connected to the form, but unlike Layout view, the design of the form cannot be altered. End users of the database typically see all forms in Form view.

- **Datasheet:** A spreadsheet-like grid.

  Essentially, this is an Access Datasheet view embedded in a form. It's appropriate when an Excel-style presentation suits your needs.

- **Print Preview:** Displays your form as it will appear on the printed page.

  Although forms can be printed, they rarely are. Typically, forms are formatted to fit the screen. Reports are your tool for the printed page. For an introduction to reports, see Chapter 16.

- **Pivot Table:** Summarizes data and allows you to interactively analyze data on the screen.

- **Pivot Chart:** A graphical analysis of data that lets you drag and drop items.

We concentrate on Layout view in these instructions because it's easier to use.

To enter Layout view, follow these steps:

1. **Right-click the form you'd like to modify.**

   The shortcut menu appears.

2. **Select Layout View from the shortcut menu.**

How can you tell whether you're in Layout view or Form view? Look at the Status Bar in the lower-left corner of your screen. It tells you the current view for an open form.

Managing form controls

A control is any design element (such as a line, label or data entry box) that appears on a form. The Form Wizard and AutoForm tools do a fine job of constructing forms but often do not place or size them just right. In this section, we'll discuss how to take charge of your controls.

Control Types

The two most common control types display data from an underlying table or query (like a text box) or supply a design element to the form (like a line).

Here are the most common form controls:

- **Text box:** The box where you type your data.

  Text boxes are *bound* (a way of saying *linked)* to a table field or unbound (contain a calculation derived from other fields in a table).

- **Label:** The descriptive text next to the text box or the title of the form.

- **Combo box:** A drop-down list of choices.

- **List box:** A box that contains a list of choices, giving the reader the ability to choose more than one item from the list.

- **Check box:** A square box that is attached to a field that can store only true/false, on/off, or yes/no answers. For example, a personnel table may have a field called Married. Either you are or you aren't.

- **Subform:** A form inside another form.

  Subforms usually display the "many" records of the "one" record when tables are in a one-to-many relationship. For details on table relationships, see Chapter 4.

If your form is *columnar* (most are) and you've created it with the Form Wizard or AutoForm tools, all text boxes and labels on the form are *anchored*. Anchored controls behave as a group when you size them. Additionally, they can be moved within the other controls in the group but cannot be moved outside of the group. The sidebar "Weighing anchor" shows how to separate controls so that you can move them anywhere your heart desires or size them independently from the rest of the group.

Weighing anchor

If you want to move a control outside of the group or size it independently from others on a form, you may need to remove control anchoring from the controls on that form. Here's how:

1. **Put the mouse pointer anywhere on the control you'd like to set free.**

   The arrow-shaped mouse pointer changes into a hand.

2. **Click to select the control.**

A thick border around the control indicates that it is selected.

3. **Select the Arrange tab on the Ribbon.**

   The layout tools appear.

4. **Click the Remove button on the Control Layout group of controls.**

   The control is now free to move about the form without any of its friends.

Moving controls

To move a control around in Layout view, follow these steps:

1. **Put the mouse pointer anywhere on the control that you want to move.**

   The mouse changes to a pointer with four-headed arrow attached. *Text boxes* and their labels stick together — just like mashed potatoes and gravy. If you want to move one, the other comes along for the ride.

2. **Hold down the left mouse button.**

   The control is *selected*, so a thick border appears around it. See Figure 7-7 for an example of a selected control.

3. **Drag the control to its new location.**

   A line follows the mouse as you drag up or down.

   If the form's controls are anchored and your form is columnar, you can move the control up or down, not left or right. Sorry!

4. **When the control is in position, release the mouse button.**

   The control drops smoothly into place.

   If you don't like an adjustment you've made, press Ctrl+Z to undo the change and start over from scratch. Access has multiple undo levels, so play to your heart's content; you can always undo any mistakes.

Sizing controls

Sometimes the Form Wizard and AutoForm tools fall a bit short (literally) when sizing your text boxes and labels. A common problem is the last part of some information is cut off on either a label or text box.

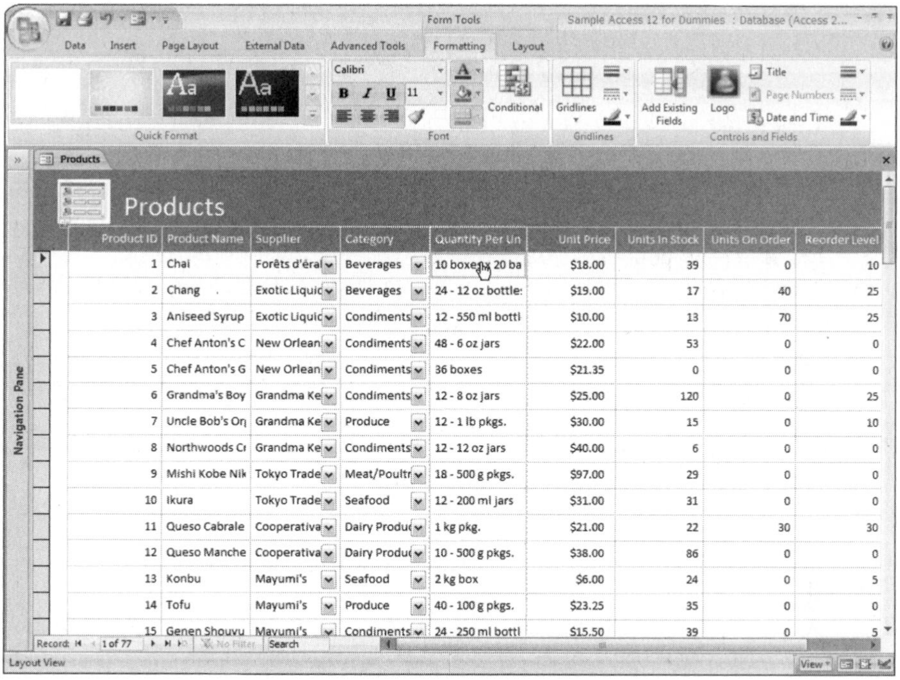

Figure 7-7:
A selected
control on
the products
form with
the hand
mouse
shape.

To size a control in Layout view (as shown previously in this chapter), follow these steps:

1. Put the mouse pointer on the control that you want to size.

The mouse changes to a pointer with four-headed arrow attached. If the controls are anchored, it doesn't matter which control you roll the mouse over.

Although data display controls such as text boxes and their associated labels *move* together, they do not *size* together. You must size labels and data display controls individually.

2. Click to select the control.

A thick border appears around the control to indicate that the control is selected.

3. Move the mouse to the edge of the selected control.

A double arrow mouse shape appears.

4. Click and drag to resize the control.

Anchored controls size together horizontally. So when you change the width of one, all are changed to that same width. If you need to change the width of an individual anchored control, the sidebar "Weighing anchor" shows how to separate it from the rest. You can size the height of an anchored control while it is still anchored to the rest of the group.

Editing labels

The Form Wizard and AutoForm tools use field names as control labels when they build your forms. If you abbreviated a field name (FName for First Name) when creating a table, that abbreviation will become the label for the control created by the Form Wizard and AutoForm tools. So if a label doesn't quite say what it should, you'll need to know how to edit the text it contains.

To edit a label, enter Layout view (as shown previously in this chapter) and try this:

1. **Put the mouse pointer anywhere on the label that you want to edit.**

   The mouse pointer changes into a pointer with four-headed arrow attached.

2. **Click to select the label control.**

   A thick border indicates that the control is selected.

3. **Click the word you'd like to edit.**

   A blinking cursor appears on the word.

4. **Edit the word.**

5. **Click outside of the label control.**

   The label is deselected and the edit is preserved.

Deleting controls

Sometimes, an Access form contains an unneeded or unwanted control:

- ✔ Maybe you selected an unwanted field while using the Form Wizard
- ✔ Maybe you added a control (like a line) and in retrospect decided it is not needed.
- ✔ Maybe you're just tired of looking at that control.

Here's how you remove the control:

1. **Put the mouse pointer anywhere on the control that you want to delete.**

   The arrow mouse pointer changes into a pointer with four-headed arrow attached.

2. **Click to select the control.**

   A thick border appears around the control, indicating that it is selected.

3. **Tap the Delete key on your keyboard.**

   The unwanted control disappears into digital oblivion.

Chapter 8

Importing and Exporting Data

- -

- -

*1*t would be nice if all computer software spoke the same language, but unfortunately this is not the case. Software applications have proprietary "languages" called *file formats.* Just as a person who speaks only English cannot easily communicate with one who speaks only Spanish, software of one file format cannot directly communicate with software of another file format.

If you're a typical business user, you'll come across a situation in which you need some data in your Access database, but it happens to be in another file format. Or, you'll get the question, "Can you put that data in a spreadsheet for me so I can play around with it?"

Do you limber up your fingers in preparation for hours of data re-entry? Not with Access! Access provides tools that speak the languages of other software applications. This chapter looks at the *import* and *export* capabilities of Access. If you work with Access and almost any other program, you need this chapter, because sometime soon, some data will be in the wrong place.

If you'd like to try the import and export techniques described in this chapter for yourself, download the sample files used in the chapter at `http://www.dummies.com/go/access2007`. There are two Access databases you can link together and a sample spreadsheet to import.

Make copies of your databases *before* trying the techniques in this chapter.

Retrieving Data from Other Sources

Access includes two ways of grabbing data from other applications:

- ✔ **Importing:** Translate the data from a foreign format into the Access database file format then add the translated data to an Access table. You can either:

  - • Create a new table in an Access database for the data. You might do this if you are creating a new database and some of your data is already in spreadsheets.

  - • Append the data as new records at the end of an existing table. Perhaps you need to import monthly expense data into your expense reporting database from your credit card company and that data can only be provided in spreadsheet format.

- ✔ **Linking:** Build a temporary bridge between the external data and Access. The data remains at its original source yet Access can manipulate it just as if it resides in the source Access database. Once a link is established, it remains until the link is deleted or the source file is moved or deleted.

When linking tables between two Access databases, the source table structure cannot be edited in the destination database (the database that contains the links). You must open the source database to edit the table structure of the tables linked to the destination database.

Translating file formats

Regardless of whether you import or link the data, Access understands only certain data formats.

Always back up your data before importing, exporting, or mowing the lawn — err, trying anything that could do serious damage to the data. The backup lesson is one of the most painful to learn and one of the most common. Make a copy of your database *before* trying the techniques in this chapter.

Tables 8-1 (databases), 8-2 (spreadsheets), and 8-3 (other file types) list the file formats that Access can understand. These tables cover the vast majority of data formats used on PCs all over the world.

Table 8-1	Compatible database file formats		
Program	*File Extension*	*Versions*	*Comments*
Access	.MDB, .ADP, .MDA, .MDE., .ADE, .ACCDB, ACCDA, .ACCDE	2.0, 7.0/95, 8.0/97 9.0/2000, 10.0/2002, 2003, 2007	Although they share the same name, these versions use different file formats.
ODBC	n/a	n/a	Use ODBC (Open Database Connectivity) to connect to other databases, such as Oracle.
Outlook/Exchange	n/a	n/a	Link your Outlook or Exchange folder straight to an Access database.
dBASE	.DBF	III, IV, 5	Many programs use the dBASE format.
Paradox	.DB	3.x, 4.x, 5.0, 7-8	A database from Borland.

Table 8-2	Compatible spreadsheet file formats		
Program	*File Extension*	*Versions*	*Comments*
Excel	.XLS, .XLSX	3.0, 4.0, 5.0, 7.0/95, 8.0/97, 9.0/2000, 10.0/2002, 2003, 2007	Although Excel is a spreadsheet program, many people use it as a simple flat-file database manager.
Lotus 1-2-3	.WKS, .WK1, .WK31, .WK4	All	Formerly, the most popular spreadsheet program.

Table 8-3	Other compatible file formats		
Program	**File Extension**	**Versions**	**Comments**
Text	.TXT	n/a	The "if all else fails" format; Access understands both delimited and fixed-width text files.
XML	.XML	All	XML (eXtensible Markup Language) stores and describes data.
HTML	.HTM, .HTML	1.0 (lists), 2.0 (tables),3.x (tables)	The Web page codes that make a Web page a Web page.
SharePoint list	n/a	n/a	Web-based data collaborative software. Replaces data access pages in previous versions of Access.

Spreadsheets

When you import a spreadsheet file (such as Excel or Lotus 1-2-3), each spreadsheet *column* becomes an Access table *field:*

- ✔ **The first row *in the spreadsheet* (the column headings) becomes the *names* of the fields.**

   You must check the First Row Contains Column Headings check box during the import process to use the first row for field names.

   An ideal spreadsheet for import will have field names in row 1.

- ✔ **Each following row becomes a *record* in the Access table.**

   An ideal spreadsheet for import will have data starting in row 2.

When you import data from spreadsheets, watch for these quirks:

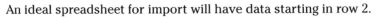

- ✔ **Double-check spreadsheet data to be sure that it's *consistent* and *complete*.**

- ✔ **Make sure that all entries in each spreadsheet column (field) are the same data type (numbers, text, or whatever).**

- ✔ **Remove *titles* and *blank rows* from the top of the spreadsheet.**

✔ **Make your spreadsheet column headings *short* and *unique*.**

I usually shorten my spreadsheet column headings to the field names I'd like Access to use so I don't get scolded during import about field name issues.

✔ **If you're adding data to an *existing Access table,* make sure the spreadsheet columns are of the same number and in the same order as the Access table fields. Your spreadsheet columns and table fields must line up exactly.**

Text files

If you have difficulty importing a format (such as a Quattro Pro spreadsheet), you may be able to import the data as text. Text is the most widely recognized form of data known to man (or computer). Try these steps to import the data as text:

1. **Open the file with the old product.**

2. **Use the old product's exporting tools to export your data into a text file.**

   Computer geeks use a text file's formal name: ASCII.

   A *delimited* text file is preferred if the old product supports this type of text file. A delimited file contains a marker character (such as a comma) between each field so that Access can easily understand where one field ends and another begins.

3. **Import the text file into Access (as shown later in this chapter).**

Importing and linking

Because Access offers two ways to get existing data in — linking and importing — a logical question comes up: Which method should you use? The method depends on the situation:

✔ **Link:** If the data in the other program must remain in that program.

   If the data is in a SQL Server database that's not going anywhere, link to the source.

✔ **Import:** If the database is replacing the source. Perhaps you are creating an Access database to replace your old spreadsheet because your spreadsheet no longer meets your needs. You should also import if the source data is supplied by an outside vendor in a format other than an Access format. For example, you receive cash register sales data from an outside vendor on a monthly basis in spreadsheet format that you'd like to bring into Access for reporting purposes.

The following section shows how to link and import data from the file formats discussed in the previous sections of this chapter.

Steps for importing

Here are the steps for importing or linking data sources to your Access database:

1. **Open the Access database that will hold the imported data.**

2. **Click the External Data tab on the Ribbon.**

   An Import group of tools appears on the Ribbon (see Figure 8-1).

   Each tool is connected to a wizard that walks you through the process:

   - Common file formats have a specific button, such as Excel or Text.
   - Obscure file formats are located on the More button.

3. **Click the tool that matches your file format.**

   A Get External Data dialog box (shown in Figure 8-2) specific to the selected file format appears on-screen.

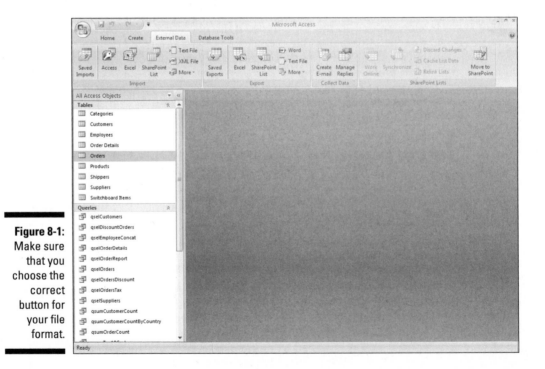

Figure 8-1: Make sure that you choose the correct button for your file format.

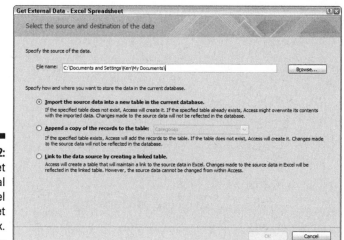

Figure 8-2:
The Get
External
Data – Excel
Spreadsheet
dialog box.

4. **Select the data source that you want to import or link to Access.**

   Usually, this is a file. It could also be a SharePoint site or Outlook folder.

   If typing filenames is not your thing, click the Browse button to locate the file.

5. **Select the method of data storage.**

   This is where you tell Access whether to *import* or *link* the data.

   The sidebar "External Data Source Storage Methods" shows the common data storage options.

6. **Follow the remaining steps in the Get External Data dialog box.**

   From this point forward the steps depend on which data format you're importing. Follow the prompts carefully. The worst that can happen is that you get an imported (or linked) table full of gibberish. If you do, check the format of the source file. For example, if the source is a text file and you get gibberish, you may need to confirm that the text file was saved as a *delimited* (character like a comma between each field) file. It is also possible that the source file is not in the correct format. For example, you may think it is an Excel spreadsheet but it is not.

   If you'll import or link to this type of file often, click the Save Import Steps check box.

   The External Data tab on the Ribbon contains a button called Saved Imports. Use this to routinely import or link data from an external data source if necessary.

External data source storage methods

When you select a method of data storage, most of the Get External Data dialog boxes ask you to select from the following storage methods:

Import the source data into a new table. This means creating a new table from the imported data.

Access warns you that this choice could overwrite an existing table with the same name as the imported data's filename. However, Access usually just creates another table with the number 1 after it. For example, if you have a Contacts table and you import a file called `Contacts.dbf`, Access creates a new table called Contacts1.

Append the data to an existing table. This choice adds the imported data to the end of existing records in an existing table.

When you append, make sure that the import file and the existing table have

✔ The same number of columns

✔ The same order of columns

✔ The same data types

Link to the data source. Access creates a table that manages the data in the external file. Depending on the source, the link may be either of the following:

✔ *Two-way link.* Edits in *either* file (the internal Access file or the external file) automatically appear in *both* files.

 A link to another Access data source is an example of a two-way link.

✔ *One-way link.* You can change the data in the external source but not in Access.

 A spreadsheet link is a one-way link. You can change the data in the spreadsheet but not in the Access table linked to the spreadsheet.

Troubleshooting

During the import or linking process, Access may have difficulties. You'll know because the import or linking process is taking a long time or Access displays an error message. This section describes some common import and linking problems and how to resolve such problems.

Slow imports and links

If importing is taking forever, Access is probably struggling with errors in the inbound data. Follow these steps to troubleshoot the problem:

1. **Press Ctrl+Break to stop the import process.**

2. **Open the source file in its native application and check the data that's being imported for errors, such as**

   • Bad or corrupt data

   • Badly organized spreadsheet data

   • Invalid index

3. **Save the corrected source file.**

4. **Start the import or linking process again as outlined in the previous section of the book.**

Bad data

If the imported table barely resembles the source, open the source file in its native program and clean up the data before importing again.

Follow the tips in the preceding "Translating file formats" section to clean up your data.

Get This Data Out of Here

Every Access object can be exported. However, exporting the data in a table or query to another program such as a spreadsheet is the most common export task. Therefore, this chapter will concentrate on exporting table and query data to other file formats.

Exporting a table or query involves reorganizing the data it contains into a different format. As with importing, Access can translate the data into a variety of file formats depending on your needs.

Every Access object can be exported. The External Data tab on the Ribbon will present you with all file formats to which the object can be exported.

Export formats

Access exports to the same formats that it imports (as listed earlier in the chapter). Access also exports to PDF (Adobe Acrobat files) and Microsoft Word.

The main problem to keep an eye out for when exporting is *data loss.* A fabulous Access table doesn't always translate to a fabulous Paradox table. Not all databases share the same rules for

- ✔ **Data types:** Special Access data types such as AutoNumber, Yes/No, Memo, and OLE are almost sure to cause problems in other programs. You may need some creative problem solving to make the data work just the way you want it to work.

- ✔ **Field names:** Each database program has its own set of rules governing field names such as the length of and the special characters (like a dollar or percent sign) allowed in the field name.

  To avoid field name problems during export, keep your field names short and use only letters and numbers while naming your Access fields. If your Access table's field names break the rules of the program you are exporting to, the export will not work properly.

Be ready to spend time tuning the export so that it works just the way you want. If you have a problem during export, consult the documentation of the software whose file format you are exporting to for field name and data type rules.

Exporting table or query data

The steps to exporting a table or query are simple:

1. **With the database open, click the table or query that you want to export.**

   The table name is highlighted.

2. **Click the External Data tab on the Ribbon.**

   The Export tool group appears on the Ribbon:

   • The common exporting tasks have their own buttons.

   • The seldom used formats are lumped onto the More button.

3. **Click the tool that matches the program to which you'll export your data.**

   An Export dialog box (see Figure 8-3) customized to your format of choice appears.

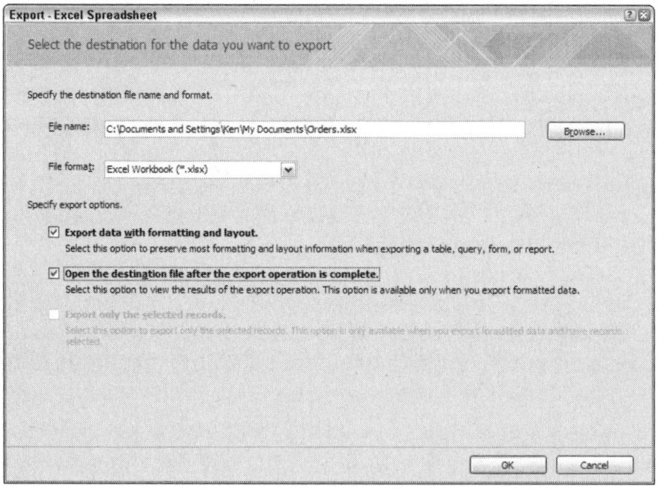

Figure 8-3:
A completed Export – Excel Spreadsheet dialog box.

Export - Excel Spreadsheet

Select the destination for the data you want to export

Specify the destination file name and format.

File name: C:\Documents and Settings\Ken\My Documents\Orders.xlsx   Browse...

File format: Excel Workbook (*.xlsx)   ▾

Specify export options.

☑ **Export data with formatting and layout.**
   Select this option to preserve most formatting and layout information when exporting a table, query, form, or report.

☑ **Open the destination file after the export operation is complete.**
   Select this option to view the results of the export operation. This option is available only when you export formatted data.

☐ Export only the selected records.
   Select this option to export only the selected records. This option is only available when you export formatted data and have records selected.

OK   Cancel

4. Follow the steps in the Export dialog box to complete the export.

The Export dialog box will display the choices for your export file format:

- Every choice will ask for a filename (including path) for your exported data.

- Some export processes also ask whether you want to open your new file after the export is complete.

This can prevent a frustrating search after you save the file.

5. Select the Save Export Steps check box if you know you'll do this export again.

The Ribbon contains a button called Saved Exports. Use this to easily export a table or query on a routine basis. Figure 8-4 shows a table.

Figure 8-4:
The exported OrderDetails table in Excel ready for some crazy calculations.

Order ID	Product	Unit Price	Quantity	Discount
10248	Queso Cabrales	$14.00	12	0.00%
10248	Singaporean Hokkien Fried Mee	$9.80	10	0.00%
10248	Mozzarella di Giovanni	$34.80	5	0.00%
10249	Tofu	$18.60	9	0.00%
10249	Manjimup Dried Apples	$42.40	40	0.00%
10250	Jack's New England Clam Chowder	$7.70	10	0.00%
10250	Manjimup Dried Apples	$42.40	35	15.00%
10250	Louisiana Fiery Hot Pepper Sauce	$16.80	15	15.00%
10251	Gustaf's Knäckebröd	$16.80	6	5.00%
10251	Ravioli Angelo	$15.60	15	5.00%
10251	Louisiana Fiery Hot Pepper Sauce	$16.80	20	0.00%
10252	Sir Rodney's Marmalade	$64.80	40	5.00%
10252	Geitost	$2.00	25	5.00%
10252	Camembert Pierrot	$27.20	40	0.00%
10253	Gorgonzola Telino	$10.00	20	0.00%
10253	Chartreuse verte	$14.40	42	0.00%
10253	Maxilaku	$16.00	40	0.00%
10254	Guaraná Fantástica	$3.60	15	15.00%
10254	Pâté chinois	$19.20	21	15.00%
10254	Longlife Tofu	$8.00	21	0.00%
10255	Chang	$15.20	20	0.00%
10255	Pavlova	$13.90	35	0.00%
10255	Inlagd Sill	$15.20	25	0.00%
10255	Raclette Courdavault	$44.00	30	0.00%
10256	Perth Pasties	$26.20	15	0.00%

Chapter 9

Automatically Editing Data

- -

- -

Correcting an incorrect entry in an Access table is pretty easy. A few clicks, some typing, and voilà — the problem is gone. But what if you need to correct 26,281 records? Manually editing so many records would involve a whole bunch of clicking and typing and clicking and typing. Editing an entire table by hand doesn't sound like an opportunity to triumphantly say, "Voilà!"

Fortunately, Access offers some handy, large-scale housekeeping and editing tools that let you make big changes to your database — all without wearing out your keyboard, mouse, or fingertips.

Please Read This First!

If you're following my not-terribly-subtle suggestion not to skip this section, you're well on your way to successful database maintenance. Why? Because the fact that you're reading this tells me that you're a careful sort who follows suggestions and instructions. These traits are key to managing thousands of records, keeping them accurate and up to date, and making the type of corrections I talk about in this chapter.

Why do I sound so serious, all of the sudden? Well, when you're making large-scale changes to a database, things can go wrong and mistakes can be made. If you're going to do anything major to your database in terms of editing and/or deleting a whole lot of records, you want a backup there behind you so that if you do make a mistake and wipe out the wrong records or edit something that should have been left alone, you can easily go back to the pre-edited version of the database and start over.

Careful people make backups of their work before starting any task with a margin for error involved. Here's how you back up the table you want to edit:

1. **Open the database file that contains the table you want to edit.**

   The list of tables in the database appears on the left side of the window.

2. **Right-click the table name in the list on the left.**

3. **Choose Copy from the pop-up menu (see Figure 9-1).**

   Access places a copy of the table onto the Windows clipboard.

4. **Right-click anywhere below the list of tables, reports, and so forth in the left-side panel (as shown in Figure 9-2).**

   A pop-up menu appears.

5. **Choose Paste from the pop-up menu.**

   The Paste Table As dialog box appears, as shown in Figure 9-3. It offers choices for how to paste your copied table data, but you don't really need to worry about them at this point.

6. **Type a name for the new table (such as** Copy Of Personnel**).**

7. **Click OK.**

   Don't worry about the options in the dialog box. The default setting (Structure and Data) works just fine.

   The dialog box closes, and you now have a copy of the original table.

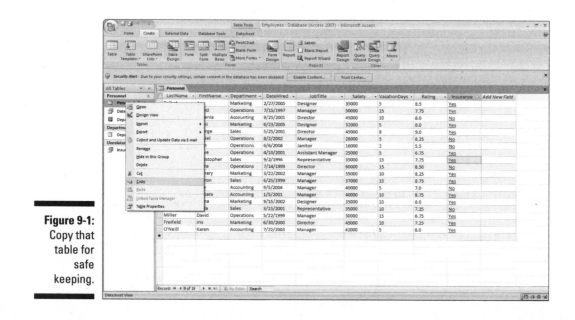

Figure 9-1:
Copy that table for safe keeping.

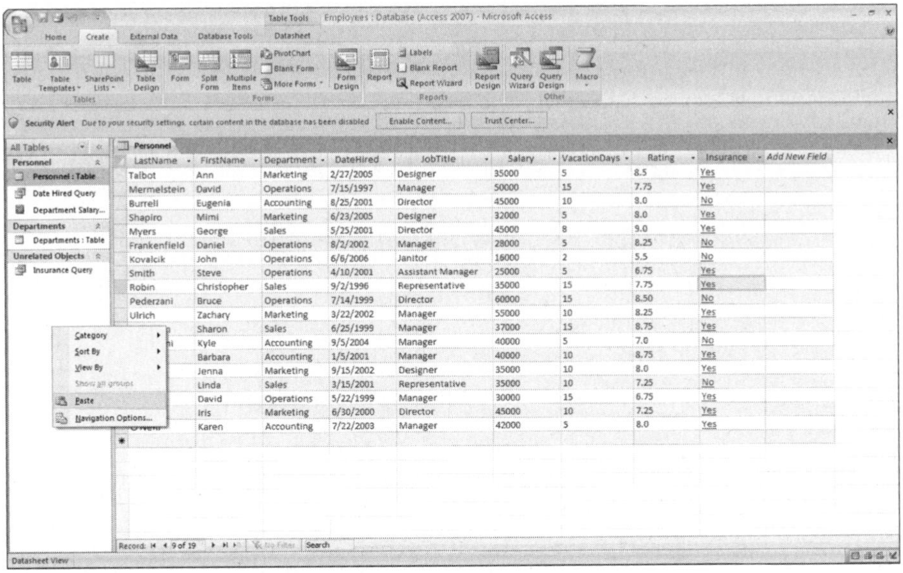

Figure 9-2: Choose Paste from the pop-up menu to make a backup version of the table.

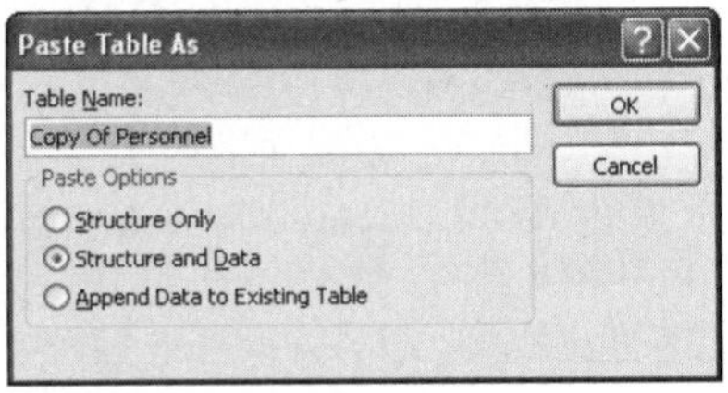

Figure 9-3: The Paste Table As dialog box.

With your table copy there to support you, you now have a backup — something to go back to should any of the steps in the rest of this chapter go awry when you apply them to your data.

Backup at the ready, it's time to move on and start editing your database — automatically.

Creating Consistent Corrections

Automated editing queries have a lot of power. But before you haul out the *really* big guns, here's a technique for small-scale editing. The technique may seem simplistic, but don't be fooled; it's quite handy.

You can practice small-scale editing by using the Replace command as follows:

1. **Open a table in Datasheet view.**

2. **On the Home tab click the Replace button in the Find section.**

   The Find and Replace dialog box appears, as shown in Figure 9-4.

Figure 9-4:
The Find
and Replace
dialog box.

Find and Replace	? ×

Find | Replace

Find What:	Oparations	Find Next
Replace With:	Operations	Cancel
Look In:	Personnel	
Match:	Whole Field	Replace
Search:	All	Replace All
Match Case	☑ Search Fields As Formatted	

3. **In the Find What box type the value you want to change. In the Replace With box type a new value.**

   With this information in place you're ready to start making changes.

4. **(Optional) Click the Look In drop-down list to choose a different table in which to search.**

   All of the tables and queries in your database appear in the drop-down list. The default table is the one that's open on-screen at the time.

5. **Click one of the buttons on the right side of the dialog box to apply the changes to your table.**

   The moment you click either the Replace or Replace All button, Access *permanently* changes the data in your table. Access lets you undo only the last change you made, so if you clicked Replace All and updated 12,528 records, Access lets you undo only the very last record that you changed — the other 12,527 records stay in their new form.

   • **To find the next record to change, click Find Next.** The cursor jumps to the next record in the table that contains the text you entered in the Find What box. No changes get made at this point — Access only finds a matching candidate. To make a change, click the Replace button, explained next.

   • **To apply your change to the current record, click Replace.** This makes the change *and* moves the cursor to the next matching record in the database. Click Replace again to continue the process. To skip a record without changing it, click Find Next.

   • **To make the change *everywhere* in your table, click the Replace All button.** Access won't ask about each individual change. The program assumes that it has your permission to correct everything it finds. Don't choose this option unless you are *absolutely certain* that you want the change made everywhere.

6. **When you finish, click Cancel or the X button in the top-right corner of the dialog box.**

   The Find and Replace dialog box closes.

If you misspell a word, any word, throughout your data (don't you *hate* it when that happens?) and need to change all its occurrences to the proper spelling, follow these steps:

1. **Open the Find and Replace dialog box.**

   Clicking the Replace button in the Find section of the Home tab will do the trick.

2. **Type the incorrect spelling in the Find What box.**

3. **Type the proper spelling in Replace With box.**

4. **Click the Replace All button.**

   Your computer goes off and does your bidding, changing each instance of the word in the Find What box to the word in the Replace With box.

Access gives you a lot of control over the process. In addition to the options of the Find command (discussed in Chapter 11), Replace offers additional options:

- **Match Whole Field:** Selected by default, Whole Field (in the Match drop-down list) makes Access look only for cases in which the information in the Find What box *completely matches* an entry in the table. That is, if the data in your table includes any additional characters in the field — even a single letter — Match Whole Field tells Access to skip it.

- **Match Any Part of Field:** If you select Any Part of Field from the Match drop-down list, Access performs the replace action whenever it finds the text in *any portion* of the matching text in the field. For instance, this setting picks the area code out of a phone number. Unfortunately, it also replaces those same three numbers if they appear anywhere else in the phone number, too.

- **Match Start of Field:** If you choose Start of Field from the Match drop-down list, Access replaces the matching text only if it appears at the beginning of the field. This option could replace only the area code in a series of phone numbers without touching the rest of the numbers.

If your editing goes awry, remember that the wonderful Undo option corrects only the *very last record* that Access changed. Just click the Undo button on the Quick Access toolbar or press Ctrl+Z.

Using Queries to Automate the Editing Process

Queries, especially those created through the Query Wizard, are exceptionally easy to create, as you'll discover in Chapter 12 In this chapter, you create a very simple and specific query not created elsewhere in the book — you create a query designed solely to look for duplicate records.

So what about correcting those 26,281 records? If Find and Replace doesn't solve the problem, you're looking at some serious querying — a topic covered in Chapters 11 through 14 — and you may find that creating the exact query you need is not within the skills imparted in those chapters. Be prepared to do some editing of individual records, maybe combined with a Find and Replace procedure to locate consistent errors and replace them with something you can spot easily (such as a big "X" in a particular field) and then replace with the correct data. This is kind of a twist on using Find and Replace to fix spelling errors (covered previously in this chapter), but instead of fixing an error, you're using Replace to flag certain records for editing.

Generally, however, Find and Replace will do what you need because a universal misspelling, a bunch of zip codes accidentally entered into another numeric field, or any repeated error of that sort can be fixed pretty quickly by searching for the erroneous content and replacing it with what should be there instead. With a backup copy of your table preserved for safe keeping (you *did* read the "Please Read This First!" section, didn't you?), feel free to experiment with Find and Replace and even some queries that you make on your own.

Looking for duplicate records

What exactly *is* a duplicate record? You will have duplicated data in your database — people who live in the same city, for example, will have the same city in their records in the City field. Products that have the same price, or that come in the same colors, will have the same data in some or nearly all of their fields. What we mean here by a duplicate *record* is an entire record that is an exact duplicate — every field is the same in one record as it is in another (or several others, as the case may be).

How do duplicate records get made? It can happen quite easily:

✔ It happens a lot when more than one person is doing data entry because two or more people might have the same list or stack of cards or other source of data that's being keyed into your Access table.

✔ If you're relying on an Excel worksheet as the source of the table data, or if some other electronic source is providing the records, it's just as easy to paste the same rows of data into the table twice as it is to accidentally enter the same records twice manually.

TIP

Duplicate records waste time and money. If you think that it's no big deal to have the same person entered into your database three times, or that the record for your Green Widget with the Deluxe Carrying Case is in the database twice, consider the extra postage you would spend mailing a catalog more than once to the people who appear in the database multiple times, or the confusion when only one instance of a product is updated to reflect a price increase. Which record is correct after they're no longer identical? So it's a good idea to not just be vigilant about avoiding duplicates from the beginning, but to ferret them out and get rid of them whenever they're found.

Running the Find Duplicates Query Wizard

The Find Duplicates Wizard can help you spot one of the most common errors in any database — duplicate records. Ever received two or three copies of the same catalogue in the mail? This happens when the database geek at the company who does the mailing has you in the database two or three times and doesn't realize it. Why is this such a big deal? Because the duplicates waste time and money, especially when the database is used for mailings or some other activity that would be reduced if the database had no duplicate records within it. Even if your database isn't used for anything expensive like a catalog mailing or to spur the efforts of a sales rep, it's still a good idea to ferret out the duplicates and keep your database clean.

To run the Find Duplicates Query Wizard, follow these simple steps:

1. **Open the table with possible duplicates you want to check and click the Create tab.**

   The Create tab's four sections — Tables, Forms, Reports, and Other — appear.

2. **Click the Query Wizard button.**

   The Query Wizard dialog box opens, as shown in Figure 9-5.

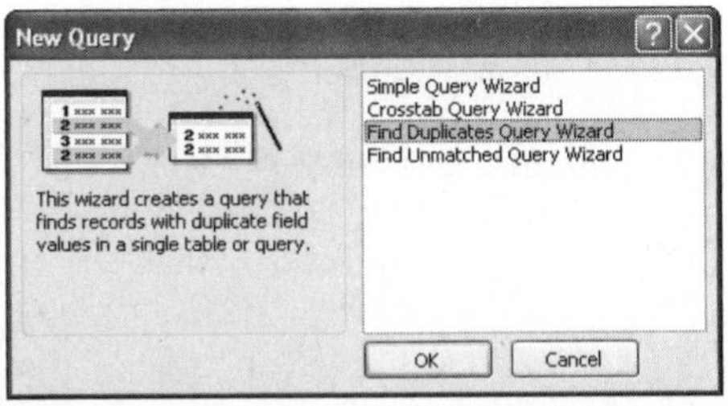

Figure 9-5:
The Query
Wizard
is here to
help you.

New Query

Simple Query Wizard
Crosstab Query Wizard
Find Duplicates Query Wizard
Find Unmatched Query Wizard

This wizard creates a query that finds records with duplicate field values in a single table or query.

OK   Cancel

3. Choose Find Duplicates Query Wizard in the list of available wizards.

A description of the Wizard's function appears on the left side of the dialog box.

4. Click OK.

The original Query Wizard dialog box closes and is replaced by the Find Duplicates Query Wizard dialog box, shown in Figure 9-6.

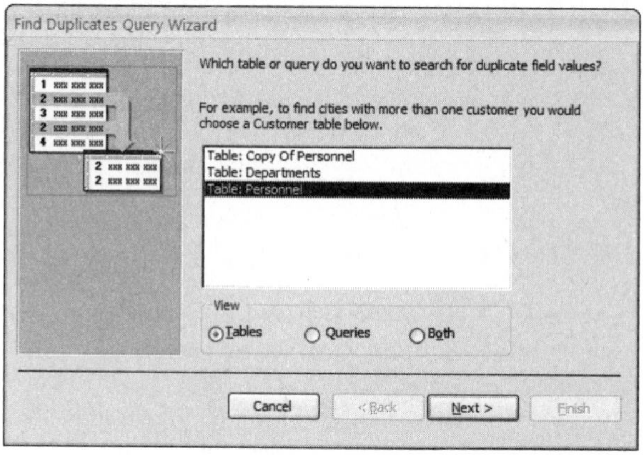

Figure 9-6: The Find Duplicates Query Wizard takes you through duplicate-finding steps.

5. Choose the table in which you want to search for duplicates.

- You can choose to see Tables, Queries, or Both in the list, so if this isn't your first query or if another user has created one for you, you can certainly search a query for duplicates, too.

- If this is your first query, and your data is only in tables that you or someone else made, simply leave Tables selected in the View area.

You'll also see your backup copy of the table in this list, so be sure you pick the right table and don't start operating on your backup!

6. Click Next.

In the Available Fields list (see Figure 9-7), double-click those fields that could have duplicate entries in them. Skip fields that should have duplicates or where duplicates, however unlikely, are no problem — such as cities, states, zip codes, or last names.

7. When the Duplicate-Value Fields list is populated with those fields that you want the query to look in, click Next.

The next step in the Wizard appears, as shown in Figure 9-8.

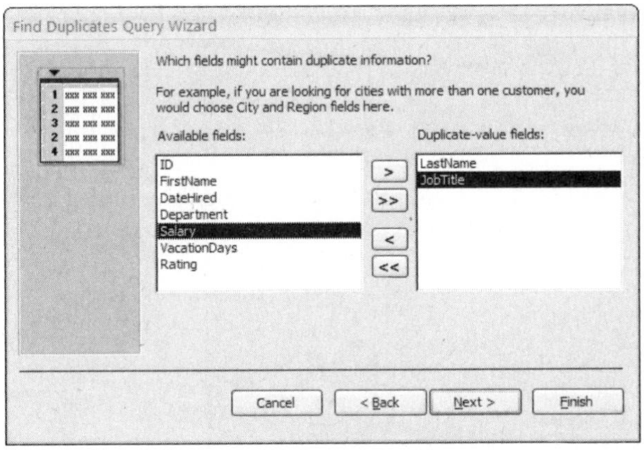

Figure 9-7:
Pick the fields that might have unwanted duplicate entries.

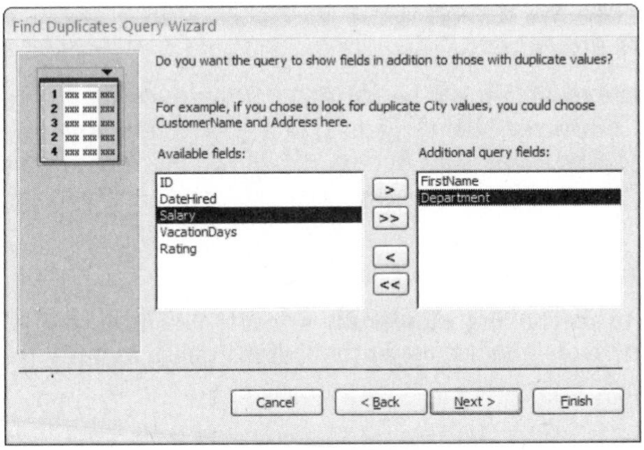

Figure 9-8:
Pick the fields that will help you choose which duplicates to keep.

8. **From the Available Fields list, double-click those fields you want to include in the query's results.**

   This typically includes those fields that will help you identify the records with duplicate data, such as First Name if you're looking for records that might have identical Last Names, or Product Numbers if you're looking for products that have the same description or price. In our example, we're looking for duplicate job titles, in case someone's promotion isn't reflected in the database or someone's title is simply wrong. By including other fields, such as Department, someone familiar with the data can spot problems that might not jump out as obviously as two records for the same person.

9. **Click Next.**

   The last step in the Find Duplicates Query Wizard appears, as shown in Figure 9-9.

10. If you don't like the default name Access gave your query, type a new name for the query.

Preferably, the name should be short but should identify the query's purpose — "Duplicate Names Query" is a good name for this example. The default query name that Access offers will be "Find duplicates for _____", where the blank is the name of the table searched for duplicates.

11. Click Finish.

The results of your query appear on-screen (see Figure 9-10). You can print the results as needed using the Quick Access menu's Print button.

Now that you know which records have duplicate data within them, you can

✔ **Edit them individually.**

✔ **Use Find and Replace to make more targeted changes such as taking all records with a particular word in a particular field and either**

- Changing that word to something else

- Appending a character or digit to that entry to make them different from the others

✔ **Delete the unwanted records.**

Chapter 10

Gather Locally, Share Globally

In This Chapter

▶ How Access works with the Web

▶ Creating and using hyperlinks

▶ Publishing your database and tables to the Web

Access can be a great resource for Internet and intranet information. If the data you're working with really needs global exposure, or if you simply yearn for fun and profit on the electronic superhighway, Access (and much of the Office suite, for that matter) is ready to get you started.

In this chapter, you take a quick look at the online capabilities of Access and uncover some of the details of hyperlinks and online database publishing. It may seem a bit daunting to think of putting your data online for all to see, but it's really a simple process with some very straightforward tools and procedures.

Access and the Web

It's almost a requirement these days that software be Web-ready, if not at least Web-friendly. Even word processors, which should never be used to create a Web page, contain "Save for Web" commands and tools (and Word is no exception on either count). Graphics software has evolved to help you create Web-ready images, leaving, in some cases, print formats in the dust in terms of support and new gadgets when the new software releases come out.

Unlike its Office sibling Word, however, Access is a natural fit for the Web — because data is something we've all come to expect to find online. Unlike graphics software, Access hasn't left any of its features in the dust just to support Web-readiness. It's the data you put on the Web, not the application, and Access makes that easy — it doesn't assume you're building any database exclusively for the Web, but once the data's there, putting it online is quite simple, thanks to Microsoft's ActiveX technology.

As I said, databases are a perfect complement to the Web, where people turn for nearly everything these days — from phone numbers to driving directions to music to job searches. The Web offers lots of interactivity and a flexible presentation medium, which makes it ideal for ever-changing, ever-growing databases. In previous years, publishing a database on the Web was a complex process requiring a great deal of time and effort, and a willingness to cheerfully rip your hair out by the roots. This is not the case anymore, though, because Microsoft makes it relatively simple to bring the Web right into Access.

To make Access do its Internet tricks, you must have

- ✔ **A version of your browser that's no more than a year old (so that it will be compatible with the current version of Office)**
- ✔ **A connection to the Internet (or to your company's intranet)**

Click! Using Hyperlinks in Your Access Database

If you've ever looked into or done any Web page design, the term *link* is probably quite familiar — it's the text or pictures that serve as jumping-off points to other data. Click a link and you go to another Web page. Click an image that's set up as a link (your mouse pointer turns to a pointing finger), and you go to a larger version of the image. Underlined text is the typical sign of the existence of a link, and another term, *tag*, is what's added to the Web page code to make the text or image a link.

So what's this *hyperlink* stuff? Although *hyperlink* makes it sound like a link that's had way too much coffee, within the context of Microsoft Office (of which Access is a part), it's actually a special storage compartment for storing the address of a resource on either the Internet or your local corporate network. Hyperlinks start with a special identification code that explains to the computer what kind of resource it's pointing to.

Table 10-1 lists the most common *protocol codes* (a harmless but scary-sounding term that simply refers to portions of the programming code that allow a browser to use a hyperlink). You'll find, along with the code itself, an explanation of the kind of resource the code refers to.

Table 10-1	Types of Hyperlink Protocol Codes in Access
Protocol Code	*What It Does*
`file://`	Opens a local or network-based file
`ftp://`	File Transfer Protocol; links to an FTP server
`http://`	Hypertext Transfer Protocol; links to a Web page
`mailto:`	Sends e-mail to a network or Internet address
`news://`	Opens an Internet newsgroup

For a complete list of hyperlinks that Access understands, press F1 to open the Access Help system and then search for the term *hyperlink*.

If you surf the Web regularly, many of these terms should be familiar. Although most of them are geared toward Internet or intranet applications, Access can also use hyperlinks to identify locally stored Microsoft Office documents (that's what `file://` does). This enables you, for example, to create a hyperlink in your Access table that opens a Word document, or a hyperlink in an Excel worksheet that opens an Access table. Links can be placed in PowerPoint slides, Outlook e-mail messages, anywhere within any file created by or for use with Office. This technology is so flexible that the sky's the limit.

Adding a hyperlink field to your table

Access provides a handy field type specifically designed for this special type of data. As you probably guessed, this type is called the *hyperlink field*.

Adding a hyperlink field to a table doesn't require special steps. Just use the same steps for adding *any* field to a table — get to Design view for your table and use the Data Type column to choose the Hyperlink field type, as shown in Figure 10-1.

The Hyperlink field type is no different than the other field types, at least in terms of applying it. When you hop back to Table view, you'll see that your entries (if any) in the hyperlink field are underlined, just like link text on a Web page.

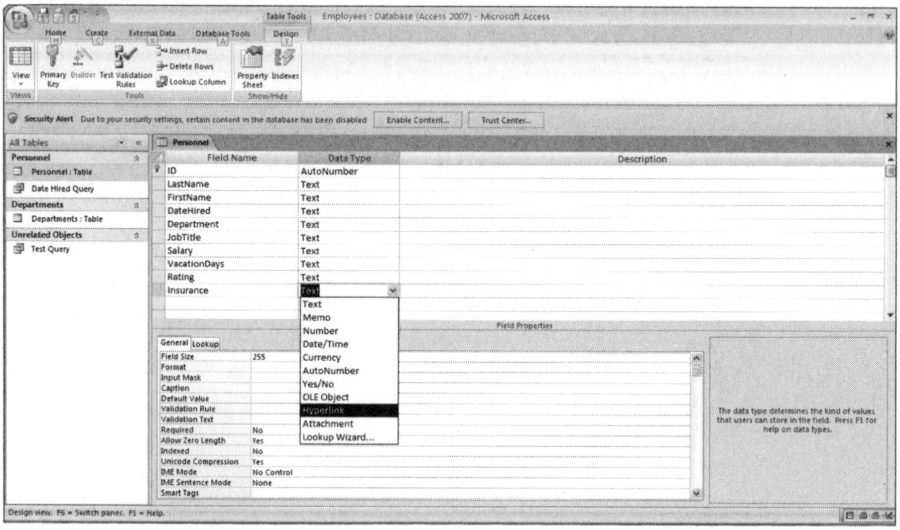

Figure 10-1:
In Design
view,
choose
Hyperlink
from the list
of data
types.

To switch between Design and Table views of your data, click the View button on the Home and Design tabs. It's the first button, and either appears as

- ✔ A table icon (a small grid)
- ✔ An icon combining images of pencil, ruler, and angle

Typing your hyperlinks

Hyperlinks in Access can have up to four parts, all separated by pound signs. In order, the parts of the hyperlink look like this:

```
display text#address#subaddress#screen tip
```

Table 10-2 lists these four parts individually and tells a little about what each one does. Most of the parts are optional, as the table shows.

Table 10-2	Formatting Hyperlinks in Access	
Hyperlink Part	**Requirement**	**What It Is**
Display text	Optional	The text that's displayed. If omitted, Access displays the URL.
Address	Required	The URL (Uniform Resource Locator), such as a Web page.

Hyperlink Part	Requirement	What It Is
Subaddress	Optional	A link on the same page or document.
Screen tip	Optional	Text that pops up if the user pauses his or her mouse cursor over the address.

Here are some examples of formatted hyperlinks and the obscure commands required to create them. (But don't fret about the complication. The following section shows an easier way to make complex hyperlinks.)

- ✔ `www.microsoft.com` displays the URL `http://www.microsoft.com` in the field.

- ✔ `Microsoft Corporation# http://www.microsoft.com#` displays the words *Microsoft Corporation* in your Access table instead of showing the hyperlink itself.

- ✔ `Microsoft Corporation# http://www.microsoft.com#Information#` displays *Microsoft Corporation* and links to a topic called Information on the Microsoft home page.

- ✔ `Microsoft Corporation# http://www.microsoft.com#Information#Bill Gates#` displays *Microsoft Corporation* and links to a topic called Information on the Microsoft home page. When the user pauses the mouse pointer over the link, the words *Bill Gates* pop up.

    This works well when referring to documentation on an in-house Web site — for example, you can set up a link that appears as "Vacation Request" and have it link to a document that lives in a folder on a network drive, the actual address of which would tell no one what the document is or is used for.

- ✔ `Microsoft Corporation# http://www.microsoft.com##Bill Gates#` displays *Microsoft Corporation*. When the user pauses the mouse pointer over the link, the name *Bill Gates* pops up.

    Because this hyperlink doesn't include a subaddress, it uses two pound signs between the URL and the tip (Bill Gates).

Fine tuning your hyperlinks

If all of those pound signs seem a little complicated, or you're afraid you'll forget where and how to use them, fear not. You can format your hyperlinks the easy way with the Edit Hyperlink menu. Follow these steps:

1. Right-click the hyperlink field you want to change in your table.

2. Choose Hyperlink⇨Edit Hyperlink from the pop-up menu.

The nifty little dialog box shown in Figure 10-2 appears.

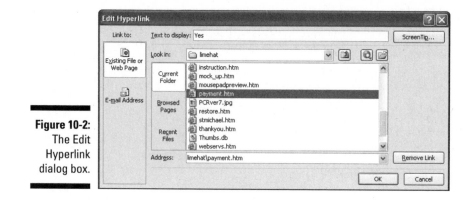

Figure 10-2:
The Edit
Hyperlink
dialog box.

3. Use the dialog box to make the following selections:

- The site address

- The text that's displayed

- The screen tip (the little text that pops up when your mouse
  hovers over a Web address). To create one, click the ScreenTip
  button and use the resulting Set Hyperlink ScreenTip dialog box to
  create your tip — then click OK to return to the Edit Hyperlink
  dialog box.

- Links for documents, spreadsheets, graphics, or even e-mail
  addresses in an Access database.

4. Click OK.

Your hyperlink is edited, with the text you chose to display pointing to
the Web address (document, or other file) that you designated. If you
chose to create a ScreenTip, you can test this by mousing over your
hyperlink and seeing what appears.

Pretty neat, huh? Experiment with the dialog box a little to find out how
everything works. It takes only a moment.

Although most hyperlinks store Web or other Internet addresses, they can
point to just about anything in the known world. Thanks to their flexible tags,
hyperlinks understand Web pages, intranet servers, database objects
(reports, forms, and such), and even Microsoft Office documents on your
computer or another networked PC.

Testing links

Hyperlinks in your table work just like the ones you find on the Web — just point and click:

1. **Either log on to your network or start your Internet connection.**

   While Internet Explorer (or whichever browser you're using) will open whenever a hyperlink that points to a Web site is clicked, if you're not online at the time, it won't go where the hyperlink points.

2. **Open the Access database you want to use.**

3. **Open the table containing those wonderful hyperlinks.**

   The fun is about to begin!

4. **Click the hyperlink of your choice.**

   - If the hyperlink is to a Web page, Internet Explorer leaps on the screen, displaying the Web site from the link.

   - If the link leads to something other than a Web site, Windows automatically fires up the right program to handle whatever the link has to offer.

Publishing Your Data to the Web

If Access contains your most desirable and important information, why not share your stuff with others in your company — or even publish it for the world? Whether you're building a commercial site geared toward fame and online fortune or an interdepartmental intranet to infuse your company with valuable information, Access contains all the tools you need to whip your data into Web-ready shape in no time.

Although you don't need to know anything about HTML (Hypertext Markup Language, the scripting language that is used to build Web pages) to build Web pages with Access, you probably need to know some HTML before your project is finished:

- ✔ For a painless introduction to HTML, check out *HTML 4 For Dummies,* 5th Edition, by Ed Tittel and Mary Burmeister (published by Wiley Publishing, Inc.).

- ✔ You can find out quite a bit online, specifically at the World Wide Web Consortium's Web site: www.w3c.org. From their home page, you can pursue any of their links to Web-related technologies.

A few words about the Web (and why you care)

Although hyperlinks may seem like just so much technohype, they really are important. Nearly all businesses have a Web presence, and many (if not most) are moving information to the Web. Companies are also creating in-house *intranets* (custom Web servers offering information to networked employees).

The capabilities of Access put it in the middle of the Web and intranet excitement — and that presents a great opportunity for you. Duties that used to belong exclusively to *those computer* *people* are landing in graphic arts, marketing, and almost everywhere else. New jobs are born overnight as companies wrestle with the Web's powerful communication features.

If you're looking for a new career path in your corporate life, knowledge of the Web may be just the ticket. Whether you move into Web site development, information management, or even your own Web-oriented consulting business, this is an exciting time full of new possibilities. Dive in and discover what's waiting for you!

✔ To focus solely on HTML, visit the W3C's markup page, which tells you all about HTML and other such languages. Check this out at `www.w3c.` `org/markup`.

✔ If you want to sample the information at other Web sites, type **HTML** at the Google search box or use any other search site you prefer. While the W3C's site offers the most accurate and up-to-date information, you can also learn a lot from Web developers who maintain Web sites pertaining to their knowledge and experience with HTML.

Microsoft provides two ways to take your data to the world (or to the next cubicle) with Access 2007:

✔ **Publish your tables individually as HTML documents.**

The rest of this chapter shows how to publish HTML tables.

✔ **Publish your whole database with Office's SharePoint services.**

SharePoint is beyond the scope of this book. To find out more about SharePoint, check out *Office 2007 and SharePoint Productivity For Dummies* by Vanessa Williams (Wiley; due out in January 2007) or visit Microsoft's SharePoint Web page at

`www.microsoft.com/windowsserver2003/technologies/sharepoint/default.mspx`

Previous versions of Access could publish your entire database through a *data access page.* That option has been dropped from Access 2007.

Publishing your Access tables

Follow these steps to make your tables and their data available with a Web browser:

1. **Open the database containing the table (or data within a table) destined for your intranet or the Web.**

   The database window hops to the screen.

2. **In the All Tables list on the left side of your window, double-click the table that you want to save as an HTML document.**

   Your desired table opens in the central part of the Access window.

3. **As needed, select the records you want to make part of the HTML document.**

   Drag through a series of records to select them. The process so far appears in Figure 10-3.

   You don't need to select individual records if you want to publish the entire table. You select a range of records if you want only those records to appear in the HTML document.

4. **In the External Data tab, locate the Export section and click the More button.**

   The available Export types, in addition to the standards, appear in a list.

Figure 10-3: Select the table and records within the table that you want to publish to the Web.

LastName	FirstName	DateHired	Department	JobTitle	Salary	VacationDay	Rating	Insurance	Add New Field
Bowling	David	7/15/1997	Operations	Manager	50000	15	7.75	Yes	
Burrell	Eugenia	8/25/2001	Accounting	Director	45000	10	8.0	No	
Fabiano	Jenna	9/15/2002	Marketing	Designer	35000	10	8.0	Yes	
Frankenfield	Daniel	8/2/2002	Operations	Manager	28000	5	8.25	No	
Freifeld	Iris	6/30/2000	Marketing	Director	45000	10	7.25	Yes	
Joubert	Christopher	9/2/1996	Sales	Representative	35000	15	7.75	Yes	
Kline	Linda	3/15/2001	Sales	Representative	35000	10	7.25	No	
Kovacik	John	6/6/2006	Operations	Janitor	16000	2	5.5	No	
Maloney	Steve	4/10/2001	Operations	Assistant Manager	25000	5	6.75	Yes	
Mermelstein	David	5/22/1999	Operations	Manager	30000	15	6.75	Yes	
Myers	George	5/25/2001	Sales	Director	40000	8	9.0	Yes	
O'Neill	Karen	7/22/2003	Accounting	Manager	42000	5	8.0	Yes	
Patrick	Kyle	9/5/2004	Accounting	Manager	40000	5	7.0	No	
Pederzani	Bruce	7/14/1999	Operations	Director	60000	15	8.50	No	
Shapiro	Mimi	6/23/2005	Marketing	Designer	32000	5	8.0	Yes	
Sorensen	Sharon	6/25/1999	Sales	Manager	37000	15	8.75	Yes	
Talbot	Ann	2/27/2005	Marketing	Designer	35000	5	8.5	Yes	
Ulrich	Zachary	3/22/2002	Marketing	Manager	55000	10	8.25	Yes	
Weller	Barbara	1/5/2001	Accounting	Manager	40000	10	8.75	Yes	

5. **Select HTML Document from the list, as shown in Figure 10-4.**

   The Export – HTML Document dialog box opens (see Figure 10-5). The current table's location and filename appear in the File Name field, with the table's file extension changed to `.html`.

6. **If needed, click the Browse button and navigate to the table you want to publish.**

   You're better off having selected the table within the Access workspace (as described in Steps 1 through 5) than trying to change horses at this point. You can also type a new name for the HTML document by editing the last segment of the File Name field content. The last segment is the actual file name, ending in ".html" — just edit the name, which appears to the left of the period.

7. **Click the box next to the Export Data with Formatting and Layout option to place a check mark there.**

   The remaining two options are now available:

   • Open the Destination File after Export Operation is Complete

   • Export Only Selected Records

8. **Click the Open the Destination File option to select it.**

   If you don't want to publish all records — that is, if you selected specific records back in Step 3 — check Export Only Selected Records, too.

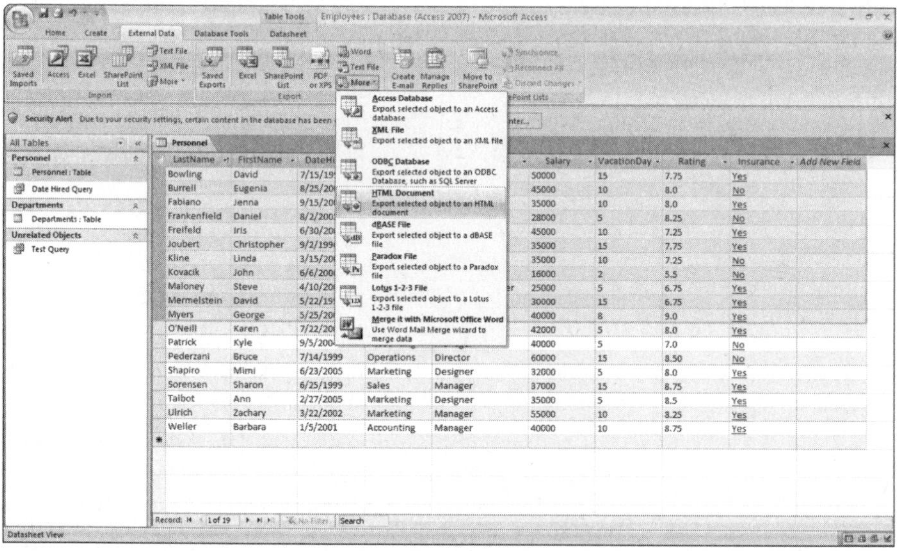

Figure 10-4:
Select
HTML
Document
from the
More list.

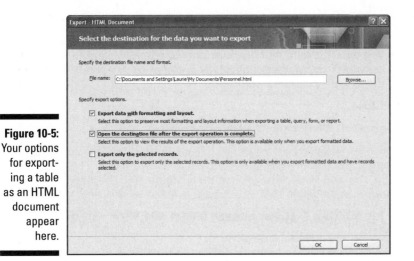

Figure 10-5:
Your options
for export-
ing a table
as an HTML
document
appear
here.

9. **Click OK.**

A second dialog box opens, entitled HTML Output Options (see Figure 10-6). The HTML document is created, and an Internet Explorer window with your HTML document name is opened, represented by a button on your taskbar.

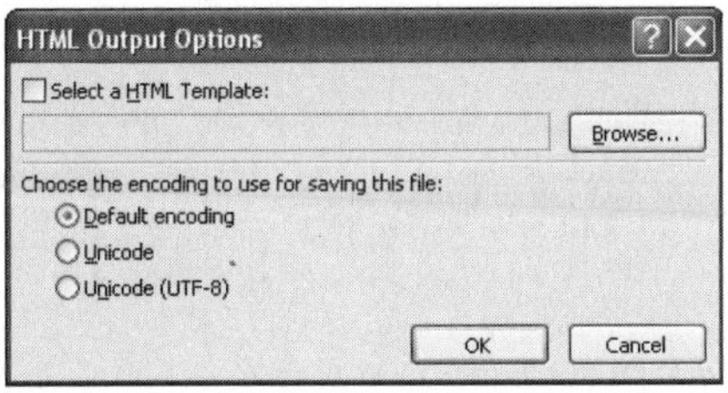

Figure 10-6:
Choose an
HTML
template or
click OK to
accept the
defaults.

10. **Select an HTML output option and click OK:**

- If you don't have an HTML template and simply want a table to appear in a browser window, just click OK.

- If you do have a template — in the form of an existing HTML document, click in the Select a HTML Template checkbox and then click the Browse button to navigate to the template, telling Access where to find it. In the resulting HTML Template to Use dialog box, click

OK once you've selected the template file to return to the Export HTML Document dialog box.

- You don't have to worry about the encoding method (unless a geek in your IT department has advised you of such a need), so accept the Default Encoding option.

11. Click Close.

The Export HTML Document dialog box closes.

Access asks you whether you want to save your Export settings. Leave the Save Export Steps option unchecked and click Close. There's no need to save the steps. The procedure is simple and there really aren't any unique steps taken that you'd want or need to skip next time.

12. Click the Internet Explorer taskbar button and view your new HTML document.

As shown in Figure 10-7, your table (or the records you chose from within it) appears in a simple grid right within the browser window.

Now all that's left to do is upload your HTML document to either

- ✔ Your in-house intranet server
- ✔ A Web server for global access (pardon the expression)

Figure 10-7:
Congratu-
lations!
You've just
created
an HTML
document!

Personnel								
LastName	FirstName	DateHired	Department	JobTitle	Salary	VacationDays	Rating	Insurance
Bowling	David	7/15/1997	Operations	Manager	50000	15	7.75	Yes
Burrell	Eugenia	8/25/2001	Accounting	Director	45000	10	8.0	No
Fabiano	Jenna	9/15/2002	Marketing	Designer	35000	10	8.0	Yes
Frankenfield	Daniel	8/2/2002	Operations	Manager	28000	5	8.25	No
Freifeld	Iris	6/30/2000	Marketing	Director	45000	10	7.25	Yes
Joubert	Christopher	9/2/1996	Sales	Representative	35000	15	7.75	Yes
Kline	Linda	3/15/2001	Sales	Representative	35000	10	7.25	No
Kovacik	John	6/6/2006	Operations	Janitor	16000	2	5.5	No
Maloney	Steve	4/10/2001	Operations	Assistant Manager	25000	5	6.75	Yes
Mermelstein	David	5/22/1999	Operations	Manager	30000	15	6.75	Yes
Myers	George	5/25/2001	Sales	Director	40000	8	9.0	Yes
O'Neill	Karen	7/22/2003	Accounting	Manager	42000	5	8.0	Yes
Patrick	Kyle	9/5/2004	Accounting	Manager	40000	5	7.0	No
Pederzani	Bruce	7/14/1999	Operations	Director	60000	15	8.50	No
Shapiro	Mimi	6/23/2005	Marketing	Designer	32000	5	8.0	Yes
Sorensen	Sharon	6/25/1999	Sales	Manager	37000	15	8.75	Yes
Talbot	Ann	2/27/2005	Marketing	Designer	35000	5	8.5	Yes
Ulrich	Zachary	3/22/2002	Marketing	Manager	55000	10	8.25	Yes
Weller	Barbara	1/5/2001	Accounting	Manager	40000	10	8.75	Yes

Personnel - Microsoft Internet Explorer
File   Edit   View   Favorites   Tools   Help
Back · · · Search · Favorites
Address C:\Documents and Settings\Laurie\My Documents\Personnel.html   Go   Links
My Computer

You'll need some FTP software (FTP stands for *File Transfer Protocol* and simply refers to the rules for uploading documents to servers) and login information for the server where your document will be stored. After the file is uploaded, you can view it online by typing the URL (Web address) for the Web site that contains your HTML document into any browser's address bar.

There's plenty of shareware and freeware available for FTP software. Just search at Google or Yahoo! (or the search site of your choice) for **FTP software**. If you're uploading files to your company's intranet or Web server, you'll probably be given software and instructions for how and where to upload your files.

Part IV
Ask Your Data, and Ye Shall Receive Answers

The 5th Wave   By Rich Tennant

"Our automated response policy to a large company-wide data crash is to notify management, back up existing data and sell 90% of my shares in the company."

In this part . . .

Data isn't very useful if you can't get at it — if you can't look for the one record you need and actually find it quickly and easily. Why would you spend hours building tables and entering data into them if you weren't going to be able to use it?

Part IV is all about the return on your database-building investment — getting the information you need out of the data you're storing. You'll find out about putting your records in a particular order and then distilling them down to just the one or two that you need to see. You'll also discover cool ways to ask your tables questions, the database version of playing "Go Fish". Instead of saying "Gimme all your eights", however, you'll be saying, "Show me everyone who lives in Idaho" or "Gimme all the gizmos that cost more than $5.00 but don't come from the Chicago warehouse."

All the various ways Access provides for getting at your data, from the painfully simple to the dazzlingly powerful, are covered here.

Chapter 11

Fast Finding, Filtering, and Sorting Data

. . . .

In This Chapter

▶ Locating data with the Find command

▶ Sorting your database

▶ Filtering by selection

▶ Filtering by form

. . . .

You probably already know what databases do. They help you store and organize the information that's important to you — your personal information, your business-related information, any kind of information you need to keep track of.

Of course, this is not a new concept. People have been storing information for as long as there've been people. From making scratches in the dirt to keep count of the number of sheep in the flock to handwritten census information to metal filing cabinets filled with typed lists and reports, man has been using databases for a long, long time.

Of course, things are a lot easier now. You can store millions of records in a single computer, and people all over the world can access them, assuming they have permission. Farmers can keep track of their sheep, countries can keep track of their populations, and you can keep track of your friends, family, employees, products, and holiday card lists — anything your little data-driven heart desires.

But what is all this "keeping track" of which I speak? It's not just storing the data — it's getting at it when you need it. Thanks to the magic of the Find, Sort, and Filter commands, Access tracks and reorganizes the stuff in your tables faster than ever and puts it literally at your fingertips whenever you need to locate one or more of the pieces of information you're storing. When you need a quick answer to a simple question, these three commands are ready to help. This chapter covers the commands in order, starting with the speedy Find, moving along to the organizational Sort, and ending with the flexible Filter.

Find, Sort, and Filter do a great job with *small* questions (like "How many people work at our Chicago office and also work in the accounting department?"). Answering big, complex questions (like "How many people attended major league baseball games in July and also bought a team hat?") still takes a full-fledged Access query (querying a database of baseball game attendees and the database of items sold in the team store). Don't let that threat worry you, though, because Chapter 10 explains queries in delightful detail.

Using the Find Command

When you want to track down a particular record *right now,* creating a query for the job is overkill. Fortunately, Access has a very simple way to find one specific piece of data in your project's tables and forms — the Find command.

Find is found — big surprise here — in the Find section of the Home tab, accompanied by a binoculars icon. You can also press Ctrl+F to open the Find dialog box.

Although the Find command is pretty easy to use, knowing a few tricks makes it even more powerful. And if you're a Word or Excel user, you'll find the tricks helpful in those applications, too — the Find command is an Office-wide feature. After you get through the Find basics (covered in the next section), check the tips for fine tuning the Find command in the "Shifting Find into high gear" section, later in the chapter.

Finding anything fast

Using the Find command is a very straightforward task. Here's how it works:

1. **Open the table or form you want to search.**

   Find works in both Datasheet view and with Access forms.

   If you want to dive into forms right now, flip to Chapter 7.

2. **Click in the field that you want to search.**

   The Find command searches the *current* field in all the records of the table, so make sure that you click the right field before starting the Find process. Access doesn't care which record you click — as long as you're on a record in the right field, Access knows exactly which field you want to Find in.

3. **Start the Find command.**

   You can either click the Find button in the Find section of the Home tab or press Ctrl+F.

   The Find and Replace dialog box opens, ready to serve you.

4. **Type the text you're looking for into the Find What box, as shown in Figure 11-1.**

   Take a moment to check your spelling before starting the search. Access is pretty smart, but it isn't bright enough to figure out that you actually meant *plumber* when you typed *plumer*.

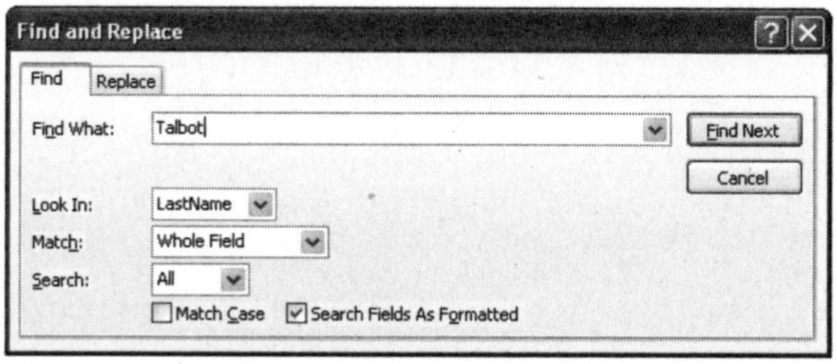

Figure 11-1:
The Find and Replace dialog box.

Find and Replace		? ✕
Find	Replace	
Find What:	Talbot	Find Next
		Cancel
Look In:	LastName	
Match:	Whole Field	
Search:	All	
	☐ Match Case ☑ Search Fields As Formatted	

5. **Click Find Next to run your search.**

   • If the data you seek is in the active field, the Find command immediately tracks down the record you want.

   The cell containing the data you seek is highlighted.

   What if the first record that Access finds isn't the one you're looking for? Suppose you want the second, third, or the fourteenth *John Smith* in the table? No problem — that's why the Find and Replace dialog box has a Find Next button. Keep clicking Find Next until Access either works its way down to the record you want or tells you that it's giving up the search.

   • If Find doesn't locate anything, it laments its failure in a small dialog box, accompanied by the sad statement, "Microsoft Access finished searching the records. The search item was not found."

If Find didn't find what you were looking for, you have a couple of options:

✔ You can give up by clicking OK to make the dialog box go away.

✔ Check the search and try again:

   a. Make sure that you clicked in the correct field and spelled everything correctly in the Find What box.

> You can also check the special Find options covered in the following section to see whether one of them is messing up your search.

b. If you change the spelling or options, click Find Next again.

Shifting Find into high gear

Sometimes, just typing the data you need in the Find What box doesn't produce the results you need:

- ✔ You find too many records (and end up clicking the Find Next button endlessly to get to the one record you want).
- ✔ The records that match aren't the ones that you want.

The best way to reduce the number of wrong matches is to add more details to your search, which will reduce the number of matches and maybe give you just that one record you need to find.

Access offers several tools for fine tuning a Find. Open the Find and Replace dialog box by either

- ✔ Clicking the Find button on the Home tab
- ✔ Pressing Ctrl+F

The following sections describe how to use the options in the Find & Replace dialog box.

If your Find command isn't working the way you think it should, check the following options. Odds are that at least one of these options is set to *exclude* what you're looking for.

Look In

By default, Access looks for matches only in the *current* field — whichever field you clicked in before starting the Find command. To tell Access to search the entire table instead, choose your table by name from the Look In drop-down list, as shown in Figure 11-2.

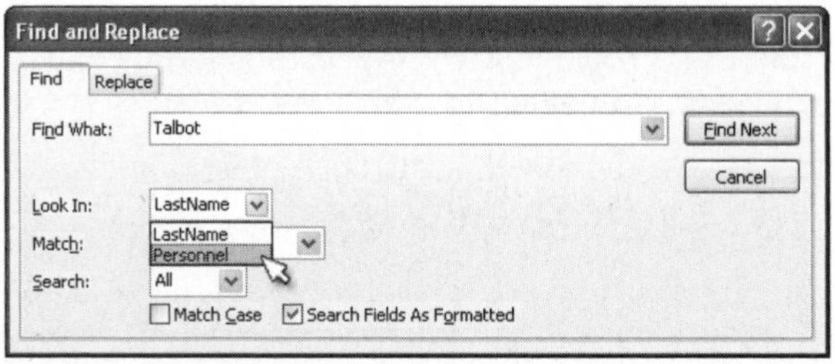

Figure 11-2: To search the entire table, change Look In.

Find and Replace	? X

Find | Replace

Find What: Talbot | Find Next | Cancel

Look In: LastName

Match: LastName / Personnel

Search: All

☐ Match Case   ☑ Search Fields As Formatted

Match

Access makes a few silly assumptions, and this setting is a good example.

By default, Match is set to Whole Field, which assumes that you want to find only fields that *completely match* your search text. The Whole Field setting means that searching for *Rich* doesn't find fields containing *Richard, Richelieu,* or *Ulrich.* Not terribly intuitive, eh? Well, you can turn up the intuition level in Access by changing the Match setting to either

- ✔ **Any Part of Field:** Allows a match anywhere in a field (finding *Richard, Ulrich,* and *Lifestyles of the Rich and Famous*).

- ✔ **Start of Field:** Recognizes only a match that starts from the beginning of the field.

    This option allows you to put in just part of a name, too — like if you only know the beginning of a name or the start of an address.

To change the Match setting, click the down arrow next to the field (see Figure 11-3) and then make your choice from the drop-down menu that appears.

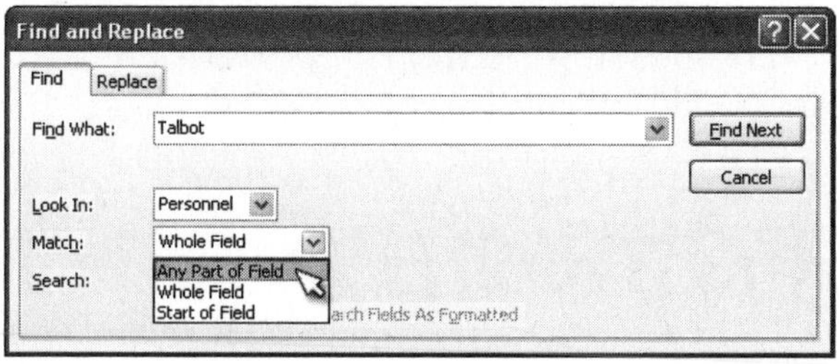

Figure 11-3:
Using the
Match
option.

Find and Replace

| Find | Replace |

Find What: Talbot ▾   Find Next

Cancel

Look In: Personnel ▾
Match: Whole Field ▾
     Any Part of Field
Search: Whole Field
     Start of Field   ...ch Fields As Formatted

Search

If you're finding too many matches, try limiting your search to one particular portion of the table with the Search option. Search tells the Find command to look either

- ✔ At all the records in the table (the default setting)
- ✔ Up or Down from the current record

Clicking a record halfway through the table and then telling Access to search Down from there confines your search to the bottom part of the table.

Tune your Search settings by clicking the down arrow next to the Search box and choosing the appropriate choice from the drop-down menu.

Match Case

Match Case requires that the term you search for is *exactly* the same as the value stored in the database, including the case of the characters.

This works really well if you're searching for a name, rather than just a word, so that *rich custard topping* is not found when you search for (capital-*R*) *Rich* in the entire table.

Search Fields As Formatted

This option instructs Access to look at the formatted version of the field instead of the actual data you typed.

Limiting the search in this way is handy when searching dates, stock-keeping unit IDs, or any other field with quite a bit of specialized formatting.

Turn on Search Fields As Formatted by clicking the check box next to it.

This setting doesn't work with Match Case, so if Match Case is checked, Search Fields As Formatted appears dimmed. In that case, uncheck Match Case to bring back the Search Fields As Formatted check box.

Most of the time, this option doesn't make much difference. In fact, the only time you probably care about this Find option is when (or if) you search many highly formatted fields.

Sorting from A to Z or Z to A

Very few databases are organized into nice, convenient alphabetical lists. You don't enter your records alphabetically, you enter them in the order they come to you. So what do you do when you need a list of products in product number order or a list of addresses in zip code order, right now?

Sorting by a single field

The solution is the Sort command, which is incredibly easy to use. The Sort command is on the Home tab, in the Sort & Filter section. The two buttons in this section (Sort Ascending and Sort Descending) do the job quite well:

✔ Sort Ascending sorts your records from top to bottom:

- Records that begin with *A* are at the beginning, and records that begin with *Z* are at the end.

- If your field contains numeric data (such as zip codes and prices), an Ascending sort puts them in order from lowest to highest.

✔ Sort Descending sorts your records from bottom to top:

- Records that begin with *Z* are at the top, and records that begin with *A* are at the bottom of the list.

- If your field contains numeric data, a Descending sort puts the records in order from highest to lowest.

Sorting on more than one field

What if you want to sort by zip code, and then within that sort you want all the people in the same zip code to appear in Last Name order?

You can sort by more than one column at a time like this:

1. **Click the heading of the first column to sort by.**

   The entire column is highlighted.

2. **Hold down the Shift key and click the heading of the last column to sort by.**

   All columns from the first one to the last one are highlighted.

3. **Choose either Sort Ascending or Sort Descending.**

   The sort is always performed from left to right.

   In other words, you can't sort by the contents of the fourth column and within that by the contents of the third column.

Sort has its own peculiarity when working with numbers in a text field. When sorting a field that has numbers mixed in with spaces and letters (such as street addresses), Access ranks the numbers as if they were *letters,* not numbers. This behavior means that Access puts "1065 W. Orange Street" before "129 Mulberry Street." (Thanks to the peculiar way that your computer sorts, the 0 in the second position of 1065 comes before the 2 in the second position of 129.)

Fast and Furious Filtering

Sometimes, you need to see a group of records that share a common value in one field — perhaps they all list a particular city, a certain job title, or they're all products that have the same cost. Always willing to help, Access includes a special tool for this very purpose — the Filter command.

Filter uses your criteria and displays all matching records, creating a mini-table of only the records that meet your requirements. It's like an instant query without all the work and planning. Of course, it's not as flexible or powerful as a query, but it's all you need when your needs are simple.

The Filter tool appears in the Sort & Filter section of the Home tab, and you have the following choices for a simple filter:

- ✔ Filter
- ✔ Selection
- ✔ Advanced, Filter by Form
- ✔ Advanced Filter/Sort
- ✔ Toggle Filter

Each type of filter performs the same basic function, but in a slightly different way. The following sections cover the first three options. The Advanced Filter/Sort option, found by clicking the Advanced button, opens a window that actually has you building a query — selecting tables and fields to filter and setting up criteria for the filter to use in finding specific records. You can read about queries and familiarize yourself with the tool Advanced Filter/Sort presents by reading Chapter 12.

Filters work in tables, forms, and queries. Although you can apply a filter to a report, filtering reports can be a daunting task, and one that we're not going to get involved with here. Of course, what you read here can be applied to that process, should you want to try it on your own. And in the following sections, what you learn to apply to a table can also be applied when you're working with queries and forms.

Filtering by a field's content

The main Filter command enables you to filter your records so that you view only records meeting specific criteria. Suppose, for example, that you wanted to see all records where employees work in the Sales Department. Here's how to do it:

1. **Click the small triangle on the field name for the field you want to filter (Department in this case).**

   Access displays a pop-up menu like the one in Figure 11-4.

   Don't right-click the header at the top of the column (where it says *Department* in the figure). Right-clicking there displays a different pop-up menu filled with wonderful things that you can do to that column of your table.

2. **If you want to omit some entries from your filter, remove their checkmarks.**

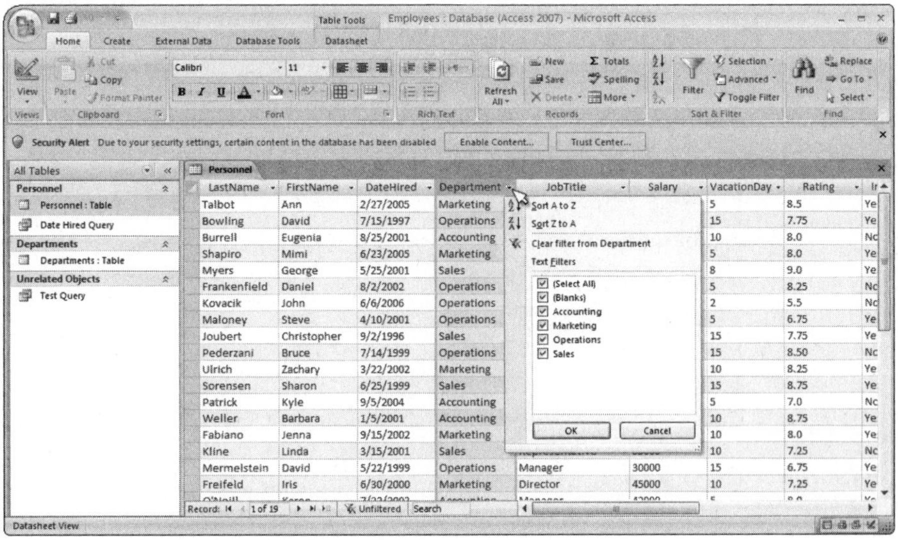

Figure 11-4:
Filter a
single field
based on
that field's
entries.

You can either

- • Remove checkmarks from individual entries.

- • Remove the Select All checkmark to uncheck all the items.

Uncheck everything so that you can easily check only those entries whose matching records you want to see. With all the entries checked, you see all the records.

3. **Place checkmarks next to those entries for which you want to filter the field.**

In this case, I mark Sales.

Access searches the column in which you checked and displays only those records that meet your Filter criteria.

4. **Click OK.**

All the records meeting the criteria set (by virtue of the items you checked) are displayed. This might be several records, a whole lot of records, or just one.

To see all of the records again, you can either

✔ Click the Toggle Filter button in the Sort & Filter section of the Ribbon.

✔ Click the field name's tiny triangle again and choose Clear Filter From *Field Name.*

The entire table, full of records, returns to view.

Filter by selection

The Selection command is the easiest of the filter commands to use. It assumes that you've found one record that matches your criteria. Using the Selection filter is a lot like grabbing someone in a crowd and shouting: "Okay, everybody who's like this guy here, line up over there."

For example, imagine that you want to find all the employees who work in the Sales Department. You can use Selection filter in this manner:

1. **Click the field that has the information you want to match.**

   In this case, it's the Department field.

2. **Scroll through the list until you find the field entry that will serve as an appropriate example for your filter.**

3. **Click the value you're searching for, click the Selection button, and then click Equals "X", where X is the value you want the filter to look for. Or you can right-click and choose Equals "X".**

   Access immediately displays a table containing only the records with X in the filtered field, as shown in Figure 11-5, where our Sales Department filter has been applied.

4. **Click the Toggle Filter button on the toolbar after you finish using the filter.**

   Your table or form returns to its regular display.

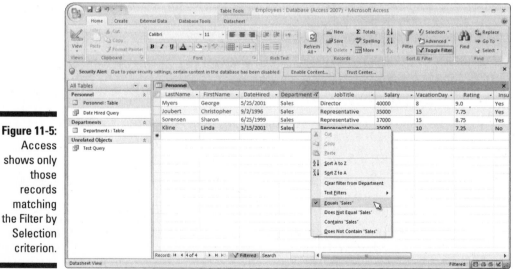

Figure 11-5: Access shows only those records matching the Filter by Selection criterion.

At this stage of the game, you may want to save a list of everything that matches your filter. Unfortunately, the Filter's simplicity and ease of use now come back to haunt you. To permanently record your filtered search, you need to create a query. See Chapter 12 for details about creating queries.

Filter by Form

You can tighten a search by using additional filters to weed out undesirable matches, but that takes a ton of extra effort. For an easier way to isolate a group of records based on the values in more than one field, try Filter by Form.

Filter by Form uses more than one criterion to sift through records. In some ways, it's like a simple query. (What's a query? See Chapter 12.) It's so similar to a query that you can even save your Filter by Form criteria *as* a full-fledged query!

Suppose, for example, that you need a list of all the employees at your company who work in a certain department and have a particular title. You can perform two Selection filters (on the Department and Job Title fields, using our employee database as an example), and write down the results of each to get your list, or you can do just *one* search with Filter by Form and see all the records that meet your criteria (based on their entries in multiple tables) in a single step.

To use Filter by Form, follow these steps:

1. **On the Home tab, click the Advanced button in the Sort & Filter section.**

   A menu appears.

2. **Choose Filter by Form from the menu.**

   The table is replaced by a single row of cells, one under each field header in your table, as shown in Figure 11-6.

3. **Click the first column that you want to filter.**

   Use the scroll bars to bring the column on the screen if it's off to the right and can't be seen.

   The down arrow jumps to the column you click.

   • Normally, Access shows a down-arrow button next to the first field in the table.

   • If you previously used a Filter command with the table, Access puts the down-arrow button in the last field you filtered, as shown in Figure 11-6.

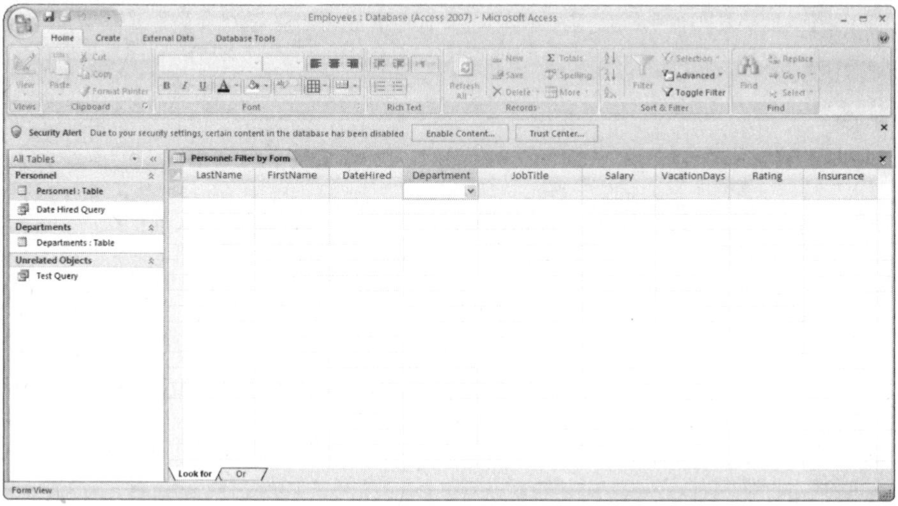

Figure 11-6:
Filter by
Form offers
a grid and
drop-down
lists to set
criteria for
each field.

4. **Click the down arrow to see a list of values that the field contains, as shown in Figure 11-7.**

5. **In the list of values, click the value that you want to use in this Filter.**

For instance, if you select Accounting from the drop-down list in the Department field, "Accounting" moves into the Department column. Access automatically adds the quotes on its own — one less detail that you need to remember!

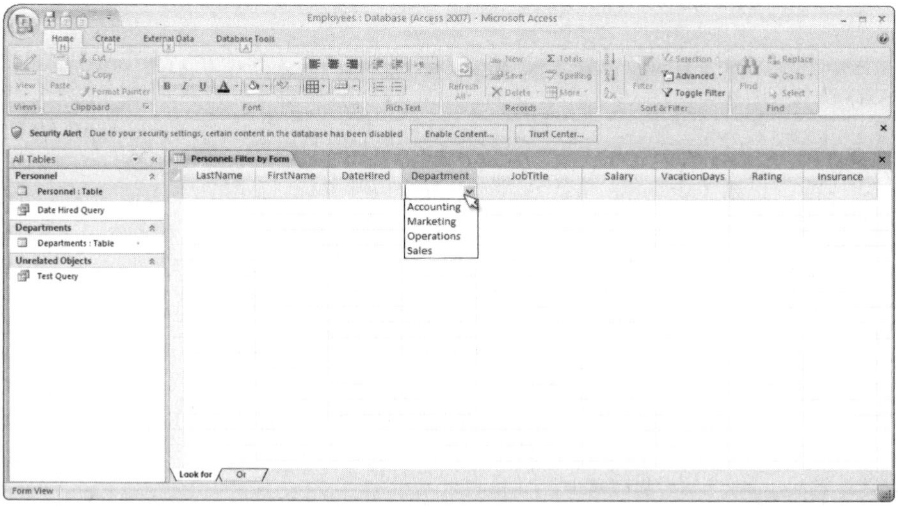

Figure 11-7:
The drop-
down list
shows all
unique
values in
this field.

6. **To add another filter option, click the Or tab in the lower-left corner of the table.**

   A new Filter by Form window appears, letting you add an alternate search condition. In addition, Access adds another Or tab to the lower-left corner of the display, as shown in Figure 11-8.

   The Filter by Form command likes to answer simple questions, such as "Show me all the records containing "Accounting" in the Department field." It also provides answers to more complex questions like "Show me all the records containing "Accounting" or "Sales" in the Department field and who have a "Manager" Job Title," and it performs both tasks easily.

   Asking a more complex question (such as "Show me all the employees in either Accounting or Sales who are Managers and earn more than $50,000") requires query. To find out about queries, flip ahead to Chapter 12.

7. **For each additional field you want to filter, repeat Steps 3 through 6.**

   In this example, the second field to be filtered is "JobTitle", and Manager is selected from the drop-down list.

8. **When you finish entering all the criteria for the filter, click the Toggle Filter button.**

   Figure 11-9 shows the results.

Figure 11-8: Use as many Or statements as you need to define the criteria.

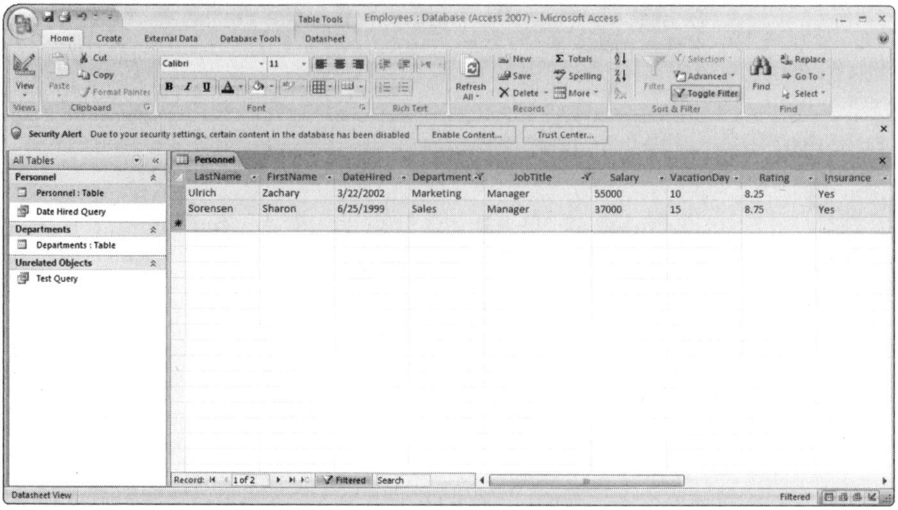

Figure 11-9:
Access
finds all
Managers
from the
Accounting
OR Sales
Department.

A final thought about Filter by Form:

> ✔ Although you can get fancy by adding OR searches to your heart's content, keeping track of your creation gets tough in no time at all. Before you go too far, remind yourself that queries work better than filters when the questions get complex. Flip to Chapter 12 for the lowdown on queries.

When you finish fiddling with your filter, click the Toggle Filter button. At that point, your table returns to normal (or at least as normal as data tables ever get).

Unfiltering in a form

What do you do when you enter criteria by mistake? Or when you decide that you really don't want to include Ohio in your filter right after you click OH? No problem — the Clear Grid command comes to the rescue!

When you click the Clear Grid command (found in the Advanced menu), Access clears all the entries in the Filter by Form grid and gives you a nice, clean place to start over again.

Filter by excluding selection

The Selection filter can also be used to exclude certain records. This works great for times when you want to briefly hide a bunch of records that all share a unique attribute (a particular zip code, a certain state, a particular price, and so on).

Here's how to make the Selection filter exclude records for you:

1. **Scroll through the table until you find the value you want to exclude.**

2. **Right-click the value and choose Does Not Equal _____ (where the blank represents the value you've right-clicked), as shown in Figure 11-10.**

   You right-click the field containing the value, just as you do when using Filter by Selection.

   Voilà! Access shows everything *except* the records containing the value you chose.

You can also click the Selection button (in the Sort & Filter section of the Home tab) and choose Does Not Equal from the menu there. You'll also notice the Contains and Does Not Contain commands — these are handy for culling records that have something in common, such as a particular word or number within them.

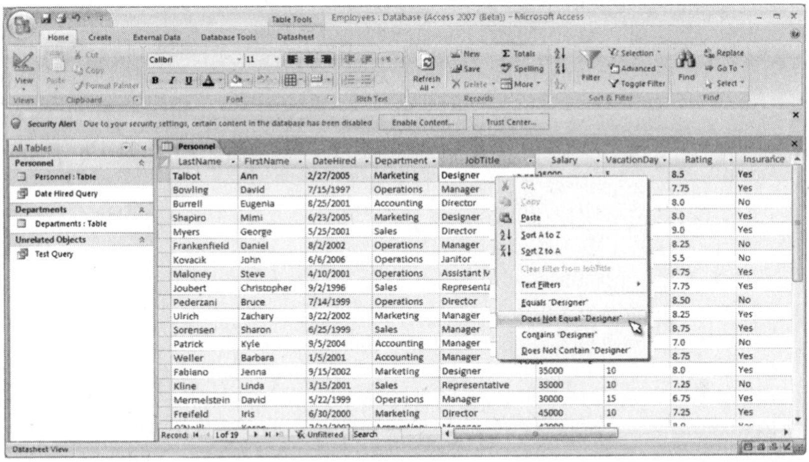

Figure 11-10: With one click, Access hides all records for employees who are not Designers.

Chapter 12

I Was Just Asking . . . For Answers

In This Chapter

▶ Defining what queries are and what they can do

▶ Posing questions (and getting answers) with filter and sort queries

▶ Asking deep questions with queries

▶ Making query magic with the Query Wizard

*Y*ou know the old saying, "The only stupid question is the one you didn't ask." It's supposed to mean that if you have a question, ask it, because if you don't, you'll be operating in the dark, and that's far sillier than your question could ever have been. Although you don't ask "meaning of life" questions of a database, you do pose questions like, "How many customers do we have in Arkansas?" or "What's the phone number of that guy who works for Acme Explosives?" Either of those questions, if you didn't ask it, would require you to scroll through rows and rows of data to find the information. That's the silly approach, obviously.

This chapter introduces you to the art of asking questions about the information in your database, using *queries*. You discover how to use the Query Wizard to pose simple questions, and then you find out about creating your own simple yet customized queries by using the bizarrely and inaccurately named Advanced Filter/Sort tool. Suffice to say, by the end of this chapter you'll be a veritable quiz master, capable of finding any record or group of records you need.

 Don't worry if your first few queries produce odd or unexpected results. Like anything new, queries, and their inherent procedures and concepts, take a little getting used to. Because they're so powerful, they can be a little complicated, but it's worth taking the time to figure things out (with the help of this book!). Take your time, be patient with yourself, and remember that old saying: "The only stupid question is the one you didn't ask."

Simple (Yet Potent) Filter and Sort Tools

Wait a minute. We were just talking about queries, and the heading above says something about *filter* and *sort*. What happened to querying?

It's all related, and it's all about asking questions. There are really two ways to find a particular record:

- *Queries* use a set of criteria — conditions that eliminate many, if not all but one, of your records — that you present to the database and that says, "Look here, here, and here, and find THIS for me!"

- *Filters* say "Sift through all these records and find the one(s) that looks like THIS!"

Of course, the exclamation point is optional, and so is the method you use — you can query *or* filter for any record or group of records you want. But it's all about asking questions.

Filter things first

We begin by explaining filters because they're more straightforward, procedurally, than queries. By starting with filters, too, you can get your feet wet with them while preparing for the deeper waters of querying.

How filters work

Filters quickly scan a single table for whatever data you seek. Filters examine all records in the table and then hide those that do not match the criteria you seek.

The filtering options are virtually unlimited, but simple:

- Want every customer in Pennsylvania? Filter the State field for **PA**.

- Want every plumber in Hollywood? Filter for City (**Hollywood**) and Occupation (**Plumber**), and there you go.

- Want to make sure you have only the plumbers from Hollywood, California, and not the ones in Hollywood, Florida? Filter for State, too.

There's a price to pay for ease and simplicity. Filters aren't *smart* or *flexible*:

- You cannot filter multiple tables without first writing a query that contains the tables.

- A filter cannot be the basis for the records seen on a report or form.

Chapter 11 covers filters in their limited but useful glory.

Fast filing with Access

Back before computers, people filed information in *file folders* and stored them in *file cabinets.*

✔ The file folders had useful information on their tabs — like letters of the alphabet, dates, or names, indicating what kind of information could be found inside.

✔ The file cabinet drawers had information on them, too — little cards with names, numbers, or letters on them, indicating which folders were stored inside them.

The figures on the file drawers and file folders helped people find information:

✔ Need an invoice from April 10, 2006? Go to the Invoice cabinet, open the drawer for April, and pull out the folder with invoices from the week of April 10. Leaf through a few sheets of paper, and voilà!

✔ Need to know how much a given customer spent in the last quarter of 2005? Go to the 2005 cabinet, open the drawer of customer folders, and pull the folder for the customer you want.

In a sans-computer environment, you'd also need a calculator, abacus, or scrap paper and a pencil to tally the expenditures by that particular customer.

Querying in Access is a lot like the process of opening a file drawer, looking at folder tabs to figure out which folder is needed, and then leafing through the pages in the folder. The process just happens a lot faster, and you don't get any paper cuts!

✔ The data stored in an Access table can be found by using a query that goes to a particular table, looks in particular fields, and pulls out certain records, based on the criteria set for the query, such as "Show me all the people with Sales in the Department field."

✔ You can even perform calculations with queries (like tallying the invoices for a particular customer). Chapter 15 shows you how.

What about queries?

Queries go far beyond filters. But to get to that great "beyond," queries require more complexity. After all, a bicycle may be easy to ride, but a bike won't go as fast as a motorcycle. And so it goes with queries. Queries work with one or more tables, let you search one or more fields, and even offer the option to save your results for further analysis, but you can't just hop on and ride a query with no lessons.

For all the differences between filters and queries, the most advanced filter is, in reality, a simple query, which makes some bizarre sense. Your first step into the world of queries is also your last step out of the domain of filters. Welcome to Advanced Filter/Sort, the super filter of Access, masquerading as a mild-mannered query.

Advanced Filter/Sort

Advanced Filter/Sort is more powerful than a run-of-the-mill filter. It's so powerful that it's like a simple query:

- ✔ You use the same steps to build an Advanced Filter/Sort as a query.
- ✔ The results look quite a bit alike, too.

Advanced Filter/Sort looks, acts, and behaves like a query, but it's still a filter at heart and is constrained by a filter's limits, including these:

- ✔ Advanced Filter/Sort works with only one table or form in your database at a time, so you can't use it on a bunch of linked tables.
- ✔ You can ask only simple questions with the filter.

  Real, honest-to-goodness queries do a lot more than that

- ✔ The filter always displays all the columns for every matching record.

  With a query, *you* choose the columns that you want to appear in the results. If you don't want a particular column, leave it out of the query. Filters aren't bright enough to do that.

Even with those limitations, Advanced Filter/Sort makes a great training ground to practice your query-building skills.

Although this section talks about applying filters only to tables, you can also filter a query. There's a good reason to filter queries: Some queries take a long time to run, so it's faster to *filter* the query results than to *rewrite and rerun* the query. Suppose that you run a complicated Sales Report query and notice that it includes data from *every* state instead of the individual state you wanted. Rather than modify the query and run it again, you can apply a filter to your query's results. *Poof!* You get the results in a fraction of the time.

Fact-finding with fun, fast filtering

Before you use the filter window, you need to take a quick look at its components and what they do. In the section that follows this one, you find out how to access and use the filter window.

The filter window is split into two distinct sections, as shown in Figure 12-1:

- ✔ **Field list** (the upper half of the window). The field list displays all the fields in the *current table or form* (the table or form that's open at the time). Not sure about forms? Check out Chapter 7!

At this point, don't worry about the upper half of the window. The field list comes more into play when you start working with full queries. The table you were working on is already shown in the upper half of the window, so you don't have to do anything with this part of the window now.

✔ **Query grid** (the lower half of the screen). When you use the Advanced Filter/Sort command, you are presented with a blank *query grid* for the details of your filter.

You're building a filter, but Access calls the area at the bottom of the screen a query grid because you use the same grid for queries. You'll see it later in the chapter in the section about building real queries.

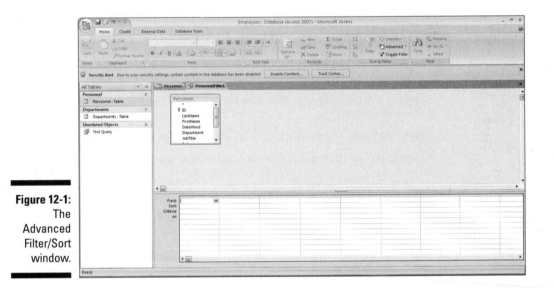

Figure 12-1: The Advanced Filter/Sort window.

To build the filter, you simply fill in the spaces of the query grid at the bottom of the window, as shown in Figure 12-1. Access even helps you along the way with pull-down menus and rows that do specific tasks. The procedure for filling in these spaces appears in the next section, along with details about each part of the grid and how it all works.

Here's the "advanced" part

The Advanced Filter/Sort tool also works on *forms*. If you feel particularly adventuresome (or if you mainly work with your data through some ready-made forms), try the filter with your form. Filtering a form works like filtering a table, so you can follow the same steps.

The following sections show how to design and use filters.

Starting the process

Start your filter adventure by firing up Access's basic query tool, the Advanced Filter/Sort.

1. **Decide what question you need to ask and which fields the question involves.**

   Because it's your data, only you know what information you need and which fields would help you get it. You may want a list of employees who use the company's insurance, customers who live in a particular state, books by your favorite author, or people whose birthdays fall in the next month (you can't put off that card-shopping forever).

   Whatever you want, decide on your question first and then get ready to find the fields in your table or form that contain the answer.

   Don't worry if your question includes more than one field or multiple options. Filters (and queries) can handle multiple-field and multiple-option questions.

2. **Open the table (or form) that you want to interrogate.**

   Assuming you have the right database open, your table or form pops into view.

3. **Click the Home tab at the top of the Access workspace.**

4. **In the Sort & Filter section of the toolbar (see Figure 12-2), choose Advanced⇨Advanced Filter/Sort.**

   The filter window appears, ready to accept your command. What you see depends on the following considerations:

   - If you previously used a filter of any kind with this table, Access puts that most recently used filter information into the new window.

   - If no filter was done previously, the Filter/Sort window looks pretty blank — for now.

   The filter window is nothing but a simplified query window. The filter looks, acts, and behaves a lot like a real query. More information about full queries comes later in the chapter, so flip ahead to the next section if that's what you need.

After you open the filter window, you're ready to select fields and criteria for your filter. The following section shows you how.

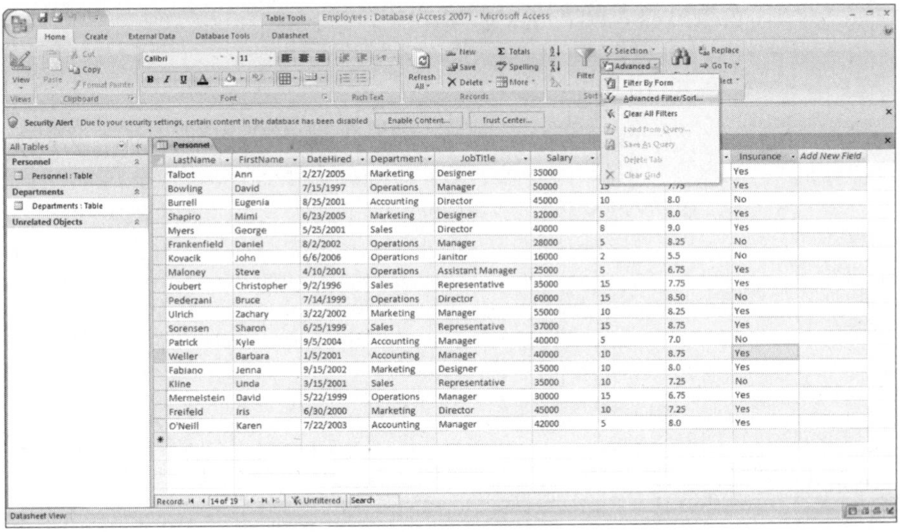

Figure 12-2:
Click the
Advanced
button to
choose
Advanced
Filter/Sort.

Selecting fields and criteria

As you begin selecting the fields you want to use in your filter and set up the criteria against which your fields' content will be compared, you'll need to follow these steps carefully:

1. **Click the first box in the Field row and then click the down arrow that appears to the right of the box.**

   The drop-down menu lists all the fields in your table (or form).

2. **Click the field (as identified in the preceding section).**

   Access helpfully puts the field name in the Field box on the query grid. So far, so good.

   If you want to see the results of your filter in the same order that your data always appears in, skip to Step 4.

3. **If you want to sort your filter results by this particular field, follow these steps:**

   a. Click the Sort box

   b. Click the down arrow that appears.

   c. Select Ascending or Descending from the drop-down menu.

   *Ascending order is lowest to highest (for example, A, B, C . . .).
   Descending order is highest to lowest (for example, Z, Y, X . . .).*

4. **Set up your criteria for the field.**

Follow these steps:

a. *Click the Criteria box under your field.*

b. *Type the criteria, such as* =**value**, *where "value" refers to a specific word or number that is represented within your data or < or > followed by a value.*

Setting the criteria is the most complex part of building a query — it's the most important part of the entire process. The criteria are your actual question, formatted in a way that Access understands. Table 12-1 gives you a quick introduction to the different ways you can express your criteria.

Table 12-1		Basic Comparison Operators	
Name	*Symbol*	*What It Means*	*Example*
Equals	=	Displays all records that exactly match whatever you type.	To find all items from customer 37, type **37** into the Criteria row.
Less Than	<	Lists all values that are less than your criterion.	Typing **<50000** in the Salary field finds all employees who earn less than $50K.
Greater Than	>	Lists all values in the field that are greater than the criterion.	Typing >**50000** in the Salary field finds all employees who I'll be hitting up for a loan because they earn more than $50K.
Greater Than or Equal To	>=	Works just like Greater Than, except it also includes all entries that exactly match the criterion.	>=**50,000** finds all values from 50,000 to infinity.
Less Than or Equal To	<=	If you add = to Less Than, your query includes all records that have values below or equal to the criterion value.	<=**50000** includes not only those records with values less than 50,000, but also those with a value of 50,000.
Not Equal To	<>	Finds all entries that don't match the criteria.	If you want a list of all records except those with a value of 50,000, enter <>**50000**.

If you're making comparisons with logical operators, flip to Chapter 13 for everything you need to know about Boolean logic, the language of Access criteria.

c. *If your question includes more than one possible value for this field, click the Or box and type your next criterion in the box to the right of the word* Or.

If you move on to a new box, the criterion you entered is automatically placed in quotes. Don't worry. This is just Access acknowledging that you've given it a specific value to look for, either to

• Make an exact match.

• Use the value with a greater-than or less-than symbol for comparison.

If your question involves more than one field, repeat the preceding Steps 1–4 for each field. Just use the next block in the grid for the additional field or fields you want to use in your filter.

With all the fields and criteria in place, it's time to take your filter for a test drive.

Running the filter

After completing the process of choosing fields and setting criteria, you're ready to run the filter. Click the Toggle Filter button in the Sort & Filter section of the Ribbon.

Access thinks about it for a moment, and then a new tab appears, displaying the record or records that met your criteria. This is shown in Figure 12-3. Pretty cool, eh?

Your filter appears on its own tab — temporarily named *OriginalTable NameFilter1*.

There are two ways to see all the data again:

✔ Click the Toggle Filter button.

The filtered records join their unfiltered brethren in a touching moment of digital homecoming.

✔ Click the Filtered button.

This button appears at the bottom of the Access window (next to the Record buttons that you use to move through your records one at a time). When you click the Filtered button, your entire table comes back, and the button changes to say Unfiltered. Click again? The results of your query return. It's a quick toggle, perhaps even toggle-ier than the Toggle Filter button!

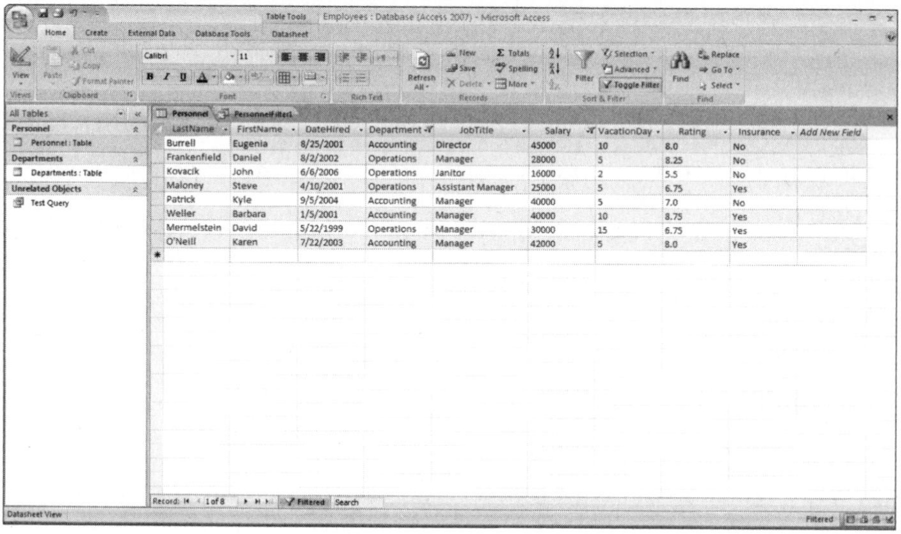

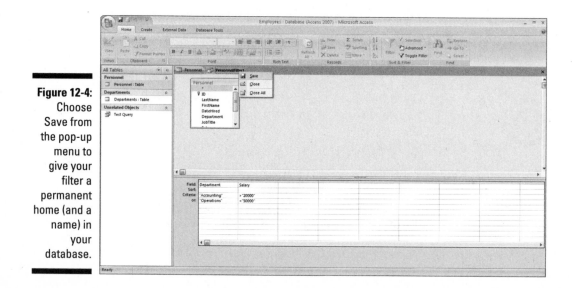

Figure 12-3:
Voilà! Your
filtered data
appears, no
abracadabra
needed.

Saving your work

If you think a filter will come in handy in the future, save it with these steps:

1. **Right click the NameFilter1 tab (the word "Filter1" preceded by your table or form name) and choose Save as shown in Figure 12-4.**

   Access displays a dialog box asking what you want to call the query.

Figure 12-4:
Choose
Save from
the pop-up
menu to
give your
filter a
permanent
home (and a
name) in
your
database.

2. **Type a name and then click OK.**

   Access saves your filter as a query. You can see the query listed in the Navigation Pane, under your table's entry in the list of elements in your database.

If you want to delete your filter and not save it, follow these steps:

1. **Right-click the filter's tab and choose Close from the pop-up menu.**

2. **When prompted, click No to saving the filter.**

Select Queries

The basic query tool, created to make your life easier, is the *Select query*. This type of query is so named because it *selects* matching records from your database and displays the results according to your instructions.

The sidebar "Secrets of the Select Query" summarizes the key differences that make Select queries more powerful than lesser filters. If upon reading these secrets, the Select Query sounds like the right tool for the job you have in mind, you may be able to use a filter instead of a query.

The best process for creating a Select query depends on the following:

✔ If you are new to writing a query, the Simple Query Wizard is a fast, easy way to get started. It walks you through the process of selecting tables and fields for the query and can even add some summary calculations (such as counting records) to your query.

✔ If you have already written some queries and are comfortable with the Query Design window, you'll probably want to bypass the Query Wizard and build your queries from scratch. Later in this chapter, "Getting Your Feet Wet with Ad Hoc Queries" guides you through the process.

Solid relationships are the key to getting it all (from your tables)

In life, solid relationships make for a happier person; in Access, solid relationships make for a happier query experience.

Secrets of the Select Query

Unlike its simplified little brother Advanced Filter/Sort (shown previously in this chapter), a Select query offers all kinds of helpful and powerful options, including these:

✔ **Use more than one table in a query.** Because a select query understands the relational side of Access, this query can pull together data from more than one table.

✔ **Show only the fields that you want in your results.** Select queries include the ever-popular Show setting, which tells Access which fields you really care about seeing.

✔ **Put the fields into any order you want in the results.** Organize your answer fields where *you* want them without changing the order of the fields in your original table.

✔ **List only as many matching entries as you need.** If you need only the top 5, 25, or 100 records, or a percentage, such as 5% or 25%, use the *Top Value setting.* (Top Value is covered in Chapter 14).

To effectively query your database, you need to know the following about your database table structure:

✔ Which tables do you need to use?

✔ How are the tables you need to use related to each other?

✔ Which fields contain the data you want to know about?

✔ Which fields do you need in the solution?

Access maintains relationships between the tables in your database. Usually you (or your Information Systems department) create these relationships when you first design the database. When you build the tables and organize them with special key fields, you actually prepare the tables to work with a query.

Key fields relate your Access tables to one another. Queries use key fields to match records in one table with their related records in another. Properly related tables allow you to pull the data for the item you seek from the various tables that hold this data in your database.

The sidebar "Solid table relationships make solid queries" shows a key field in action.

Solid table relationships make solid queries

The figure in this sidebar shows a key field in action. You see two related tables from the Northwind database:

✔ The *Customers* table stores contact information for everyone who purchases goods from the company.

To prevent mixing up customers who have identical names, the company assigns each customer a unique number (the CustomerID). No two customers can have the same CustomerID; it's the key field in the Customer table.

✔ The *Orders* table lists the details of a specific order the customer has placed.

To keep the orders straight, each order gets a unique OrderID.

Because every order comes from someone listed in the Customers table, the company puts the customer's number (the number stored in the CustomerID field of the Customer table) in the CustomerID field of the Orders table. That connects the two tables. Through that connection,

✔ Every CustomerID in the Orders table matches a CustomerID in the Customers table.

✔ All the orders placed by a particular customer can be found.

Cool, huh?

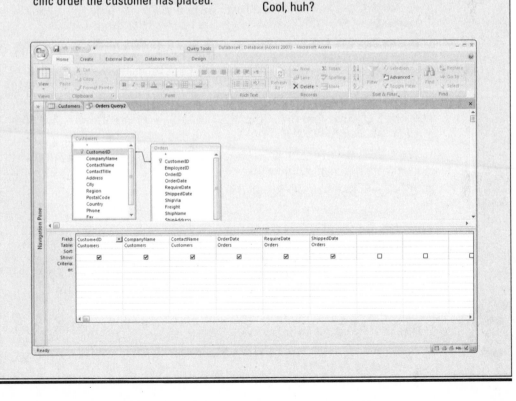

If you don't relate your tables via the Relationships window, you'll have to do so for each multiple-table query you build in Access. As a general rule, put in the time to properly design and relate your tables. With proper table design and relationships, you'll get the results you want in a shorter amount of time.

Running the Query Wizard

You can rely on the Simple Query Wizard for a real dose of hands-free filtering. With the Simple Query Wizard, you enter *table and field information*. The wizard takes care of the behind-the-scenes work for you.

Access isn't psychic (that's scheduled for the next version); it needs *some* input from you!

To create a query with the Query Wizard, follow these steps:

1. **Lay out the data you'd like in your query results on a piece of paper.**

   A query returns a datasheet (column headings followed by rows of data), so make your layout in that format. All you really need are the column headings so that you'll know what data to pull from the database.

2. **Determine the table location of each piece of data (column heading) from your paper.**

   Write down the table and field name that contains the data matching the column heading on the paper above the column heading.

3. **In the Database window, click the Create tab on the Ribbon and then click the Query Wizard button from the Other button group.**

   The New Query Wizard dialog box appears, asking you what kind of Query Wizard you'd like to run.

4. **Choose Simple Query Wizard and click OK.**

   The Simple Query Wizard window opens (see Figure 12-5) and offers you choices for the tables you want to query and which fields from within those tables you want to work with.

5. **Click the down arrow in the Tables/Queries box.**

   A list of all tables and select queries in the database appears.

6. **Select the fields for your query.**

   Repeat these steps to select each field:

       a. Click the down arrow next to the Tables/Queries drop-down list (as shown in Figure 12-6).

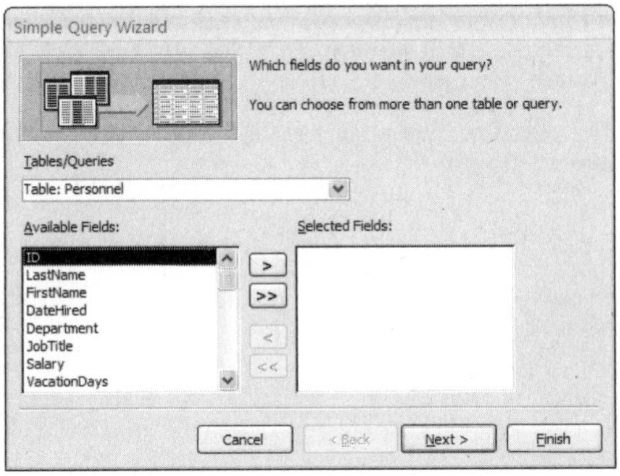

Figure 12-5:
The Simple
Query
Wizard
starts out
with a
simple,
necessary
question
about which
table(s) you
want to
query.

b. *Click the name of the table or query to include in this query.*

The Available Fields list changes and displays the fields available in the table.

c. *In the Available Fields list, double-click each field that you want to include in the query from this table or query.*

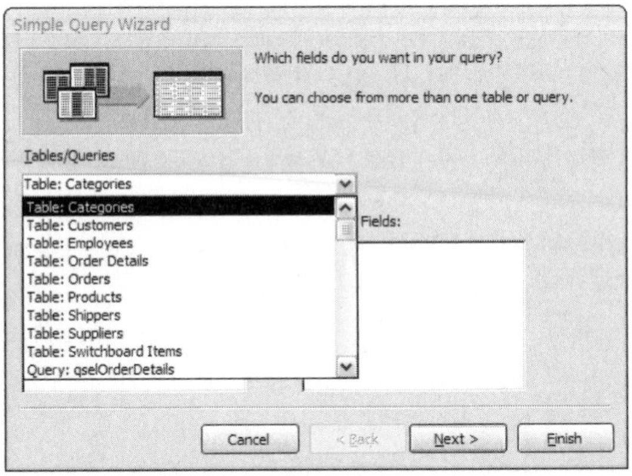

Figure 12-6:
The Tables/
Queries
drop-down
list.

If you add the wrong field, just double-click it in the Selected Fields list. It will go back home. If you just want to start all over, click the double-left *chevron* (that's what you call symbol that looks like a less-than sign) and all the selected fields will go away.

7. After you select all the fields, click Next.

The window in Figure 12-7 will appear if the Wizard can determine the relationships between the tables you selected.

If you don't see the window, not to worry. Access wants you to name the query instead. Skip to Step 8.

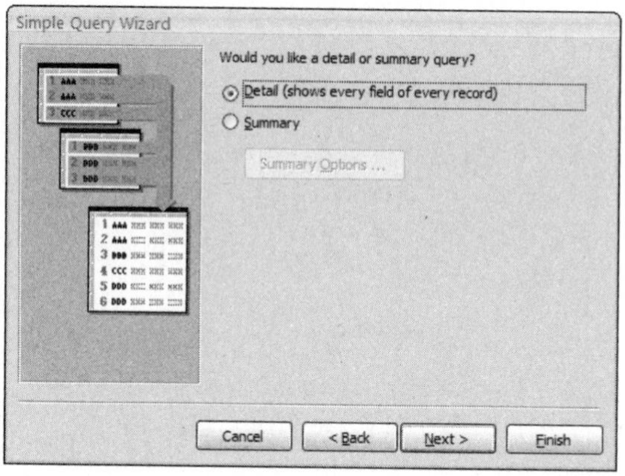

Figure 12-7:
The Query
Wizard may
give you the
chance to
summarize
your data.

Simple Query Wizard

Would you like a detail or summary query?

⊙ Detail (shows every field of every record)

○ Summary

Summary Options ...

Cancel   < Back   Next >   Finish

If you include fields from two tables that aren't related, a warning dialog box appears (see Figure 12-8). The dialog box reminds you that all of the selected tables must be related and suggests that you correct the problem before continuing. In fact, it won't let you go any further until you either

- Remove all the fields selected for your query from the unrelated tables.

- Fix the relationships so that all tables you've selected in your query are related.

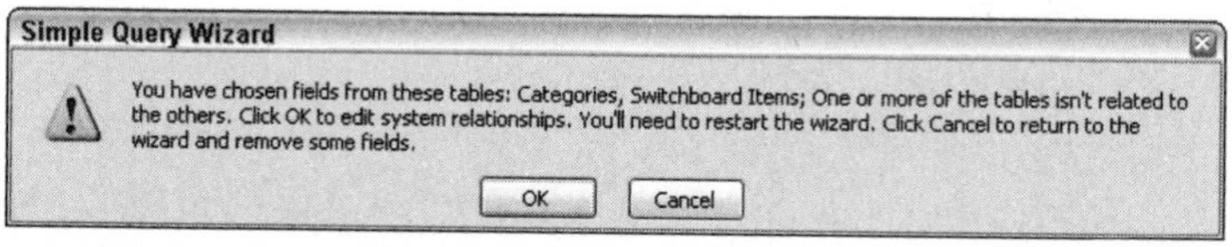

Figure 12-8:
The Simple
Query
Wizard
warning
dialog box.

Simple Query Wizard

⚠ You have chosen fields from these tables: Categories, Switchboard Items; One or more of the tables isn't related to the others. Click OK to edit system relationships. You'll need to restart the wizard. Click Cancel to return to the wizard and remove some fields.

OK   Cancel

8. If the wizard asks you to choose between a Detail and a Summary query, click the radio button next to your choice and then click Next.

- *Detail* creates a datasheet that lists all the records that match the query. As the name implies, you get all the details from those records.

- *Summary* tells the wizard that you aren't interested in seeing every single record; you want to see a summary of the information instead.

A summary query can perform calculations on numeric fields like sums and averages. If text fields are selected, Access can count the records or pull the first and last item from the field alphabetically.

If you want to make any special adjustments to the summary, click Summary Options to display the Summary Options dialog box shown in Figure 12-9. Select your summary options from the list and then click OK.

If you're curious about how the wizard decides whether to display the detail or summary step, the sidebar "To summarize or not to summarize" tells the story.

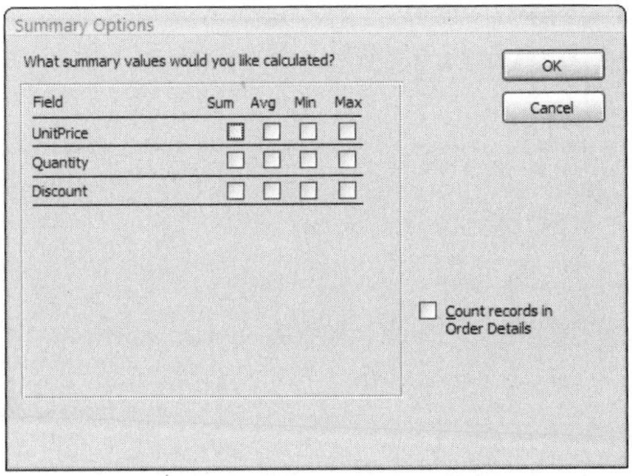

Figure 12-9:
Access
offers
different
ways of
summarizing
the data.

Summary Options				
What summary values would you like calculated?				OK
Field	Sum	Avg	Min	Max
UnitPrice	☐	☐	☐	☐
Quantity	☐	☐	☐	☐
Discount	☐	☐	☐	☐

Cancel

☐ Count records in Order Details

9. **Select a radio button for what you want to do next:**

- *Make your query snazzy:* Select the Modify the Query Design option.

The wizard sends your newly created query to the salon for some sprucing up, such as the inclusion of sorting and totals.

Clicking the check box at the bottom of the screen opens a Help file that explains how you can customize your query.

- *Skip the fancy stuff:* Select the Open the Query to View Information option to see the datasheet view.

The wizard runs the query and presents the results in a typical Access datasheet.

To summarize or not to summarize

How does the wizard choose whether or not it feels like summarizing things? Computers are a lot like people. Things that seem arbitrary usually have reasons behind them.

The wizard displays the detail or summary step (shown previously in Figure 12-7) if *either* of these statements is true:

✔ Fields for your query are selected from two tables that have a *one-to-many* relationship with each other. (Chapter 4 explains one-to-many relationships.)

✔ A selected field contains numeric data.

10. Type a title for your query in the text box and then click Finish.

The Wizard builds your query, saves it with the title you entered, and Access displays the results, as shown in Figure 12-10.

Cigars for everyone! You've given birth to a query.

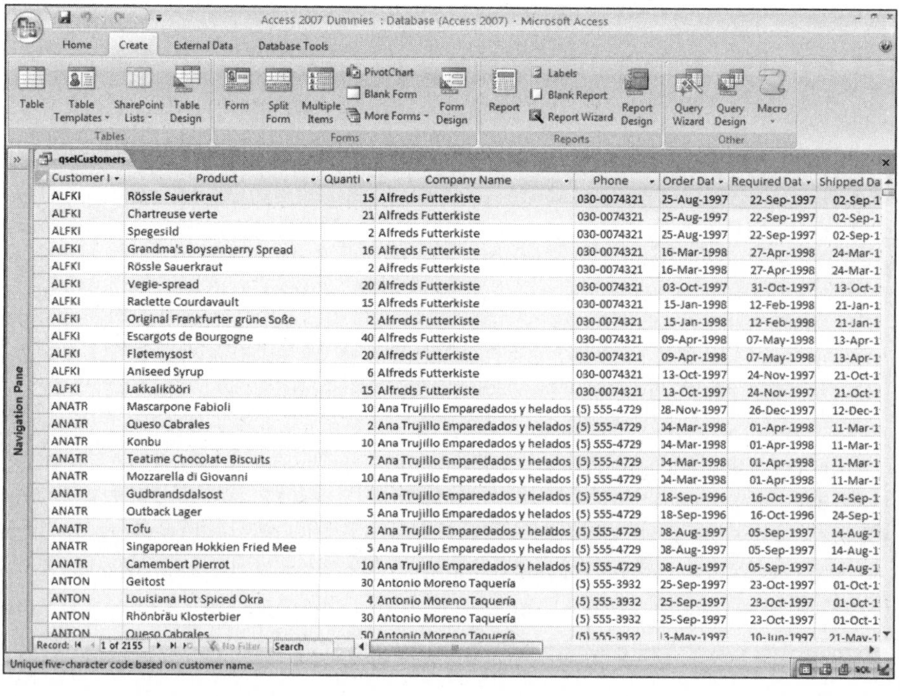

Figure 12-10: The results of a query built with the Query Wizard.

When you finish the steps in this section, the Query Wizard automatically saves your query with this name.

Use this list to modify or use a query created with the Query Wizard:

- ✔ To write complex AND and OR criteria, see Chapter 13.
- ✔ To add calculations like sums and averages, see Chapter 14.
- ✔ To add custom formulas (like a sales tax calculation), see Chapter 15.
- ✔ To attach the query to a report, see Chapter 16.

But what about the other query wizards?

Besides the Simple Query Wizard, Access offers three other query wizards.

- ✔ *Crosstab Wizard* summarizes multiple rows of data into a spreadsheet-like format.

  A Crosstab is similar to an Excel Pivot Table.

- ✔ *Find Duplicates Query Wizard* helps you locate duplicate records in a table or query.

  Talk about stating the obvious! How is this wizard useful? You've received two pieces of the same junk mail right? In my case, one is usually addressed to Ken Cook and the other to Kenneth Cook. The mailer's database thinks we are two different people. If the mailer was using an Access Database to generate customer lists, the mailer could run a find duplicates query on its Customers table on the last name and street address fields. The wizard will locate all records in the customer table that have the exact same last name and street address. Any results returned by that query

are most certainly the same person, or at least two people in the same family. Either way, one can be deleted to eliminate the duplicate mailings.

- ✔ *Unmatched Query Wizard* finds unrelated records in two tables that share a common field.

  If an Orders table contains orders for a customer who isn't in the Customers table, you have yourself a problem — orders in the system and no one to bill. Sounds like a recipe for the unemployment line! How can such a thing happen? *Referential integrity* prevents a child table from containing a record without a corresponding record existing in its parent table. (Chapter 4 covers referential integrity.) If you don't turn Referential Integrity on, it's quite possible to put in an order for a non-existent customer. The Find Unmatched Query Wizard can find records with reference problems and help you get to the bottom of such a dilemma.

Getting Your Feet Wet with Ad Hoc Queries

If you use Access regularly, you need to know how to build a query from scratch. This is where Design view comes into play. Design view may look daunting, but it's really not that bad. I promise!

Figure 12-11 shows a query in Design view:

✔ The top half of the view is where you place the tables you want to query.

✔ The bottom half is called the Design Grid; it contains the field, table, sort, show, and criteria rows used to generate the results.

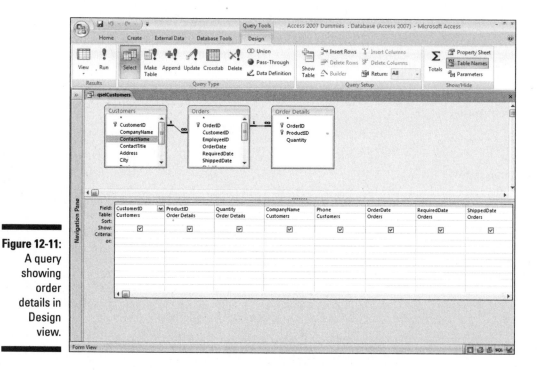

Figure 12-11:
A query showing order details in Design view.

To build a multiple-table query by hand in Design view, follow these steps:

1. **Click the Create tab from the Ribbon.**

   A series of buttons grouped by object type appears on the Ribbon.

2. **From the Other button group, click the Query Design button.**

   The Show Table dialog box appears listing all tables and queries available for your new query.

   Yes, you can query a query.

3. **Add the tables you want in your query:**

   a. *In the Show Table dialog box, double-click the names of each table or query you want.*

   After you double-click a table, a small window for the table appears in the Query Design window (see Figure 12-12).

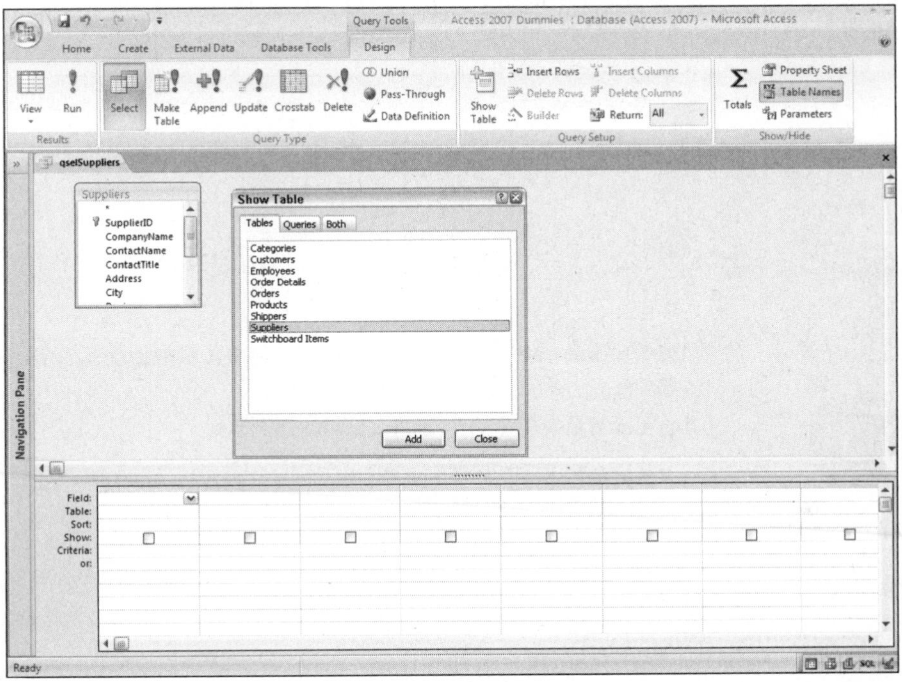

Figure 12-12:
The Suppliers table is added to the ad hoc query.

   b. *After you add the last table you want, click Close.*

   The Show Table dialog box is dismissed.

   In the query window, lines between your tables (as shown in Figure 12-13) show *relationships* between the tables. The sidebar, "Get the right tables," explains how to add and remove tables from a query in Design view.

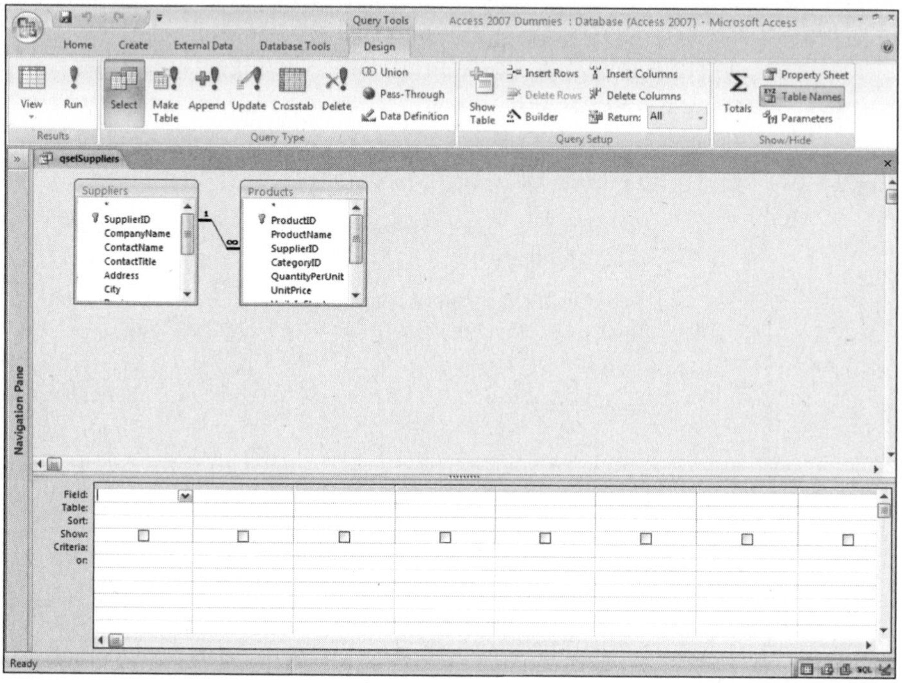

Figure 12-13:
Access
knows how
to link the
Suppliers
and
Products
tables.

4. Double-click each field you want in the list at the top of the Query window.

Consider the following while choosing fields:

- Choose your fields in the order you want them to appear in the query results.

- You can include fields from any or all of the tables at the top of the query window (the tables you selected in the preceding step).

Figure 12-14 shows fields selected form multiple tables in Query Design view.

If you accidentally choose the wrong field you can easily correct your mistake:

a. Click the field name's entry in the query grid.

b. Select the Delete Columns button from the Ribbon.

The field is removed from the query grid.

Now you're ready to put the finishing touches to your query by adding functionality such as sorting. The following section shows you how.

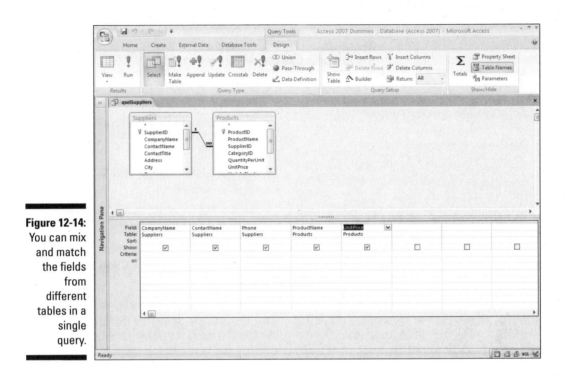

Figure 12-14:
Figure 12-14:
You can mix
and match
the fields
from
different
tables in a
single
query.

Adding the finishing touches

To sort your query results, follow these steps:

1. **Repeat these steps for each field you want to use for sorting:**

   a. Click the Sort box under the field name.

   b. Click the down arrow that appears at the edge of the Sort box.

   c. Click either Ascending or Descending (as shown in Figure 12-15).

   The sidebar "Just these, and in this order" shows how to arrange sort fields. For all you need to know about sorting, see Chapter 11.

2. **In the Criteria row for each field you want to use as criterion, type the criterion appropriate to that field.**

   For example, to show product quantities ordered greater than 50, you would type >**50** in the criteria row under the Quantity field column heading. Table 12-1 shows some criteria examples.

Get the right tables

If you've been a faithful reader from page 1 of this book, you've probably related your selected tables together and saved yourself an extra step when building a query.

That's one of the reasons table relationships are important. Each time you create a new query and select multiple tables, the relationship lines will already be in place for your queries. Database geeks call these relationship lines *join lines* or just plain old *joins*. Without the relationships you'll have to join the tables manually for each new query.

What happens if you create a query but no line appears between the tables? Access is telling you that it doesn't have a clue how to relate the tables. It's possible that you selected the wrong tables — they don't share a common field and therefore cannot be related. If you've selected the wrong tables, follow these steps to delete the unwanted tables and add the correct tables to your query:

1. **Click the title bar of the table that doesn't belong.**

   The * from the table's field list will highlight, indicating that the entire table list window is selected.

2. **Tap the Delete key on your keyboard to remove the table.**

   Repeat Steps 1 and 2 for each table you'd like to remove from the query.

   The Show Table dialog box appears.

3. **Select the correct table or tables for your query.**

If you select the right tables and still get no join lines, then you can go back to the Relationships window and relate the tables correctly. Chapter 4 shows you how. (You can also join tables in Query Design view, but I don't recommend it.)

3. **If you don't want that field to appear in the final results, deselect the check box in the Show row for that field.**

   The Show setting really stands out in your query grid. There's only one check box in there, and that's the Show option.

After you tell the query how to sort and select data, you're ready to see your query results by running the query.

Saving the query

After you create your query, you're ready to save it. Follow these steps:

1. **Review your work one more time. When you're sure it looks good, click the Save button on the Quick Access toolbar to save your query.**

   The Save As dialog box appears.

Just these, and in this order

Access has a nice tool for sorting the results from a query. After all, queries don't get much easier than clicking a little box labeled *Sort* and then telling the program whether Ascending or Descending is your choice for sort-flavor-of-the-moment.

The only problem with this little arrangement is that Access automatically sorts the results from *left* to *right*. If you only request one sort, this order is no big deal. But if you request *two* sorts, the column that's closest to the *left* side of the query automatically becomes the primary sort, with any other field playing second (or third) fiddle.

Taking control of the sort order isn't hard, but it also isn't obvious. Because Access looks at the query grid and performs the sorts from left to right, the trick is to move the column for the main sorting instruction to the left side of the grid. Follow these steps to move a column in the grid:

1. **Put the tip of the mouse pointer in the thin gray box just above the field name on the query grid.**

2. **When the mouse pointer turns into a black downward-pointing arrow, click *once*.**

All of a sudden the chosen field is highlighted and the mouse pointer changes from a downward-pointing black arrow to an upward-pointing white arrow.

3. **While still pointing at the thin gray box just above the field name, hold down the mouse button and drag the field to its new position on the grid.**

As you move the mouse, a black bar moves through the grid, showing you where the field will land when you let up on the mouse button.

4. **When the black bar is in the right place, release the mouse button.**

The field information pops into view, safe and happy in its new home.

This moving trick also changes the order in which the fields appear in your query results. Feel free to move fields here, there, or anywhere, depending on your needs.

Is this some great flexibility or what?

2. **In the Save As dialog box, type a name for the query and then click OK.**

You are saving the design of the query and not the results returned by the query. So as records are added, edited, and deleted from your data tables, the query always returns the data as it is at the moment the query is run.

Running your query

After you create your query and save it, you're ready to run it. Follow these steps:

1. **Take one last look to make sure it's correct.**

   Inspect the fields you've chosen and your other settings in the query grid. The sidebar, "Query troubleshooting," lists common query problems.

2. **Click the Run button (the huge red exclamation point).**

   Did you get the answer you hoped for? If not, take your query back into Design view for some more work. To do so, click the Design View button on the Quick Access toolbar.

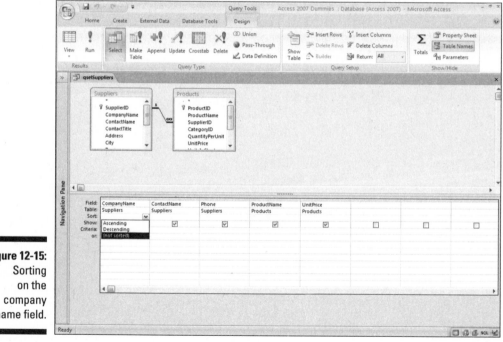

Figure 12-15:
Sorting on the company name field.

TIP

Query troubleshooting

If your query results *aren't* exactly what you thought you asked for (isn't that just like a computer?), double-check your query design for errors. Common design errors include

✔ Mixing up the greater than (>) and less than (<) signs

✔ Leaving out an equals sign (=) in your greater-than-or-equal-to statements

✔ Misspelling criteria such as region name, state, or postal code

✔ Entering criteria in the wrong field

Chapter 13

I'll Take These AND Those OR Them

....

In This Chapter

▶ Understanding the process of setting criteria for your queries

▶ Working with the AND and OR operators

▶ Including AND and OR in the same query

....

As you build larger and more complex databases with Access, your questions about that data become larger and more complex. Changing the order of your records — sorting from A to Z and then from Z to A and filtering it from one or more perspectives — just isn't enough for you or your database. You want more, or to be more accurate, you *need* more from your database, and you need it quickly.

What to do? You can use queries that ask questions (present criteria to the database to see which records meet it) to help you ferret out those records that you need to *access* (pardon the expression) right now.

This chapter shows how to set more specific criteria for your queries, controlling the answers to your database questions with ease and speed. You find out about two very powerful Access operators: AND and OR. what the operators do, how they do it, and (most importantly) when and why to use them.

If AND and OR are not the solutions to your query-building needs, Chapter 12 shows the basics of querying, and may help point you in the right direction. You can create queries automatically, or you can build them from scratch. Chapter 12 gives you some more advanced ideas about queries and helps you craft specialized queries for your specific needs..

Working with AND and/or OR

AND and OR are the most powerful and popular of the *Boolean* terms.

In written language, you probably know when to use *and* versus *or*. If you're not sure how this knowledge can be transferred to your use of Access, read on:

- ✔ AND is used when all the items in a list are to be chosen. For example, "bring a salad, side dish, and a dessert to the potluck dinner" would tell the person to bring all three items to the dinner.

- ✔ OR creates a list wherein each item is a choice — "bring a salad, side dish, or a dessert to the potluck dinner." In this example, the person reading the instruction would know that only one item need be brought, but they can bring one or more (or all) of the items if they so choose.

  With the OR example, you'll be spending less time in the kitchen, and with OR in your query, you'll be making it possible for more of the records to meet your criteria. Using our employee database as an example, your query might say, "Give me all the people who work in Accounting AND Operations" — and none of the employee records would meet that criteria, because nobody works in two departments at the same time. However, using OR would work: "Give me all the people who work in Accounting OR Operations" would provide a list of all the employees in the two departments.

Boolean logic (named for the guy who invented it) allows you to use words like AND, OR, NOT, LESS THAN, GREATER THAN, and EQUAL TO to search a database. In Access, these terms are called *operators*.

If you're not sure you can remember when to use AND versus OR, think of it this way:

- ✔ AND **narrows your query.** Fewer records match.

  In normal usage, *and* gives you no options. You do *everything* in the list.

- ✔ OR **widens your query.** More records match.

  In normal usage, *or* gives you more options because you can pick and choose which items from the list you want to do.

As an example, in Access, if you're searching a customer database and you say you want customers who live in a particular city *and* who live in a particular zip code *and* who have purchased more than $50,000 worth of items in the past year, you're probably going to end up with a short list of customers — you'll have fewer options. On the other hand, if you want customers who are in a particular city *or* a particular zip code *or* who have purchased more than $50,000 in goods this year, you'll get many more choices — everyone from the city, zip code, and over that purchasing level — probably many more customers than the *and* query will give you.

Data from here to there

One of the most common Access queries involves listing items that are between two values.

Here's an example. You may want to find all the people in an employee database who were hired between January 1996 and January 2006. For this list of records, you need to use AND criteria to establish the range. Here's how you do it:

✔ Put the two conditions (on or after December 31, 2005 and before January 2, 2006) together on the same line.

✔ Separate the conditions with an AND operator.

Figure 13-1 shows the query window for this range of DateHired dates.

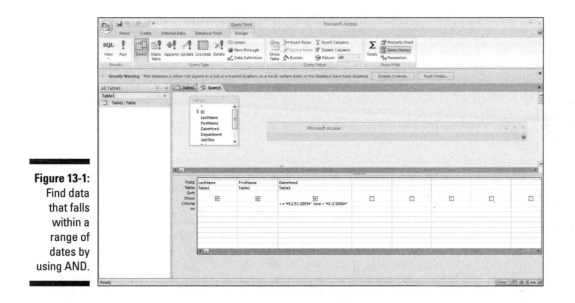

Figure 13-1: Find data that falls within a range of dates by using AND.

Don't worry about the pound signs (#) — Access puts those in automatically for you.

Here's what's going on in x:

1. Access begins processing the query by looking through the records in the table and asking the first question in the criteria:

   Was the record entered on or after December 31, 2005?

   - If the record was entered before this date, Access ignores the record and goes on to the next record.
   - If the record was entered on or after the date, Access goes to Step 2.

2. If the record was entered on or after December 31, 2005, Access asks the second question:

   Was the record entered before January 2, 2006?

   - If yes, Access includes the record in the results.
   - If no, the record is rejected, and Access moves on to the next record.

   Access repeats Step 1 and Step 2 for all of the records in the table

3. When Access hits the last record in the database, the query's results appear.

You could also use "less than" (>) for the first date which would allow the query to include only records for those employees hired after December 31st, 2005 — the omission of the equal sign (=) eliminates those records with a December 31st 2005 date in the Date Hired field.

This type of "between" instruction works for any type of data. You can list numeric values that fall between two other numbers, names that fall in a range of letters, or dates that fall in a given area of the calendar.

You could also search for dates by using the BETWEEN operator (see Figure 13-2 for an example of BETWEEN in action). The criteria BETWEEN #12/31/2005# AND #1/1/2006# selects records if the dates land on or between December 31, 2005, and January 1, 2006, a span of three days.

Using multiple levels of AND

Overall, Access lets you do whatever you want in a query — and for that reason, flexibility really adds to the application's power.

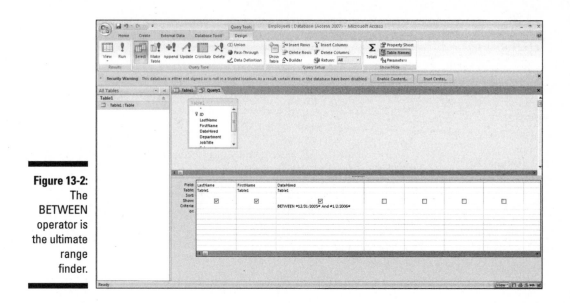

Figure 13-2:
The
BETWEEN
operator is
the ultimate
range
finder.

Access doesn't limit you to just *one* criterion in each line of a query — you can include as many criteria as you want, even if by adding more and more criteria you end up whittling your results down to one record, or even no records. When you add multiple criteria, Access treats the criteria as if you typed an AND between each one.

All that power can backfire on you. Each AND criterion that you add must sit together on the same row. When you run the query, Access checks each record to make sure that it matches all the expressions in the given criteria row of the query before putting that record into the result table. Figure 13-3 shows a query that uses three criteria. Because all the criteria sit together on a single row, Access treats the three criteria as if they were part of a big AND statement. This query returns only employees who were hired before January 1, 2006, AND who make more than $20,000 per year, AND who work in the Accounting department.

When you have a very large database and want to restrict your results to a minimum of records, combining a few criteria is the most useful way to go.

Really want to whittle that list of records down? Because Access displays the query results in datasheet view, all the datasheet view tools work with the query — including filters! Just use any of the filter commands (use the Filter tool group's buttons to filter by Selection, for example) to limit your query results. (If you need a quick refresher on filters, flip back to Chapter 11.)

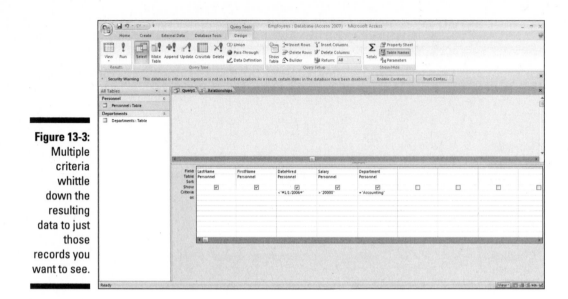

Figure 13-3:
Multiple criteria whittle down the resulting data to just those records you want to see.

Establishing criteria with OR

When you want to find a group of records that match one of several possibilities, such as employees who work in *either* Sales *or* Marketing, you need the OR criteria. It's the master of multiple options.

Access makes using OR criteria easy. Because the OR option is built right into the Access query dialog box, you can just

✔ Choose the field on which to query the data.

✔ Indicate which values to look for.

To make a group of criteria work together as a big OR statement, list each criterion on its own line at the bottom of the query, as shown in Figure 13-4. Here you see that employee records for those people in the Sales OR Marketing OR Operations department will meet the query's criteria.

Each line can include criterion for whichever fields you want, even if another line in the query *already* has a criterion in that field. (This is easier than it sounds.)

Of course, you can list the criteria in different columns, as shown in Figure 13-5. Here, we see a query that searches for people working in the Sales department (Department field) OR who earn more than $50,000 per year (Salary field).

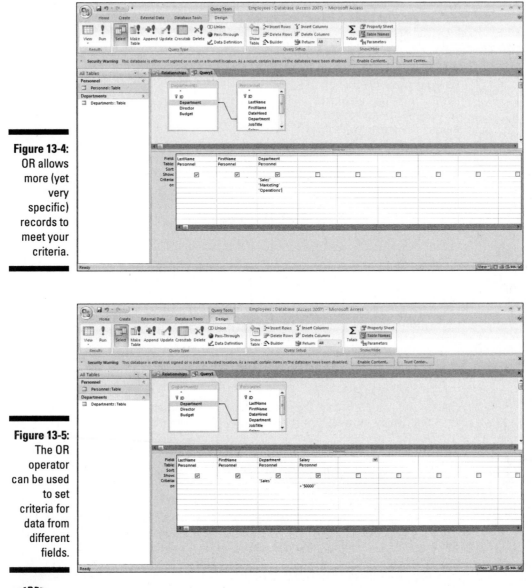

Figure 13-4: OR allows more (yet very specific) records to meet your criteria.

Figure 13-5: The OR operator can be used to set criteria for data from different fields.

Each OR criterion is on a separate line. If the criteria are on the same line, you are performing an AND operation — only records that match both rules appear.

Combining AND with OR and OR with AND

When it comes to combining the use of AND and OR operators, Access can bend like a contortionist (ouch!). When the AND and OR operators by themselves aren't enough, you can combine them within a single field or in multiple fields in one or more tables.

These logically complex queries get really complex, really fast. You can end up confused as to why certain records came back in your results — or worse, why certain records didn't make the cut. If a query grows to the point that you're losing track of which AND the last OR affected, you're in over your head, and it's time to start over again.

Instead of adding layer upon layer of conditions into a single query, you can break down your question into a series of smaller queries that build on each other:

1. **Begin with a simple query with one or two criteria.**

2. **Build another query that starts with the first query's results.**

3. **If you need more refining, create a third query that chews on the second query's answers.**

   Each successive query whittles down your results until the final set of records appears.

   This procedure lets you double-check every step of your logic, so it minimizes the chance of any errors accidentally slipping into your results. You can also use it to build on an existing query, adding more criteria and including more or different fields in the query — just open the previously-created query and begin working on it as though it was a new query in progress.

Each OR line (each line within the query) is evaluated separately, so that all the records that are returned by a single line will appear in the final results. If you want to combine several different criteria, make sure that each OR line represents one aspect of what you're searching.

For example, in the Employees database, querying which people earn less than $50,000 or more than $20,000 per year requires the OR condition, and using an OR condition means that the criteria go on separate lines.

Imagine, however, that you want to find only the people who earn within that range (querying the Salary field) but who also work in a particular Department or who have received a particular Rating at their last review. For such a query to work, you need to repeat the Salary information on each OR line.

To set up this query, you need criteria on separate lines:

✔ One line asks for people who earn within the stated range (Salary).

✔ The other criteria gives you people based on the Department (Sales or Marketing) or Rating (greater than 7.5) field.

Because the criteria are on different lines, Access treats them as a big OR statement. Figure 13-6 shows this combination of AND and OR operators in action.

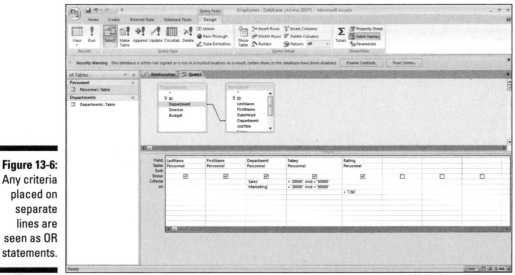

Figure 13-6: Any criteria placed on separate lines are seen as OR statements.

When reviewing your query criteria, keep these points in mind:

✔ Separately, make sure each line represents a group that you want included in the final answer.

✔ Check that the individual lines work together to give you the answer you're seeking:

• AND criteria all go on the same line and are evaluated together.

• OR criteria go on separate lines. Each line is evaluated separately.

• Criteria that you want to use in each OR statement must be repeated on each separate line in the query grid.

Chapter 14

Queries That Think Faster Than You

*E*ver need to know how many orders were placed in the past month? Or total dollar sales for last year? How about the top ten best-selling products for the current year? If you answered yes to any of these questions or have similar questions that need answering, then this chapter is for you. Here I discuss the ever-wonderful Total row. The Total row slices, dices, and makes julienne fries out of your data! Well, actually, it summarizes your data via the select query. If you don't know what a select query is or how to create one, I suggest you go back and read Chapter 12 before beginning the material in this chapter.

Kissing That Calculator Goodbye via the Total Row

In Chapter 12, I show you how simple select queries can fetch data, such as a list of customers who reside in California or all the details of tofu sales. The Total row takes the select query one step further and summarizes the selected data. The Total row can answer questions like, "How many of our customers reside in California?" and "How much money did we make in tofu sales last month?" It can also do statistical calculations, such as standard deviations, variances, and maximum and minimum values. For a complete list of what the Total row can do, see Table 14-1.

To coerce Access into performing these calculations, you must group records together by using the Total row's Group By function. The Total row is seen in Figure 14-1. As you might imagine, Group By treats multiple repeated information as one. It puts all the Californians together on one row so that you can count the number of Californians in your database. Typically, you apply Group By to a text or ID field and the remaining functions in the total row on numeric fields.

Table 14-1	Total Row Functions
Function	**What It Does**
Group By	Groups the query results by the field's values
Sum	Totals all the values from this field in the query results
Avg	Averages the values in this field in your query results
Min	Tells you the lowest value found in the field
Max	Reports the highest value found in the field
Count	Counts the number of records that match the query criteria
StDev	Figures the statistical standard deviation of the values in the field
Var	Calculates the statistical variance of the values in the field
First	Displays the first record that meets the query criteria
Last	Displays the last matching record that Access finds
Expression	Tells Access that you want a calculated field (See Chapter 15 for the different calculations Access can perform.)
Where	Uses this field for record selection criteria but doesn't summarize anything with it

The most commonly used tools among the Total row's offerings are Group By, Sum, Avg, Count, and the odd-sounding option Where. Later sections in this chapter go into more depth about these items, explaining what they do, how to use them, and why you really *do* care about all this stuff.

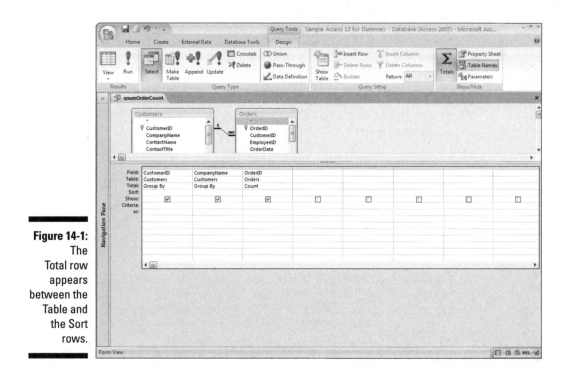

Figure 14-1:
The
Total row
appears
between the
Table and
the Sort
rows.

Adding the Total Row to Your Queries

By default, Access always thinks you want a simple select query. You must specifically tell it you want to summarize your data by adding the Total row to your query.

Okay, enough chatter about the Total row; it's time to get busy. Make sure you are in design view, then follow these steps to create summary queries with the Total row:

1. **Create a new select query or open an existing select query that contains the data you want to summarize..**

   If you're scratching your head at this point, go to Chapter 12 for an explanation of creating select queries.

2. **Turn on the Total row by clicking the Totals tool in the Show/Hide group of tools.**

   The Total row appears between the Table and Sort rows on the query grid. For every field already in your query Access automatically fills the Total row with its default entry, Group By.

The Totals button displays the Greek letter sigma (Σ). Mathematicians, engineers, and others with questionable communication skills use this symbol when they mean "give me a total."

3. **To change a field's Total entry from Group By to something else, click that field's Total row.**

   The blinking-line cursor appears in the Total row, right next to a down-arrow button.

4. **Click the down-arrow button in the field's Total row and then select the new Total entry you want from the drop-down list.**

   The new entry appears in the Total row.

5. **Make any other changes you want and then run the query.**

   With the Total line in action, the query results automatically include the summary (or summaries) you selected. How about that?

The following section shows how to use the most popular and useful Total row options.

Giving the Total Row a Workout

This section focuses on the most commonly used options in the Total row's toolbox: Group By, Sum, Count, and Where.

Unless you are a statistician or scientist, the information in this chapter should suffice for all your Total row needs. However, even though we don't discuss standard deviations or variances, they work the same way as Sum or Count. Check the Access help system (press F1 on your keyboard) for more on the less-popular Total row functions.

Most of the Total row options perform well by themselves, but they also work well with others. When running multiple queries, try mixing different options together to save yourself time. It takes some practice to ensure that everything works the way you want, but the benefits (more information with less effort) make up for the investment.

Organizing things with Group By

The Group By instruction has two functions:

✔ To organize your query results into groups based on the values in one or more fields.

✔ To eliminate duplicate entries in your results.

When you turn on the Total row in your query grid, Access automatically puts in a Group By for every field on the grid. Group By combines like records so that the other Total row instructions, such as Sum and Count, can do their thing. So to make effective use of the Total row, your query must return one or more fields that contain duplicate information across records.

✔ Putting a single Group By instruction in a query tells Access to total your results by each unique value in that field (by each customer number or product name, for instance). Each unique item appears only once in the results, on a single line with its summary info.

✔ If you include more than one Group By instruction in a single query (like the one shown in Figure 14-2), Access builds a summary line for every unique combination of the fields with the Group By instruction.

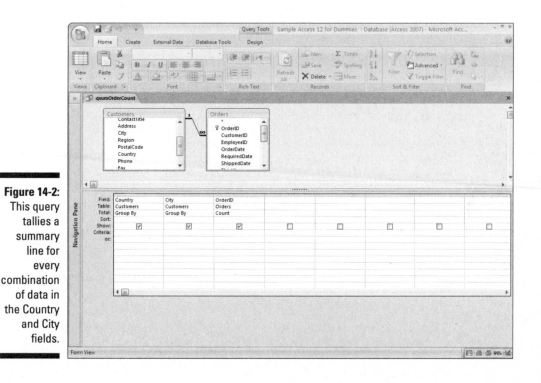

Figure 14-2:
This query tallies a summary line for every combination of data in the Country and City fields.

Don't see what you expect in your results?

Sometimes when I run a summary query a few lines are "missing." I expect to see them, but they just aren't there. That begs the question "Why?" Usually it's because of the type of *join* between tables in my query. The default join is called an inner join. This means that there must be matching records in both tables for a row to display in the query. So for a customer to show on an orders count query that joins the customer and order tables, the customer must have at least one order in the orders table. If I want a query to show customers who do not yet have an order placed, I need to change the type of join to what is called an *outer* join.

To change join types, display the Join Properties dialog box by double-clicking the line that connects the two tables. You have to be good with the mouse on this one. If you miss the join line, nothing will happen. This can be one of those throw-a-brick-at-your-computer moments. However, don't despair. Just point to the line once again and double-click. If the tip of the mouse is on the line, the Join Properties dialog will pop up.

Read options 2 and 3 carefully and select whichever one is appropriate for your situation. Each option will create an outer join. In my example above, the option that reads "2: Include ALL records from 'Customers' and only those records from 'Orders' where the joined fields are equal" would be correct. This option displays all customers regardless of their order situation. So, I'll see 0 next to each customer who has yet to order plus an order count next to those who have ordered.

Put the Group By instruction into the field you want to summarize — the one that answers the question, "What do you want to count *by?*" or "What needs totaling?" For example, to count California customers you need to group on the State field in your table. To produce a list of total dollar sales by product within each state or province you need to group by the State and Product fields.

When you use Group By, Access automatically sorts the results in order based on the field with the Group By instruction. If you put Group By in the State/Province field, for example, Access sorts your results alphabetically by the contents of that field. To override this behavior and choose a different sorting order, use the Sort row in your query grid, as shown in Figure 14-3:

1. **Choose the field that you want to sort everything by.**

2. **Put the appropriate sorting command (ascending or descending, depending on your needs) in that field's Sort row.**

   Access automatically organizes the query results in the right order.

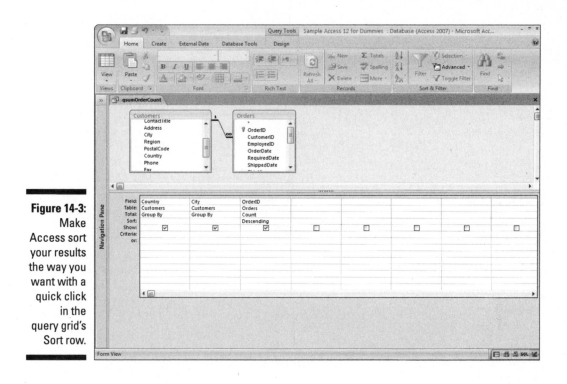

Figure 14-3:
Make
Access sort
your results
the way you
want with a
quick click
in the
query grid's
Sort row.

Performing sums

Sum finds the total value of numeric fields:

- ✔ When you put the Sum instruction in a field, Access totals the values in that field.

- ✔ If you use the Sum instruction all by itself in a query grid, Access calculates a grand total of the values in that field for the entire table.

- ✔ By pairing a Sum instruction with a Group By instruction (as shown in Figure 14-4), your results display a sum for each unique entry in the Group By field.

- ✔ Pair the Sum instruction with any other Total row option to get more than one summary for each line of your results. Count and Sum naturally go together, as do Sum and Avg (Average), Min (Minimum value) and Max (Maximum value).

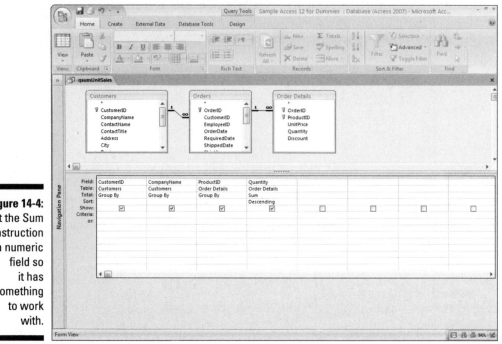

Figure 14-4:
Put the Sum instruction in a numeric field so it has something to work with.

To limit the range of the records totaled in Sum, use the Where instruction (described later in this chapter).

Counting, the easy way

Use the Count instruction in the query when you want to know how many entries are in the group, not how much.

Because Count doesn't attempt any math on a field's data, it works with any field in your tables.

When used by itself in a query (as shown in Figure 14-5), Count tallies the number of entries in a particular field across every record in the entire table and then displays the answer. By using Count with one or more Group By instructions in other fields, Access counts the number of items relating to each unique entry in the Group By field.

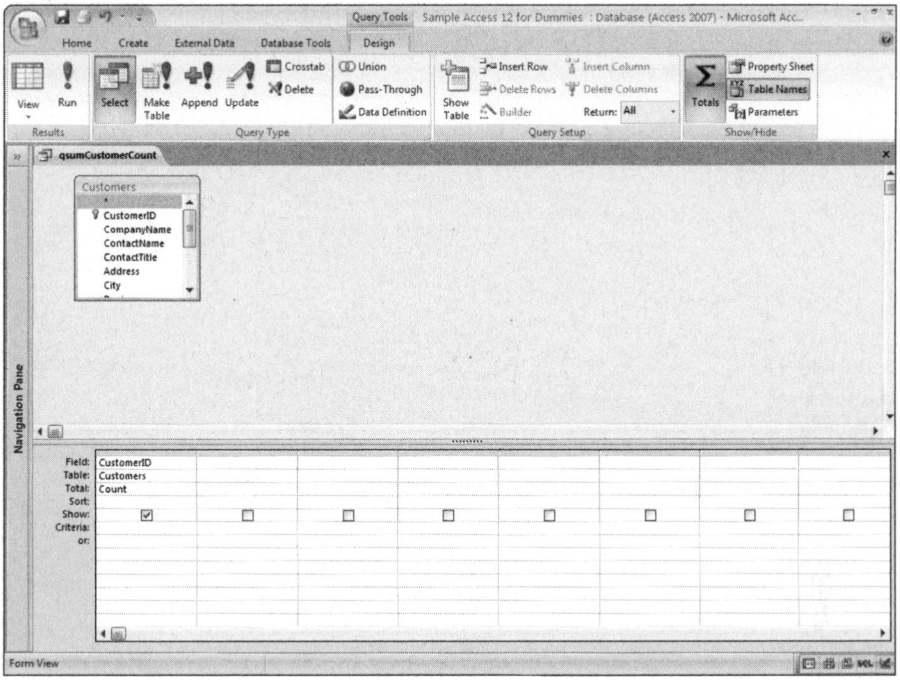

Figure 14-5:
Use Count
on a single
field to
easily count
the number
of records in
a table.

For a quick and accurate count of the number of records in a group, point the Group By and Count instructions at the same field in your query grid, as shown in Figure 14-6. To be part of the group, the records need matching data in a certain field. Because you *know* that the field for your Group By instruction contains something (namely, the data that defines groups for the query results), that field is a perfect candidate for the Count instruction as well. Add the field to your query grid a second time by choosing the same field name again in a new column and then selecting Count in the Total row.

Apply a calculation to a field and Access tacks on a newfangled word like SumOf or CountOf or <insert calculation name here>Of to the beginning of the field name in Datasheet view. To insert your own more meaningful column heading, type the heading followed by a colon (as in Order Count:) in front of the field name on the query grid (see Figure 14-7).

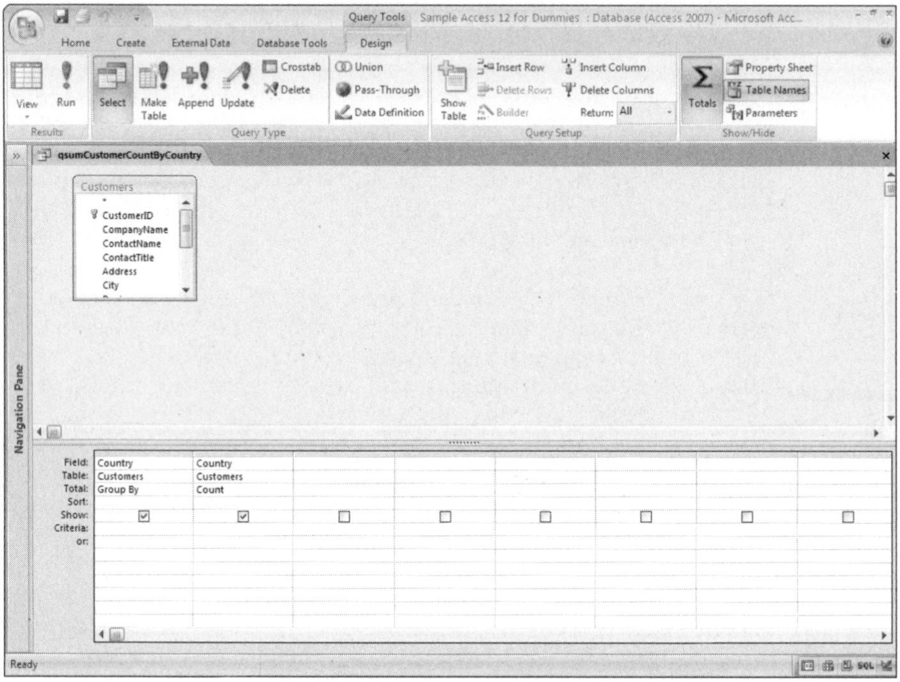

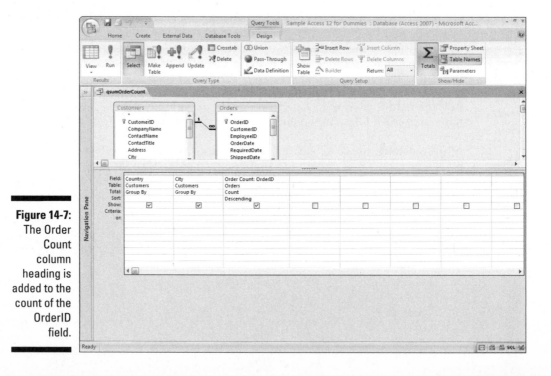

Figure 14-6:
This query
easily
counts the
number of
customers
in each
country.

Figure 14-7:
The Order
Count
column
heading is
added to the
count of the
OrderID
field.

Narrowing the results with Where

The Where instruction works a bit differently than the other options in the Total row. The Where instruction lets you add criteria to the query (such as showing customers from certain states, or including orders placed only after a certain date) without including additional fields in your results. In fact, Access won't allow you to show a field in your query results that contains the Where instruction.

The query in Figure 14-8 uses a Where instruction to limit which records appear in the query results. Normally, that query would count orders by customer using every record in the table. Adding a Where instruction to the Country field tells the query that it needs to test the data before including it in the results. In this case, the Where instruction's criteria include records for those people living in the United States or Great Britain (the data in Country matches either USA or UK).

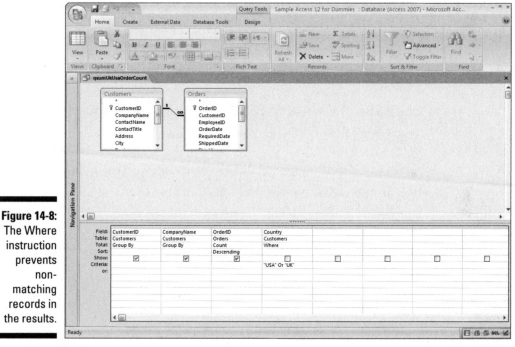

Figure 14-8: The Where instruction prevents non-matching records in the results.

Creating Your Own Top-Ten List

Here's a problem that is a snap to solve with Access. You need a list of the top ten customers in dollar sales. Or a list of the top five best-selling products last year. Or a list of the top whatever. The query property Top Values takes all the dirty work out of this chore. Simply set it and forget it — the dirty work that is! You can return the top values (like top 5 which will return top 5 out of a list of 40) or top percentage of values (like top 5% which will return top 2 out of 40) with the Top Values properly.

Follow these instructions to make a top-ten (or whatever number you choose) list:

1. **Open the query containing the data for your top values list in Design view.**

   The query must contain at least one numerical field so that a set of top values can be selected. Usually, it is a summary query such as total dollar sales by customer.

2. **Right-click an open area on the top half of the grid (away from any table or query windows).**

3. **Choose Properties from the shortcut menu.**

   The Property Sheet window appears, chock-full of query properties.

4. **Click in the Top Values box on or near the default of All.**

   The cursor blinks in the row and a drop-down list arrow appears to the right.

5. **Select a choice from the list or type your own number in the box.**

   Because 10 isn't on the list, you'll need to type **10** in the box to generate a top-ten list (see Figure 14-9).

6. **Switch to Datasheet view.**

   The list is limited to the top values based on the number or percentage you entered in the box.

The Top Values property doesn't automatically sort the results. If you tell Access to show you the top 10 customers in dollar sales based on a field called DolAmount, you'll get them — but not necessarily in the correct order. Choose Descending in the Sort row of the DolAmount field to have Access order them for you from highest to lowest.

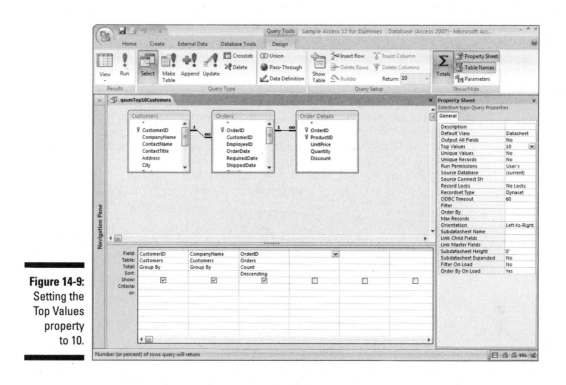

Figure 14-9:
Setting the
Top Values
property
to 10.

Choosing the Right Field for the Summary Instruction

Deciding which field gets a Sum, Count, or other Total row instruction *greatly* affects your query results. If you choose the wrong field, Access fails to tally things correctly.

Follow these guidelines when choosing fields for your summary queries:

✔ Don't apply summary functions that require numbers to calculate (such as Sum and Avg) to a text field. You'll get the ever popular "Data type mismatch" error if you do.

✔ Fields with repetitive information (such as order date or customer ID) make excellent group by fields. For example, if you group by order date and count the customer ID field, you'll get a count of orders per day.

✔ When counting records, choose a field that contains data for each record. If you don't, Access will exclude the blank fields in its count.

Figure 14-10 shows a summary query that has been written to count customers. The Count instruction has been applied to both the Region and CustomerID fields of the Customers table. The Region field returns 31, while the CustomerID field returns 91. Which is right? The latter is correct because each record in the table has a customer ID. Not every record has a region specified. So, Access counts only the records for which Region has been entered for a customer. Choose your fields wisely to avoid this problem.

The Totals row takes some getting used to. But in no time, you'll master the power of this tool in your queries. When that day comes, say goodbye to your old friends, Mr. Spreadsheet and Mr. Calculator, forever!

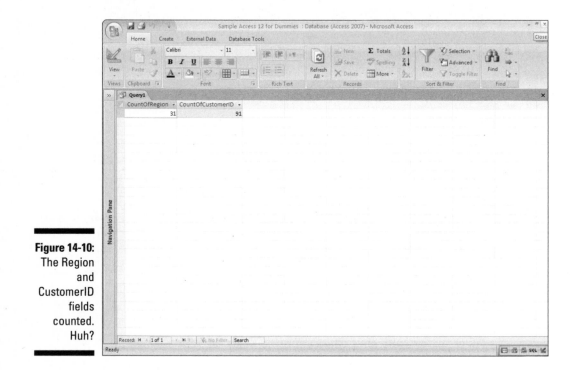

Figure 14-10: The Region and CustomerID fields counted. Huh?

Chapter 15

Calculating with Your Data

*E*fficient database design requires that tables contain only necessary fields. Too many fields can cause a table to load slowly — you won't notice the difference with a few hundred records, but you certainly will with a few hundred thousand. Too many fields can also eat up precious disk space. So what fields are often added to a table's design unnecessarily? Fields that could be generated from calculations on data stored in other fields.

For example, suppose you have a products table with a unit price field and an orders table with number of units ordered field. You may be tempted to add an amount field to your orders table that stores the product of the unit price and the quantity ordered. This is unnecessary because Access can perform these calculations on the fly in what's called a *calculated field*.

A *calculated field* takes information from another field in the database and performs some arithmetic to come up with new information. In fact, a calculated field can take data from more than one field and combine information to create an entirely new field if that's what you want. You can perform simple arithmetic, like addition and multiplication, or use Access's built-in functions, such as Sum and Avg (average), for more difficult calculations. For more on using the built-in functions, see Chapter 14.

In this chapter, you build all kinds of calculations into your queries. From simple sums to complex equations, the information you need is right here.

Although the examples in this chapter deal with calculated fields in queries, the same concept applies to calculated fields in forms and reports.

A Simple Calculation

The first step when creating a calculated field (also know as an *expression* by Access) in a query is to include the tables that contain the fields you need for your calculation. In the preceding example, the product unit price was in the products table, and the quantity ordered was in the orders table. So, a query to calculate unit price multiplied by product price must include both the products and orders tables. Access can't pull the numbers out of thin air for the calculation, so you must make sure the fields that contain the numbers are present in your query.

Access uses a special syntax for building calculated fields. Here's how to create a calculated field:

1. **Click an empty column in the Field row of the query grid.**

   The good old cursor will blink in the row. Access puts the results of the calculation in the same grid position as the calculation itself, so if the calculation sits in the third column of your query grid, the calculation's results will be in the third column, too.

2. **Enter a name for your calculation followed by a colon (:).**

   Access will refer to this calculation from now on by whatever you enter before the colon. Keep it short and sweet, like **Amount** or **Tax**, so it's easier to refer to later on. If you don't name your calculation, Access will put the generic Expr (followed by a number) as its name. It has to be called something, so why not Expr1 or Expr2, right?

3. **Enter your calculation, substituting field names for the actual numbers where necessary.**

   My Amount calculated field would look something like (well, exactly like) the calculation in Figure 15-1.

You don't have to exclusively use field names in your calculations. You can also enter formulas with numbers, like this:

```
Tax: Quantity * UnitPrice * .06
```

If a field name contains more than one word, put square brackets around it. Access treats anything else it finds in the calculation as a constant (which is the math term for *it is what it is and it never changes*). If the field name contains no spaces, Access will put the square brackets in for you after you enter the field name. That's why I always use one-word field names — so I don't have to type those darned square brackets.

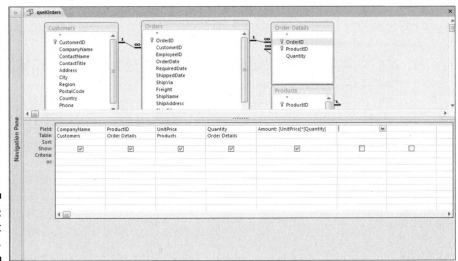

Figure 15-1:
The Amount
calculation.

When creating formulas, keep these general guidelines in mind:

- ✔ **You must manually type the field names and constants into your formula.** You can't just drag and drop stuff from the table list.

- ✔ **Don't worry if your calculation grows past the edge of the Field box.** Access still remembers everything, even if it doesn't appear on the screen.

  To make the query column wider, aim the mouse pointer at the line on the right side of the thin bar above the calculation entry. When you get it right over the line, the pointer changes into a line with a horizontal arrow through it. When that happens, click and drag the mouse to the right. As you do, the column expands according to your movements. To fit the width to just the right size, position the mouse to size the column as described above then double-click!

- ✔ **If it's a really, really, really long calculation, press Shift+F2 while the cursor is somewhere on the calculation.**

  This opens the Zoom dialog box so that you can easily see and edit everything in a pop-up window.

When you run a query containing a calculation, Access

- ✔ Produces a datasheet showing the fields you specified

- ✔ Adds a new column for each calculated field

In Figure 15-2, the datasheet shows the customer name, product, unit price, quantity, and the calculated field amount for each item ordered.

Company Name	Product	Unit Pric	Quanti	Amount
QUICK-Stop	Chai	$18.00	45	$810.00
Rattlesnake Canyon Grocery	Chai	$18.00	18	$324.00
Lonesome Pine Restaurant	Chai	$18.00	20	$360.00
Die Wandernde Kuh	Chai	$18.00	15	$270.00
Pericles Comidas clásicas	Chai	$18.00	12	$216.00
Chop-suey Chinese	Chai	$18.00	15	$270.00
Queen Cozinha	Chai	$18.00	10	$180.00
La maison d'Asie	Chai	$18.00	24	$432.00
Princesa Isabel Vinhos	Chai	$18.00	15	$270.00
Lehmanns Marktstand	Chai	$18.00	40	$720.00
Wartian Herkku	Chai	$18.00	8	$144.00
Tortuga Restaurante	Chai	$18.00	10	$180.00
Mère Paillarde	Chai	$18.00	20	$360.00
Du monde entier	Chai	$18.00	3	$54.00
Wolski Zajazd	Chai	$18.00	6	$108.00
Blondel père et fils	Chai	$18.00	25	$450.00
Hungry Owl All-Night Grocers	Chai	$18.00	15	$270.00
Berglunds snabbköp	Chai	$18.00	35	$630.00
QUICK-Stop	Chai	$18.00	30	$540.00
Save-a-lot Markets	Chai	$18.00	5	$90.00
LINO-Delicateses	Chai	$18.00	50	$900.00
North/South	Chai	$18.00	8	$144.00
LINO-Delicateses	Chai	$18.00	4	$72.00
Save-a-lot Markets	Chai	$18.00	80	$1,440.00
HILARIÓN-Abastos	Chai	$18.00	20	$360.00

Record: 1 of 25   No Filter   Search

Figure 15-2: The results of the amount calculation in Datasheet view.

Complex Calculations

After getting the hang of simple calculations, you can easily expand your repertoire into more powerful operations, such as using multiple calculations and building expressions that use values from other calculations in the same query. This stuff really adds to the flexibility and power of queries.

Calculate until you need to calculate no more!

Access makes it easy to put multiple separate calculations into a single query. After building the first calculation, just repeat the process in the next empty Field box. Keep inserting calculations across the query grid until you've calculated everything you need.

You can use the same field in several calculations. Access doesn't mind at all.

Using one calculation in another

One of the most powerful calculated field tricks involves using the solution from one calculated field as part of another calculation in the same query. This is sometimes called a *nested* calculation. The calculation both

- ✔ Creates a field in the query results
- ✔ Supplies data to other calculations in the same query, just like a real field in the table

Figure 15-3 shows an example of a nested calculation in Design view.

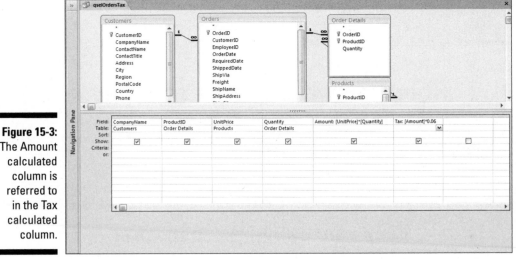

Figure 15-3: The Amount calculated column is referred to in the Tax calculated column.

Figure 15-4 shows the actual results of the calculations.

Although this technique seems simple, tread carefully. A small error in one calculation can quickly trickle down to other calculations that are based on it, compounding a simple error into a huge mistake.

To use the results from one calculation as part of another, just use the name of the first calculation as if it were a field name. In short, treat the first calculation like a field in your table.

qselOrdersTax

Company Name	Product	Unit Pric	Quanti	Amount	Tax
QUICK-Stop	Chai	$18.00	45	$810.00	$48.60
Rattlesnake Canyon Grocery	Chai	$18.00	18	$324.00	$19.44
Lonesome Pine Restaurant	Chai	$18.00	20	$360.00	$21.60
Die Wandernde Kuh	Chai	$18.00	15	$270.00	$16.20
Pericles Comidas clásicas	Chai	$18.00	12	$216.00	$12.96
Chop-suey Chinese	Chai	$18.00	15	$270.00	$16.20
Queen Cozinha	Chai	$18.00	10	$180.00	$10.80
La maison d'Asie	Chai	$18.00	24	$432.00	$25.92
Princesa Isabel Vinhos	Chai	$18.00	15	$270.00	$16.20
Lehmanns Marktstand	Chai	$18.00	40	$720.00	$43.20
Wartian Herkku	Chai	$18.00	8	$144.00	$8.64
Tortuga Restaurante	Chai	$18.00	10	$180.00	$10.80
Mère Paillarde	Chai	$18.00	20	$360.00	$21.60
Du monde entier	Chai	$18.00	3	$54.00	$3.24
Wolski Zajazd	Chai	$18.00	6	$108.00	$6.48
Blondel père et fils	Chai	$18.00	25	$450.00	$27.00
Hungry Owl All-Night Grocers	Chai	$18.00	15	$270.00	$16.20
Berglunds snabbköp	Chai	$18.00	35	$630.00	$37.80
QUICK-Stop	Chai	$18.00	30	$540.00	$32.40
Save-a-lot Markets	Chai	$18.00	5	$90.00	$5.40
LINO-Delicateses	Chai	$18.00	50	$900.00	$54.00
North/South	Chai	$18.00	8	$144.00	$8.64
LINO-Delicateses	Chai	$18.00	4	$72.00	$4.32
Save-a-lot Markets	Chai	$18.00	80	$1,440.00	$86.40
HILARIÓN-Abastos	Chai	$18.00	20	$360.00	$21.60

Record: 1 of 25 No Filter Search

Figure 15-4: The results of the Amount and Tax calculated columns.

Using parameter queries to ask for help

At times, you may want to include a value in a formula that doesn't exist anywhere in your database (for example, the number .06 for 6 percent tax rate in the calculation example earlier in this chapter). If you know the value, you can type it directly into the formula.

Keep your calculations in order

You've written your formula and don't see the answer you expect to see. You double check the formula and it seems correct. How can the formula be correct yet the result wrong? If you have more than one mathematical operation in a calculated expression, Access will follow these rules (called the *order of operations*) when determining the results of your expression.

- All operations in parentheses are calculated first.
- Exponents (^) are calculated second.
- Multiplication (*) and division (/) are calculated third.
- Addition (+) and subtraction (-) are calculated fourth.

For example, you might expect the formula 2+3*6 to equal 30. However, due to the order of operations (multiplication before addition), Access will return 20. To make Access generate the expected result, the formula must be entered as (2+3)*6.

But what if the number changes all the time? You don't want to constantly alter a query. That's a big waste of time and effort. Instead of building the ever-changing number into your formula, why not make Access *ask* you for the number (called a *parameter*) when you run the query? This is an easy one:

1. **Think of an appropriate name for the value (such as Tax Rate, Last Price, or Discount).**

   When choosing a name for your parameter, don't use the name of an existing field in your table — Access will ignore the parameter if you do. Instead, go with something that describes the number or value itself. As you can see in the query grid shown in Figure 15-5, entering something like `[Enter discount as decimal]` makes it very clear what is required from the user. When you look at this query months (or even years) from now, you can easily recognize that something called `[Enter discount percentage as decimal]` probably is a value that Access asks for when the query runs, not a normal field.

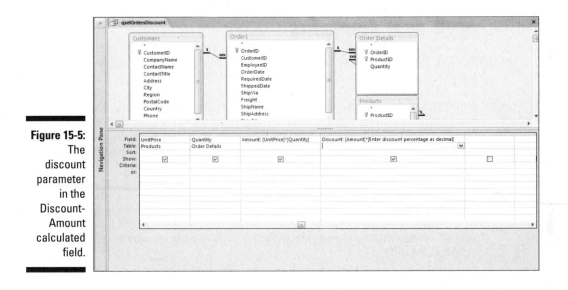

Figure 15-5: The discount parameter in the Discount-Amount calculated field.

2. **Use the name in your formula as if it were a regular field.**

   Put square brackets around it and place it into your calculation, just like you did with the other fields.

3. **Run the query.**

   Access displays a dialog box like the one shown in Figure 15-6.

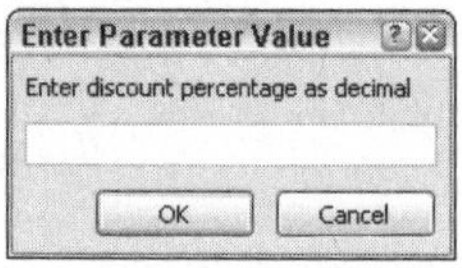

Figure 15-6:
Access
asks for a
discount.

Enter Parameter Value

Enter discount percentage as decimal

OK   Cancel

4. **Enter the prompted information.**

> For this example, just enter the value of your discount (as a decimal value). Access does the rest.

This option means that you can use the same query with different values to see how changing that value affects your results.

Daisy chaining your words with text formulas

Number fields aren't the only fields you can use in formulas. Access can also use the *words stored in text fields*.

A classic formula comes from working with names. If you have a Contacts table with FirstName and LastName fields, you will at some point want to string those names together on a form or report. A text formula can do this for you. It can add the first name to the last name so that the result is the person's full name in one column.

The syntax for text field formulas is similar to the syntax for number field formulas — the field name is still surrounded by square brackets and must be carefully entered by hand. Include literal text in the formula (such as spaces or punctuation) by surrounding it with quotation marks (like "," to insert a comma).

You connect text fields with the ampersand character (&). Microsoft calls the ampersand the *concatenation operator*, which is a fancy way to say that it connects things.

Figure 15-7 shows a text field formula. This example solves the problem I describe earlier in this section: making one name out of the pieces in two separate fields. The formula shown in the figure combines the FirstName and LastName fields into a single full name, ready to appear on a mailing label, report, or some other useful purpose you devise.

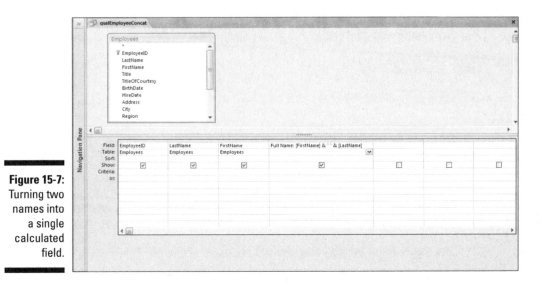

Figure 15-7:
Turning two
names into
a single
calculated
field.

This formula consists of the FirstName field, an ampersand, a single space inside quotation marks, followed by another ampersand, and then the LastName field:

```
[FirstName]&" "&[LastName]
```

When you run this query, Access takes the information from the two fields and puts them together, inserting the space between them so they don't run straight into each other. Figure 15-8 shows the results of this query.

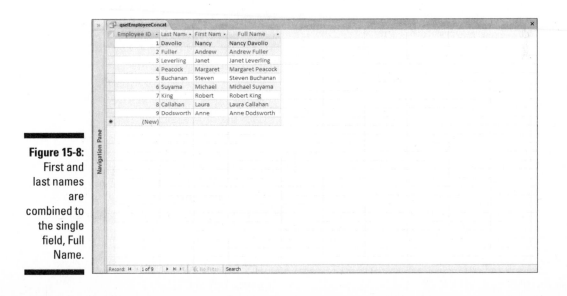

Figure 15-8:
First and
last names
are
combined to
the single
field, Full
Name.

Expression Builder (Somewhat) to the Rescue

Creating calculated fields presents you with two basic challenges:

- ✔ Figuring out what the formula should say
- ✔ Entering the formula so Access recognizes it

Although Access can't help you with the first problem, it tries hard to offer some assistance with the second. When all else fails, and you just can't assemble a calculated field exactly the way Access wants it, click the Builder button on the Design tab of the Ribbon to open the Expression Builder.

The Expression Builder has several parts, as shown in Figure 15-9:

- ✔ You create the expression in the big window at the top.
- ✔ Immediately below the big window, a bunch of buttons show the mathematical and comparison operators available to your formula.

Don't rely on Expression Builder

In theory, Expression Builder walks you through the frustrating syntax of building a calculation (what Access calls an *expression*) that meets all the nitpicky requirements Access puts in place. Unfortunately, Microsoft chose not to improve the Expression Builder for Access 2007. It does present you with the tools to build the formula, but you have to wade through lists of every object, field, control, and function in the database to find what you need. What would be helpful is limiting each list to just those items that will work for the current situation. Just show me fields and functions I can use in my current query. Don't show me fields from unrelated tables, queries, forms, and reports that will just generate an error if used.

I find Expression Builder helpful for locating a list of built-in Access functions or for referring to a field properly in an expression, but beyond that, it isn't much help. For me, it's faster to type my numerical operators rather than click the tiny little buttons that contain those operators in Expression Builder.

Before resorting to Expression Builder, try a little troubleshooting on your own. If your formulas don't work the way you think they should, double-check the spelling of every field. Most problems come from simple field name spelling errors. If all else fails and you're feeling adventurous, then give Expression Builder a try. With any luck, it might actually solve your problem.

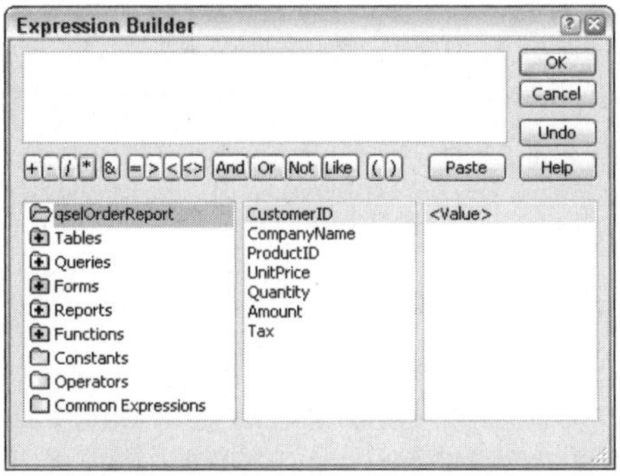

Figure 15-9:
The
Expression
Builder in all
its easy-to-
use glory.

From left to right, these are the operator groups and buttons:

- Simple mathematical actions: addition, subtraction, division, and multiplication.

- Ampersand (&)

  This combines two text fields.

- Mathematical comparisons: =, >, <, <>

- Boolean comparisons: And, Or, Not, and Like

  Use comparisons to develop expressions for the Criteria section of your queries, when you need a response of *True* or *False*.

- Left and right parentheses

✔ The lower half of the dialog box contains three windows that work as a team.

- The first window on the left lists folders for all the tables, queries, forms, and other stuff in the current database.

- When you click something in the left window, its contents spill into the center and right windows, depending on how much stuff Access needs to display.

✔ Near the bottom of the list in the first window, Access also includes a few items for the Truly Technical Person. These folders contain

- Constants (values that never change such as *true* and *false*)

- Another list of operators available for comparisons and formulas.

- A folder called Common Expressions, which contains stuff that makes sense only when building a report.

Expression Builder works like a big calculator crossed with a word processor:

- ✔ At the bottom, double-click items in the center or right window to include them in your expression at the top.
- ✔ Click once on the buttons just below the top window to include different operators in the expression.
- ✔ Click anywhere in the big pane on top and type whatever you feel like typing.

TIP

Expression Builder can refer to controls on a form in your query so that you can easily control what criteria are used to run the query. Figure 15-10 shows a simple form called Order Report with one combo box called Customer listing all customers in the customer table.

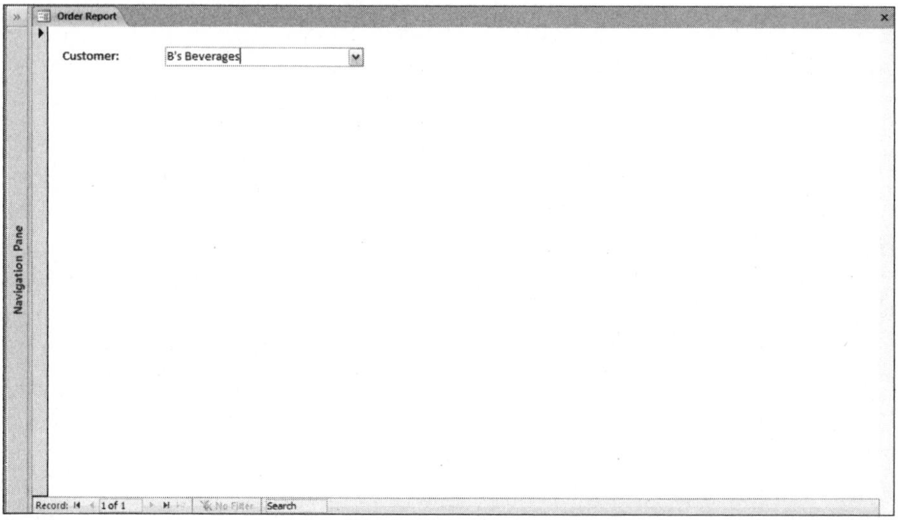

Figure 15-10:
The Order Report form with the Customer combo box.

Order Report

Customer: B's Beverages

Record: 1 of 1 No Filter Search

Figure 15-11 shows how the Expression Builder finds and uses the combo box on the form.

Finally, Figure 15-12 shows the expression in the criteria row of the order report query. So how does all this work? Open the form and select a customer. Run the query and the query will be limited to just the orders for the customer selected on the form. Cool, huh?

Figure 15-11:
The
Expression
Builder is
used to
select the
Company
Name
combo
box from
the Order
Report form.

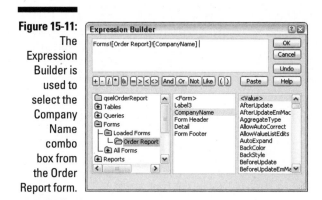

Figure 15-12:
The
expression
as it
appears in
the criteria
row of the
order report
query.

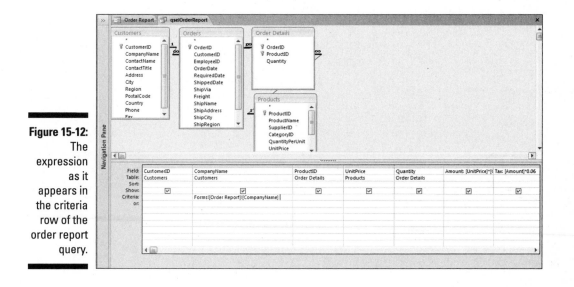

Part V
Plain and Fancy Reporting

The 5th Wave
By Rich Tennant

"Yes, I know how to query information from the program, but what if I just want to leak it instead?"

In this part . . .

*P*lain *and* fancy? How can this be? Can Access really give you both? Sure it can. You can create a quick report that's a simple display of every record in a single table, or you can craft beautiful reports that use multiple tables and specific records from within them. You can also create reports that fall somewhere in between — call them "Flain" or "Plancy" — and you can create them with a stress-preventing tool called the Report Wizard.

You'll find out about the simple and powerful ways that Access provides for generating reports, and even ways to do a mass mailing from your database of names and addresses, or to create product labels from your database of . . . um . . . products.

Chapter 16

Quick and Not-So-Dirty Automatic Reporting

*T*hat fact that you're reading this chapter right now tells me that either you've already been asked to create a report or you're afraid that might happen. Yes, I used the word *afraid* — because the idea of reporting on a database seems daunting to many users. You might be wondering, "Do I have to learn some really complex Access features? Do I have to master some word processing program so that I can make the report look like more than just a list of records?"

The answers to those questions are no and no. You don't have to learn anything other than a couple of quick mouse clicks in the Access workspace in order to whip up a snazzy report in seconds. And you don't have to master Word or any other word processing program to dress up your report and make it look serious and important. No, you have all you need to make a quick, simple, yet professional-looking report, right here in Access 2007.

But what if your boss/customer/business partner is standing over your shoulder right now and he or she wants a report on your department/products/expenses *right now?* There's no time to figure out how to do anything; you just need a report this minute. Have no fear — the Report button is here! Located on the Create tab, all you have to do is open the table — the one that's the source of the much-sought-after report — and then click the Report button. Lickety-split, you'll have a report you can print immediately. Or if you have a laptop or a nice, big monitor, you can invite the report-seeker over to your desk for a look-see.

That's quick, but what if you have to report on more than one table? What if your boss/customer/partner needs a report on data from table A and table B, and you know he or she does *not* want to see certain pieces of data from those tables anywhere on the report? In situations such as these, the Report Wizard comes in handy, allowing you to choose multiple tables as the sources for your report and also letting you pick and choose which fields to include from those tables.

Knowing that there are two very simple paths to follow, depending on the report you're looking for (or that someone else is hounding you for), it's time to take a look at the two paths and figure out which one is right for you.

Chances are, you'll need both of Access's simple reporting tools (the Report button and the Report Wizard) over time, so it's worth checking them both out now. I start with an analysis of them both and then get into the procedural specifics of the simplest one first.

Fast and Furious Automatic Reporting

The Access Report and Report Wizard tools make reporting on your database extremely simple. If you click the Report tool, your table, the open and active one at the time you click the Report button, is used to generate a report, instantly. You can then go in and tweak margins, fonts, and other formatting so that it looks more like you'd imagined and/or fits on the number of pages you prefer.

If you use the Report Wizard, you get taken step by step through the process of choosing which fields (and which tables) to include in your report, how the report will look, and how the content will flow over one or more pages.

Each method has its merits in different situations:

- ✔ **If you want every field in your single table included in your report,** and you don't mind if your report looks a lot like a worksheet or the way your table looks on-screen while you're in Table view, then the Report tool is for you. It's quick, and it gives you a report without any formatting or other fanfare required.

- ✔ **If you want to choose which fields to include in your report,** and maybe want your report to include fields from more than one table, the Report Wizard is for you. It takes a little longer than the Report tool, but the flexibility and ability to customize the report's appearance through a series of dialog boxes (rather than using multiple tabs and buttons) is a real plus.

Creating a quick, one-table report

All you have to do is click your mouse twice to generate a report on an open table:

1. **Open the table that you want to report on.**

2. **Click the Create tab and then click the Report button (see Figure 16-1).**

Report Wizard

Figure 16-1:
The Report button is found on the Create tab.

The open table is now a report, laid out exactly as it appeared in Table view — as a series of rows and columns. It has a heading and a small graphic in the upper-left corner, and some color has been added, using a default template, to the field names and the report's title (which is the same as the table name).

3. **Use the Office button on the upper left of your screen to access the Print command (or press Ctrl+P) if you want to print the report you see on-screen.**

You can also display the report on-screen, now and in the future, so there's no requirement that you print the report.

If you save your database right now, the report (now with its own tab, as shown in Figure 16-2) becomes part of the database and will be there next time you open it.

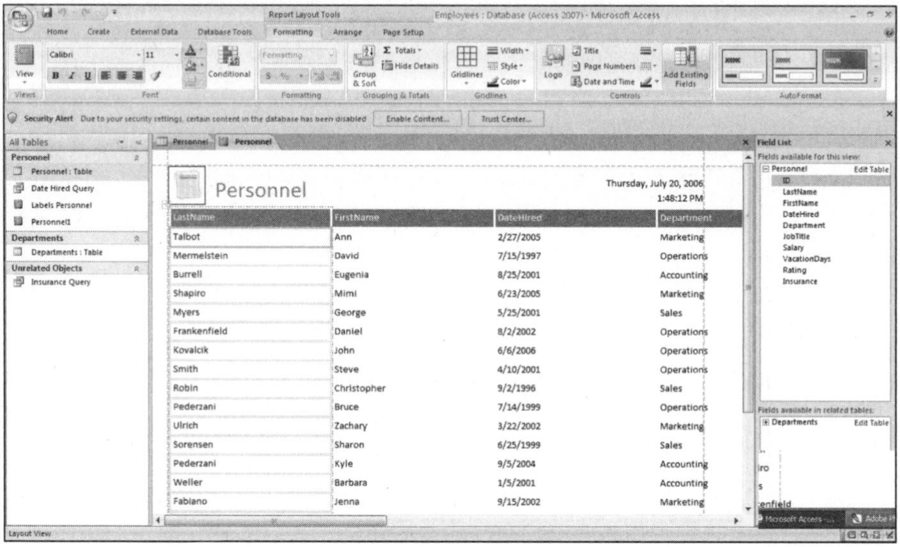

Figure 16-2:
Now your
single-table
report has
a tab of its
own and
can be
saved as
part of the
database.

Your instant report formatting options

Although the Report tool works with only one table or query at a time, it still offers some choices for the way the report looks and how the fields appear in the report.

On the Arrange tab (displayed after you use the Create tab to generate the quick, one-table report) you can choose from a variety of options for the tabular layout of your report. You can have each record listed on its own row, as a series of columns, or you can stack your fields so that, for example, last name and first name fields are paired up vertically, as shown in Figure 16-3.

Can't find the buttons to change your report's tabular settings? Look at the Control Layout section (far left) of the Arrange tab, found in the Report Tools area, also shown in Figure 16-3. To arrange your fields so that they appear in a vertical stack, click the field name that you want to stack under the field to its left and then click the Stacked button. You can also click the Tabular button to display one control per field, and one record per page. My advice? Experiment with different layouts, and when you like what you see on-screen, print. If you hate what you've done, just keep clicking the Undo button (up on the Quick Access toolbar) until the report is back at its pre–I Don't Like That state.

You can also remove your layout controls, reverting a report back to the simple series of rows, one field per column, that's the default for this type of report. Just click the Remove button until you're back to the original layout.

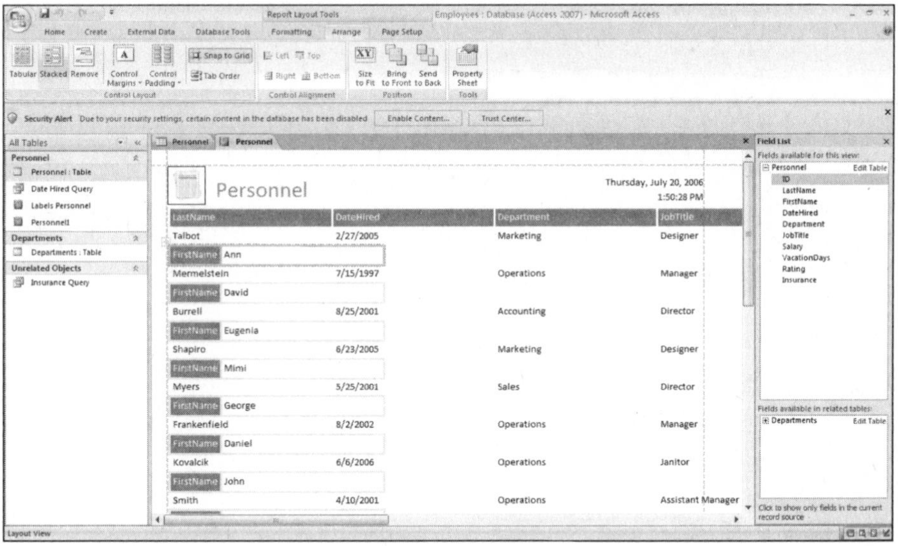

Figure 16-3:
Stack your
fields to
narrow your
report and
pair up
related
fields.

Rearranging columns

Not only can you pair up your report's fields vertically, stacking them to keep relevant fields together, but you can rearrange your columns so that your report's readers see what they want to see first (assuming they read from left to right) and so that you can horizontally pair up things that relate to each other. As shown in Figure 16-4, all you have to do to rearrange columns is drag the headings — the columns' data comes along with them — and when you release your mouse the fields are rearranged.

Sizing columns to fit the data

One thing that can be very appealing about a quick report on a single table is the ability to put the entire report on a single page (if you have only 20 or 30 records) or on a series of pages that include all the table's fields on each page (for large databases with hundreds or thousands of records). This can be difficult on a report that uses all the fields in a table because many tables have a lot of fields and rarely do they fit across an 8½-x-11-inch sheet of paper. That is, unless you resize the fields, narrowing them so that they're no wider than they have to be to display the widest entry in the column.

When stacking fields doesn't reduce the horizontal dimensions of your report, try the Size to Fit button — also found on the Arrange tab (see the Position section of the Arrange tab, shown in Figure 16-5), the Size to Fit button takes each column and makes it fit, sizing it to accommodate the widest entry in the field. Typically, this cuts the allocated horizontal space for a field by 50 percent or more.

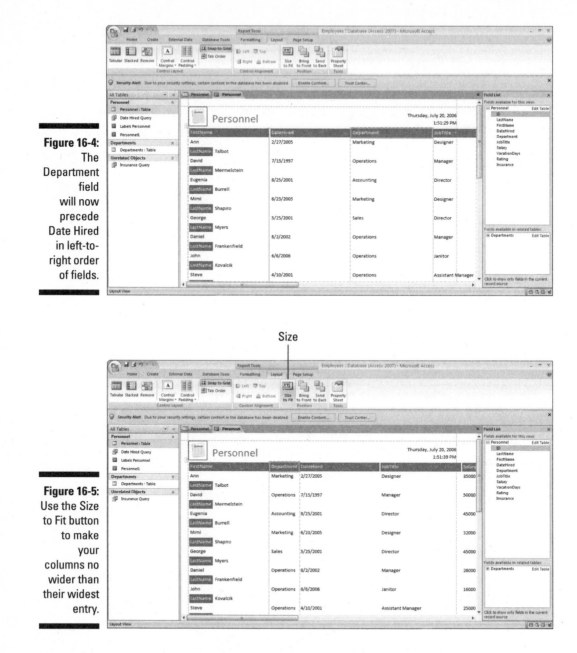

Figure 16-4: The Department field will now precede Date Hired in left-to-right order of fields.

Size

Figure 16-5: Use the Size to Fit button to make your columns no wider than their widest entry.

To use Size to Fit, click the heading for the column you want to resize (working, of course, in the report, not in your actual table) and click the Size to Fit button. The column changes width, usually becoming narrower. If you've manually narrowed the column and now you can't see the wider entries, you can also use Size to Fit to make the column wider, accommodating these larger entries.

 What's that about manually widening a column? Yes, you can manually narrow (or widen) any column by clicking the column's heading and then using the two-headed arrow that appears when you mouse over the column's right seam. Drag, as shown in Figure 16-6, until the column width shown by the grid is the width you want for that field's portion of the report.

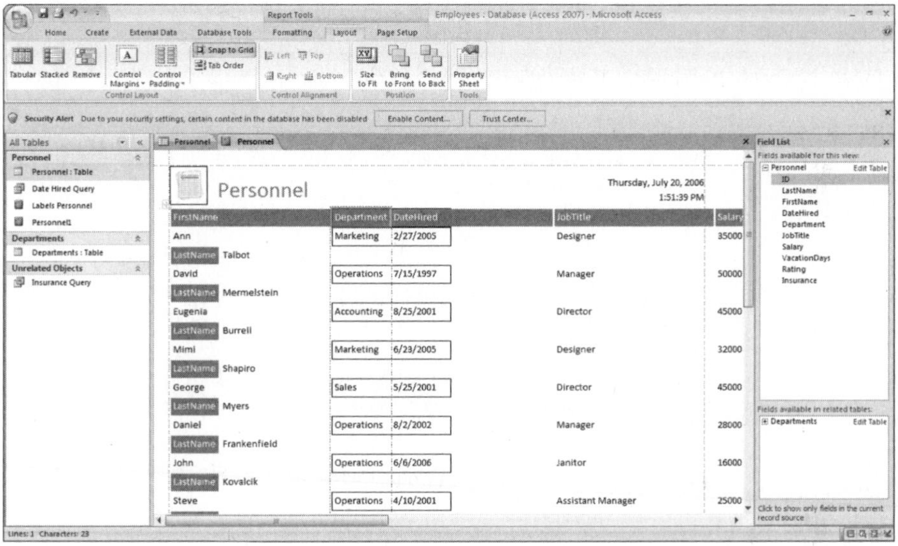

Figure 16-6:
Click and
drag to
widen or
narrow your
report's
columns,
one at a
time.

Starting the Report Wizard

So you've decided to take things step-by-step, perhaps because you want to include multiple tables and/or queries in your report. Or maybe you're still deciding what the best path is and want to see what's involved in the process.

The Report Wizard is simple. It requires a few more steps and decisions from you than the Report tool does, but it's much more flexible than the instant Report tool. Here goes:

The query advantage

The fact that Access lets you base a report on a query is wonderful. When you build a report on a table, you get a report containing each and every record in the table. But what if you want only a few of the records? Access makes it easy. Create a query and then base the report upon that query. (Chapter 12 shows how to make a query.)

The advantages don't stop there. If you create a query based on multiple tables, Access neatly

organizes your results into a single datasheet. This allows you to use the quick, one-click Report tool to report on multiple tables — essentially duping Access into giving you a quick report on more than one table because the tables are part of a single query, and that single query is your Report source. If you're unclear on the process of creating a query on multiple tables, take a look at Chapter 12.

1. **In your database window, click the Create tab and then click the Report Wizard button.**

   The Report Wizard dialog box appears, listing all the fields in the active table. As shown in Figure 16-7, the dialog box offers

   • A drop-down list from which you can choose other tables and queries

   • Two columns of Selected and Available fields, which you use to determine which fields from the selected table(s) will be used in your report

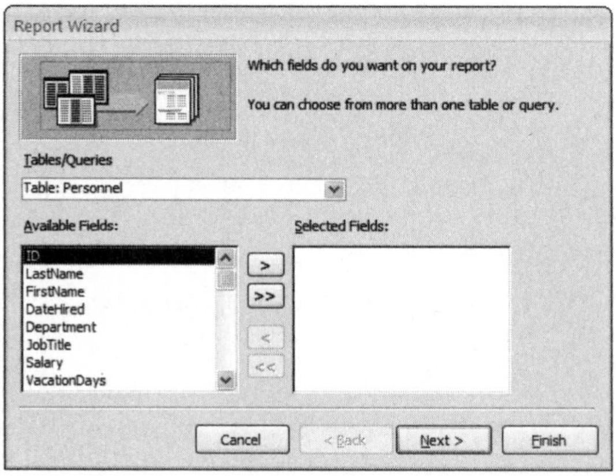

Figure 16-7: The Report Wizard starts by offering you tables and the fields within them to use in your report.

Report Wizard

Which fields do you want on your report?

You can choose from more than one table or query.

Tables/Queries

Table: Personnel

Available Fields:

ID
LastName
FirstName
DateHired
Department
JobTitle
Salary
VacationDays

Selected Fields:

Cancel < Back Next > Finish

2. Use the Tables/Queries drop-down list to choose the table you want to start with.

The fields from the table you select appear in the Available Fields box.

3. Add fields to your report by double-clicking them in the Available Fields box.

By double-clicking, you add the fields to the Selected Fields box, and they become part of the report. You can also click once on a field and then click the button with a > symbol on it, as shown in Figure 16-8.

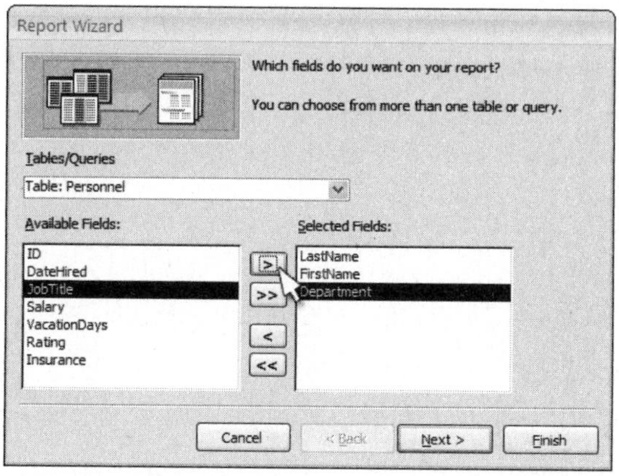

Figure 16-8:
Add fields
by double-
clicking
them or by
using the
buttons
between the
Available
and
Selected
Fields
boxes.

4. Repeat Steps 2 and 3 for each table and/or query in the database that you want to include in the report.

If at any point you want to add all of the fields in a given table or query, click the >> button to add all the Available Fields to the Selected Fields list.

5. Click Next twice to move on with the Report Wizard.

This bypasses grouping issues, which, for a simple report are often unnecessary. To explore this step of the Report Wizard in greater detail, check out Chapter 18.

6. Choose a sort order for your report — typically sorting on the field by which people will look up information in the report, as shown in Figure 16-9.

For example, if your report documents a list of employees, Last Name might be a good choice. A report on product sales would be useful in

Product Number or Product Name order. You can sort by more than one field, choosing up to four fields to sort by and either Ascending or Descending for the sort order on each field.

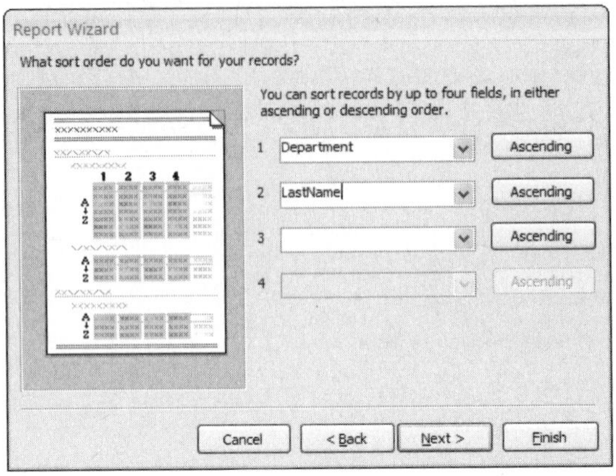

Figure 16-9:
Sort by the most important field in the table, and as needed, by three additional fields.

Sorting is best done on fields that have either very few or a lot of duplicate entries:

- In a name and address list, sorting by Last Name (which may have very few duplicates) will put the list in an order for which there's very little opportunity for subsequent sorting — because the unique records in Last Name don't create any groups that can be further sorted.

- If you sort that name and address list by City or State (which may have lots of duplicate entries), a subsequent sort can be done on Last Name, putting each group of people living in the same city or state in last-name order.

- To choose between Ascending (the default) and Descending sort order, you'll either leave the Ascending button alone (for A-Z sorting) or click it to change it to Descending (for Z-A sorting).

7. **Click Next to display your options for Layout and Orientation.**

8. **Choose a Layout and an Orientation from the two sets of radio buttons and click Next.**

- Layout options (Tabular or Columnar) are simple — you either want to see your report as a list (Tabular) or in sections (Columnar), in which each record appears in a section on its own. Justified is similar to Tabular, but groups the fields in a sort of stacked jumble.

- Orientation decisions (Portrait or Landscape) are generally made by envisioning the report in your head — are there more fields than will fit across a sheet of 8.5" wide paper? If so, choose Landscape to give yourself 11" of paper (or 10", to allow for the smaller margin possible) across which your fields will appear.

You probably don't want to use Justified unless your report has very few fields per record.

Figure 16-10 shows this stage of the Report Wizard and a Tabular format chosen.

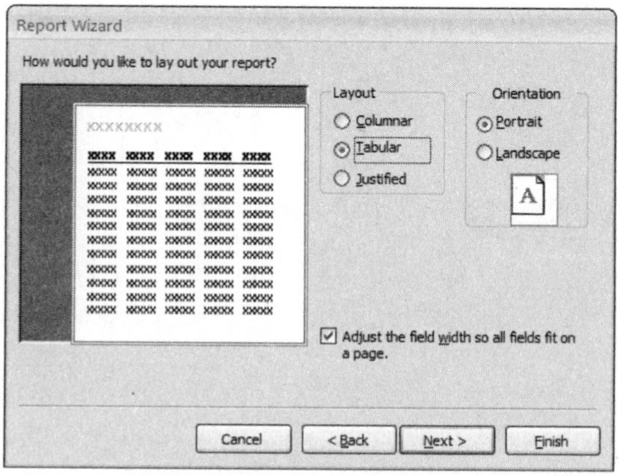

Figure 16-10:
Choose your report's layout in terms of field structure and orientation.

If you leave the Adjust the Field Width So All Fields Fit on a Page option checked, you run the risk of data being chopped off in the report and rendering the report unusable. If you have more than four or five fields, and if any of your fields have very long entries, turn this option off.

9. **Select the Style of your report and click Next.**

   You can pick from six preset designs (plus None, which applies no special formatting). Click them by name in the box on the right side of the dialog box to see a preview on the left (see Figure 16-11).

   After making a choice (by clicking the style name), you're ready to name and finish your report.

10. **Give your report a Name.**

    Type a name in the long box at the top of the dialog box.

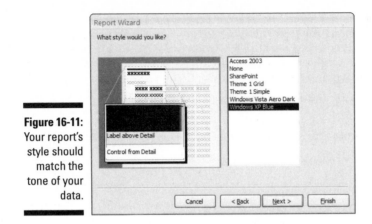

Figure 16-11:
Your report's
style should
match the
tone of your
data.

11. Click Finish.

The report appears in a Preview window, at which point you can print it or close and save it for future use. Figure 16-12 shows a preview of a report that lists employees sorted by Department, and each employee's last name, date hired, director, and rating are displayed.

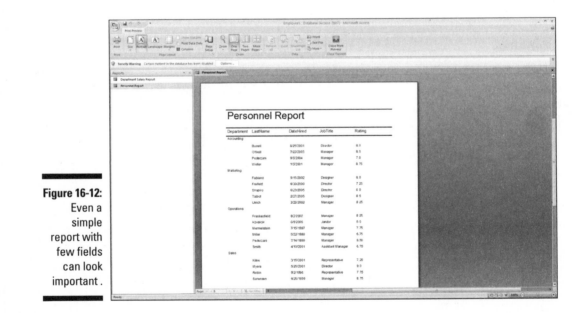

Figure 16-12:
Even a
simple
report with
few fields
can look
important .

Previewing Your Report

When you're in Print Preview mode (which results from having clicked Finish to complete the Report Wizard process, as described in the steps in this chapter's previous section), you can't do a whole lot with your report except print it. But Print Preview shows exactly what your document looks like. Table 16-1 shows the tools Print Preview provides to help with your inspection.

Table 16-1		Print Preview Tools
Tool	*What It Is*	*What It Does*
	Print button	Opens the Print dialog box
	Size button	Allows you to choose a paper size for your report
	Portrait button	Converts your report to Portrait mode
	Landscape button	Converts your report to Landscape mode
	Margins button	Allows you to set Normal, Wide, or Narrow Margins for your report
☑ Show Margins	Show Margins	Click the check box to display or hide the margins
☐ Print Data Only	Print Data Only	Click the check box to include only your data in the report
▦ Columns	Columns button	Opens the Page Setup dialog box with the Columns tab chosen, allowing you to setup a columnar report
	One Page	Previews one page of your report at a time

(continued)

Table 16-1 *(continued)*

Tool	What It Is	What It Does
	Two Pages	Previews your report two pages at a time
	Page Setup	Opens the Page Setup dialog box
	More Pages	Click this to choose to preview four, eight, or twelve pages at a time
	Refresh All	Refreshes the report to display the latest data in the table(s) included in the report
	Excel	Exports your report to an Excel worksheet
	SharePoint List	Exports your report to a SharePoint list
	PDF or XPS	Exports your report in either of these file formats
	Word, Text File, More	These three buttons (stacked vertically) allow your report to be exported as various document types
	Close Print Preview	As you might have guessed, this closes the Preview window.

Zooming in and out and all around

In Figure 16-12, where the preview of our Report Wizard creation appeared, you can't see the entire page. The parts you can see look okay, but how can you commit to printing if you don't know how the whole page looks? In Figure 16-13, by clicking the magnifying glass mouse pointer that appears whn you move your mouse over the preview of your report, Access displays the report full-size, just like it looks on the printed page.

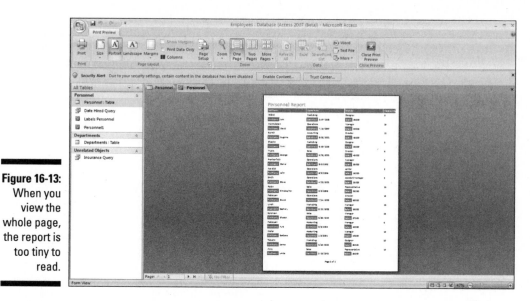

Figure 16-13:
When you view the whole page, the report is too tiny to read.

When you move your mouse pointer over the preview of your report, your pointer changes into a magnifying glass. Use this to zoom in to the report and check individual sections:

✔ Just click what you want to see, and Access swoops down, enlarging that portion of the report so you can see it clearly.

✔ Click again, and your view changes back to the previous setting.

Clicking any of the page-number buttons (One Page, Two Page, More Pages) sets the Zoom view to the Fit view setting. When you have two pages showing, the odd-numbered page is always on the left, unlike book publishing, which puts the odd-numbered page on the right — unless the typesetting department is having a very bad day.

If you use the Zoom section of the Print Preview tab, Access offers quite the selection of page view options, as you see in Figure 16-14. Set your system to show either 1 page, 2 pages, or click the More Pages button drop list to choose up to 12 pages per screen — of course you won't be able to read anything at this setting, but you'll at least see how the whole report lays out on the page/s.

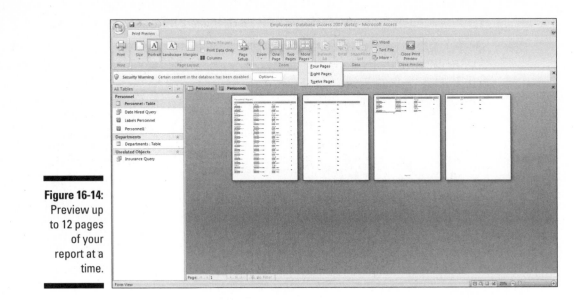

Figure 16-14:
Preview up
to 12 pages
of your
report at a
time.

Pop goes the menu

You can right-click anywhere on the Print Preview screen to see a pop-up
menu that gives you the choice of switching the zoom or viewing a specific
number of pages, as shown in Figure 16-15. When you click the Zoom button
drop list in the Zoom section of the Print Preview tab, you get a similar pop-
up menu offering various zoom percentages, from 10% to 1000%.

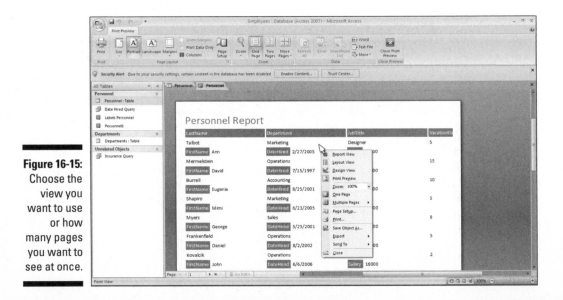

Figure 16-15:
Choose the
view you
want to use
or how
many pages
you want to
see at once.

Other than the Zoom submenu, the following useful commands are available when you right-click the Print Preview screen:

- ✔ **Report, Layout, Design, or Print View:** These four options appear at the top of the pop-up menu and give you lots of ways to look at your report.

- ✔ **One Page and Multiple Pages:** If you choose to see Multiple Pages, you must tell Access how many by using the submenu that appears when you make that pop-up menu selection. Drag through the grid (it appears as 6 blocks to start with) and the grid expands as you drag. Release your mouse when the number of pages you want to see is displayed selected in the grid.

- ✔ **Page Setup:** This opens the handy Page Setup dialog box.

- ✔ **Print:** This opens — yep, you guessed it — the Print dialog box.

- ✔ **Save Object As:** Choose this command to save your report with a new name and choose what type of object to save it as — Report is the default.

- ✔ **Export:** Choose this command to save your Access report in a format used by another program, such as a Word document, a PDF (Portable Document Format) file, a Text file, an XML document, or an HTML document.

- ✔ **Send To:** Choose this command and then select an e-mail recipient to send the report to.

Beauty Is Only Skin (Report) Deep

After looking at your report in the Print Preview window, you have a decision to make. If you're happy with how your report looks, great! Go ahead and print the document. However, a few minutes of extra work does wonders for even the simplest reports.

Start with the basics in the Page Setup dialog box. To get there, right-click anywhere on the report and choose Page Setup from the pop-up menu (this command and others are briefly explained in the preceding section of this chapter).

The Page Setup dialog box allows you to fine tune your report in terms of its Print Options, Page, and Columns settings. Adjust margins, change orientation, and control how many vertical columns your report content is divided into — all from within this handy dialog box.

The Print Options tab

The Margins section of the Page Setup dialog box controls the width of the margins in your report — no surprises here.

Figure 16-16 shows your margin options. The page has four margins so the dialog box includes a setting for each one (Top, Bottom, Left, and Right).

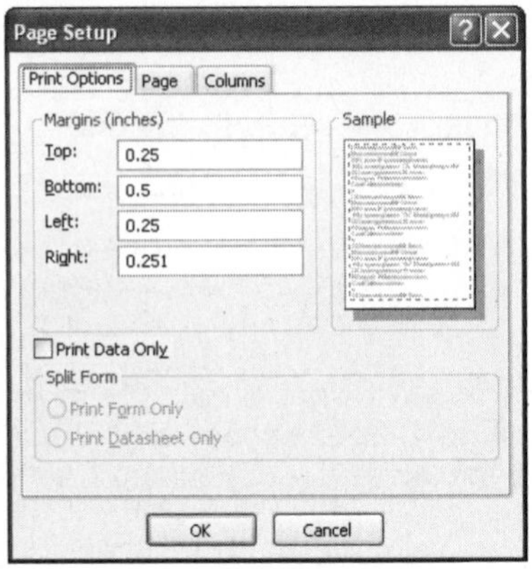

Figure 16-16:
Choose how much white space will surround your report by adjusting your margins.

Here is how you set or change margins:

1. **Double-click in the appropriate box (Top, Bottom, Left, or Right) and type a new setting.**

   When you double-click the box, the current entry is selected. Access automatically uses whatever Windows thinks is your local unit of measurement (inches, centimeters, or whatever else you measure with). On the right side of the dialog box, Access displays a sample image, which shows you how your current margin settings work on a page.

2. **Make all the changes you want to your report's layout, and then click OK.**

3. **Look at your report in Print Preview to check your adjustments.**

   If you need to tweak the report, simply go back to Page Setup and play with the options until everything looks just right.

The last item on the Print Options tab is the Print Data Only check box. I guess the programmers can't think of anywhere else to put this box because it has nothing to do with margin settings. If you select this option by checking its box, Access prints only the data in your records; field headings won't appear on the printed document. Use Print Data Only if you plan to use preprinted forms. Otherwise, leave it alone, because your report looks pretty odd without any field labels.

The Page tab

The Page tab tells Access about the sheet of paper you print your report on, including its size and layout, as well as what printer you keep the paper in. You make some of the most fundamental decisions about how your report looks from the Page tab of the Page Setup dialog box (see Figure 16-17).

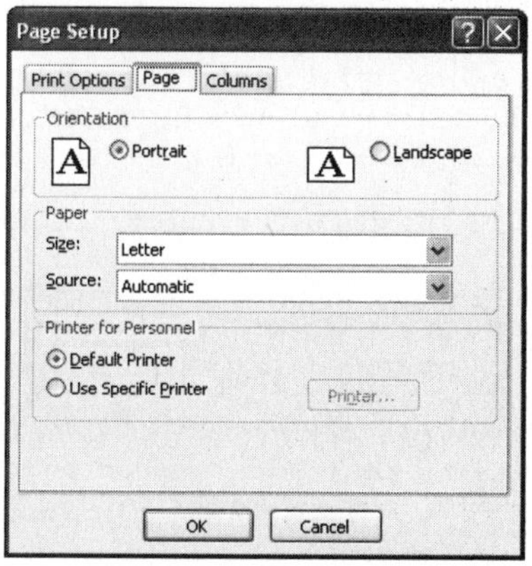

Figure 16-17: The Page tab enables you to choose a printer, page size, and more.

The Orientation box sets the direction that your report prints on paper:

- ✔ Portrait (the way that this book and most magazines appear) is the default choice.

- ✔ Landscape pages lie on their side, giving you more horizontal room (width) but less vertical space (height).

Deciding whether to use Portrait or Landscape is more important than you might think:

- ✔ For tabular reports, landscape orientation displays more information for each field, thanks to the wider columns. Unfortunately, the columns get shorter in the process. (After all, that piece of paper is only so big.)

- ✔ Columnar reports don't do very well in a landscape orientation because they usually need more vertical space than horizontal space.

Your other choices for the Page tab are determined by your printing capabilities:

- ✔ The Size drop-down list in the Paper section of the tab enables you to choose the size of the paper you want to use (refer to Figure 16-17).

- ✔ The Source drop-down list gives you the option to

  - Use your regular paper feed (the Automatic choice)

  - Use another automatic source, should your printer be equipped with multiple trays.

  - Manually feed your paper into the printer

- ✔ The last part of the Page tab lets you choose a specific printer for this report.

  Most of the time you can leave this setting alone; it's useful only if you want to force this report to always come from one specific printer at your location. You can choose either

  - The Default Printer option (Access uses whatever printer Windows says to use)

  - Use Specific Printer option (you choose the printer yourself).

    If you click the Use Specific Printer option, the Printer button comes to life. Click this button to choose from among your available printers.

The Columns tab

You get to make more decisions about your report's size and layout on the Columns tab, as shown in Figure 16-18.

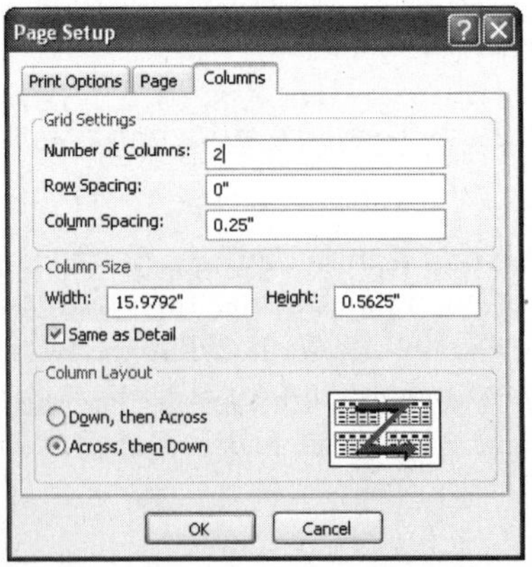

Figure 16-18:
The Column Layout area of the Columns tab enables you to format a report with vertical columns.

Page Setup

Print Options | Page | Columns

Grid Settings

Number of Columns: 2

Row Spacing: 0"

Column Spacing: 0.25"

Column Size

Width: 15.9792"   Height: 0.5625"

☑ Same as Detail

Column Layout

○ Down, then Across
◉ Across, then Down

OK | Cancel

The Columns tab of the Page Setup dialog box is divided into three sections:

- ✔ **Grid Settings:** Controls how many columns your report uses and how far apart the different elements are from each other

- ✔ **Column Size:** Adjusts the height and width of your columns

- ✔ **Column Layout:** Defines the way that Access places your data in columns (and uses an easy-to-understand graphic to show you as well)

The default number of columns is one column to a page, but you can easily change the setting to suit your particular report. Just keep in mind that with more columns, your report may show less information for each record. If you use so many columns that some of the information won't fit, Access conveniently displays a warning.

If the number of columns you select fits (or if you're willing to lose your view of the information in some of your fields), click OK to see a view of how your document looks with multiple columns.

The Grid Settings section of the Columns tab also adjusts

- ✔ **Row Spacing:** Adjusts the space (measured in your local unit of distance) between the horizontal rows. Simply click the Row Spacing box and enter the amount of space that you want to appear between each row. Again, this setting is a matter of personal preference.

- ✔ **Column Spacing:** Adjusts the width of your columns. If you narrow this width, you make more room, but your entries are more difficult to read.

The bottom section of the Columns tab, called Column Layout, lets you control how your columns are organized on the page. You have two options here:

- ✔ **Down, then Across:** Access starts a new record in the same column (if the preceding record has not filled up the page). For example, Record 13 starts below Record 12 on the page (provided there's enough room), and then Records 14 and 15 appear in the second column.

- ✔ **Across, then Down:** Access starts Record 13 across from Record 12, and then puts Record 14 below Record 12, and Record 15 below Record 13, and so on.

If your columns don't look exactly right the first time, keep trying. Small adjustments to the row and column spacing produce big changes across a long report. The on-screen preview gives you an easy check on how the report looks — and prevents you from killing multiple trees in the quest for perfection.

Chapter 17

Dazzling Report Design

. . . .

In This Chapter

▶ Understanding report sections

▶ Using text boxes and labels

▶ Previewing your changes

▶ Putting AutoFormat to work

▶ Drawing lines and boxes

▶ Adding pictures

. . . .

*T*he Report Wizard does most of the dirty work of report creation. However, it has its shortcomings. Most of the Report Wizard's shortcomings have to do with text. Sometimes the text is cut off, not aligned properly, too small, too big — you get the idea.

Along the way, you may not like the Report Wizard's color choices or design elements as well. Don't despair (hopefully, you're not despairing over an Access report, but I have to throw some drama in here somewhere). Design and layout views hold the key to unlocking the report of your dreams (I know, who isn't dreaming about Access reports)!

In this chapter, I discuss some of the most popular report design and layout view tasks. With this knowledge, you can create professional-quality reports and be the envy of the office.

Taking Your Report In for Service

Design and Layout views are the places to be for tweaking reports — but which view to use and when? Usually, these are the best options:

✔ **Design view:** Adding new elements such as lines , titles, and subtitles to the report.

Figure 17-1 shows a report in Design view.

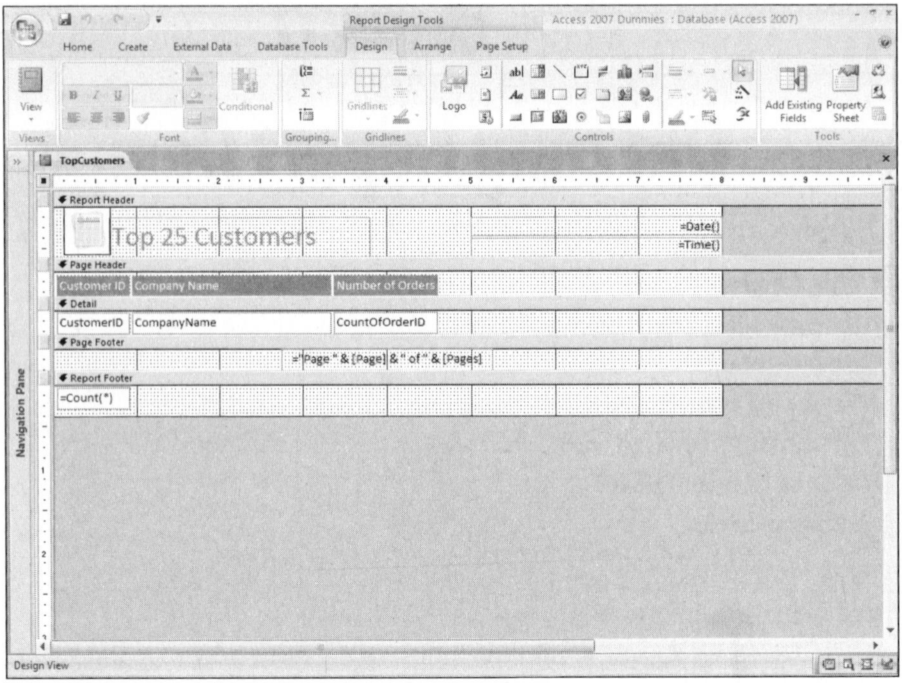

Figure 17-1:
Design view
is best for
adding new
design
elements to
your report.

✔ **Layout view:** Formatting existing elements. (Layout view shows you actual data as it will appear on the printed page.)

Figure 17-2 shows the same report in Layout view.

You have many ways to change report views. Here are some of the most common:

✔ **After creating a report with the Report Wizard:** The wizard asks whether you want to

- *Preview the report*

- *Modify the Report's Design*

 Click the Modify the Report's Design option to send the wizard's creation straight into Design view.

✔ **While a report is print previewed on the screen:** Use the row of view buttons on the lower-right corner of your screen:

- *Design view* is the last button from the right

- *Layout view* is the second-to-last button from the right.

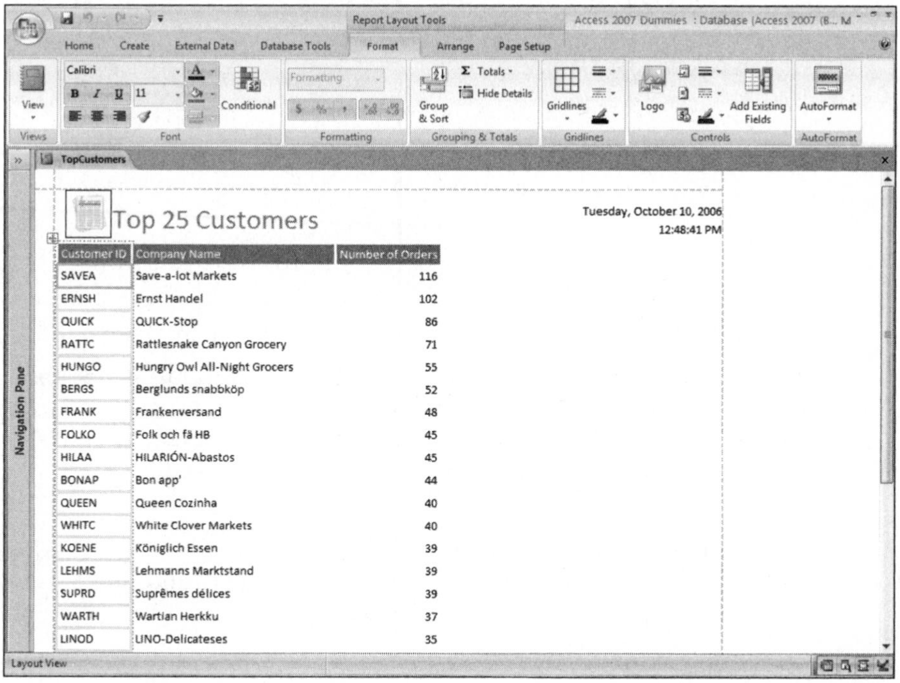

Figure 17-2:
Layout view is best for modifying existing report elements.

✔ **To open a report in Design or Layout View from the navigation pane:** Follow these steps:

1. *Right-click the report you want to work on.*

   A shortcut menu pops up.

2. *Select Design View or Layout View from the shortcut menu.*

Report Organization

Access provides the following design tools to control the layout of your report — where the report data appears on the printed page and where the pages break.

Structural devices

When you look at a report in Design or Layout view, Access displays a ton of markers (called *controls* by Access) that are grouped into several areas (called *sections* by Access). Together these design elements make up the layout of your report — where the report data appears on the printed page.

Controls

In Design or Layout View, *controls* show the following:

- ✔ Where Access plans to put the report elements (such as text, lines, or logos) on the printed page.
- ✔ How the program plans to format each element.

Access uses two kinds of controls for text depending on what information the report includes:

- ✔ **Text boxes:** Boxes that display a particular field's data in the report.

  Every field you want to include in the final report has a text box in Design view. If the report doesn't include a text box for one of the fields in your table, the data for that field won't end up in the report.

- ✔ **Labels:** Plain, simple text markers that display a text message on the report.

  Sometimes labels stand alone (such as "Ken Cook Enterprises – Monthly Sales."). Often they accompany a text box to show people who read the report what data they're looking at ("Customer ID," or "Product," for example).

Sections

The *sections* (like report header) determine *where* and *how often* the elements will print.

The report design in Figure 17-3 displays the most common sections (in order of appearance on the page).

Chapter 18 shows how to slice, dice, and make julienne fries out of your sections. The following information is a summary of the report sections.

Headers

Access provides a pair of header sections for the top of reports.

The header section you need depends on whether you need to print information at the *beginning* of the report or on *every page:*

- ✔ **Report Header:** Anything in the Report Header prints just once at the very start of the report — the top of the first page.

  Typically, a report title appears in the report header.

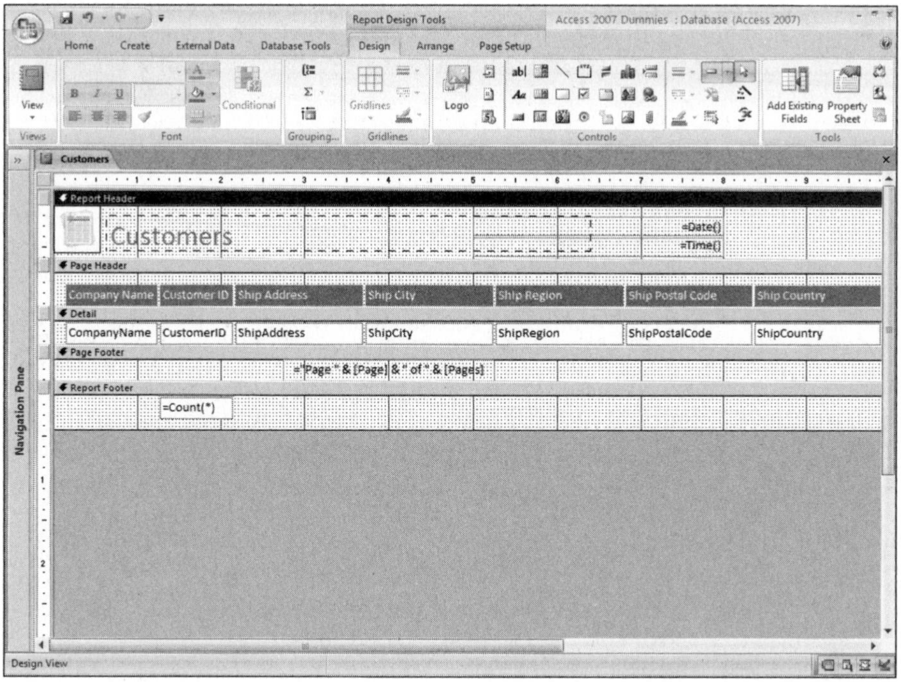

Figure 17-3:
Common
report
sections.

✔ **Page Header:** Information in the Page Header prints at the top of every page.

On the report's first page, the Page Header appears *below* the Report Header.

Typically, the page header contains column heading labels. You can also add design elements such as lines or shaded rectangles to the page header to separate the data rows from the column headings.

Detail

The Detail section displays the essence of the report — the actual database records. The Detail section appears only once in Design View. However, the Detail section is *repeated* for every record in the actual report as seen in Layout View.

The report automatically fits as many Detail sections (records) as possible between the header and footer sections on each page of your report.

The data in the Detail section usually fills the majority of each report page.

Footers

Access provides a pair of footer sections for the bottom of reports.

The footer section you need depends on whether you need to print information at the *end* of the report or on *every page:*

- ✔ **Page Footer:** When each page is nearly full, Access finishes it off by printing the Page Footer at the bottom.

  Common Page Footer elements are the date and page number.

- ✔ **Report Footer:** At the bottom of the *last* page, immediately following the Page Footer, the Report Footer is the last thing that prints on the report. This information prints only once.

  Typically, the Report Footer contains summary formulas that calculate grand totals for numeric columns such as total dollar sales.

Page breaks

By default, Access automatically fills each report page with as many records as possible and then starts another page. But there are a couple of ways that *you* can control how Access reports start new pages:

- ✔ **Grouping.** Places like records together.

  For example, you are printing an order report by month and you want each month to start at the top of a page. If you group the report by month and add a group footer, you can tell Access to start a new page after each month footer prints.

  For more about putting records into groups, see Chapter 18.

- ✔ **Page Break control.** Starts a new page from the point where the control is placed in the report layout.

  The following sections show how to add and remove page breaks.

Inserting a page break

Here's how to add a page break in Design View:

1. **Click the Page Break button in the toolbox.**

   The mouse pointer changes to a crosshair with a page next to it.

2. **Position the crosshair wherever you want the page break and then click.**

A small horizontal line appears on the left side of the report. What you are seeing is actually the *selected* page break control. Click somewhere away from the line and that line will become a series of dots, as shown in Figure 17-4. From now on, a new page always begins at the spot of the marker.

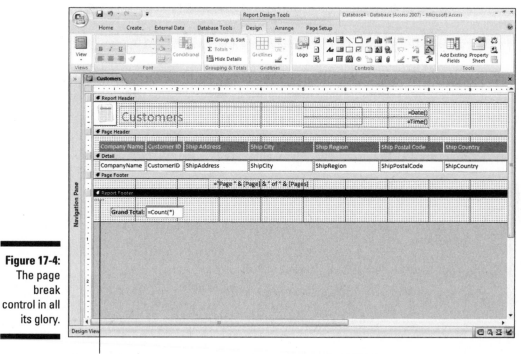

Figure 17-4:
The page break control in all its glory.

Page Break

Removing a page break

If you want to remove a page break, just follow these steps:

1. **With the report in Design View, click the page break marker.**

2. **Press the Delete key on the keyboard.**

   Goodbye Mister Page Break!

This will not remove any page breaks that are *automatic* or created with *grouping*. This will only remove page breaks created using the Page Break control

Formatting This, That, and the Other

You can change almost any existing item in a report's design with the help of the Format tab, which is shown in Figure 17-5. With the Format tab, you can change item properties such as fonts, colors, borders, and alignment. In addition, you can add common report elements such as a logo, page number and date.

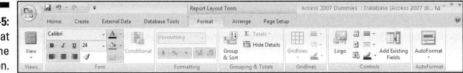

Figure 17-5:
The Format tab on the Ribbon.

The Formatting tab is visible only while a report is in Layout view.

To adjust items in your report with the tools on the Format tab, follow these steps:

1. **Switch to Layout view.**

   The Format tab appears on the Ribbon.

2. **Click the item you want to format.**

   A thick border will appear around the item, as in Figure 17-6.

3. **Click the button for the formatting effect you want.**

   The appropriate buttons will be enabled for the item you've selected. There are two kinds of buttons:

   • **Toggle buttons** (like *Bold*): They are either on or off.

   • **Pull-down arrows** (like *Font*): Many available choices.

   I cover these options in detail later in the chapter.

   Repeat Steps 2 and 3 for all of the items you want to modify.

   If you make a mistake while formatting, click the Undo button on the Quick Access toolbar or press Ctrl+Z. Your mistake will be whisked away to cyber-neverland.

The following sections step through some of the most common formatting tasks. Just follow the instructions, and your report will look like a million bucks in no time. Now, if you could only sell it for a million bucks!

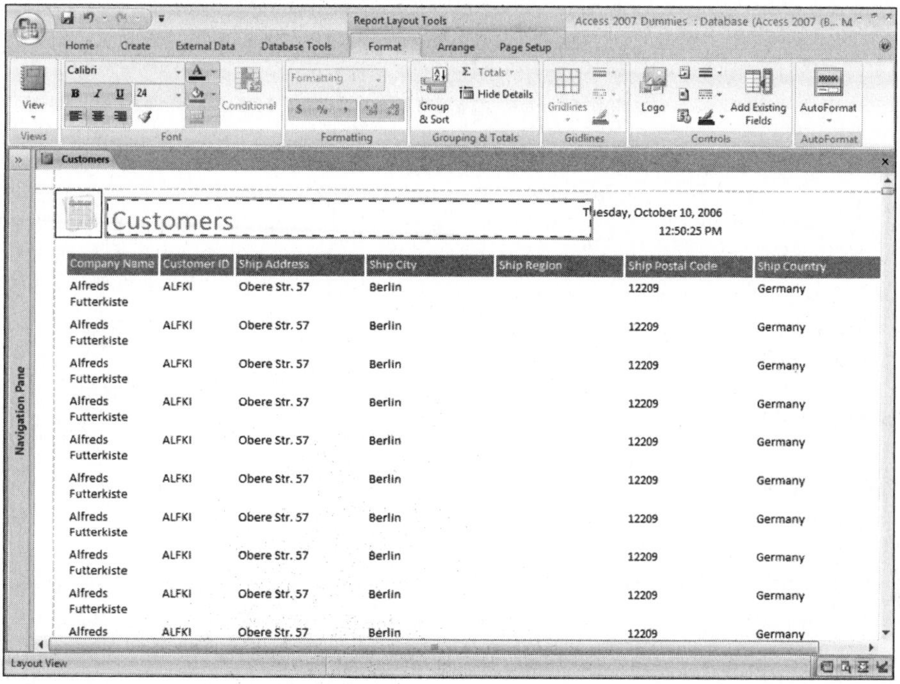

Figure 17-6:
The
Customers
label is
selected.

Adding color

A little color can help keep report readers awake as they browse through 300 pages of data.

These buttons change the color of label and text box controls in your report:

- **Font Color:** Changes the color of text in a text box or label marker.
- **Fill Color:** Changes the control's background color, but not the text.

These buttons are located in both

- **Layout view:** In the Font group on the Format tab of the Ribbon

  I think you'll find these buttons are easier to work with in Layout view.
- **Design view:** On the Design tab

When a text control is selected, the buttons will show you the current font and fill colors for the control. To change colors, follow these steps:

Taking control of your report

In addition to label and text box controls, more controls are available in Design view by using the tools from the Controls group of the Ribbon's Design tab.

Some controls work with specific types of fields. For example, a check box can graphically display the value of a Yes/No field.

Some of these controls can be a bit complicated to set up. However, Access includes several control wizards to take the pain out of the process. These wizards walk you through the steps for building your controls in the usual wizardly step-by-step process. Just answer the questions, and the wizard does the rest.

The control wizards *usually* pop on-screen automatically after you place a control in the report. If you create a new control but the control wizard doesn't show up to help, make sure that the Use Control Wizards button at the right of the Controls group of tools on the Design tab (the button with a magic wand on it) is turned on. If it's on, the Control Wizards button looks like it's pushed down a bit.

Here is a list of the report controls covered in this book and where you can find information on them:

✔ The line, rectangle, page break, and image controls are covered elsewhere in this chapter.

✔ Using controls to create summaries in your report is covered in Chapter 18.

1. **Click the control to select it.**

   The control has a thick border around it.

2. **Click the arrow to the right of the Font Color or Fill Color button.**

   The menu of colors appears.

3. **Click the color you want to use.**

   The colors are divided into sections:

   - *Theme:* Colors that the experts at Microsoft have determined work well together

   - *Standard:* All the colors that have been created for you.

   - *Recent:* All the colors that have been used in the current Access session on the report

If you make the text and background colors the same, the text seems to disappear! If this happens, just click the Undo button on the Quick Access toolbar to bring back the original color setting.

Relocation, relocation, relocation

Don't like that column where it is? The position of your report title got you down? Your line won't stay in line? You can easily move just about any element (text box, label, line, and such) in a report.

- ✔ Most elements can be moved in Layout view. Since you see your data in Layout view, I recommend you start there.

- ✔ If you have trouble in Layout view, switch to Design view. For example, I find lines easier to work with in Design view.

The amount of space between the controls determines the space between items when you print the report:

- ✔ Increasing spacing gives your report a less crowded look.

  This is appropriate if you have only a few columns on your report and you want to spread them out to fill up the width of the page. For example, a report that shows annual sales by product might have a column for the product description and a column for both the unit and dollar sales. Spread the three controls out to fill up the page width.

- ✔ Decreasing the space enables you to fit more information on the page.

  This is appropriate when you have many columns on your report and you want to fit them all on the width of one page. For example, a report that shows dollar sales by month might have fourteen columns — one for the product description, twelve for each month and a Total column. Crowd the fourteen controls together to fit the page width.

Moving a single control

To move a line, box, label, or text box, follow these steps:

1. **Point the tip of the mouse arrow to the item you want to move.**

2. **Press the left mouse button.**

   The mouse will change to a four-headed arrow.

3. **Drag your item to a new position.**

   As you move the mouse the four-headed arrow drags an outline of whatever object you selected.

4. **Release the mouse button when the item is in the right place.**

   If you make a mistake while moving, click the Undo button on the Quick Access toolbar or press Ctrl+Z. This will put the item back where it started.

In most Access reports, text box controls are grouped with corresponding labels. If you move one, the other comes along for the ride. If your report is tabular, this makes it easy to move the whole column of data to the left or right of an adjacent column. If your report is columnar, this makes it easy to move a row of data with its corresponding label up or down.

Moving a group of controls

In a columnar report, you can move an entire group of controls in the Detail section. Here's how:

1. **Click one of the controls in the Detail section.**

   A thick border appears around the item and select all box containing a four-headed arrow appears toward the upper-left corner of the group of controls (see Figure 17-7).

The select all box

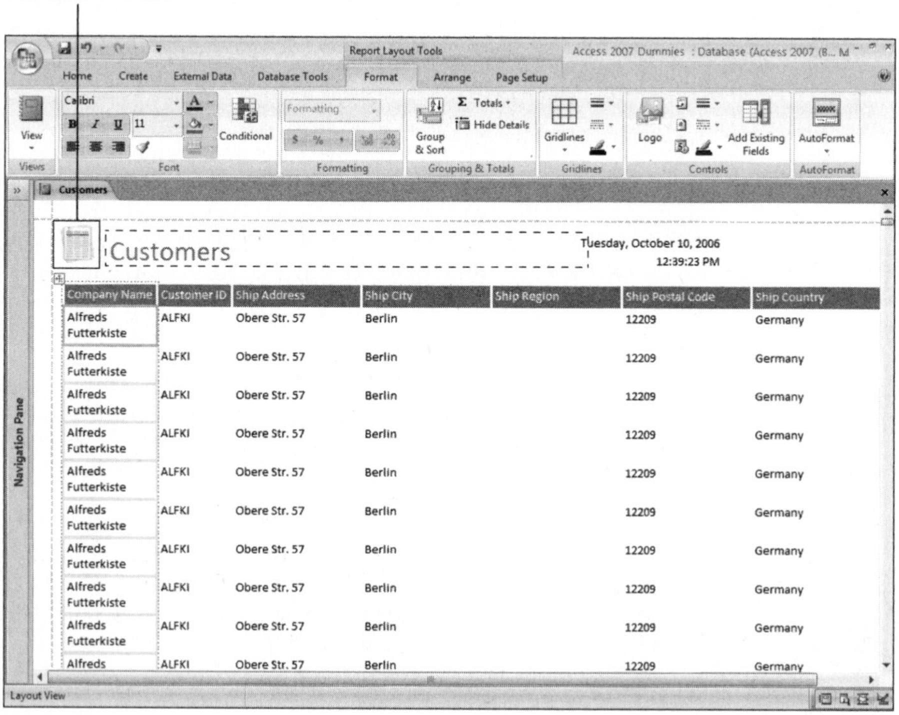

Figure 17-7:
Use the select all box with the four-headed arrow in it to move a group of controls.

2. **Roll the mouse over the box icon containing the four-headed arrow.**

   The mouse will change to a four-headed arrow.

3. **Drag the group of controls to a new position.**

   All the controls in the group will move at one time. Everything stays in alignment.

One size does not fit all

The Report Wizard and basic Report button do their best to size your report items properly. Very often, however, neither gets it right. A column will be too narrow or too wide, causing the space on the page to be used inefficiently. Do you throw your hands in the air and curse at the computer gods? Of course not. You can size any control to your exact needs.

I find that sizing works best in Layout view because you can see data in the controls as you are sizing them. However, sizing can be done in Design view as well.

Follow these steps to size a control:

1. **Select the item you want to size by clicking it.**

   The item will have a thick border around it.

2. **Roll the mouse to the edge of the selected item.**

   The mouse cursor changes to a two-headed arrow. See Figure 17-8 for a picture.

3. **Drag your item to its new size.**

   As you drag with the mouse, the two-headed arrow drags an outline of whatever object you selected to show you its new size.

4. **Release the mouse button when the item is the right size.**

   The item stretches or shrinks to its new size.

Text boxes and labels can be scaled to the exact size required to display the longest piece of text. To do this, follow Steps 1 and 2 above and then double-click instead of dragging. Like magic, Access figures out the correct size for the item and sizes it accordingly.

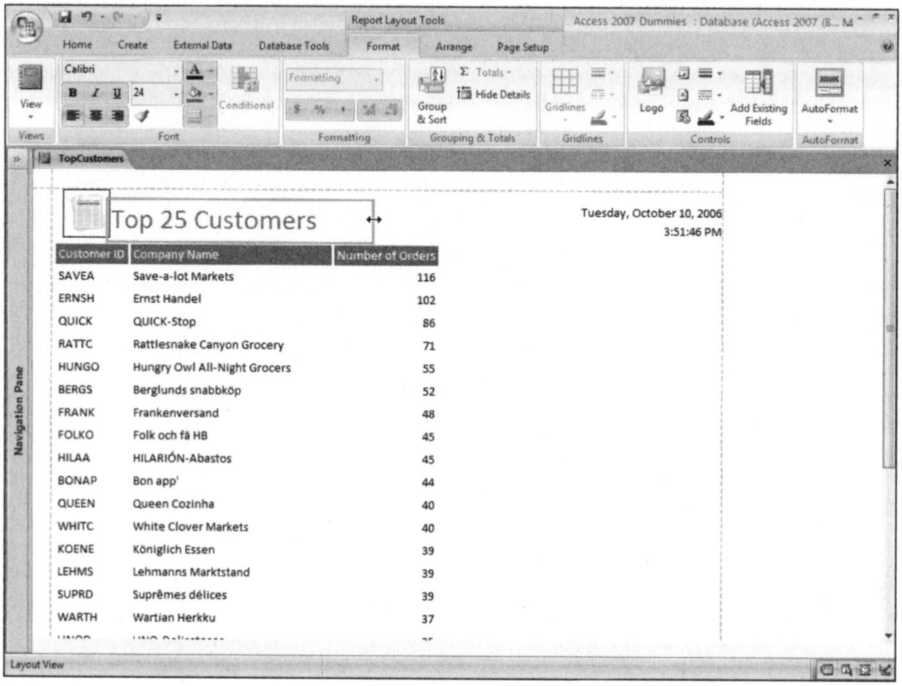

Figure 17-8:
The two-
headed
mouse
arrow at the
edge of the
Top 25
Customers
label
control.

Spaced out controls

The spacing of columns is a common problem in tabular reports. The report wizards tend to butt columns up against each other, sometimes making data difficult to read. If this is the case for you, you can use the Control Padding tool located on the Arrange tab of the Ribbon to space everything out a bit.

This adjustment can be done in either Layout or Design view, but I think you'll find Layout view is easier.

Follow these steps to add space between your columns in Layout view:

1. **Click the Select All box.**

   The labels and text boxes for all the columns are selected.

2. **Switch to the Arrange tab on the Ribbon, if necessary, by clicking it.**

The Arrange tools appear, including the Control Padding tool located in the Control Layout group (see Figure 17-9).

3. Click the arrow in the lower right of the Control Padding tool.

Four padding choices drop down.

4. Select one of the last three choices to add spacing between the columns.

Check your changes in Print Preview (see "Sneaking a Peek," later in this chapter). Sometimes adding too much space between columns pushes one or more of them off the page. If this happens, experiment with the different choices on the Control Padding tool until everything fits correctly.

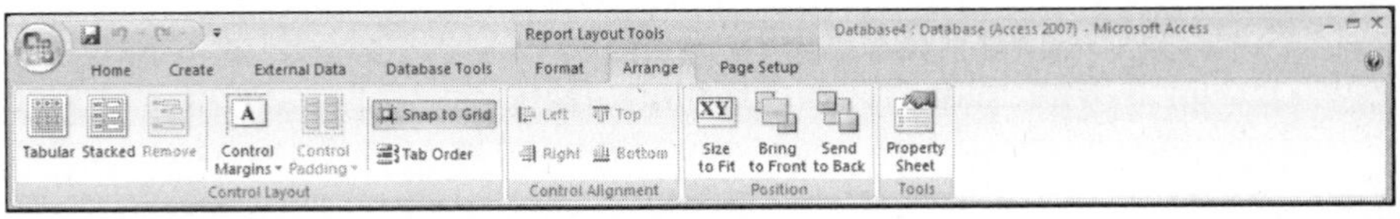

Figure 17-9:
The Ribbon's Arrange tab.

Borderline beauty

Organizationally speaking, lines and borders are great accents to

✔ Draw your readers' eyes to parts of the page.

✔ Highlight sections of the report.

✔ Add some pizzazz.

The Format tab on the Ribbon contains three buttons that work with lines:

✔ Line Color

✔ Line Type

✔ Line Thickness

You can use these tools on a line control to change the appearance of the line or on label and text box controls to add a border to the control. The three tools are in the Controls group on the Format tab.

Coloring

The Line Color button changes the color of lines that mark a text box's border and lines you draw on your report by using the Line tool.

This button works just like the Fill Color and the Font Color buttons for text.

- ✔ Lines are easier to work with in Design view.
- ✔ Text boxes and labels are easier to work with in Layout view.

To change the color of a line or control border, follow these steps:

1. **Click the item to select it.**

   The item has a thick border around it.

2. **Click the arrow next to the Line Color button.**

   A drop-down display of color choices appears, as shown in Figure 17-10. The colors are divided into sections:

   - *Theme:* Colors that the experts at Microsoft have determined work well together.
   - *Standard:* All the colors that have been created for you..
   - *Recent:* All the colors that have been used at one time or another on the report.

3. **Click your color choice from the myriad options.**

Thickening

In addition to colorizing lines and borders, you can also control their thickness:

1. **Click the line or text control you want to work with.**

2. **Click the arrow next to the Line Thickness button to display line and border thickness options.**

   Seven line thickness choices drop down, starting from thin and moving to thick, as shown in Figure 17-11.

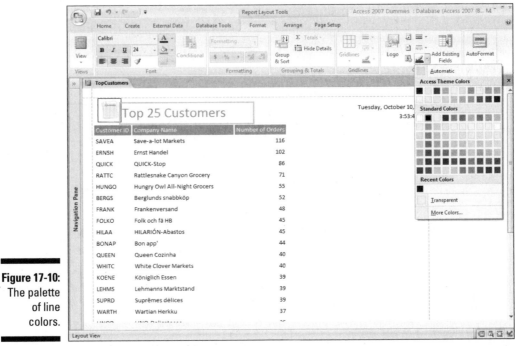

Figure 17-10:
The palette
of line
colors.

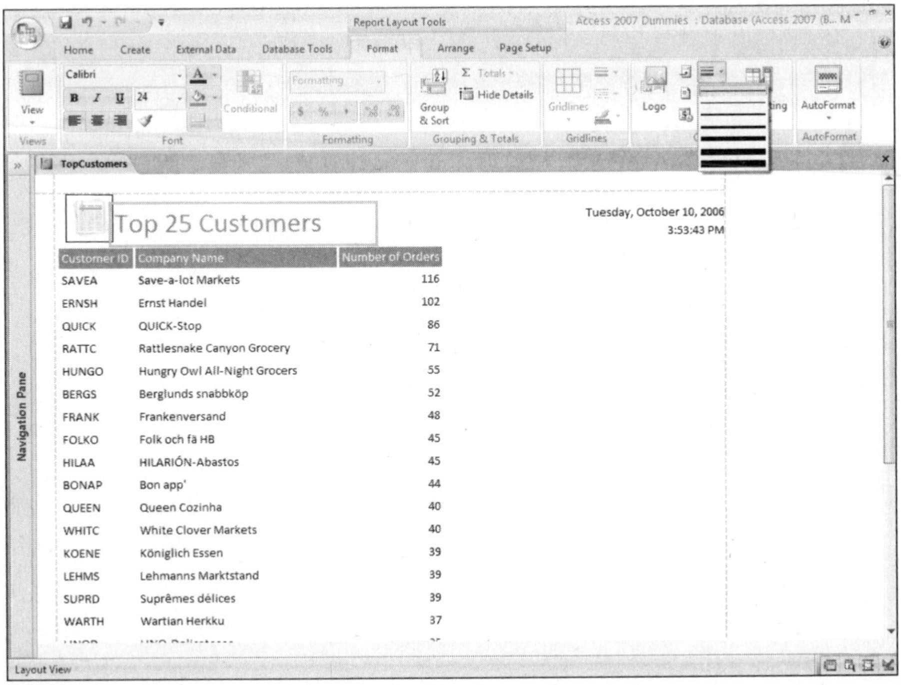

Figure 17-11:
The seven
line
thickness
options.

3. Click the line thickness option you want.

Like magic, your line or border thickness changes.

If you make a mistake, click the Undo button on the Quick Access toolbar or press Ctrl+Z to undo your mistake.

Changing the type

You can change the type of line displayed by your line control or text control border. The Line Type button handles that job for you. Seven choices are available under this button, as shown in Figure 17-12.

To change the line type of a control, follow these steps:

1. Click the control whose line type you want to change.

2. Click the arrow next to the Line Type button to display the options.

3. Click the line type you want.

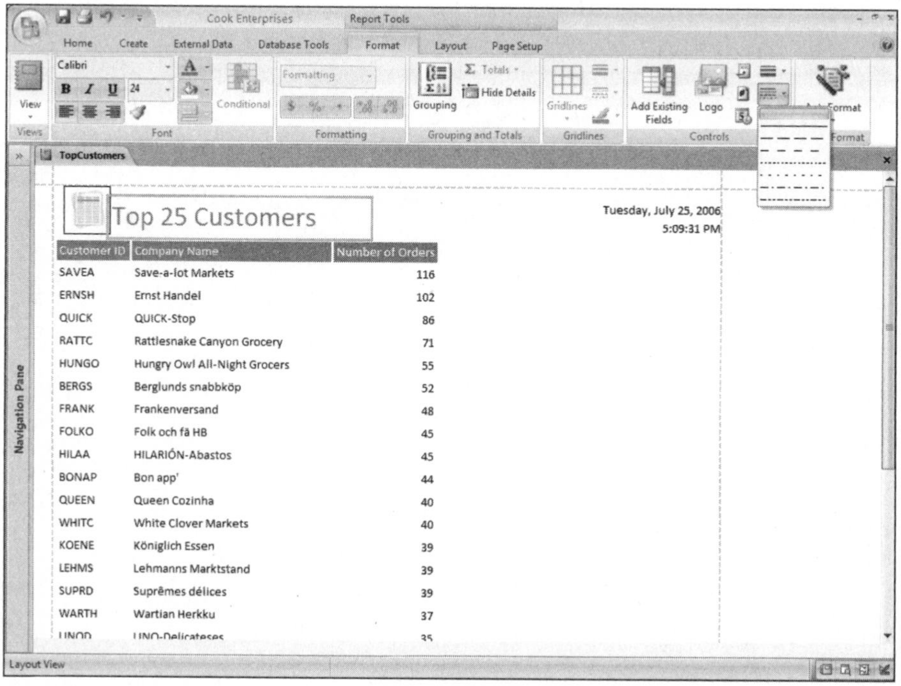

Figure 17-12:
The seven line type options.

Customer ID	Company Name	Number of Orders
SAVEA	Save-a-lot Markets	116
ERNSH	Ernst Handel	102
QUICK	QUICK-Stop	86
RATTC	Rattlesnake Canyon Grocery	71
HUNGO	Hungry Owl All-Night Grocers	55
BERGS	Berglunds snabbköp	52
FRANK	Frankenversand	48
FOLKO	Folk och fä HB	45
HILAA	HILARIÓN-Abastos	45
BONAP	Bon app'	44
QUEEN	Queen Cozinha	40
WHITC	White Clover Markets	40
KOENE	Königlich Essen	39
LEHMS	Lehmanns Marktstand	39
SUPRD	Suprêmes délices	39
WARTH	Wartian Herkku	37
LINOD	LINO-Delicateses	35

Top 25 Customers

Tuesday, July 25, 2006
5:09:31 PM

Tweaking your text

You must select the text you'd like to tweak before using any of the formatting tools. With Access labels, all of the text in the label must be formatted the same way. You cannot format one word differently from another. The same is true with the contents of a text box.

Fonts

To change the font or the font size,

1. **Select the text you want to change.**

2. **Click the arrow to the right of the Font or Font Size list box.**

3. **Make a selection from the drop-down list that appears.**

To turn on or off the bold, italic, or underline characteristics, select a block of text and click the appropriate button from the Font group on the Ribbon's Format tab. The characteristic *toggles* (switches) between on and off each time you click the button.

Alignment

You can control the alignment of the text within labels and text boxes. To change the alignment of the text for a label or text box, follow these steps:

1. **Select the control.**

2. **Click one of the three alignment buttons on the toolbar.**

   Figure 17-13 shows the alignment buttons. Pictured from left to right:

   - Align left
   - Center
   - Align right

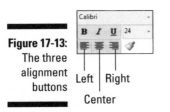

Figure 17-13:
The three alignment buttons

Make sure your reports follow these simple rules for your reader's pleasure:

- ✔ Align numeric data and dates to the right so that the numbers line up correctly.
- ✔ Align text to the left.
- ✔ Align your column headings to the data in the column:
    - Text column headings should align left.
    - Number column headings should align right.

Sneaking a Peek

Neither Layout view nor Design view give you a perspective on how the report will look on the printed page. So, where can you go to see how the report will print?

Access provides a command called Print Preview that does the trick. To preview your report, click the Print Preview button from the set of four view buttons on lower-right part of your screen. The Print Preview button is the second from the left with the magnifying glass on it.

Figure 17-14 displays a report in Print Preview. Here's how to navigate it:

- ✔ **Zoom:** Click anywhere on the report to zoom in or zoom out.
- ✔ **Page buttons:** Find these on the lower-left part of the Print Preview screen.
    - The right arrows move to the next or last pages.
    - The left arrows move to the first or previous pages.
    - Type a page number in the Current Page box (the one with the number in it), and Access will take you to that page.
- ✔ **Page Layout group** (on the Ribbon): The buttons change page orientation, margins, and paper size.
- ✔ **Zoom group** (on the Ribbon): The buttons change the number of pages that appear in Print Preview.
- ✔ **Close Print Preview button** (on the Ribbon): Exits print preview.

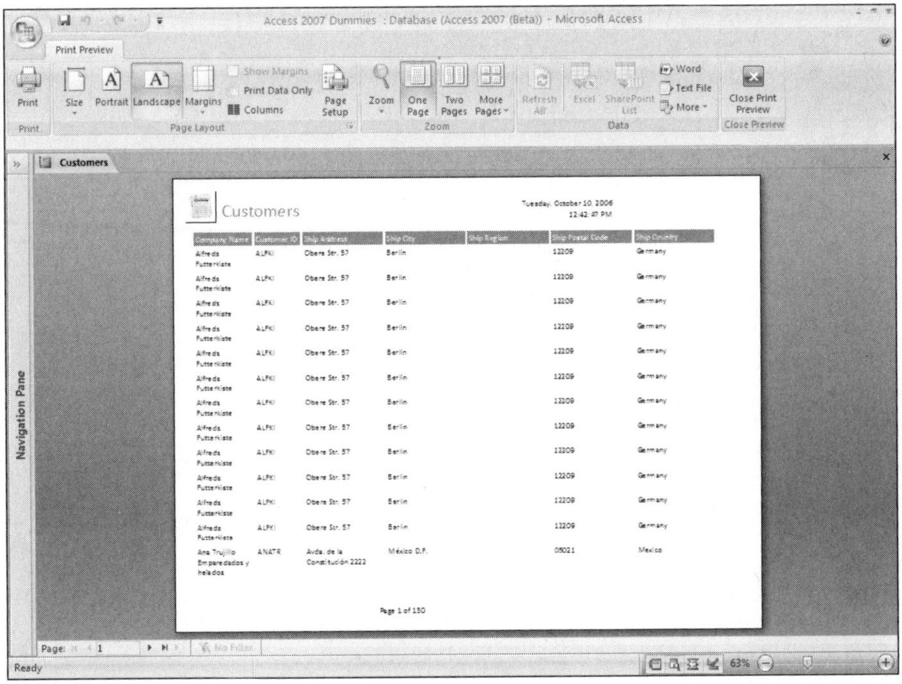

Figure 17-14:
A report in
Print
Preview.

For details on setting margins, paper size, and page orientation, see Chapter 16.

Getting an AutoFormat Makeover

When you want to change the look of the entire report in a few easy clicks, check out the AutoFormat button. When you click this button, Access offers several different format packages that reset everything from the headline font to the color of lines that split up items in the report.

AutoFormat is available in either

 ✓ **Layout view:** On the Format tab

   Layout view is best because actual data is present in this view.

 ✓ **Design view:** On the Arrange tab

Follow these steps to AutoFormat your report:

1. **Select the whole report (or the report sections you want to format).**

   The following steps select the whole report for formatting:

   • *Layout view:* Click in the margin area (above the dotted line) at the top of the report.

   • *Design view:* Click the small gray box with black dot in it at the upper-left corner of the report.

2. **Click the arrow on the AutoFormat toolbar button.**

   A palette of formatting choices drops down with a variety of color schemes, as depicted in Figure 17-15.

3. **Click the format you want.**

   Access updates everything you selected in your report with the new look.

   If just part of the report changes, go back and try Step 1 again. The odds are good that you had only part of the report selected when you clicked AutoFormat.

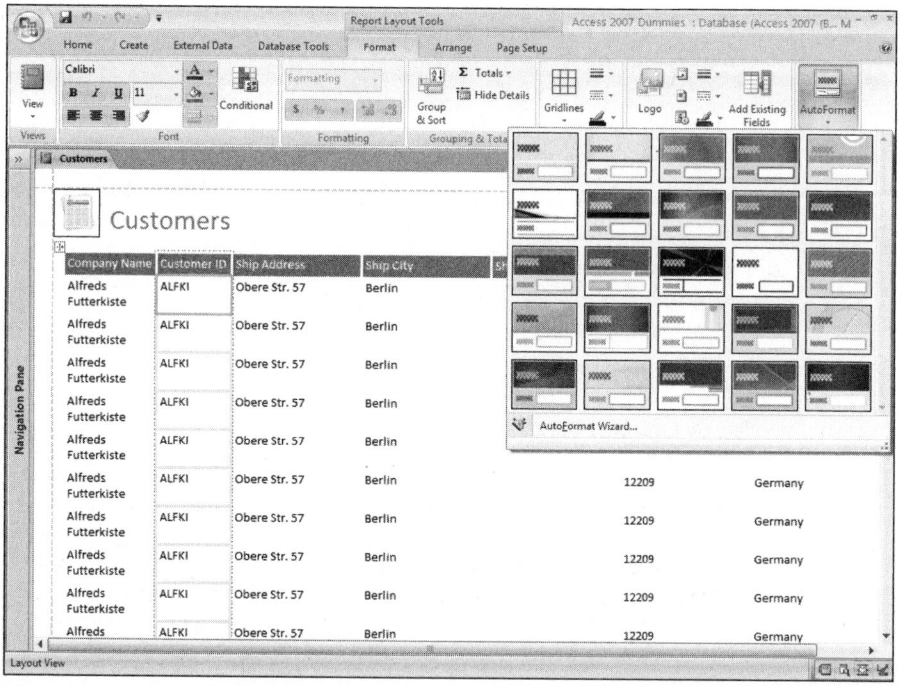

Figure 17-15:
Choose the look that you like and apply it to the entire report.

Adding Additional Design Elements

Use the controls we discuss in this section to enhance the appearance of your report. You'll see suggestions for the control's use in each section.

Drawing lines

An easy way to make your report a bit easier to read is to add lines that divide the sections. Lines can only be *added* in Design View.

You can use the various toolbar buttons (discussed earlier in this chapter) to dress up your lines, such as

✔ Line Color

✔ Line Thickness

✔ Line Type (solid, dashed, or dotted line)

You must switch to Design view to add lines.

Straight lines

To add straight lines to your report, follow these steps:

1. **Click the Line tool (the one with the diagonal line on it) in the Controls group of tools on the Design tab.**

   Your cursor changes to a crosshair with a line trailing off to the right.

2. **Repeat these steps for each line you want:**

   a. Click where you want to start the line.

   b. Drag to the location where you want to end the line

   c. Release the mouse button.

Rectangular boxes

The Rectangle tool draws boxes around separate items on your report. Rectangles can only be *added* in Design View. Follow these steps:

1. **Click the Rectangle tool (the one below the line tool, with a rectangle on it) in the Controls group of tools on the Design tab.**

2. **Repeat these steps for each rectangle you want:**

   a. *Click where you want to start the upper-left corner of the rectangle.*

   b. *Drag the rectangle shape down to the lower-right corner.*

   c. *Release the mouse button.*

Pretty as a picture

By default, the report wizards place an icon in the upper-left corner of reports they create, as shown in Figure 17-16. This icon is a logo placeholder should you want to add a logo to your report. Microsoft calls it the Auto_Logo.

If you're not going to add a logo to your report, you should *remove* the Auto_Logo icon because the icon will print on the report.

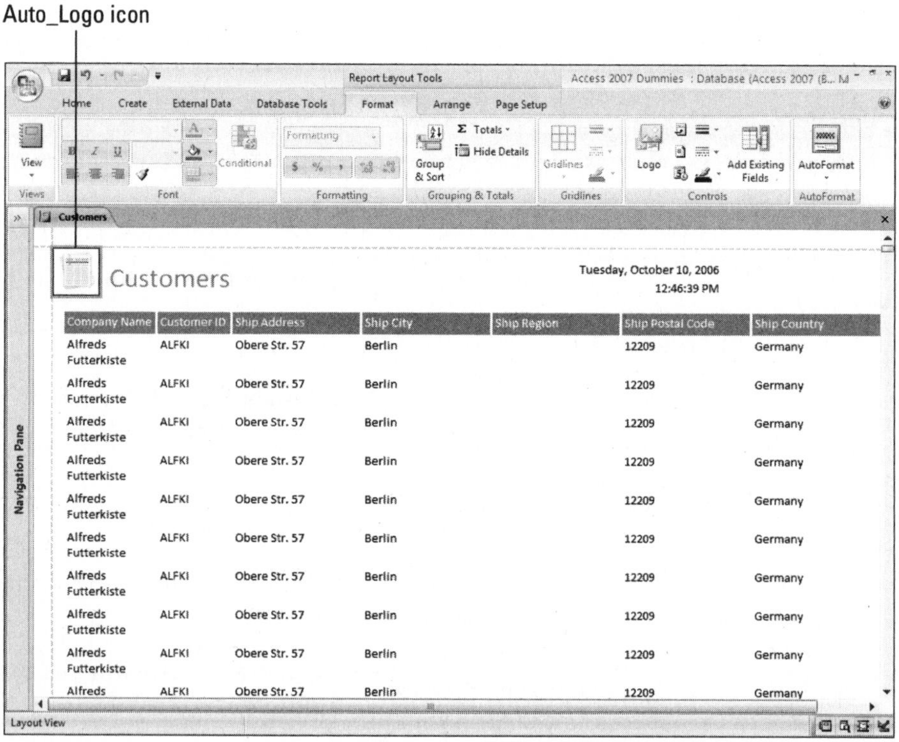

Auto_Logo icon

Figure 17-16:
The
Auto_Logo
icon.

Removing the Auto_Logo icon

It's easy to remove a logo. Here's how:

1. **In Design or Layout View, click the Auto_Logo icon.**
2. **Tap the Delete key on your keyboard.**

Adding a logo

You can replace the Auto_Logo icon with your logo in both Layout and Design views.

Pages that contain logos take longer to print. Use your logos wisely:

- ✔ *Headers* and *footers* are the best places for logos.
- ✔ The *Detail* section is not a good place for logos.

   In the Detail section, you get one copy of the logo for *each* record on the report. This could greatly slow the printing of your report.

Hitting the Office links

You can do a lot with Access, but sometimes you may want to use a different program because Access cannot do what you need. For example, you may need to calculate a median on a report. Access does not contain a built-in median function. To resolve this issue, you can export your data via the Excel Office Link button to Excel and use Excel's Median function to perform your calculation.

Access provides tools for converting reports to file formats that can be opened and modified in other programs (including other Office programs):

1. **In the Navigation Pane, locate and then right-click the report.**

2. **Choose Print Preview from the shortcut menu.**

   The Data group of tools on the Print Preview tab has a tool for each file format to which you can export your data.

3. **Click the tool for you desired format.**

   An Export dialog box will appear.

4. **Use the Browse button to assist you in entering a file name in the File name box.**

   The File name box should contain a path and file name when you're finished.

5. **Check the Open the destination file after the export operation is complete check box.**

   Do this so you won't have to remember where you stored the exported file and what you called it.

6. **Click the OK button to begin the export process.**

   The report will be exported to your selected file format then opened in the exported format's application.

If you want to replace the Auto_Logo icon with your logo, switch to Design view and follow these steps:

1. **Right-click the Auto_Logo icon on the page.**

   The icon is selected, and a shortcut menu appears.

2. **Choose Properties from the shortcut menu.**

   The Property Sheet window appears to the right of the report.

3. **Click in the Picture property row (see Figure 17-17).**

   A build button showing three dots appears.

4. **Click the build button.**

   The Insert Picture dialog box appears.

5. **Select the logo file you'd like to add and click OK.**

   The logo appears in the spot occupied by the Auto_Logo icon.

After you add a logo, you can size and move the logo as described earlier in this chapter.

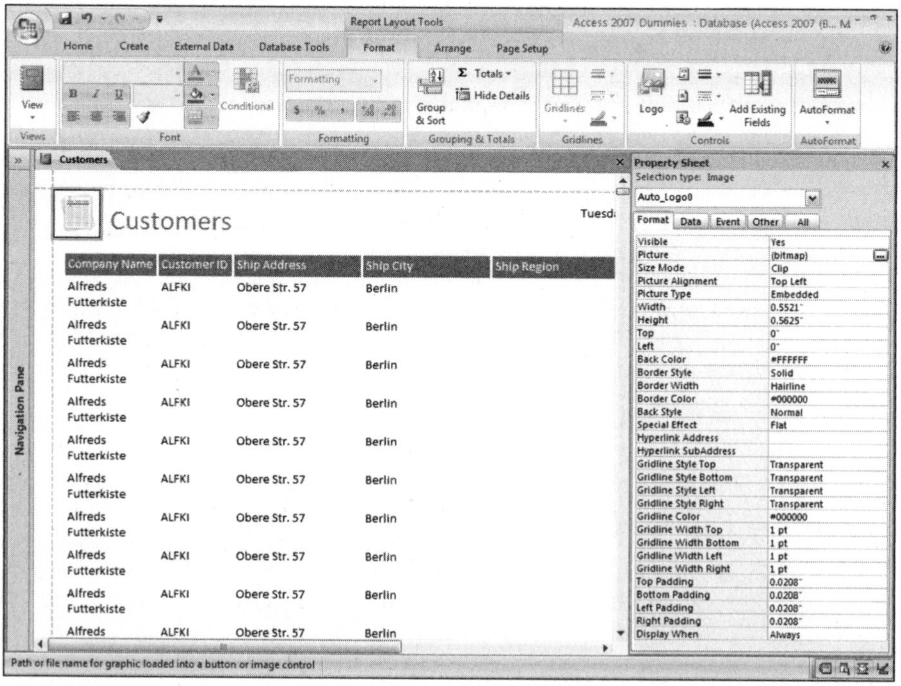

Figure 17-17:
The Picture property row showing the build button.

Chapter 18

Headers and Footers and Groups, Oh My!

The Report Wizard takes much of the stress and decision-making out of creating reports. This is also true of the Report tool which asks no questions at all and just turns your table into a report — bang, zoom, no fuss, no muss. The Report Wizard is almost that simple; it asks just a few simple questions that you won't have any trouble answering.

Well, *maybe* no trouble. A few of the questions, which I address in this chapter, may give you a moment's pause, if only because you may not understand what's being asked or how your answer can affect your report. Given that this book is all about eliminating any stress or concern for the Access user, my goal, then, is to explain those questions and to help you make the Report Wizard even more wizardly.

In addition to simplifying the already-simple Report Wizard, this chapter also covers the use of two very convenient and powerful report features — headers and footers. These stalwart additions appear at the top and/or bottom of your reports, performing whatever role you dictate — from eye candy to outright informers. They can be very spare and simply tell your readers what the name of the report is, or they can be really useful and tell people when the report was created when it was last printed. What you include in your headers and footers is entirely up to you.

A Place for Everything and Everything in Its Place

The secret to successful report organization lies in the way you set up the information included in the report. Access enables you to choose how your fields are laid out on the report, enabling you to achieve the most effective layout for the data in question.

A report is effective when the reader can glance at it and see exactly what information is offered:

- What data is included
- How much detail is available
- Where to look on the page to find specific pieces of information

Achieving an effective layout is simple, as Access's automatic reporting tools create a very basic, no-confusion-here layout by default.

Layout basics

Reports come in two layouts, *Columnar* or *Tabular*.

The layout that's right for your report is totally subjective. You can preview your report in both layouts and make your decision accordingly.

In either layout, each of the fields you choose to include in your report appears in two parts:

- Fields
- Labels (a name for the field, essentially)

The fields and labels are paired and laid out in either Columnar or Tabular format.

This chapter shows how you can take the default layouts that Access's automatic reporting features give you and tweak them by working in Design view. You can drag labels and fields around to achieve a completely custom report layout.

Here's the skinny on how Columnar and Tabular layout options look and work:

✔ **Columnar layout**

- Field descriptions print with every record's data (side by side), as shown in Figure 18-1.

  The layout behaves this way because both the field descriptions and data area are in the report's Detail section.

- The report title prints only once, at the very beginning of the report (because the title is in the Report Header section).

✔ **Tabular layout**

- Field descriptions print once per page in the Page Header section, as shown in Figure 18-2.

- The data areas are in the Detail section.

- The title prints, only at the top of the report.

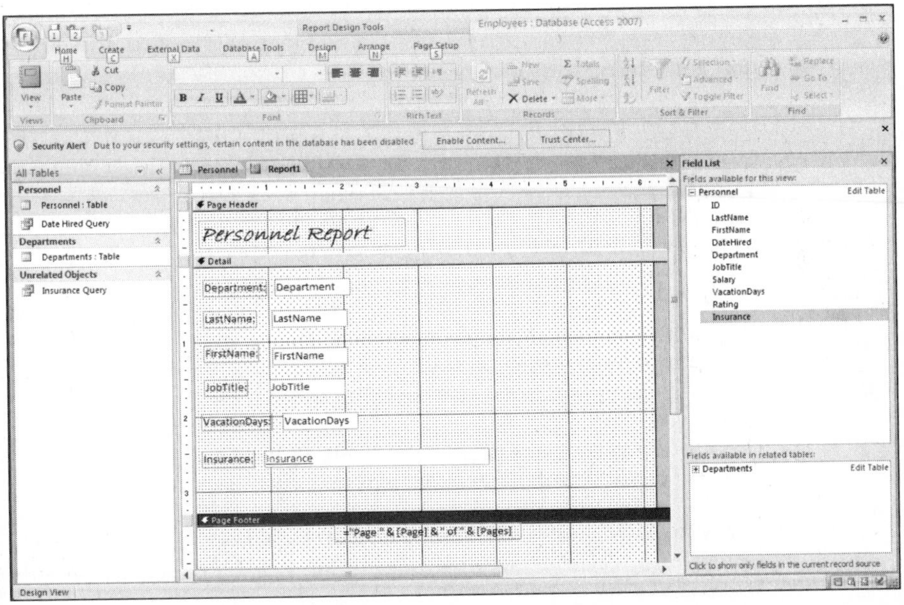

Figure 18-1:
In a columnar report, labels are to the left of the fields and repeat for each record.

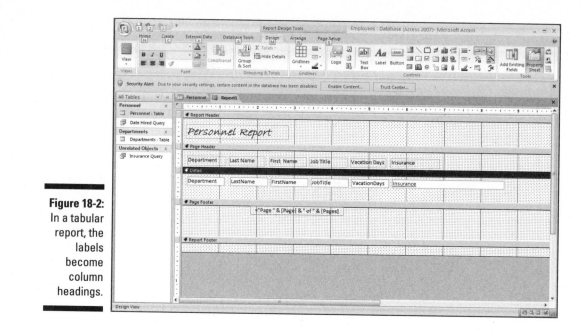

Figure 18-2:
In a tabular
report, the
labels
become
column
headings.

Sections

Reports are divided into sections. The information that appears in each section is dictated by your chosen layout.

Understanding the section concept is a prerequisite for performing any serious surgery on your report or for running off to build a report from scratch. Otherwise, your report groupings don't work right, fields are out of place, and you end up with a very frustrating, unfriendly report that neither you nor anyone else will want to read.

The most important point to understand about sections is that the contents of each section are printed *only* when certain events occur. For example, the information in the Page Header is repeated at the top of each page, but the Report Header prints on only the first page.

Getting a grip on sections is easy when you look at the *innermost section* of your report first and work your way outward, like so:

- ✔ **Detail:** Access prints items in this section each time it moves to a new record. Your report includes a copy of the Detail section for each record in the table.

- ✔ **Group headers and footers:** You may have markers for one or more *group sections.*

In Figure 18-3, information in the report is grouped by Department.(You can tell by the section bar labeled Department Header — the section bar identifies which field is used for grouping.)

Group sections always come in pairs:

- The *group header* section is above the Detail section in the report design.

- The *group footer* is always below Detail.

Information in these sections repeats for every unique value in the groups' fields. For example, the report shown in Figure 18-3 reprints everything in the Department Header for each employee. Within the section for each department, Access repeats the information for each person who works for the company.

✔ **Page Header and Page Footer:** These sections appear at the top and bottom, respectively, of every page. They're among the few sections not controlled by the contents of your records.

Use the information in the Page Header and Footer sections to mark the pages of your report.

✔ **Report Header and Footer:** These sections appear at the start and end of your report. They each make only one appearance in your report — unlike the other sections, which pop up many times.

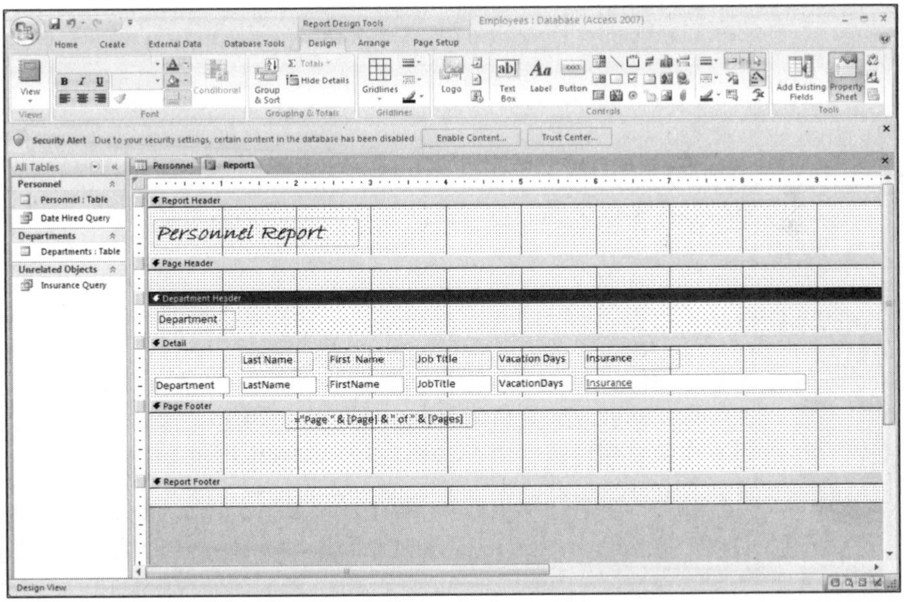

Figure 18-3:
Grouping
records by
Department.

Reporting, Step by Step

When Access produces a report, what does it do with all these sections? The process goes this way:

1. Access begins by printing the Report Header at the top of the first page.

2. Access then prints the Page Header, if you choose to have the Page Header appear on the first page. (Otherwise, Access reprints this header at the top of every page except the first one.)

3. If your report has groups, the Group Headers for the first set of records appear next.

4. When the headers are in place, Access prints the Detail lines for each record in the first group.

5. After it's finished with all the Detail lines for this group, Access prints that group's Group Footer.

6. If you have more than one group, Access repeats Steps 3, 4, and 5 for each group.

7. At the end of each page, Access prints the Page Footer.

8. When it finishes with the last group, Access prints the Report Footer — which, like the Report Header, appears only once in a given report.

Here's what you can do with headers and footers:

✔ The Report Header provides general information about the report. This is a good place to add the report title, printing date, and version information.

✔ The Page Header contains any information you want to appear at the top of each page (such as the date or your company logo).

✔ The headers for each group usually identify the contents of that group and the field names.

✔ The footers for each group generally contain summary information, such as counts and calculations. For example, the footer section of the Department group may hold a calculation that totals the minimum bids.

✔ The Page Footer, which appears at the bottom of every page, traditionally holds the page number and report date fields.

✔ The footer in your report can be a good place to put things like

• Confidentiality statements

• Information regarding the timeliness of the data in the report

• The name(s) of the report's author(s).

• An e-mail address or phone number to contact the person who made the report.

Grouping your records

When the Report Wizard creates a report for you it includes a header and footer section for each group you want. If you tell the Report Wizard to group by the Department field, for example, it automatically creates both the Department Header and the Department Footer sections. You aren't limited to what the wizard does, though. If you're a little adventuresome, you can augment the wizard's work with your own grouping sections.

Before making any big adjustments to the report, take a minute to save the report (choose Save from the Quick Access bar). That way, if something goes wrong and the report becomes horribly disfigured, just close it (click the X in the upper-right corner of the report window) without saving your changes. Ahhh. Your original report is safe and sound.

The key to creating your own grouping sections is the Group, Sort, and Total panel, which is available after you've created a report with the Report Wizard or while you're in Design view working on a customized report. To display the panel, shown in Figure 18-4, click the Design tab and then click the Grouping button in the Grouping and Totals section.

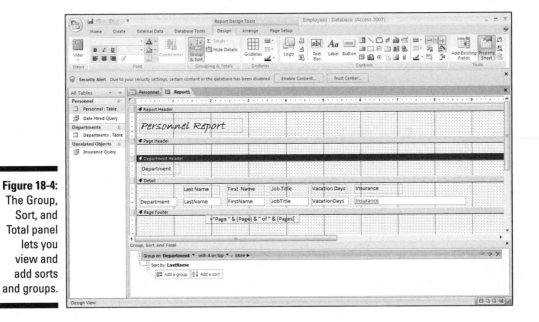

Figure 18-4: The Group, Sort, and Total panel lets you view and add sorts and groups.

This panel allows you to control how Access organizes the records in your report, augmenting the sorting and grouping you may have already set up through the Report Wizard dialog box or when you're building a report from scratch in Design view.

You can completely customize how your report's records are grouped and sorted and sort by multiple fields quickly and easily. The next set of steps shows you how.

To build your own groupings and add sorting with the Group, Sort, and Total panel, follow these steps:

1. **Click the Design tab (while you're in Design view of an existing or in-progress report).**

2. **Click the Grouping button in the Grouping and Totals section.**

   The Group, Sort, and Total panel appears.

3. **View any existing grouping or sorting, each represented by a Sort By or Group On bar, as shown in Figure 18-5.**

   The tree-like display shows the hierarchical groups and sorting set up for your report.

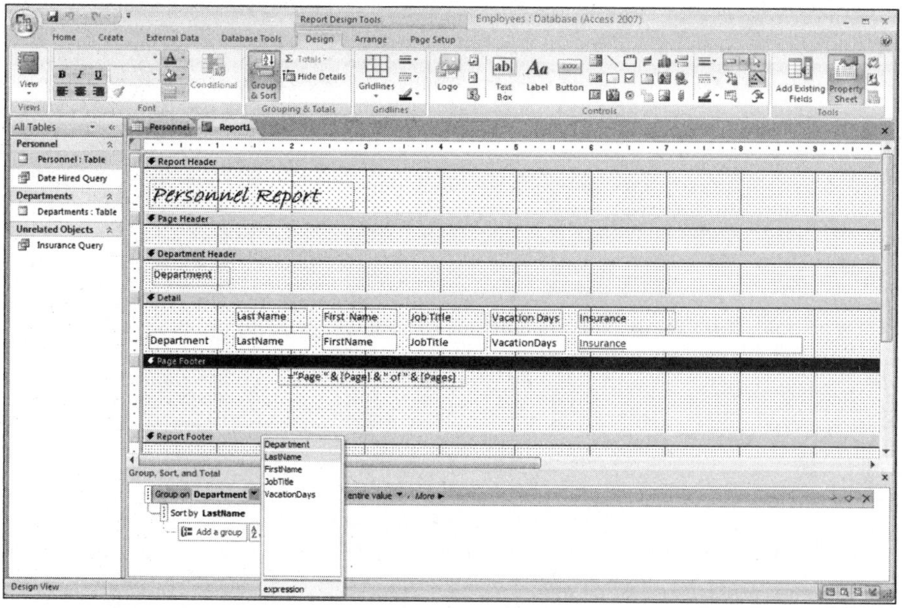

Figure 18-5:
Choose a new field by which to group or sort your records.

4. **Click Add a Group and select a field by which to group from the pop-up menu.**

   Access displays a list of available fields from which you can choose to group your report's records.

5. **Click Add a Sort and select a field by which to sort from the pop-up menu**

   Again, a list of fields appears. You can click a field to choose a new field on which to sort your records.

   If you've already sorted by a field within the report, your subsequent sorting will be applied to the sort already applied — using the employee database as an example, if you already elected to sort by Department (say, while you were setting up the report through the Report Wizard), that sort will appear in the panel. If you click Add a Sort, your next logical field on which to sort might be JobTitle or LastName. The resulting sort would then put the list, already in order by Department, in further order, putting each department in order by the field chosen for the added sort. All the Accounting department people will be in order by that second field, all the Operations people, and so on. It's a lot like the phone book — all the records in that book are in order by last name, and for those listings with the same last name, the records are in order by first name. If the first names are the same, a third order, by street, is applied, so if there are two John Smiths, the one on Elm Street comes before the one on Walnut Street.

6. **To change the settings for an existing group or sort, click the Group On or Sort By bar and change the sort order or pick a different field by which to sort.**

   As shown in Figure 18-6, you can

   • Change the sort order from ascending "with *A* on top" to descending "with *Z* on top."

   • Change the field on which the group or sort is based by clicking the currently-selected field and choosing another one from the list.

7. **Close the Group, Sort, and Total panel.**

   You can close the panel after you've finished using it by either

   • Clicking the X in its upper-right corner.

   • Clicking the Group button again (in the Grouping and Totals section of the Design tab)

To remove a group, click the X on the far right end of the Group On or Sort By bar. There is no confirming prompt; when you click that X, your group or sort is gone. Of course, you can re-group or re-sort by using the Add a Group or Add a Sort buttons.

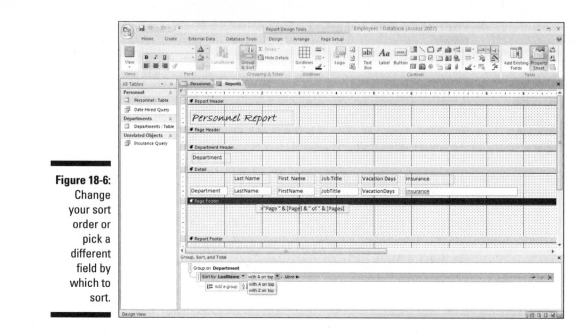

Figure 18-6:
Change
your sort
order or
pick a
different
field by
which to
sort.

So you want more?

In addition to adding and removing groups and sorts with the Group, Sort, and Total panel, you can also make the following adjustments/selections:

- ✔ **On the Sort By bar, click More** and view a list of options, including "by entire value," "with no totals," "with title" (click the "click to add" link to insert a title), and options for adding headers and footers for the sorted records.

  To hide these options, click Less.

- ✔ **On the Group On bar, click More** to make the same choices as to how to group the records, whether or not to include totals, and how to use headers and footers.

  Click Less to hide the options on the bar when you've finished using them.

With the appropriate fields in the correct header, footer, and detail sections, you've successfully finished the biggest step in building your report. Now you're down to the little things — tweaking, adjusting, and touching up the details of how your report presents itself. The properties described in the following sections govern the visual aspect — the look and feel — of your report.

Some of the stuff in the coming paragraphs looks a little technical at first glance because these settings dig deep into the machinery of report-making. Don't let the high-tech look scare you. By organizing your headers, footers, and detail rows, you have already conquered the hard part of building the report. This stuff's just the window-dressing.

Customizing Properties

In an amazing stroke of usability, Access keeps all properties settings for your report in a single panel, the Property Sheet, which appears to the right of your report in Design view, as shown in Figure 18-7, which shows the daunting All tab. But before you can start using the Property Sheet, you have to have it on your screen:

✔ To start adjusting the details of any component of your report, either

   • Double-click the item you want to modify.

   • Right-click the item and choose Properties from the pop-up menu.

   • You can also display the Properties panel by clicking Property Sheet in the Tools section of the Design tab, under Report Tools.

✔ To display the controls for the entire report, double-click the little box where the two rulers meet, just to the left of the Report Header.

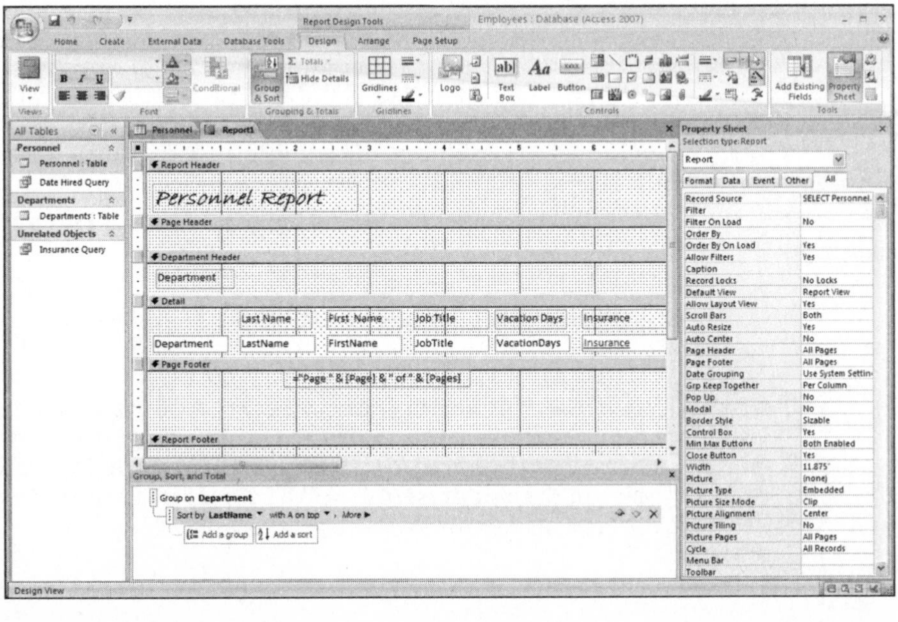

Figure 18-7:
Double-click any piece of the report to see that item's properties.

No matter where you double-click, up pops a very useful panel, also known as the Property Sheet.

When the Property Sheet appears, its title bar indicates which part of the report you're about to tweak. You can also click the drop-down list (which repeats the name of the currently displayed portion of the report's properties) and choose a different component to work with.

The Property Sheet is very long and a bit scary looking. Regardless of which report component you choose to tweak (or if you're looking at the properties for the entire report), some of the settings won't need to be tweaked, and you'll probably have no idea *how* to tweak them anyway. And that's fine at this stage of the game. Seasoned Access users often leave many of these properties in their default state.

The Property Sheet has five tabs along the top of the list of properties — *Format, Data, Event, Other,* and All (which was the active tab in Figure 18-7). The only tab that's really worth looking at is Format; the others are really only of interest to programmers, and All is just plain frightening because it lists every possible property you can adjust.

So, with the Format tab clicked, as shown in Figure 18-8, feel free to tweak away. Change the Caption, decide whether you want scroll bars on the report when viewed on-screen, decide which pages should have a header or footer, and so on. Most of the properties' names are pretty self-explanatory, so you should be fine.

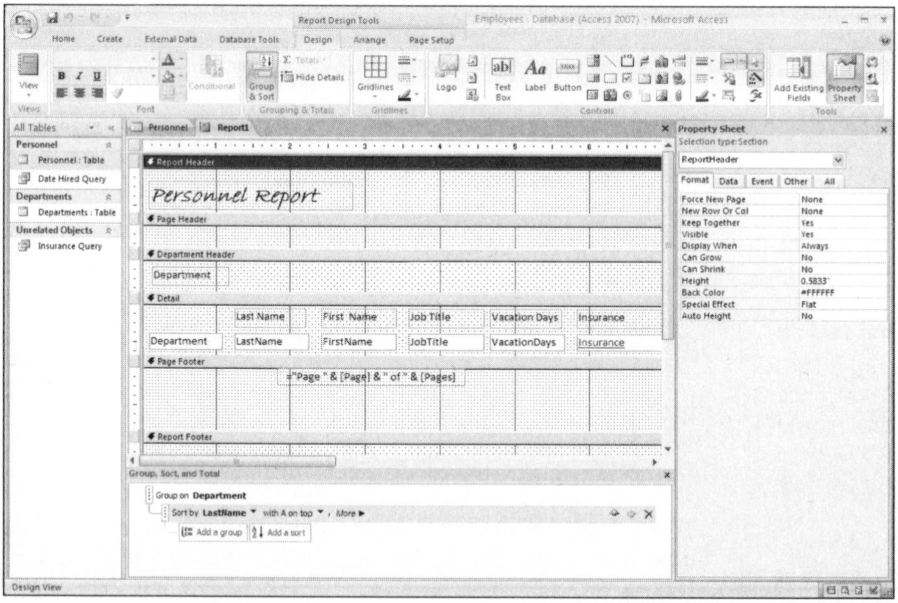

Figure 18-8:
The Format tab's properties list varies depending on which report component you're working with.

If you're at a loss as to what one of the properties does or means, click the setting on the right and see the drop-down arrow appear, as shown in Figure 18-9 — use the drop-down list to see the options for the chosen property. In many cases, seeing those options clarifies what the property is and does.

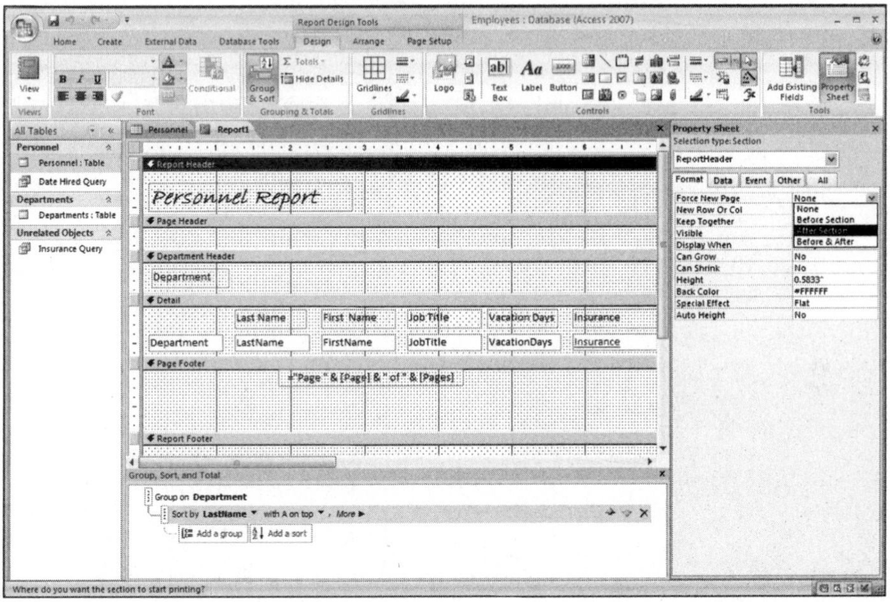

Figure 18-9:
Find out more about a particular property by using its drop-down list to make alternate selections.

Does the Properties panel look a bit cramped? Resize it:

1. **Point to the frame on its left side, where it meets the report itself.**

   Your mouse pointer turns into a two-headed horizontal arrow.

2. **Drag the arrow to the left until your Properties panel is the right width for your needs.**

Controlling report and page headings

To adjust when various headings appear in your report, start with the Property Sheet. After the panel appears (open it by double-clicking the report component of your choice), try these settings:

✔ The default setting for both the Page Header and the Page Footer is All Pages, meaning that Access prints a header and footer on every page in the report.

✔ Choose Not with Rpt Hdr (or Not with Rprt Ftr for the footer) to tell Access to

- Skip the first and last pages (where the Report Header and Report Footer are printed)

- Print the Page Header on all the other pages.

✔ The Keep Together option affects the Keep Together entry, which you set in the Sorting and Grouping dialog box (see "Grouping your records," earlier in this chapter):

- Choose Per Page to apply the Keep Together setting to pages.

- In a report with multiple columns, choose Per Column to apply the Keep Together setting to columns.

The Page Header section comes with a bunch of options, too. Double-click the Page Header to display the PageHeaderSection panel, as shown in Figure 18-10.

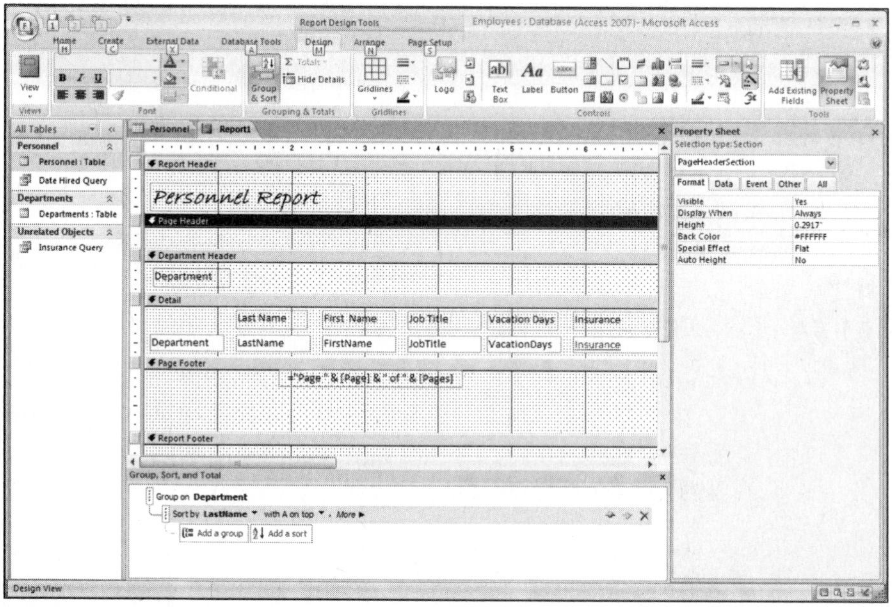

Figure 18-10:
Display
PageHeader
Section
properties
from the
Property
Sheet drop
list.

Click the Format tab on the Property Sheet for the following options:

- ✔ **Visible:** Controls whether the Page Header appears at all.

- ✔ **Display When:** This is set to Always by default, but allows you to choose from Print Only or Screen Only, should those options appeal to you.

- ✔ **Height:** Access automatically sets this property as you click and drag the section header up and down on the screen.

  To specify an exact size (for example, if you want the header area to be *precisely* 4 centimeters tall), type the size in this section. (Access automatically uses the units of measurement you chose for Windows itself.)

- ✔ **Back Color:** If you want to adjust the section's color, follow these steps:

  1. *Click the currently-selected color.*

  2. *Click the small gray button that appears to the right of the entry.*

     This button displays a color palette.

  3. *Click your color choice.*

     Let Access worry about the obnoxious color number that goes into the Back Color box.

  An easier method is to click the section in Design view and use the drop-down list on the Formatting toolbar.

- ✔ **Special Effect:** This property adjusts the visual effect for the section heading, much as the Special Effect button does for the markers in the report itself. Your choices are limited, though. Click the Special Effect box and then click the down arrow to list what's available. Choose Flat (the default setting), Raised, or Sunken.

- ✔ **Auto Height:** This option is set to Yes, but you can choose No if you'd prefer not to have an automatic height setting applied to your page heading.

Adjusting individual sections

If you want to change the format for just one section of the report, double-click GroupHeader to display the Property Sheet shown in Figure 18-11.

If your report doesn't include any groups, GroupHeader won't be in the list of components for which you can view properties, nor will there be a Group heading to double-click in Design view.

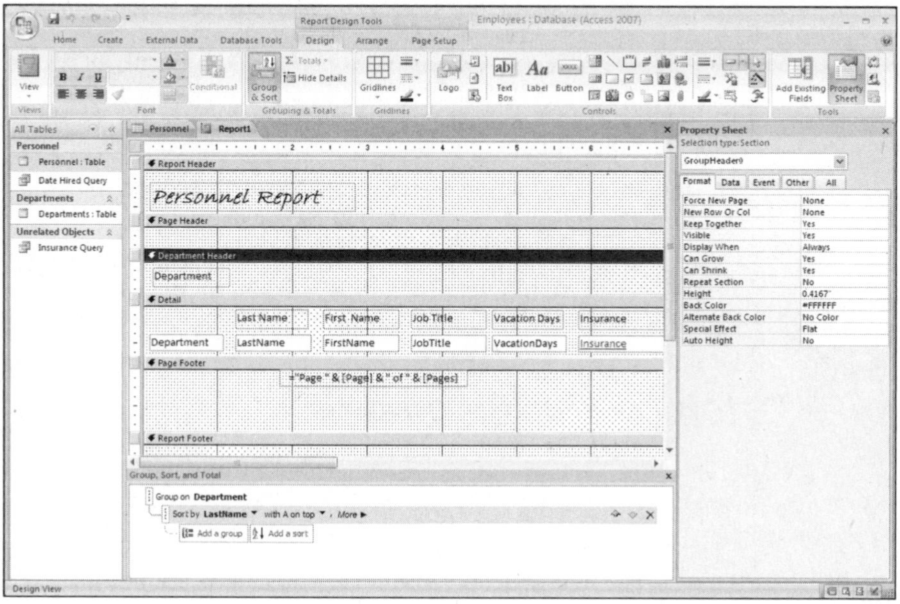

Figure 18-11:
Choose to
adjust any
section of
your report
by double-
clicking the
section in
the report.

If your report does have a group in it, you can tweak thirteen different
GroupHeader settings. The settings you're most likely to want to adjust
include the following:

✔ **Force New Page:** This option controls whether the change for that
group automatically forces the information to start on a new page. When
you set this option, you can determine whether this page break occurs

  • Only before the header

  • Only after the footer

  • In both places

You can control the way in which section beginnings and endings are
handled for multiple-column reports (such as having the group always
start in a separate column). You can control whether

  • The group is kept together.

  • The section is visible.

✔ **Can Grow:** The section expands as necessary, based on the data in it.

Can Grow is particularly useful when you're printing a report that contains a Memo field:

1. Set the width of the field so that it's as wide as you want.

2. Use the Can Grow property to enable Access to adjust the height available for the information.

✔ **Can Shrink:** The section can become smaller if, for example, some of the fields are empty.

To use the Can Grow and Can Shrink properties, you need to set them for both the section and the items in the section that can grow or shrink.

✔ **Repeat Section:** Controls whether Access repeats the heading on each page when a group is split across pages or columns.

Itemized adjustments

Double-clicking works for more than sections. When you want to adjust the formatting of any item of your report — a field, a label, or something you've drawn on your report — just double-click that item in Design view. Access leads you to a marvelous dialog box from which you can perform all manner of technical nitpicking.

Customizing headers and footers

Although Access includes several default settings for headers and footers, those settings aren't personalized or imaginative. You can do much more with headers and footers than simply display labels for your data. You can build expressions in these sections or insert text that introduces or summarizes your data. Now those are the kinds of headers and footers that impress your friends, influence your coworkers, and win over your boss.

A good header on your report's shoulders

How you place the labels in the report's header sections controls how the final report both looks and works, so you really need to put some thought into your headers. You want to make sure that all your headings are easy to understand and that they add useful information to the report.

When you're setting up a report, feel free to play around with the header layouts. Experiment with your options and see what you can come up with — the way the information repeats through the report may surprise you.

For example, when you use a wizard to create a grouped report, Access puts labels for your records into the page header by default. Figure 18-12 shows such a report in action. Notice that the Department heading is printed above the site name. This appears at the top of each and every page because that label is in the Page Header section. This example is just one way to make use of the header section, however, as shown in Figure 18-13, where the Job Title label is now in the PageHeader section. How did it get there? By dragging the label onto that section of the report. It's as simple as that!

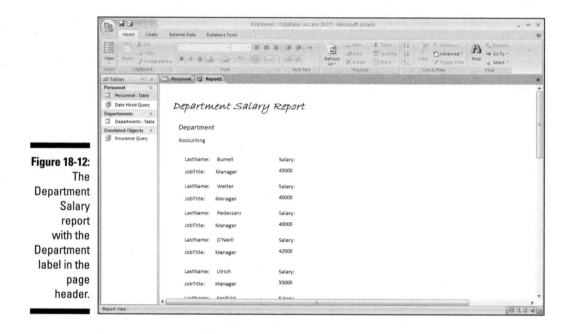

Figure 18-12:
The Department Salary report with the Department label in the page header.

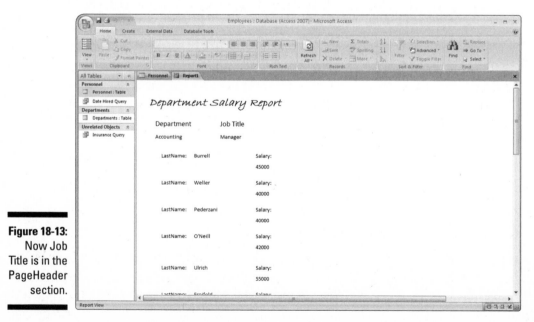

Figure 18-13:
Now Job Title is in the PageHeader section.

Solid footing with page numbers and dates

Access can insert certain information for you in either the header or the footer. Most notably, Access can insert

✔ **Page numbers.** Insert them by using the Page Number command found in the Controls section of the Design tab.

✔ **Dates.** Click the Date and Time command, also found in the Controls section of the Design tab.

And this is page what?

If you click the Page Numbers button on the Controls section of the Design tab, the Page Numbers dialog box appears (as shown in Figure 18-14).

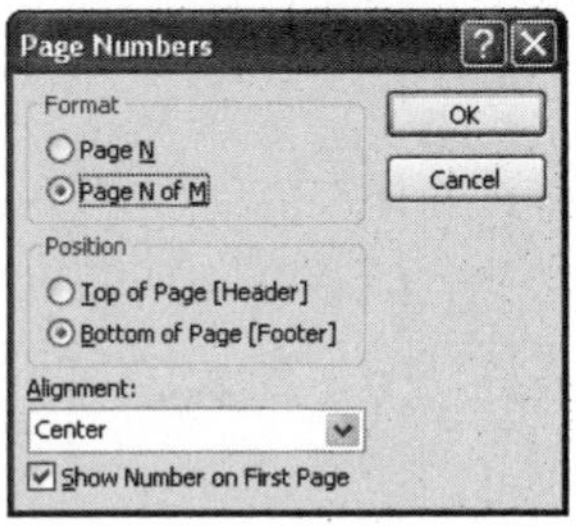

Figure 18-14: Control your report's page numbers.

The Page Numbers dialog box has several options for your page-numbering excitement:

✔ **Format:**

• *Page N:* Prints the word *Page* followed by the appropriate page number.

• *Page N of M:* Counts the total number of pages in the report and prints that number with the current page number (as in *Page 2 of 15*).

✔ **Position:** Tell Access whether to print the page number in the Page Header or the Page Footer.

✔ **Alignment:** Set the position of the page number on the page.

Click the arrow at the right edge of the list box to see your options.

✔ **Show Number on First Page:**

• Select this option to include a page number on the first page of your report.

• Deselect this option to keep your first page unnumbered.

To change how the page numbers work on your report, follow these steps:

1. **Manually delete the existing page number field.**

   To delete the field, click it and press the Delete key.

2. **Click the Page Numbers button in the Controls section of the Design tab.**

3. **Set up new page numbers.**

Time-stamping your reports

Click the Date and Time button, found in the Controls section of the Design tab, to display the Date and Time dialog box (shown in Figure 18-15).

The most important options are

- ✔ Include Date
- ✔ Include Time

Select the exact format of your date and/or time from the set of choices. The dialog box displays a sample of your settings in the section cleverly marked *Sample.*

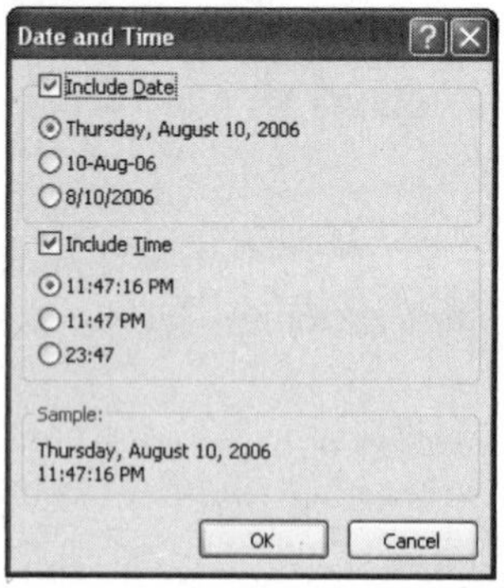

Figure 18-15:
Choose
dates and
times here.

> **Date and Time** ? X
>
> ☑ Include Date
> ⦿ Thursday, August 10, 2006
> ○ 10-Aug-06
> ○ 8/10/2006
>
> ☑ Include Time
> ⦿ 11:47:16 PM
> ○ 11:47 PM
> ○ 23:47
>
> Sample:
> Thursday, August 10, 2006
> 11:47:16 PM
>
> [OK] [Cancel]

Including the date and time makes a *huge* difference with information that changes regularly. By printing the information at the bottom of your report pages, Access automatically documents when the report came out. It never hurts to build a date stamp or a time *and* date stamp into your report footers.

Chapter 19

Magical Mass Mailings

· ·

In This Chapter

▶ Creating labels quickly and easily

▶ Formatting labels for specific situations

· ·

The Report Wizard (covered in Chapter 16) is just the tip of the Access report iceberg. If you're so inclined, you can use Access to generate useful printouts that you probably never thought of as reports — mailing or product labels. Don't be scared, though — we're off to see the wizards again, as Access provides friendly and magical helpers to see you through.

Massive Mailings with the Label Wizard

So you have 5,000 catalogues, newsletters, or some other mailable item printed and ready to go out to your adoring (or soon-to-be adoring) public. You also have a big Access database full of names and addresses. How can you introduce these two and get them started on what will surely be a wonderful relationship?

With the Access Label Wizard, your sheets of labels and your database will be married in no time flat. With the Label Wizard, you can quickly and easily generate labels that will work with just about any commercial label product on the market. If your local stationery or office supply store carries them, Access can print your data on them. All you need to know is what kind of label you have, which data should go on the labels, and who's going to slap the labels on the mailings after you've finished your part of the job.

When it comes to labels, names and addresses are just part of the story. You can also print product labels, with product names, numbers, and inventory locations on them, helping your warehouse personnel find and put away products. If you have the data and the blank labels, you can bring the two together to print labels for just about any purpose.

Microsoft engineers built the specifications for hundreds of labels from popular manufacturers right into the Label Wizard. If you happen to use labels from Avery, Herma, Zweckform, or any other maker listed in the wizard's manufacturer list, just tell the wizard the manufacturer's product number. The wizard sets up the report dimensions for you according to the maker's specifications. Life just doesn't get much easier than that.

Before firing up the Label Wizard, decide on information for the labels:

✔ The Label Wizard uses the active table's fields by default.

✔ You can create a query that includes only those fields you want to print, drawing those fields from the tables that currently house them.

Chapters 11 through 14 show the procedures for creating queries. It can be as simple as selecting the table that contains the label-bound data and querying for all the records but choosing to include only some of the fields. Or, query for certain records, again specifying which fields to include, and you're good to go. Again, check out the query chapters — especially Chapter 12 for the basics — before you embark on this process.

Of course, if your label information can all be found in a single table, just be sure that table is open and follow these steps to build a label report:

1. **In the database window, click the Create tab and then go to the Reports section of the tab.**

   The Create tab's many tools appear, including the Reports buttons that we discuss in Chapter 17.

2. **Click Labels to start the Label Wizard.**

   The Label Wizard dialog box opens, as shown in Figure 19-1.

Figure 19-1: The Label Wizard is prepared to make label magic!

Label Wizard		

This wizard creates standard labels or custom labels.

What label size would you like?

Product number:	Dimensions:	Number across:
C2160	1 1/2" x 2 1/2"	3
C2163	1 1/2" x 3 9/10"	2
C2241	1 1/4" x 7 31/50"	2
C2242	2" x 2"	3
C2243	1 1/2" x 1 1/2"	4

Unit of Measure: ⊙ English ○ Metric

Label Type: ⊙ Sheet feed ○ Continuous

Filter by manufacturer: Avery

[Customize...] ☐ Show custom label sizes

[Cancel] [< Back] [Next >] [Finish]

3. **Click the Filter by Manufacturer drop-down list and select your label manufacturer.**

   Access assumes you have Avery labels, and if you do, there's no need to perform this step — move on to Step 4.

4. **Scroll through the list of label types and find your label's product number — once you locate it, click it to select it.**

   The three-column list includes Product Number, Dimensions, and Number Across information.

   Find the product number on your package of labels in the list. If you don't see it, check the packaging for an equivalent product number that the manufacturer recommends. Often, if you buy a generic or store brand of labels, the Avery equivalent is printed right on the packaging, and you can look for that number in the list.

5. **Click Next.**

   The Label Wizard asks you for your font choices, as in Figure 19-2.

6. **Choose the font, size, weight, and text color you want for your labels and click Next.**

   The Label Wizard lets you choose which fields from the active table you want to include in your labels.

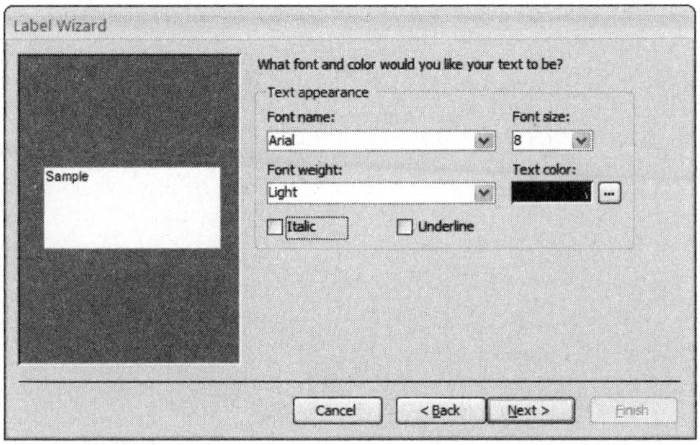

Figure 19-2:
Choose the font, size, weight, and text color for your labels.

7. **Double-click the first field you want to include on the labels.**

   As shown in Figure 19-3, when you double-click a field in the Available Fields box, it appears on the right, in the Prototype Label box.

8. **After the field name appears in the Prototype Label box, type a space after it so there's a space between the first field and the second one.**

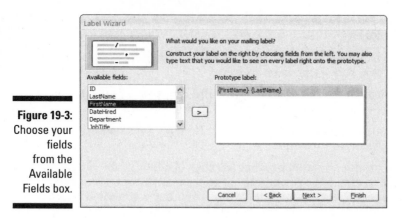

Figure 19-3:
Choose your
fields
from the
Available
Fields box.

9. **Double-click the next field to insert into your label and place a space or press Enter after the field, as in Step 8.**

   Continue double-clicking fields to add them to the Prototype, being careful to put spaces between fields and to press the Enter key to move to a new line in the Prototype box, as needed. Figure 19-4 shows a completed address label.

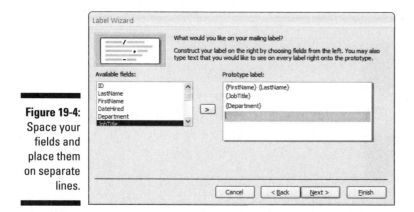

Figure 19-4:
Space your
fields and
place them
on separate
lines.

10. **Click Next.**

    Now the dialog box changes to offer choices for sorting your labels.

11. **Select the field by which to sort your labels — such as by last name or by zip code.**

    As shown in Figure 19-5, you can sort by more than one field, and the order in which you add them to the Sort by box dictates the sort order.

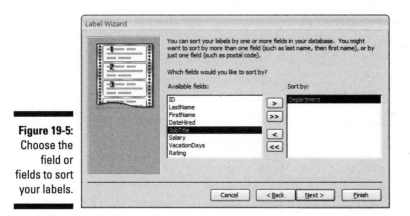

Figure 19-5:
Choose the field or fields to sort your labels.

If you plan a bulk mailing with discounted postage, check with your local postal authority for details about how to organize your mail. They often want the mail in zip code order; check first, as each post office may handle things differently. Rather than drive a postal worker over the edge, bring your mail in sorted the way *they* want it.

12. Click Next.

The next step in the Wizard process appears, as shown in Figure 19-6.

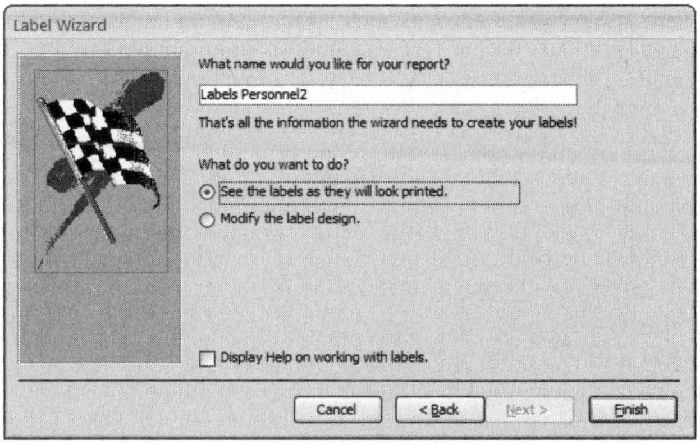

Figure 19-6:
Name your labels report.

13. Type a name for your labels report.

14. Leave the default option chosen (See the Labels as They Will Look When Printed) and click Finish.

The labels report appears on-screen, as shown in Figure 19-7, and you can print as desired (by using the Print command, as usual). You can also save your work for future reprintings of the same report.

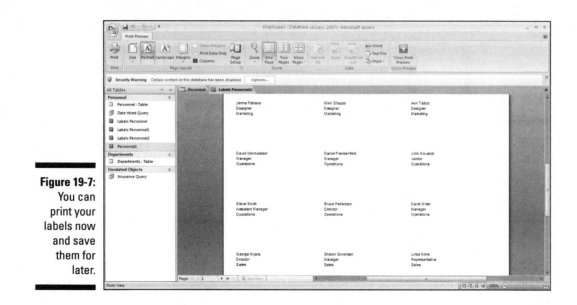

Figure 19-7:
You can
print your
labels now
and save
them for
later.

So you want to create a chart?

In previous versions of Access, charting (or graphing, depending on your terminology preference) tools were part of the action — you could transform your data into a bar, pie, or other lovely chart, suitable for any presentation purpose or venue. Sounds great, right? Well, in Access 2007, the Chart Wizard no longer exists. If you want to create a chart, you need to use either

✔ **PowerPoint, the presentation application from the Microsoft Office suite:** If you want to use PowerPoint, you can use the datasheet that appears automatically in a PowerPoint chart slide, and you can type your chart data (such as department names and total salary expenses for a given time period) into that datasheet. Alternatively, you can paste your data from an Access table.

✔ **Excel, the Microsoft Office spreadsheet application:** You can paste or import your

Access table data into Excel and then use Excel's charting tools to create a chart based on those numbers.

If you're feeling discouraged about Access' reduced charting capabilities, don't be. Access isn't really the place to build charts. If you have Office, PowerPoint and Excel offer much better tools for this purpose, because these two applications use charting more naturally than a database application ever could. PowerPoint's presentations are a perfect place for charts, as is an Excel workbook, where rows and rows of numeric data are often better explained with pictures, in the form of a nice, clear pie chart. Because you can easily use your Access table data to populate a PowerPoint datasheet or an Excel worksheet (and therefore base a chart on the data), there's no reason to have all those charting tools in Access — so they're no longer there . . .

Part VI
More Power to You

The 5th Wave
By Rich Tennant

"I couldn't get this 'job skills' program to work on my PC, so I replaced the motherboard, upgraded the BIOS and wrote a program that links it to my personal database. It told me I wasn't technically inclined and should pursue a career in sales."

In this part . . .

More power. Who doesn't want that? Part VI gives it to you in the form of the Access Analyzer, a tool that tunes up your database for better performance. It also gives you more power by showing you how to create a user interface that controls what people see, which tables they can edit, and how they work with your database overall. If you've got people doing data entry for you or using your database on their own for any reason, this will be a really powerful weapon in your Access arsenal.

Chapter 20

Making It All Better with the Analyzer Tools

In This Chapter

▶ Converting a flat file to relational tables with Table Analyzer

▶ Documenting your database

▶ Fine tuning your database with Performance Analyzer

T he Access Analyzer tools promise to help you set up, document, and fine tune the performance of your database. Sound too good to be true? Well, like most software tools that promises to automate, the Analyzer tools do some things well and others not so well.

Here is what the Analyzer tools promise to do:

✔ Convert flat files into relational databases automatically

✔ Document the database and all its parts (including tables, queries, forms, and reports)

✔ Analyze the structure of your tables to make sure that everything is set up in the best possible way

So, which Analyzer tool makes good on its promise? It would have to be the Database Documenter. To manually do what the Database Documenter does would take the average person hours if not days. If you're using the Analyzer tools for the other two tasks, they don't quite deliver on their promise. They do have merit, though, so we cover them as well.

Convert Your Flat Files to Relational Tables with Analyzer

Doesn't this sound great? The Table Analyzer promises to take a messy flat file table (such as an imported spreadsheet) with all its repetitive data and convert it to an efficient set of relational tables. But, as the bromide goes, promises made are promises broken. Unless your flat file follows some strict rules, the Table Analyzer won't quite get it right. I would love to tell you what those rules are, but only Microsoft knows the mysterious rules of the Table Analyzer.

Sometimes you get a perfect set of relational tables, and sometimes the Table Analyzer doesn't suggest a new table when it should or suggests a new table when it shouldn't. My advice to you is to give it a try and see what happens. Best case, it works right and you've just saved yourself a boatload of time. Worst case, it doesn't work right and you wasted a few minutes of your time.

The Analyzer works best with a flat file table that contains plenty of duplicate information. For example, imagine a flat file table for a video rental store. Each record in the table contains customer and movie data. If the same customer rents six movies, the table contains six separate records with the customer's name, address, and other information duplicated in every one. Multiply that by 1,000 customers, and you have precisely the kind of flat file mess that the Analyzer loves to solve.

With that thought in mind, here's how to invoke the Table Analyzer Wizard:

1. **Open your database and select the table you'd like convert from the Navigation Pane.**

2. **Click the Database Tools tab on the Ribbon.**

   The Analyze tool group appears on the Ribbon.

3. **Click the Analyze Table tool from the Analyze group.**

   The Table Analyzer Wizard dialog box appears, as shown in Figure 20-1.

4. **Read the first two screens if you want (they're strictly educational); click Next after each one.**

   Another Table Analyzer Wizard screen appears, as shown in Figure 20-2.

5. **The name of the table you selected in the Navigation Pane should be selected in the Tables list. If it is not, click the name of the table you'd like to convert.**

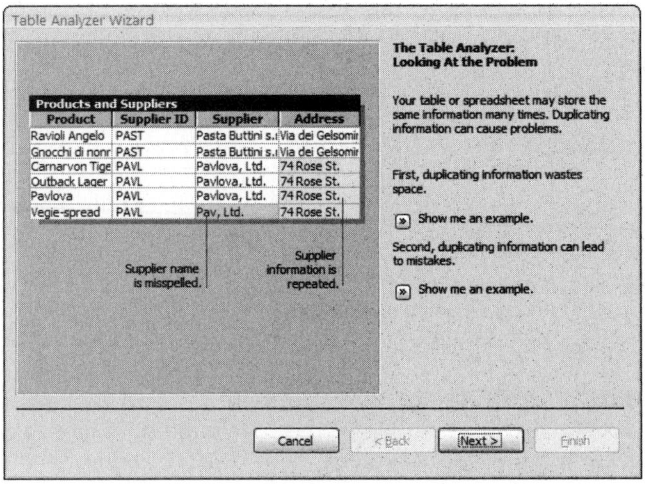

Figure 20-1:
Here comes
the Table
Analyzer.

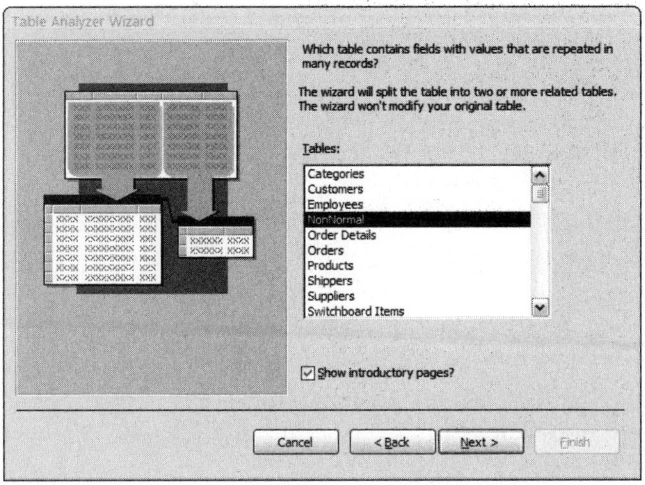

Figure 20-2:
Select a
table to
analyze.

6. **Click Next.**

   In the dialog box that appears, the wizard asks whether you want to just let the wizard do its thing (the wizard will decide how the flat file table should be arranged into multiple tables) or if you want to decide which fields go to what tables .

7. **Click the Yes option (if it's not already selected) to give the wizard full power in deciding the fate of your table; then click Next.**

If the wizard recommends that you not split your table, click the Cancel button and pat yourself on the back for a job well done. This message means that the wizard thinks your table is fine just as it is.

If the wizard does split your table, it will analyze your table and show you its findings. The results look like those shown in Figure 20-3.

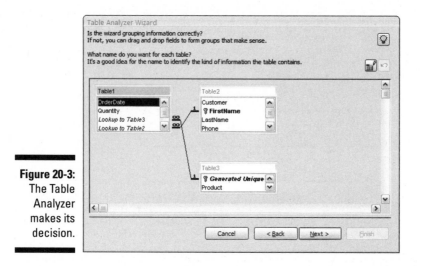

Figure 20-3:
The Table
Analyzer
makes its
decision.

8. **Make sure the information from your flat file table is grouped correctly into new tables:**

   • *If the information is grouped correctly,* name the tables by double-clicking each table's title bar and typing a new name in the resulting dialog box.

   • *If the information is not grouped correctly,* use your mouse to drag and drop fields from table to table and then double-click each table's title bar to rename the tables.

   • *If you want to create a new table,* drag a field into any open space between or around the existing tables.

9. **When you're finished arranging and naming your tables, click Next.**

   The wizard automatically selects a key field for each table that it thinks needs a key field. Should the wizard select a field incorrectly as a key field, you can correct the error.

10. **If the wizard does not designate a key field properly, you can:**

    • *Designate an existing field as a key field* by selecting the field and clicking the Set Unique Identifier button (looks like a key).

- *Change a key field designation* by selecting the proper key field then clicking the Set Unique Identifier button (looks like a key).

- *Add a key field* by clicking the Add Generated Key button (contains a plus sign and key).

11. **Click Next for the final step in the process.**

    The wizard offers to create a query that looks and acts like your original table. If you have reports and forms that work with the flat file, they'll work with the new query.

12. **Choose Yes to have the wizard create the query or No to skip query creation.**

    Yes creates a query that runs against the new tables. The query looks and acts like the original table. The original table is renamed with an _OLD slapped on the end, and any reports and forms automatically use the query instead of the original table. No generates the new tables but leaves the original table with its original name.

13. **Click Finish to exit the wizard.**

    The wizard completes the process of splitting the flat file table into a set of relational tables.

The Table Analyzer is unlikely to correctly split a flat file database into a properly designed relational database, especially if the flat file is complicated. You're much better off bringing the database to a qualified human and letting him or her properly redesign it — or figuring out how to do it yourself!

Record Database Object Details with the Documenter

In the world of database development, the last thing on the to-do list — if it's done at all — is database documentation. You're probably asking yourself, why do I need to create a mountain of paper about my database? Well, if you are the developer of that database and something were to happen to you — you were promoted or you left the company — someone else would take over responsibility for the database. A well-documented database is easier to maintain than one that is not documented.

Why is this important step rarely done? Because it takes time and money — both of which are in short supply for most businesses. Enter the Database Documenter. It browses through everything in your database and records the minutest of details about each item, be it a table, field, form, query, or report. The Documenter collects information so obscure that I'm not even sure the programmers know what some of it means.

The Documenter is fast and easy. All you have to do is turn it on and it does the rest. Before you know it, the timely and costly job is done!

Here's how to document your database:

1. **Open your database and select the Database Tools tab from the Ribbon.**

    The Analyze tool group appears on the Ribbon.

2. **Click the Database Documenter tool in the Analyze tool group.**

    The Documenter dialog box appears.

3. **In the Documenter dialog box, click the All Object Types tab, as shown in Figure 20-4.**

Figure 20-4:
Click the
All Object
Types
tab and
then click
Select All.

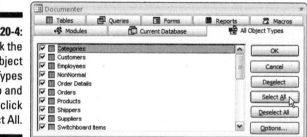

4. **Click the Select All button to document every object in your database, then click OK to start the process.**

    The Documenter begins by examining all the objects in your database, starting with the tables and moving on to the queries, forms, reports, and so on.

    During the process, your forms and reports may appear on the screen for a moment — that's normal.

    The process can take a while, depending on the size and complexity of the database you are documenting. So you might want to run the Documenter before a coffee or lunch break. There's nothing more satisfying than "working" on a break. When the Documenter finishes, it creates a lengthy report about your database, as shown in Figure 20-5.

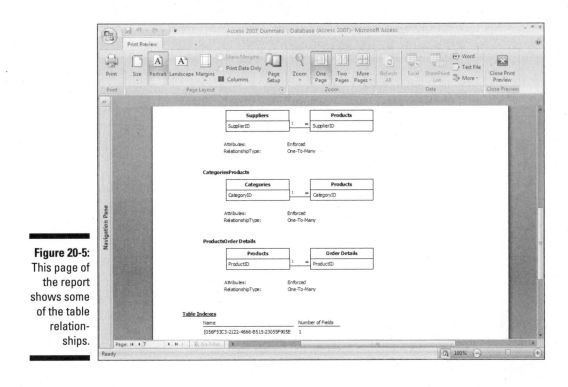

Figure 20-5:
This page of
the report
shows some
of the table
relation-
ships.

5. Click the Print button on the Ribbon to get a paper copy.

Access doesn't care a whit about trees or how much paper costs, so it generates hundreds of documentation pages about your database. For a small to mid-sized database, this can be 500 to 1,000 pages of information. If you don't want a couple reams of paper describing your database, consider saving the report and then referring back to it later. To store the report electronically, right-click the report while it is in Print Preview and choose, Export To➪Word RTF File. Select the destination folder and file name then click the OK button. The resulting exported file can be opened in Word when needed.

If you run the Documenter and find that it has generated too much detail, you can control what is documented and thereby reduce the detail (and number of pages) in the resulting report. The following instructions will remove object properties (such as field properties like the Field Size property) from the Documenter's report:

1. Click the Database Documenter tool form the Database Tools tab on the Ribbon.

The Documenter window opens.

2. **Click the All Object Types tab.**

3. **Click the Select All button.**

   Steps 2 and 3 tell the Documenter that you want to document all objects in the database.

4. **Repeat these steps for each object type (tables, queries, forms, reports) in the Documenter window:**

   a. *Click the tab for the desired object type (like the Tables tab).*

   b. *Click the Options button in the Documenter window.*

      The print definition dialog box for the object selected will appear. Figure 20-6 shows the Print Table Definition dialog box.

   c. Uncheck all the check boxes in the Include for <object type> section.

      In the Print Table Definition dialog box, for example, this section will be labeled Include for Table.

   d. *In the remaining Include for sections, select the second radio button — the one below Nothing (as illustrated in Figure 20-6).*

      In the Print Table Definition dialog box for example, these sections are labeled Include for Fields and Include for Indexes.

   e. *Click the OK button to close the print definition dialog box.*

5. **Click OK in the Documenter window to start the documentation process.**

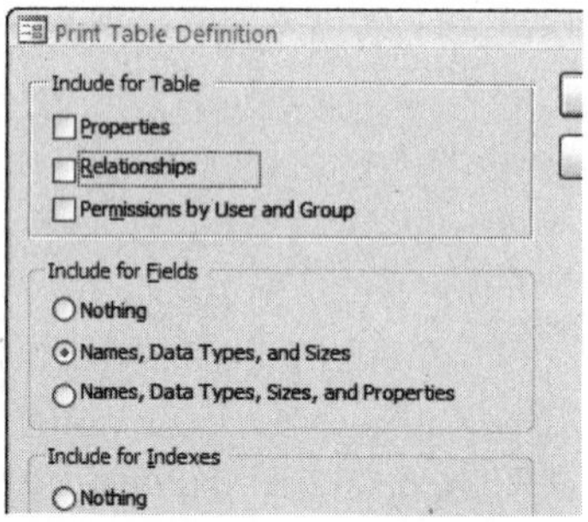

Figure 20-6:
The Table
Options
dialog box
within
Docu-
menter.

Print Table Definition

Include for Table
☐ Properties
☐ Relationships
☐ Permissions by User and Group

Include for Fields
○ Nothing
◉ Names, Data Types, and Sizes
○ Names, Data Types, Sizes, and Properties

Include for Indexes
○ Nothing

Improve Database Performance without Steroids

The Performance Analyzer is an Access tool that reviews each database object you designate and makes suggestions on how to improve the object's performance. It might for example, tell you to break up a complex form that loads slowly on screen into several smaller forms that will load faster. Use the Performance Analyzer to locate problem objects affecting database performance and improve those objects. This, in turn, improves performance.

Like the Table Analyzer, the Performance Analyzer is far from perfect. When you run it (and you should), review its recommendations carefully before implementing them.

Here's how to use the Performance Analyzer:

1. **Open your database and click the Database Tools tab on the Ribbon.**

   The Analyze tool group appears on the Ribbon.

2. **Make sure all database objects (such as forms and reports) are closed so that the only remaining window is the Navigation Pane.**

3. **Click the Analyze Performance tool from the Analyze tool group.**

   The Performance Analyzer dialog box appears.

4. **Choose the database objects (such as forms and reports) that you want to analyze.**

   I recommend clicking the All Object Types tab and then clicking the Select All button. The Performance Analyzer dialog box is similar to the Documenter dialog box shown in Figure 20-4.

5. **Click the OK button to run the Performance Analyzer.**

   You'll see a dialog box flash on screen listing each database object as it is analyzed. Eventually, the results of the analysis will appear in a dialog box.

6. **Select each result (as shown in Figure 20-7) and review the comments.**

   If Access can make the changes for you, the Optimize button is enabled. Otherwise, use a pencil and paper and jot down any good thoughts that Access may offer.

7. **To implement a task from the results list, select it and click the Optimize button.**

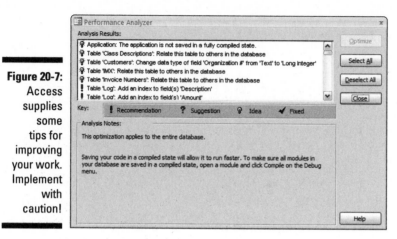

Figure 20-7:
Access
supplies
some
tips for
improving
your work.
Implement
with
caution!

After Access performs the task, a blue check mark appears next to the task on the list.

8. **When you've completed your review of the Analyzer's suggestions, click the Close button to exit the Performance Analyzer dialog box.**

If you're not sure a result should be implemented, don't implement it. Ask your local Access expert for his or her opinion before implementing such a result.

Chapter 21

Hello! Creating an Interface to Welcome Data Users

*I*f you plan for others to use your database, you may want to provide them with navigation tools so that they can easily find their way around your database (especially if they know nothing about Access). You might even want this luxury for yourself. It's much easier to move around a database with a menu system in place. Fortunately, the Switchboard Manager makes it easy to build such a system. Why it's not called the Menu Manager I'll never know, but for some reason, Microsoft likes the word *switchboard* — so switchboard it is! This chapter explains all there is to know about making your database user friendly via the Switchboard Manager.

To see a switchboard in action, download the sample files at `http://www.dummies.com/go/access2007`. Open the file Access 2007 `Dummies.accdb` and open the form Switchboard.

The Comings and Goings of a Switchboard

Before you create your switchboard, take a few minutes to plan out your database navigation. How do you want you and your users to navigate to the various forms and reports you've created?

✔ **If you have a simple database with a few data entry forms and several reports,** it might be best to have a switchboard for the data entry forms and a switchboard for the reports.

✔ **If your database is more complex, you may need to break the forms and reports into several categories — one switchboard for each category.**

For example, you might have a series of sales reports and a series of inventory reports. You may need to create two switchboards — one for each series or reports

Several switchboards for data entry and several for reports can make the object you're looking for easier to find.

Whatever you decide, you can always modify your switchboard design at any time. We discuss switchboard editing later in the chapter.

Creating a switchboard

Here's how you build a switchboard:

1. **Open the database file that will contain the switchboard.**

2. **Click the Database Tools tab on the Ribbon.**

   The Database Tools group appears toward the right end of the Ribbon.

3. **Click the Switchboard Manager tool near the top of the Database Tools group.**

   A message box appears, asking whether you'd like to create a switchboard, as shown in Figure 21-1.

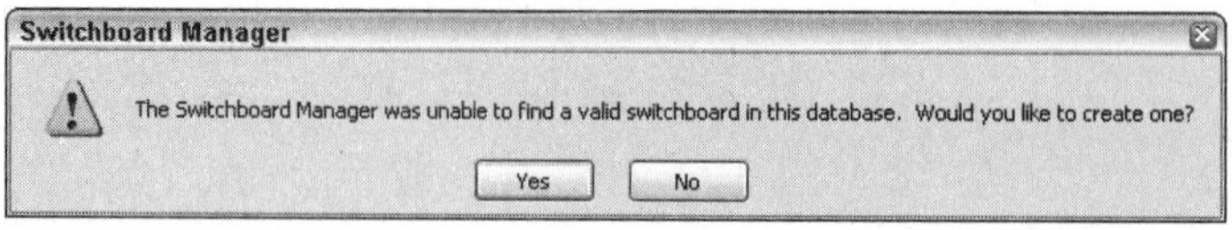

Figure 21-1:
The Switchboard Manager asks whether you'd like to create a switchboard.

Switchboard Manager

⚠ The Switchboard Manager was unable to find a valid switchboard in this database. Would you like to create one?

[Yes] [No]

4. **Click Yes.**

    The Switchboard Manager dialog box appears, ready for action (see Figure 21-2). By default, it creates a Main Switchboard (kind of like a home page) to which you can add secondary switchboards. If you like to keep it simple, you can add all your switchboard commands directly to the Main Switchboard.

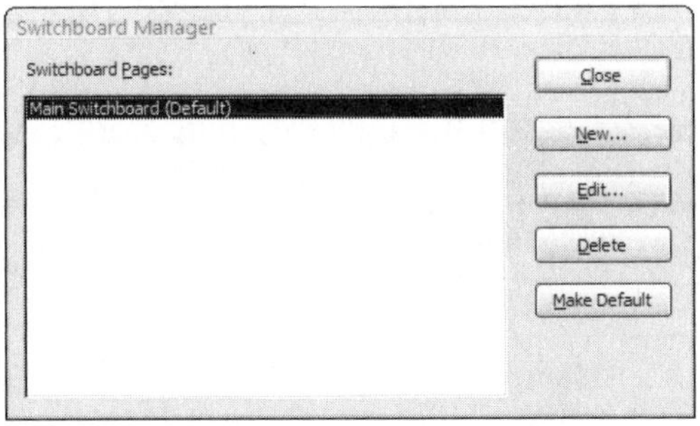

Figure 21-2:
The
Switchboard
Manager
dialog box.

5. **Click the New button to add a secondary switchboard.**

    The Create New dialog box appears, waiting patiently for your secondary switchboard name.

6. **Type a name (like** Data Entry**) and then click OK.**

    The secondary switchboard is added to the Switchboard Pages list of the Switchboard Manager dialog box. See Figure 21-3.

7. **Repeat Steps 5 and 6 for each secondary switchboard you'd like to create.**

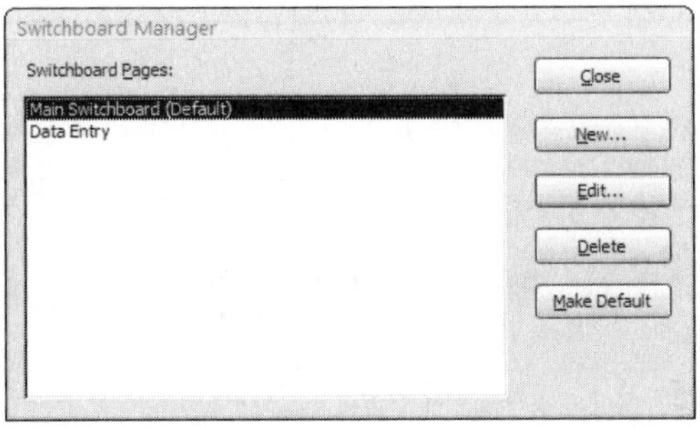

Figure 21-3:
The Data
Entry
switchboard
is added
to the
Switchboard
Pages list.

Adding switchboard items

After you've built your switchboards (see the preceding section), you must add items (you might be more familiar with the term *menu commands*) to those switchboards. Without switchboard items, you'll be staring at a pretty form with nothing on it beyond a title! The items perform tasks like opening forms and reports in your database and appear on the switchboard as command buttons. See Table 21-1 for a complete list of commands available via the Switchboard Manager.

Table 21-1	Switchboard Commands
Command	*What It Does*
Go to Switchboard	Opens a secondary switchboard
Open Form in Add Mode	Opens the form so that only new records can be added
Open Form in Edit Mode	Opens the form so that any record can be added or edited
Open Report	Opens the report in Print Preview
Design Application	Opens the Switchboard Manager
Exit Application	Closes the current database file
Run Macro	Runs a macro (series of commands strung together)
Run Code	Runs a Visual Basic function (custom command)

Both macros and Visual Basic functions are advanced topics beyond the scope of this book.

Here's how to add an item to a switchboard. These instructions assume that the Switchboard Manager dialog box is still open. If it is not, check out the steps in the preceding section to open it.

1. **On the Switchboard Pages list, select the switchboard to which you'd like to add an item.**

2. **Click the Edit button.**

   The Edit Switchboard Page dialog box appears (shown in Figure 21-4).

3. **Click the New button.**

   The Edit Switchboard Item dialog box appears.

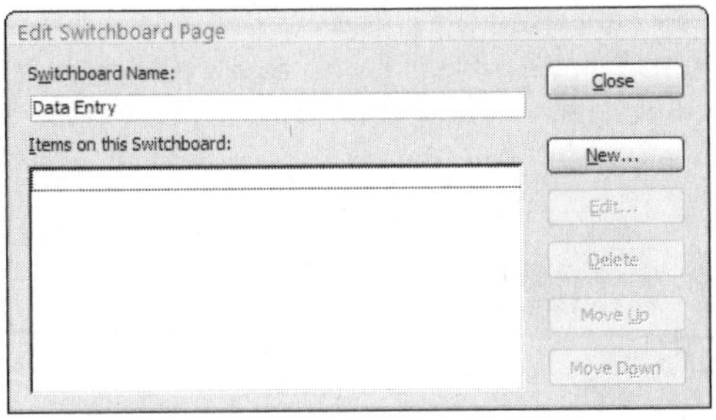

Figure 21-4:
The Edit
Switchboard
Page
dialog box
in all its
splendor.

Edit Switchboard Page

Switchboard Name:
Data Entry

Items on this Switchboard:

Close

New...

Edit...

Delete

Move Up

Move Down

4. **In the Text box , type the name of your command item.**

5. **From the Command list, select the command that fits the item.**

   For example, if the item is Manage Customers, then the command for this item is Open Form in Edit Mode.

   - For some commands, a third list may appear. The list will be labeled according to the command you select.

   - If a third list doesn't appear, skip to Step 7.

6. **If a third list is visible, select the appropriate item from the list.**

   For example, if you select the Open Form in Edit Mode command, the third list will be labeled Form. In this instance, you select the name of the form you want opened. Figure 21-5 shows a completed switchboard item.

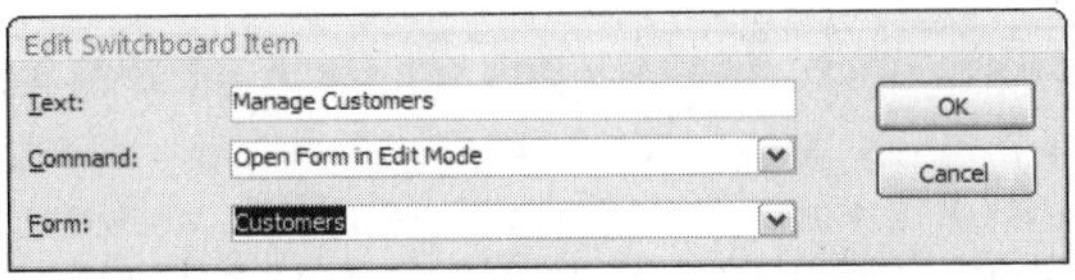

Figure 21-5:
The Edit
Switchboard
Item
dialog box
completed
to open the
Customers
form.

Edit Switchboard Item

Text: Manage Customers

Command: Open Form in Edit Mode

Form: Customers

OK

Cancel

7. **Click OK.**

   The Edit Switchboard Item dialog box closes, and your command is added to the Items on this switchboard list.

8. **Repeat steps 1–7 until you've added all the commands you'd like to each switchboard you've created.**

If you've created secondary switchboards, make sure each contains a command to go back to the Main Switchboard. If you don't have a "go back" command, your users will be stuck in a virtual hole with no way out!

Am I in the Right Place? Switchboard Testing

After you've created your switchboard, be sure to test it before turning your database loose on your users. You'll want to test for both

- ✔ The accuracy of the commands you've created (for example, does the Manage Customers button open the Customers form?)
- ✔ The intuitiveness of your switchboard

Put yourself in the shoes of someone who knows nothing about Access. Could you figure out how to run a report or enter a new order just by navigating your switchboard? If the answer is no, then you need to make some modifications. If the answer is yes, pat yourself on the back for a job well done!

Present your switchboard to someone who knows nothing about your database or Access. See if your "tester" can perform the basic tasks you'd like your users to perform without any special instructions. Use your tester's feedback to tweak your switchboard if necessary.

Of course, to do any testing, you'll need to know how the heck to launch the switchboard. Here's how:

1. **From the Navigation pane, double-click the form labeled Switchboard.**

   Your switchboard opens. It should contain buttons and labels like the sample in Figure 21-6. If you don't see any command buttons, go back to the Add Switchboard Items section of this chapter and make sure you add some items to the Main Switchboard.

   If you don't like the title the Switchboard Manager has given your switchboard, you can change the title to anything you'd like. For details on changing a form's title, see Chapter 7.

2. **Click a command button to launch one of your custom commands.**

   The command signified by the button label should run. If it does, you've done everything right! If it doesn't, you need to make some modifications, which I discuss in the next section.

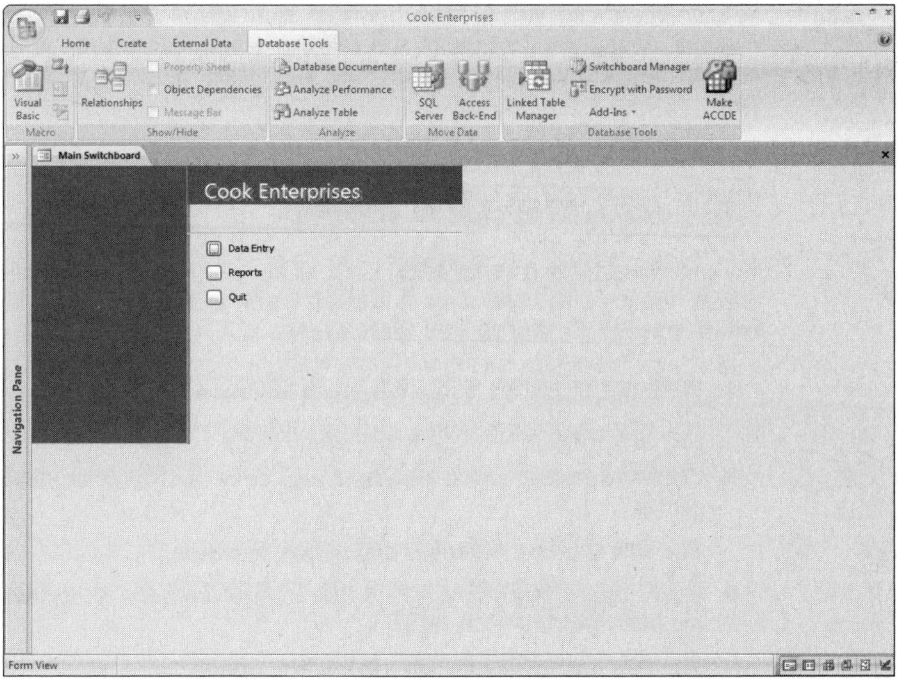

Figure 21-6:
A sample switchboard for that multimillion-dollar conglomerate Cook Enterprises.

3. **Repeat Step 2 for every custom command you've created.**

   If everything checks out, your switchboard is ready for launch.

Maintaining the Switchboard

Almost without fail, a switchboard will need modifications. Modifications may be required to

✔ Correct mistakes made during initial switchboard creation.

✔ Open new database objects such as a new report.

The Switchboard Manager allows you to

✔ Add, edit, delete, and move switchboard items.

✔ Create new switchboards.

See the previous section, "The Comings and Goings of a Switchboard," for more on adding switchboards and switchboard items. Since I've already covered those topics, I'll just concentrate on editing, deleting, and moving items here.

Edit switchboard items

If a command label is misspelled or does not perform the expected command, you need to know how to fix that command. If a switchboard is mislabeled, you can fix that as well. Here's how:

1. **Click the Database Tools tab on the Ribbon.**

   The Database Tools group appears toward the right end of the Ribbon.

2. **Click the Switchboard Manager tool near the top of the Database Tools group.**

   The Switchboard Manager dialog box appears.

3. **Select the switchboard you'd like to edit from the Switchboard Pages list and click the Edit button.**

   The Edit Switchboard Page dialog box opens.

4. **To edit the switchboard name, click in the Switchboard Name box and make your edits.**

   When you close the Edit Switchboard Page dialog box, your changes will take effect.

5. **To edit an item on the selected switchboard, select that item from the Items on this Switchboard list and then click the Edit button.**

   The Edit Switchboard Item dialog box appears.

6. **Make the necessary changes to the text or command assigned to the item in the appropriate boxes.**

   For a refresher on the commands, see Table 21-1, earlier in this chapter.

7. **Close all dialog boxes.**

   Your changes to the switchboard are saved.

Delete a switchboard or switchboard item

If a switchboard or switchboard item is no longer needed, the Switchboard Manager makes it a snap to send that bugger off to cyber heaven.

WARNING!

If you delete a switchboard, all the items assigned to that switchboard will be deleted as well.

Here are the steps for deleting a switchboard item:

1. **Click the Database Tools tab on the Ribbon.**

   The Database Tools group appears toward the right end of the Ribbon.

2. **Click the Switchboard Manager tool near the top of the Database Tools group.**

   The Switchboard Manager dialog box appears.

3. **Select the switchboard you'd like to delete or that contains the item you'd like to delete from the Switchboard Pages list.**

   Make sure you've selected the correct item from the list.

4. **To delete a switchboard, skip to Step 6. To delete an item, click the Edit button.**

   The Edit Switchboard Page dialog box appears.

5. **Select the item you'd like to delete from the Items on this Switchboard list.**

   I know I'm repeating myself, but since you're deleting, make sure you've selected the correct item from the list.

6. **Click the Delete button.**

   A confirm delete message box appears.

7. **Click Yes.**

   Say bye-bye to that switchboard or switchboard item.

8. **Close all dialog boxes.**

   Your changes are saved to the switchboard.

Move a switchboard item

If the item order on a switchboard is not quite right, the Switchboard Manager can help you. You can move items up or down so that they are in whatever order you deem appropriate. So, let's get moving!

1. **Click the Database Tools tab on the Ribbon.**

   The Database Tools group appears toward the right end of the Ribbon.

2. **Click the Switchboard Manager tool near the top of the Database Tools group.**

   The Switchboard Manager dialog box appears.

3. **From the Switchboard Pages list, select the switchboard that contains the item you'd like to move.**

4. **Click the Edit button.**

   The Edit Switchboard Page dialog box appears.

5. **From the Items on this Switchboard list, select the item you'd like to move.**

6. **Click the Move Up or Move Down button.**

   The item moves up or down on the list.

7. **Close all dialog boxes.**

   Your changes are saved to the switchboard.

Displaying the Switchboard at Startup

The last step in implementing a switchboard is to have that switchboard open when the database opens. It wouldn't be very intuitive to have your users try to find the switchboard form and open it themselves, would it? So you'll have to do it for them — automatically. Does this sound too good to be true? Well, it isn't. You can actually do it, and it's easy. Here are the steps:

1. **Click the Microsoft Office button on the upper-left part of the screen.**

   The Microsoft Office button menu drops down.

2. **Click the Access Options button in the lower-right corner of the menu.**

   The Access Options dialog box appears.

3. **Click Current Database from the list on the left.**

   The Current Database options appear. Note the Application Options section near the top of the dialog box.

4. **Select Switchboard from the Display Form drop-down list as shown in Figure 21-7.**

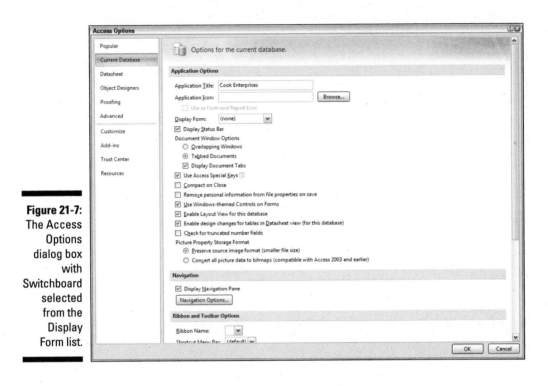

Figure 21-7:
The Access
Options
dialog box
with
Switchboard
selected
from the
Display
Form list.

5. **Click the OK button to save the change.**

   Access will now open the switchboard form when the database file is opened.

6. **Close the database file and then reopen it.**

   The Switchboard form opens automatically for the entire world to see.

Part VII
The Part of Tens

The 5th Wave   By Rich Tennant

"Look-what if we just increase the size of the charts?"

In this part . . .

What the heck is a *Part of Tens*? I remember years ago, the first time I picked up a Dummies book, and that's what I asked, too. Of course, I didn't ask this out loud, as people tend to look at you funny if you talk to yourself in the bookstore.

What I found out is that the Part of Tens is a section of the book that has cool lists of ten things related to the book's topic. If this were a book called *Avoiding Dismemberment For Dummies*, there might be a list of Ten Ways to Lose Your Head, or Ten Ways Not To Use a Chainsaw.

This, of course, is not about how to keep all the appendages you have, but rather a book on Microsoft Access. Therefore, the two Part of Tens that are offered in Part VII pertain to databases — Ten Common Problems and Ten Uncommon Tips.

Chapter 22

Ten Common Problems

Yes, even so-called "experts" have problems with computers. I've chosen ten of the most common Microsoft Access problems and presented them to you in this chapter — with their solutions of course!

Don't despair if your problem is not on my list. I find many solutions to my computing problems by searching the Access newsgroups online. Chances are, if I'm having the problem, someone else has already had it and figured out the solution. That's why the newsgroups are a valuable resource. The Appendix lists a few more valuable help resources.

Speaking of valuable resources, check out the ten problems in this chapter.

You Type 73.725, but it Changes to 74

Automatic rounding can frustrate the living daylights out of you, but correcting it is easy. By default, Access sets all number fields to accept *long integers*. As you may remember from your high school math days, an integer is a negative or positive *whole number*. You need to change the field size setting to one that accepts decimals. Here's how:

1. **Open the table in Design view and then click the field that's not cooperating.**

2. **On the General tab of the Properties area at the bottom of the screen, click the Field Size box.**

3. **Click the down arrow on the end of the box, and then select Single, Double, or Decimal from the drop-down menu that appears.**

4. **Save the table, and your automatic rounding problem is over.**

For details about the difference between Single, Double, and Decimal field sizes, check out Chapter 4.

The Words They Are A-Changing

Sometimes those "helpful" features in Access can become a nuisance. One such feature is called AutoCorrect. You may be familiar with it from Microsoft Word where it is often a great thing. Databases, however, often contain acronyms, part numbers, and the like. AutoCorrect can have a field day with such "words." You may not even realize it as you enter your data.

You have two choices to resolve this problem.

- **Undo AutoCorrect's effects as they occur.** Press Ctrl+Z right after AutoCorrect has botched your data entry. Access puts the data back to the way you typed it. Unfortunately, for this to work you actually have to notice that Access has changed what you entered.

- **Turn AutoCorrect off entirely.** To turn off AutoCorrect, follow these steps:

    1. *Click the Microsoft Office button in the upper-left corner of the Access screen.*

       The Office menu drops down.

    2. *Click the Access Options button in the lower-right portion of the menu.*

       The Access Options dialog box appears.

    3. *Click Proofing from the list on the left.*

       The proofing choices appear.

    4. *Click the AutoCorrect Options button.*

       The AutoCorrect dialog box appears.

5. *Uncheck some or all of the check boxes in the AutoCorrect dialog box.*

You can disable some or all of the AutoCorrect features depending on what AutoCorrect is doing to annoy you at present.

6. *Click OK to save your changes.*

You can now type your problem text without AutoCorrect's interference.

The Record Was There and Now It's Gone

I've heard this one a lot over the years: "The database deleted my record!" Well, I've got news for you. The database doesn't do anything without us humans commanding it. And humans can make a couple of mistakes:

- **Accidental deletion:** There are several ways to accidentally delete a record. Usually a delete keyboard shortcut is pressed, such as Ctrl+ Shift+– or Ctrl+X.

  The Undo command (Ctrl+Z) will not reverse the deletion of a record.

- **Data error:** A record may *appear* deleted if someone inadvertently changes a key piece of information. For example, suppose the record in question contains an order date of 12/15/06, and someone inadvertently changes the date to 12/15/04. The order date isn't what is expected so the record may appear to be deleted.

  If a data error makes the record appear deleted, there are several possible fixes, as I outline in the following sections.

Undo

Don't panic. Before doing anything else, press Ctrl+Z. That's the Undo command. If the record comes back, you're in luck. Undo reverses data entry errors that may cause the record to appear deleted. However, this will only work if you Undo right after the data entry error takes place.

Search for the missing record

If you try the Undo command and the record doesn't come back, there is still a chance that a data entry error is hiding it from where you expect it to be.

Open the table that contained the record and search for it in a different way than you normally would. Look for anything out of the ordinary on similar records:

- ✔ If you normally search for orders by date, search by client. See if a similar order (to the missing one) exists for that client with an unusual date (like same month and day as the missing order but year is off).

- ✔ Try looking at all orders on the date in question to see if the client on each order seems to be correct. It could be that the client was inadvertently changed on the missing order.

Backup recovery

If you can't find the record anywhere, copy the record from a backup of the database file.

This solution works only if you've backed up your database since the record was originally added. If you back up at night and the record was entered during the same day it went missing, that record will not be in your backup.

You Run a Query, but the Results Aren't What You Expect

Query writing is an art form. Even the experts spill their paint every now and then. Here are some common solutions to unexpected query results:

- ✔ **Check criteria for accuracy.** A single misplaced keystroke is all it takes to turn your query into a dud. Check your criteria for spelling or syntax errors and then run the query again.

- ✔ **Try the Unique Values property.** Ever see two copies of each record in your query results when you were expecting just one? A quick fix often comes with using the Unique Values properly. This property tells Access to stop with the doubling already. The Unique Values property tells Access to return only one rows from the group if a group of exact duplicates are present in the query results. Here's how to use it:

    1. *Open the problem query in Design view.*

       The Design tab on the Ribbon appears.

    2. *Click the Property Sheet button from the Show/Hide Ribbon group.*

       The Property Sheet window opens to the right of the query grid.

3. *Click in the Unique Values row of the Property Sheet.*

   A drop-down list arrow appears at the end of the Unique Values row.

4. *Select Yes from the drop-down list and run the query.*

   The doubling disappears.

✔ **Correct the selection logic.** Juggling a bunch of AND and OR connections in a query quickly messes up even the hardiest of database designers. Chapters 15 and 16 have tips on untangling the mess.

✔ **Fix table joins.** If your query results show *way* too many records, and the query uses two or more tables, improper joining is the likely cause. Flip back to Chapter 15 for more about joining one table to another.

✔ **Check table join types.** If your query involves two or more tables, and you get fewer records than you expected, this is the likely cause. For example, if you have an order entry database and run a query listing all customers and their orders, by default, you would see only those customers who have placed an order. To see all customers whether or not they have placed an order, do the following:

1. *In the Design view, right-click the join (the line connecting the two tables) and choose Join Properties.*

   For a quick refresher about joining tables in the Design view, check out Chapter 15.

2. *Examine the types of joins offered and choose the one that says something like "Include ALL records from 'Customers' and only those records from 'Orders' where the joined fields are equal."*

   The actual text you see differs according to the names of your tables. To query aficionados, this is called an outer join. Very cool.

3. *Click OK and run the query.*

   You should now have all records from the Customers table whether or not there are corresponding records in the Orders table.

If your query involves several criteria, some calculated fields, and numerous joins, try breaking the task into several smaller steps instead of trying to solve the problem all at once. The step-by-step approach lets you focus on each piece one at a time, making sure each works perfectly before moving on to the next one.

If your query still doesn't work no matter what you do, ask someone else to take a look. I've often wrangled with a tough query problem for hours, shown it to someone else, and heard those magical words: "That's simple. Just do this." And the problem is solved. Getting a fresh pair of eyes on the problem often solves things fast.

The Validation That Never Was

Validations are a great feature in Access that we discuss in great detail in Chapter 8. But validations can cause problems if they're not used properly.

The biggest concern is a validation rule that *can't* be valid. For example, suppose someone wants to limit a particular field so that it accepts entries between 0 and 100. To accomplish this feat, the person creates a validation that says <0 AND >100. Unfortunately, that rule won't work — ever! The person mixed up the symbols and created a rule that accepts only a number that's both less than 0 *and* greater than 100. No such number exists, but Access isn't smart enough to know that.

 Don't let this problem happen to your validations. To avoid such errors, write your rule on paper and then test it with some sample data. Be sure to include examples of both good and bad entries to make sure that the rule works just like it's supposed to.

The Slowest Database in Town

An Access database may end up on the shared drive of a business so that it is available to everyone who needs it. The problem with placing the entire Access database on the shared drive is that it often runs slowly on each user's individual workstation (that's a fancy word for their computer). The complaints start rolling in and you don't know what to do.

The solution to this problem lies in splitting the Access database file into two separate files:

- ✔ **Front end:** Contains all the database objects *except* the tables.

  The front end resides on the user workstation.

- ✔ **Back end:** Contains just the tables.

  The back end resides on the shared server.

  The front end is linked to tables in the back end (see Chapter 10 for more on table linking).

All you are really sharing is the data, so that is all that should go on the shared drive. By setting things up this way, the only information that must travel across the network is the data requested by the user. Such a setup dramatically speeds database performance.

Splitting the dataset is not as hard as you might think. Access makes it a snap with the Database Splitter Wizard. Follow these steps to split your database:

1. **Back up the database you'd like to split.**

   If anything goes wrong (unlikely, but hey, you can never be too safe when it comes to data!), you can try again with the backup copy.

2. **If necessary, move the database you'd like to split to a folder on your shared drive.**

   This step will allow the Database Splitter to set up table links properly for you.

3. **Open the database file you'd like to split from the shared folder.**

   Make sure you have a backup copy of this database before going any further.

4. **Click the Database Tools tab on the Ribbon.**

   The Move Data tool group appears on the Ribbon. It contains a tool called Access Back-End.

5. **Click the Access Database tool from the Move Data group in the Ribbon.**

   The Database Splitter Wizard dialog box appears.

6. **Click the Split Database button and let the wizard do its thing.**

   You will be prompted for a back-end database filename. Enter a name, sit back, and watch the fun unfold before your very eyes.

7. **Copy the front-end file to each user workstation.**

   Have each user open the file from his or her workstation, and see how they marvel at the improved speed of the database!

Your Database File Is as Big as a Whale

As time goes by, you find your database file growing larger and larger. This is a result of deleting objects and records over time. If for example, you create a query and then later delete it because it is no longer needed, Access doesn't automatically remove the space occupied by that query from the database file. The same is true for records. As you delete records from a table, the space that those records occupied in the database file remains. Eventually, the file can become four or five times its actual size.

Why should you care if the file size increases? Here are a few reasons:

✓ **A smaller database file runs faster.** Performance is a key component to happy database users. You want your forms to load quickly and your queries and reports to run as fast as possible.

✓ **A regularly compacted database is more stable.** If the database is used often, compacting regularly helps keep file and table corruption from occurring.

✓ **A regularly compacted database recovers disk space.** I think we all know that's a good thing.

The Compact and Repair command removes the excess. It is good practice to compact your database regularly (once a week is usually fine). Always compact it after making any design changes. Here's how:

1. **Open the bloated database and click the Microsoft Office button.**

   The Office menu appears.

2. **Select Manage from the menu.**

   The Manage Your Database submenu appears.

3. **Click Compact and Repair Database from the submenu.**

   The status bar (lower left of your screen) displays a progress bar notifying you of how the compact process is progressing. When the progress bar disappears, compacting is complete, and you'll be left with a much trimmer (faster and more stable) database file.

You Get a Mess When Importing Your Spreadsheet

It's common practice to upgrade a collection of spreadsheets to an Access database after the spreadsheet solution no longer suits your needs. It's also common to find the imported spreadsheet (now table) data in a state of disarray. The easiest way to solve this problem is by cleaning up the spreadsheet before you import it. Here are a few tips for a tidy import:

✓ **Double-check information coming from any spreadsheet program to be sure that it's *consistent* and *complete*.** Above all, make sure that all entries in each column (field) are the same type (all numbers, text, or whatever).

✔ **Remove any titles and blank rows from the top of the spreadsheet.** An ideal spreadsheet for import will have field names (column headings) in row 1 and data starting in row 2.

✔ **Make sure your spreadsheet column headings are short and unique** so Access can easily translate them to field names during import.

We're Sorry; Your Database File Is Corrupt

It started out as a day just like any other. However, on this day, when you try to open your beloved database file, Access tells you that the file is corrupt. It's funny how one little message can ruin your day. You start wondering if you backed up the file last night and when the file was actually corrupted. Then you start wondering how you'll get out of this mess.

Fear not. There is a simple solution to a corrupt database. Here are the steps:

1. **Launch Access and click the Microsoft Office button.**

   The Office menu appears.

2. **Select Manage from the menu.**

   The Manage Your Database submenu appears.

3. **Click Compact and Repair Database from the submenu.**

   The Database to Compact From dialog box appears.

4. **Navigate to and select the corrupted file. Then click the Compact button.**

   The Compact Database Into dialog box appears.

5. **Select the corrupted file once again. Then click the Save button.**

   You are prompted to replace the existing file.

6. **Click Yes to replace the existing file.**

   The database is compacted and repaired.

7. **Open the repaired file.**

   The file should now open.

 If, after following the preceding directions, the file still does not open, you have a serious problem that could take some effort to clean up. The next step is to resort to a backup copy of the database. Check what data is missing between the backup and your recollection of the corrupted file. Yes, you'll have to reenter any missing data. Sorry!

If you don't have a backup, all hope is not lost. You can buy software that is designed specifically to repair corrupted Access database files. Try searching the Web for **"repair corrupt Microsoft Access database files"**. Make sure the software works with Microsoft Access 2007.

The Program Won't Start

After launching Access, the fancy Access splash screen flows smoothly onto the screen, notifying you of what's to come. But this time, you don't see the friendly Getting Started with Microsoft Office Access home page. Instead, the Access splash screen fades, and you're back to the Windows desktop.

This sequence really does happen from time to time. Honestly, such events are just part of life with computers.

Computer software is just a series of files. Files go bad.

You don't need to play computer repair person to fix this problem. All of the Microsoft Office 2007 products come with diagnostic tools that can scan your hard drive for problems with the Office software and correct such problems if found. Here's how to use the diagnostics:

1. **Click the Microsoft Office button in the upper-left corner of the Access screen.**

   The Office menu drops down.

2. **Click the Access Options button toward the lower-right portion of the menu.**

   The Access Options dialog box appears.

3. **Click Resources — the last choice from the list on the left.**

   The resource choices appear.

4. **Click the Diagnose button.**

   The Microsoft Office Diagnostics dialog box appears. Follow the on-screen instructions to test and repair your Access problems.

If Access lives on your company's network, contact your Information Systems support people. In that case, the problem is likely out of your hands, so you'll have to move on to something else until the problem is resolved.

Chapter 23

Ten Uncommon Tips

Technical experts — the geeks/gurus who really know Access — might be annoying (perhaps simply because they exist and know way more about databases than a human should), but they're important. They're important to average Access users because they provide invaluable advice, and they're important to Access because they drive the way Microsoft continuously improves its products. They're the people who test Office products before they hit the shelves, and they're the ones who write books (like this one and more advanced books for more advanced users).

So, the people who develop databases for a living are an essential resource to the average user, to the "power user," and to the software manufacturer as well. This chapter is a compilation of some of the best advice gathered from a host of Access experts. Knowing they were offering suggestions for new users, nothing you read here is going to make your head spin or make you doubt that after reading this book, you really can use Access. To the contrary, the advice found here will help you be more confident and effective in your use of Access because you'll have done the right amount of planning and organizing of your efforts, and you'll have solid plans for moving forward with your development and use of the databases you build with Access.

So here's the sage advice — in ten quick bites.

Document Everything as Though You'll be Questioned by the FBI

Don't skimp on the time spent documenting your database. Why? Because you'll be glad you didn't skimp later. You'll have all your plans, your general information, and all your ideas — those that you acted on and those that remained on the drawing board — ready the next time you need to build a database. You'll also have them to refer to when or if something goes awry with your current database. You accidentally deleted a saved query? No problem. Refer to your documentation. Forgot how your tables were related? Check the documentation and rebuild the relationships.

So what should this glorious documentation include? Well, everything. But here's a list to get you started:

✔ **General information about the database.**

- File locations (with specific network paths, not just drive letters)
- Explanation of what the database does
- Information on how it works

✔ **Table layouts, including field names, sizes, contents, and sample contents.**

If some of the data comes from esoteric or temporary sources (like the shipping report that you shred right after data entry), note that fact in the documentation.

✔ **Summary of reports:**

- Report names
- An explanation of the information on the report
- A list of who gets a copy of the report when it's printed

    Jot down the job title and department in the documentation as well as the current person in the position.

If you need to run some queries before creating a report, document the process. (Better, get a nerd to help you automate the work.)

✔ **Queries and logic:** For every query, provide a detailed explanation of how the query works, especially if it involves multiple tables or data sources outside Access (such as SQL tables or other big-time information storage areas).

✔ **Answer the question "Why?":** As you document your database, focus on *why* your design works the way it works. Why do the queries use those particular tables? Why do the reports go to those people? Granted, if you work in a corporate environment, you may not *know* why the system works the way it does, but it never hurts to inquire.

✔ **Disaster recovery details:**

- The backup process and schedule

- Where backup tapes are located (you *are* making backups, right?)

- What to do if the computer isn't working

If your database runs an important business function, such as accounting, inventory, point-of-sale, or order entry, make sure that a manual process is in place to keep the business going if the computer breaks down — and remember to document the process!

If you need help with any of these items, *ask someone!* Whether you borrow someone from your Information Systems department or rent a computer geek, get the help you need. Treat your documentation like insurance — no business should run without it.

Every 6 to 12 months, review your documentation to see whether updates are needed. Documentation is useful only if it's up to date and if someone other than you can understand it. Likewise, make sure you (or your counterparts in the department) know where the documentation is located. If you have an electronic version, keep it backed up and have a printout handy.

Keep Your Fields as Small as Possible

As you build tables, make your text fields the appropriate size for the data you keep there. By default, Access sets up text fields to hold 50 characters — a pretty generous setting, particularly if the field holds two-letter state abbreviations.

Forty-eight characters of space aren't anything to write home about, but multiply that space across a table with 100,000 customer addresses in it, and you get 4.8MB of storage space that's very busy holding nothing.

Adjust the field size with the Field Size setting on the General tab in Design view.

Use Number Fields for Real Numbers

Use number fields for numbers, not for text pretending to be a number. Computers perceive a huge difference between the postal code 47999 and the number 47,999. The computer views a postal code as a series of characters that all happen to be digits, but the number is treated as an actual number that you can use for math and all kinds of other fun numeric stuff.

When choosing the type for a new field with numbers in it, ask yourself a simple question: Are you *ever* going to make a calculation or do anything math-related with the field?

- ✔ If you'll calculate with the field, use a *number* type.
- ✔ If you won't calculate with the field, store the field as text.

Validate Your Data

Validations can help prevent bad data from getting close to your tables. Validations are easy to make, quick to set up, and ever vigilant (even when you're so tired you can't see straight). If you aren't using validations to protect the integrity of your database, you really should start. Flip to Chapter 6 and have a look at the topic.

Use Understandable Names to Keep Things Simple

When building a table or creating a database, think about the database file, field, and table names you use:

- ✔ Will you remember what the names mean three months from now? Six months from now?
- ✔ Are the names intuitive enough that someone else can look at the table and figure out what it does long after your knowledge of Access puts your career on the fast track?

Windows allows long filenames. Use them. You don't need to get carried away, but now you have no excuse for a file called *06Q1bdg5*. Using *2006 Q1 Budget Rev 5* makes much more sense to everyone involved.

Delete with Great Caution

Whenever you're deleting field values from a table, make sure that you're killing the values in the right record, check again, and then — only when you're sure — delete the original. Even then, you can still do a quick Ctrl+Z and recover the little bugger.

Why all the checking and double-checking? Because after you delete a field value *and do anything else in the table,* Access completely forgets about your old value. It's gone, just as if it never existed. If you delete a record from a table, the record is really gone because there is no Undo available for an entire record. If that record happened to be important and you don't have a current backup file, you're out of luck. Sorry!

Backup, Backup, Backup

Did I make that clear enough? Backup your work! There's no substitute for a current backup of your data, particularly if the data is vital to your personal or professional life. Effective strategies often include maintaining backup copies at another location in case a disaster destroys your office, be it a home office or an office at your employer's location.

If you're thinking that you've never needed a backup before, so why bother, think about floods. Think about newscasters saying that an area currently underwater has never flooded before. Picture people's lives floating down the street. Whether you're faced with a real disaster of hurricane proportions, a fire, or your computer's hard drive deciding to die (and that does happen — even if it has never happened to you before), you'll be much happier if you have a backup of your database.

Think, Think, and Think Again

You know the carpenter's slogan, "Measure twice, cut once"? The same can be said for thinking when it comes to your database. Don't just think about something, come to a quick conclusion, and then dive in. Wait, think it through again, and then maybe think about it a third time. *Then* draw a conclusion and begin acting upon it. With all of the power Access gives you, coupled with the ability to store thousands of records in your database, a relatively simple mistake can be quite costly because of the potential ramifications in terms of the loss of data or an un-undo-able action that you took in error.

Get Organized and Stay Organized

Although the suggestions to get organized and to keep it simple may seem to be at odds, these two pieces of advice are really companions. Keeping things simple can often be a way to avoid the need for a lot of organization. While you probably got tired of hearing your parents remind you that "there's a place for everything, and everything in its place" (or if they're less poetic, *"Clean your room!!!"*), they were right.

If you keep your database organized, you'll save yourself time and grief. A well-planned, well-organized table will be easier to query, report on, and include in a form. It'll also sort and filter like lightning.

Yes, you can get *too* organized. In fact, overorganizing is altogether too easy. Temper your desire to organize with a passion for working with as few steps as possible. On your computer, limit the number of folders and subfolders you use — a maximum of five levels of folders is more than enough for just about anybody. If you go much beyond five levels, your organization starts bumping into your productivity (and nobody likes a productivity loss, least of all the people who come up with those silly little slogans for corporate feel-good posters).

There's No Shame in Asking for Help

If you're having trouble with something, swallow your ego and ask for help. Saying "I don't know" and then trying to find out holds no shame. This rule is especially important when you're riding herd on thousands of records in a database. Small missteps quickly magnify and multiply a small problem into a huge crisis. Ask for help before the situation becomes dire.

Not sure how to ask for help? Check the Appendix. This little chapter helps you get help through the installed Office suite, through Microsoft's online help, and through third-party sources that offer help on the Web 24/7. Crying "Uncle!" has never been easier.

Appendix

Getting Help

In This Chapter

▶ Finding help within Access

▶ Asking for help online

▶ Contacting live human beings for help

I admit it, I'm one of those twits who likes to be prepared — for anything. My handbag contains all sorts of "But what if . . . ?" objects intended to help me out of just about any situation. I have adhesive bandages, a Swiss army knife, a small flashlight, lots of pens, paper, cosmetics (you don't think pale lips is an emergency?), and my complete address book. Why the address book? In case I need help from my family, friends, accountant, doctor, veterinarian, clients, or Microsoft.

Microsoft? Yes, I have Microsoft's phone numbers in my address book, even though I'm not on its payroll, and I've never met Bill Gates. I have numbers that you, too, can call (I share them with you shortly) to get help with Microsoft Office. Of course, it's often easier to use the Help files that come installed with the Office suite, and Access gives you several ways to tap that help within the application.

It can also be faster and more effective to tap into various online sources for help — from the online help offered by Microsoft to various third-party sources of assistance. Your situation (if you've got an Internet connection, if you have a phone handy, if you're in a big hurry) will dictate which one is best, as will the question or problem you're having.

Access 2007 For Dummies is made to save you from that searching. The information you need usually should be on the pages of this book.

Asking Access for Help

No matter where you are in Access, help is there, ready to give you tips, tricks, and answers to your questions.

Installed help files

When you have questions, Access helps you to

✔ Navigate the automatically installed Access Help files.

✔ Find help at the Help database on the Microsoft Web site

Asking the right questions

Access 2007 gives you two quick ways to ask for help at any time:

✔ *Press F1* for *context-sensitive* help on what you're doing.

Context-sensitive help tries to pick the most appropriate help articles for you, based on what you're doing within the Access workspace at the time.

✔ *Click the little question mark* in the upper-left corner of the Access window (as shown in Figure A-1) to open the Microsoft Access Help window.

Figure A-1 shows the main Help categories, plus a drop-list of ways to get help — Access Help, a Developer Reference, and Offline Help (plus links to online training).

Access-ing Help Online

Access Help works best if your computer links to the Internet through an always-on, high-speed connection such as DSL, cable, or a corporate network at the office. With those connections, the Access Help system can always find the best, most recent answers to your questions. Of course, you can still reach Microsoft's online help if you're on a dial-up connection, but it will take longer to get the help you need. If you are on a dial-up connection to the Internet and you find the delays too long to deal with at Microsoft's help pages, you can always use the installed help that comes with Access or use the phone to speak to a human — using the contact numbers listed later in this appendix.

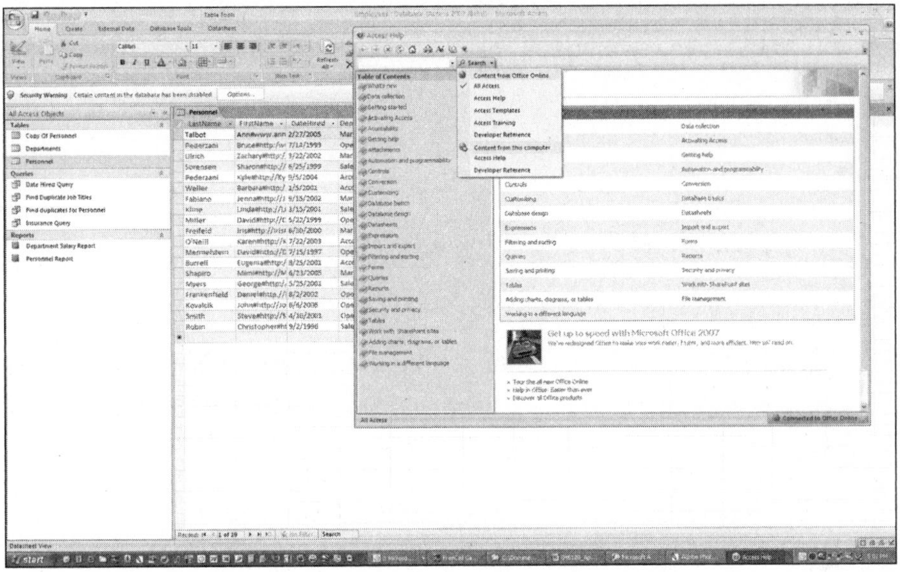

Figure A-1:
Access
hopes
you're
online when
you ask for
help, but
you can
always
access
offline help.

To find the right help article from within the Access Help window, follow these steps to pick your poison:

1. **Click a topic area from the Table of Contents list on the left.**

   Usually, this spawns a new list of subcategories.

2. **Click and follow through the subcategory links until you find the topic you need.**

If you want to use the Search field to look for help based on keywords, follow these steps:

1. **Type a word or words (keywords in a list or a simple question) in the text box to the right of the Search button.**

2. **Click the Search button.**

   The resulting list of links takes you to articles that may help you.

3. **Click the Help article that looks most promising.**

   The full article appears in either

   • The Help window (as shown in Figure A-2)

   • A new browser window (if you're on line)

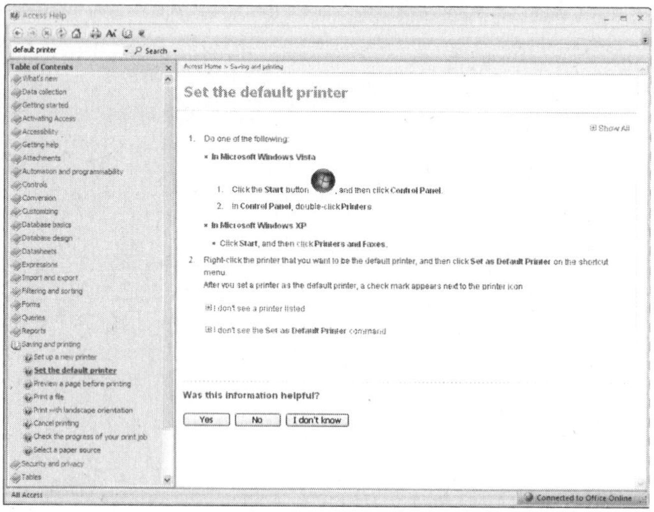

Figure A-2:
Help on
selecting a
default
printer,
complete
with links to
follow if the
help was or
wasn't
helpful.

Online Help

If you're connected to the Internet, the world truly is your oyster — and you can find some pearls of wisdom out there if you're willing to poke around, comb through mailing list postings, and read a lot of online content that may not help.

The online world includes Web sites with "official" information from Microsoft and "unofficial" information from the global community of Access users. You'll find it handy when you can't find what you need through the installed Access Help files, or if you simply want to tap into a more diverse range of insights.

Of course, "unofficial" doesn't mean inaccurate or unreliable, but rather that the sources are not representing or working for Microsoft when they offer their information. For example, the authors of this book, technically, are "unofficial" sources of information on Access, yet you (and the publishers) trust them to help you.

When you do go for "unofficial" sources of help, although much (if not most) of it is perfectly useful, accurate, and reliable, not *all* of it is. If the advice you're about to take or the steps someone has suggested you follow will affect the data in your tables, it's probably wise to backup your database before trying it. This little fail-safe procedure is probably a good idea even when using official help sources. Not sure how to do a backup of your data? Check Chapter 21.

> ## Books Are Our Friends
>
> Whether you're a new Internet user or a veteran, books can help you learn an application in a general way and also serve as a reference for specific features, topics, and questions.
>
> ✔ If the idea of using the Internet to get help is a bit daunting, kiss your scaredy-cat days goodbye. Check out *The Internet For Dummies,* 10th Edition, by John Levine, Carol Baroudi, and Margaret Levine Young (Wiley). You'll feel much more comfortable with the whole process of searching the Internet, and you'll find out stuff you never knew you didn't know!
>
> ✔ If you're already pretty Web-savvy but want to be a more proficient researcher, grab a copy of *Google For Dummies,* by Brad Hill (Wiley) or any of the other Google-related titles you'll find at Amazon or in your local bookstore.

Microsoft.com

For the "official" sort of help that Microsoft can provide, you'll find support areas for each of the Office suite applications on the Microsoft Web site.

Once you've accessed (pardon the expression) the Access pages at Microsoft.com, follow these steps to get help:

1. **To enter keywords or an actual question as a way of getting help, type the text into the Search text box at the top of the Access main page.**

2. **Click the Go button to execute the search.**

3. **View the resulting list of articles, and click on any that seem appropriate.**

   If, after clicking on an article, you don't find it useful, use your browser's Back button to return to the list of articles and try a different one. If none of them seem right, try rewording your question or changing your keywords.

Search engines and other sites

More often than not, the "unofficial" Access help you find at sites other than Microsoft's is helpful — often posted by people who've had the very problem you're experiencing. Bona fide experts are out there, ready and waiting, and continuously updating their Web sites to provide lots of help to those willing to look for it.

You may wonder why they don't have actual lives and something more fun to do, but hey, it's a good thing those experts are there, right? And maybe maintaining a Web site loaded with tips for using Access is fun for them.

The following list has sites to try and ways to search for the help you need by using Google, Yahoo!, or any other search engine you fancy:

✔ America Online: Keyword **Home and Office**

Look for *MS Access* in the message boards.

✔ Search engines (such as `www.google.com` and `www.yahoo.com`) can help you find Access assistance:

   • Search for "Microsoft Access Help."

     Hundreds of pages to check out, created by everyone from training centers to database developers and programmers. Help for users of all levels is out there.

   • Type your question in quotation marks.

     Any site that contains the phrase you typed, such as **Access table relationships,** will appear in the list of links you can follow. Some of the help is from established, published experts, while some of it is provided by people just like you — users who had a problem, solved it, and want to share the wealth.

✔ About.com: `http://databases.about.com/od/access/`

You find all sorts of Access help, including mailing lists and postings on Access topics that go for miles on the information highway.

Who's Our Next Caller?

Live technical support isn't extinct. At the other end of your phone, a live person who works for Microsoft can answer just about any question when:

✔ You can't phrase your question to get the help you need from either installed or online help sources.

✔ The answer you find is either too basic or too far over your head.

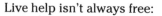

Live help isn't always free:

✔ Questions about basic installation are answered for free by Microsoft.

✔ If you want help with anything else, it's gonna cost you.

Except for the line that answers basic sales questions, Microsoft live technical support is available seven days a week, except holidays:

✔ Monday through Friday: 5 a.m. to 9 p.m. (Pacific time)

✔ Saturdays and Sundays: 6 a.m. to 3 p.m. (Pacific time)

Here's your handy-dandy Microsoft phone directory.

Voice calls

The cost and phone number to speak with a Microsoft expert in the United States and Canada depends on what you need to know about Access.

Basic installation

Microsoft provides free installation help at this number:

> 800-642-7676

You'll have to press a few more numbers to get to the tech support people, but the wait time isn't bad. If the person you get can't help you, he or she will be able to connect or direct you to the person or department who can.

Non-technical questions

If you have a light, non-technical question, such as "What's the current version number of Microsoft Access?" call the Microsoft sales department:

> 800-426-9400

You'll find people waiting for your call from 6:30 a.m. to 5:30 p.m. Pacific time, Monday through Friday.

Technical questions

For answers any Access questions involving using the software (beyond simple questions like "How do I install Access?"), you can call the following number from the United States or Canada:

> 800-936-5700

Solutions from this number aren't free, even though the initial call is. There are two ways to pay:

- ✔ A support contract from Microsoft (usually through your company)
- ✔ A flat $35 fee per *incident*.

  According to Microsoft, an incident is *all the calls related to the same problem* (or something close to that). If you call several times trying to solve the same problem, you pay for only one incident.

TDD/TT calls

If you are deaf or hearing-impaired and have a TDD or TT modem, call this number for all questions about Access (and all other Microsoft products):

800-892-5234

Unless you (or your company) have a Microsoft support contract, TDD/TT help calls cost $35 per *incident*, just like the technical voice line.

Index

Notes

Notes

Notes

Notes

Notes